Cosmic Shift

Cosmic Shift

Russian Contemporary Art Writing

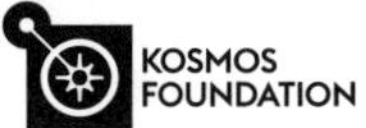 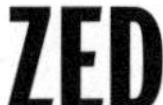

Contents

Foreword

A REPORT FROM THE CENTER OF THE WORLD

Strangely enough, the center of the world is out of view at this moment. This makes it very different from those other places that may claim this status for both historical and contemporary reasons. Beijing may be foggy but is somehow visible, and certainly present. New York now tends to be slightly obsolete and outdated, greyish and fading out, much like its historical predecessor, London. But they are present in our mind as concrete cities all the same. Unlike those places, Moscow, the center of the world, is at present virtually invisible.

With its 20 million inhabitants it is by far the largest city of Europe, but it is largely left to the Muscovites themselves. Hardly any image or word is getting out. This is not because the empire forbids visits, and nor is it because communication lines are cut by a big divide. It must be because of both of us, because of you and me, the readers of this book. Until now we were not curious and outspoken enough, we did not care enough about the well-being of our shared world spirit, however important that became in times in which both ecological challenges and ballistic missiles are shared globally. We are on the right track now, though; we can read this book and are actually doing so.

It is impossible to write the stories of modern and contemporary art in any meaningful way without including Russia in a major way. Over the past decades, we have become increasingly aware of the multitude of narratives and perspectives that have to be acknowledged alongside the traditional master narrative of contemporary art. There are still grand moments that remain unavoidable foundational references, if not for the history, then at least for the capacity of art as an emancipatory field after the bourgeois long nineteenth century. Russia can claim two of those moments, of the greatest magnitude for the role art continues to search in relation to societal change. To start with, there is obviously the intense engagement of constructivism with the new state that had to find its own shape after the 1917 revolution.

At the end of the Soviet epoch, there is a second moment. In many ways it is the opposite pole of the grand publicness of its predecessor, yet it is equally powerful as an example of how art can position itself in the heart of societal change. When Mikhail Gorbachev launches his attempt to "reconstruct" his country in 1985, the "dissident" artists of Moscow conceptualism see their position drastically changed almost overnight. Up to that point, their marginal but highly articulated positions in visual art and literature are – certainly at home – determined by an internal emigration in which the audience is limited to their own little community and the KGB, the Committee for State Security. With perestroika, these intellectuals become a concrete reference for a new ethos that is needed instantly; they are suddenly seen to be a new, contemporary symbol for a spirit to identify with.

In the tidal wave of a general enlivened global interest at
the end of the 1980s, the unofficial late Soviet avant-garde gets
some international interest as part of a blossoming art scene.
It is to a substantial extent export-driven like the Chinese
scene of the same period, but it is rife with the radicalism of
Moscow conceptualism. A symbolical work of the period is the
Brobdingnag performance by Anatoly Osmolovsky, an artist who
opposes Moscow conceptualism. He sits on the shoulders of
the giant statue of the revolutionary poet Vladimir Mayakovsky,
referring both to Jonathan Swift and to Isaac Newton, from
whom he borrows the phrase "If I have seen further, it is by
standing on the shoulders of giants." This new art scene initially
represents the radiating hope of a new Russia, like its loss of
international clout comes to stand for the loss of that hope.

That loss is strange, and not only because Moscow is the
center of the world, and the largest city in Europe. It also
continues to be home to a complex artistic scene, with a
setup from which many of us may learn. In its present state
of relative abandonment it may remind us of the Brazilian art
scene at the end of the 1980s, when the art world preferred
not to consider the possibility of there being valid art in Brazil.
That was, obviously, before it was integrated into the North
American market system and validated on its own behalf as a
proper perspective adding substantial complexity to the global
art reality.

What is the specificity of the space of Russian contemporary
art? This book bears witness to a crucial dimension of that
space. Russia is an intellectual and a literary culture. Its early
avant-garde is that of Vladimir Mayakovsky as well as that
of the constructivists, just like Moscow conceptualism is the
movement of the poet Dmitri Prigov as well as that of Andrey
Monastyrsky or Ilya and Emilia Kabakov. The present art scene

is a scene that is marvelously embedded in intellectual terms,
as is for already more than a decade proved by the *Moscow Art
Magazine*, published by the critic and thinker Viktor Misiano.
It is a thoroughly international framework, represented by the
philosopher Boris Groys, who is one of the iconic references of
global reflection in the field of contemporary art, or in a very
different way by Anton Vidokle, the founder of e-flux.

Yet what makes the Russian scene unique is not the
traditional discursive frame that over the past three decades
became a standard instrument to position and market art,
to the extent that also artists are now trained to develop it.
The relation between language and art is in this field not
predominantly discursive, and certainly not discursive in an
instrumental way. It is far wider and far more open than that.
One might say that it remains part of the artistic gesture –
indeed, by far the largest part of the authors in this book are
artists – but that would risk leading to another simplification.

The field of thinking-through-language surrounding
art is related to those possibilities and to much more. It is
both informed by the canonical philosophical network that
surrounds art in Western Europe – where even sidetracks are
neatly positioned in that network – but it has beside those a
second, completely different field of philosophical or quasi-
philosophical potential references, often consciously critical of
the canon when formulated. This second world, mirroring the
international references, remains hidden behind the Cyrillic
alphabet, the Russian language, and a different mapping, but
on the other hand also by our lack of interest. It is heterodox
to Western Europe but often orthodox to Russia. These
autonomous developments lead to a parallel intellectual world,
one that is well related to the global canon yet at the same time
superbly resistant to it, connections turning into idiosyncrasy

and back into connections. The result of this is a continuous possibility of reconfiguration, different from the Atlantic system that is the basis for the 'globalized' one, because that has only one coherence, a history of ideas that is only slowly being reedited.

We may know of glimpses of it, we may for example have heard of the noosphere of the geochemicist Vladimir Vernadsky, the sphere of human awareness, because of his influence on the French theologian Pierre Teilhard de Chardin. The present book is in its structure – starting with the future and ending with posthumanism – influenced by one of those strands that recently has seemed to rise again from the past, cosmism, the philosophical and cultural movement initiated by the Russian Orthodox philosopher Nikolay Fedorov, of influence on the avant-garde as well as on space travel. Cosmism itself and the wide span of its influences are prototypical to the proper capacity of the space for thinking in Russia. Cosmism is embedded in a holistic tradition. One may say that it continues to have a spiritual resonance. One may, however, just as well link it to the early-modern, sixteenth-century thinking in cities such as Antwerp, Augsburg, London or Florence. There too, art and science were part of one space of curiosity, research and reflection. There too, the more mundane sides of the world were a real fact, like they are here. It is utterly precise that there is a chapter in this book that has politics as a prime reference. It is precise also that this chapter spans a thinking space from the sharp analytical capacity of Ilya Budraitskis over the activist commitment of Dmitry Vilensky up to the hyperrefined reflections of Yevgeny Granilshchikov. But one might be aware also that actors from the artistic scene have over the past decades sometimes been providers of know-how for election campaigns.

The texts refuse to behave according to the simple and standardized formats expected today – one might call this a book of essays in the initial sense that Michel de Montaigne gave to the notion. They should not be seen as autonomous products, even if they may have that quality. This book, in the end, is only a series of samples, and those go with artistic trajectories that often deserve epithets that are at this point out of fashion such as "vast," "grand," or "committed." Grand not in terms of visual power, but rather in terms of aspiration. From each text in this book one should go to the corpus of texts it comes from, and to the circle of people the author represents, but also beyond that, to the abundance of artworks around and in between those. In many different ways these artworks forget to become commodities, because they are engaged in their own quest, like the texts are.

If we do want to follow cosmism, and it seems that we do, it is our duty to reflect on scientific methods to realize life extension, immortality and even resurrection of the dead. In that case the present moment of lack of knowledge on the part of the rest of the world is less of a catastrophe because it is not the market but the cultural system that may be our tool for eternity. It is good all the same that this book reports in English from that amazing area, a center of the world of sorts, and, to start with in the sense of Jimmie Durham, who situated centers of the world in places like Middelburg in the Netherlands or Yakutsk in Yakutia. Moscow is a center of the world in many ways and also, for certain, a center of futures.

Bart De Baere
Antwerp

Acknowledgements

This book has been a collective project: its ideas, structure, and development were established through the dialogue with its authors. Almost all of the authors, besides contributing a unique piece of text or artwork, were sharing their critique, knowledge, and contacts. We are grateful to every single artist and theorist whose name you can see in the table of contents for the opportunity to work in continuous dialogue with them.

We would like to express our particular gratitude to Emilia Kabakov: her kind support and advice were very helpful throughout the whole journey from the initial idea to submitting the manuscript. Arseny Zhilyaev has supported us since we first discussed the idea of publishing an anthology of art writing from Russia, and he was our committed colleague, supporter and collaborator throughout the development of the project. We are grateful to the the late Dmitry Prigov's family – Nadejda Bourova and Andrey Prigov, who, with the help of Professor Mark Leiderman, provided lesser-known texts by Dmitry Prigov.

Very important for us was support from Kosmos Foundation, received at the crucially important stage of the production of this book. We would like to say thank you to Aliya Prokofyeva, the president of the Kosmos Foundation.

The co-editors of this book met in Goldsmiths College, University of London, and the initial development of it started with the support of Goldsmiths. We would like to thank Dr Simon Sheikh, Dr Helena Reckitt, Dr Ele Carpenter, Kirsty Ogg, and Chris Hammond for their critique and advice and Dr Gilda Williams for generously sharing her outstanding experience in writing and publishing.

We would also like to say thank you to Kika Sroka-Miller, Dominic Fagan, and all the Zed Books team – and Joseph Choonara who put us in touch. Zed Books is a unique publishing collective that takes egalitarian, nonhierarchical, and nonconsumerist ethics of labor as a principle for organizing their work, which we found fitted very well to the book we assembled. Zed Books' attentive exploration of the world's diversity of histories, philosophies, and politics puts our work in an appropriate context.

The book's chapters that needed translation from Russian were translated by Andrew Bromfield; his accurate, nuanced and elegant way of treating languages made our mutual work highly enjoyable.

Many authors of this book are regular contributors to the *Moscow Art Magazine*, established and led for many years by Viktor Misiano. The magazine has been the major source of contemporary art writing in Russia which we looked at in our research. We have also looked at Former West publications for inspiration.

We would like to thank Elena Walker who generously shared her experience and who provided us with some useful contacts and information. We would like to express gratitude to Professor Averil Mansfield-Bradley for her kind and atentive support.

Both of us are grateful to our families and friends who provided help unconditionally when it was needed.

Alex sends her love to Galina Anikina and Alexander Anikin for their unwavering support and affection, and to Katya Savchenko for the gift of her friendship and invaluable advice on the matters of life and work.

Elena would like to express gratitude to Russell Bradley, who voluntarily spent hours and days helping with the editing that contributed to the clarity and rigor of thought we hope we have achieved in our work. And, special thanks to Alexander Bradley for his attentive interest and for treating this work with a sense of its importance.

Elena Zaytseva and Alex Anikina

Introduction

ELENA ZAYTSEVA

This collection of texts was assembled in the year of the centenary of the Russian Revolution to explore the aesthetic and moral legacy of the Revolution in the field of contemporary art in Russia. This is the first anthology of Russian art writing published outside Russia. Its authors, mostly artists, in different periods of our time, have had a living experience in the domain where the attempt to build utopia was conducted, and these historical circumstances to a large degree influence the critical debates of today.

The contribution to art theory and creative writing made by artists is a recognized part of the system of art. Contemporary art theory would not be what it is without the passionate writings of artists such as Liam Gillick, Hito Steyerl, Seth Price, Frances Stark or Jimmie Durham. And yet the situation of art writing in Russia is distinctively different from that in the rest of the world.

Language becomes an important medium for visual artists in periods when the relations between art and society are particularly intense, or complex. Such was the time around the First World War when a number of artists' manifestos were issued in Europe, or the 1970s when a large body of feminist and conceptual artists' texts were written. In the turmoil of Russian history, art has often had to establish its own autonomy within a dominant culture sponsored by the prevailing power – whether the power of tsars, of the Communist Party or of state capitalism. Perhaps this is why Russia produced such a large body of artists' writing during the twentieth century. Perhaps writing is a vehicle for artists to question their place within society. Or a means to establish themselves within history.

As it always has, the world continues to change, and the outcome is uncertain. To the features of contemporary global change, such as the anthropocene, accelerating technologies and the crises of Western democracies, Russia adds into the mix resurgent nationalism, growing state conservatism and dissolution of the welfare system. The contemporary art scene in Russia is vibrant and diverse, but its support from new financial elites on the one hand and state power on the other presents the very real risk of art becoming compliant with neoliberalism. In this situation the emerging generation of artists not only criticises the dominant political forces, but takes a moral position of radical autonomy from the art institutions these forces support. This position of radical autonomy is rooted in the Soviet past, in the high-spirited 1960s when, following a brief period of Khrushchev's "Thaw", independent unofficial art survived within tight circles of artists from the ardently dissident Lianosovo Group in the north of Moscow to cerebral gatherings in studios around Sretensky Boulevard, the typographical center of Moscow conceptualism. The latter created an elaborate body of writings around the autonomy of art that was understood, in the terms of the Frankfurt School, as a necessary condition that can give art social significance. Being far from the ivory tower of art for art's sake, autonomy was the ethical position that allowed art to be the "social antithesis of society" (Adorno, 1997, p. 8).

In the circles of Moscow conceptualism, the binary oppositions of a world divided into 'them' and 'us' were at the core of theoretical debates – and writing. The global opposition of 'us' and the West was no less important for these artists than the 'us' and 'them' within the Soviet domain – the local opposition between the official social realism and the unofficial realm of freedom and friendship. (Kabakov and Groys, 2010, pp. 25–37.)

It is different now. Since 1989 the West is no longer quite 'them' to Russian artists. The end of the Cold War, the deconstruction of the notion of the West and questioning of the Eurocentric model of knowledge reduces the perception of the West as point of reference. At the same time, the growing nationalist forces both in Russia and in the former West leaves a fine line between the pitfalls of noncritical perception.

Publishing such a project comes with responsibilities. The collection comprising solely of Russian authors is liable to the representational risks that come with transcultural communication. The key words and names, familiar to many Western readers, might appear in unfamiliar discussions and the irony inherent to many texts might go unnoticed. It is important to remember that this collection is only a glimpse into the ongoing conversation. The post-Soviet context, as the included theoretical texts explain well, is a space of complexity and debate. Hopefully, the book will accomplish its modest goal of enticing the reader to investigate further.

Some of the authors of this anthology are well known to the English-speaking public, such as Ilya and Emilia Kabakov, Boris Groys, and members of the Chto Delat? group Dmitry Vilensky, Gluklya/Natalia Pershina-Yakimanskaya, Artemy Magun and Oxana Timofeeva. However many of the authors, despite their many contributions to *Moscow Art Magazine*, established and run for more than twenty years by Viktor Misiano, are less known, and primarily because of the language barriers. Perhaps the most striking example of these barriers concerns Dmitry A. Prigov (1940–2007) whose published books in Russian number a dozen, none of which are available in translation at the time of writing. There is a similar situation with Andrey Monastyrsky and the Collective Actions group's volumes of "Trips to the Countryside", which are classics of Russian art literature – as well as with novels and collections of short stories by Pavel Pepperstein. Within the new generation, writings by Arseny Zhilyaev are better known because of his regular contributions to *e-flux journal* and an English translation of his monumental research into avant-garde museology (Zhilyaev, 2015).

This book is constructed in five parts. The first and the last parts address notions of the future. The first looks at philosophical and political constructions of the future such as Cosmism and communism; they are past concepts of the future. The last section, Part Five, written mostly by authors of a younger generation, addresses the current moment of rethinking the human subject and its future; *anthropocene*, *automation* and *posthumanities* become key words here. In between, parts Two and Three address the aesthetics and ethics inherited from the utopian past and the archive that becomes a charged place of collision between the private and the public, between history and the individual. Part Four addresses the politics of the present and the choices that artists have to make now. Most of the book's chapters are essays, often written in theory-fiction format, but the last chapter in each part is purely creative writing: a film script, a short story, a poem. Together, these parts present a cross section of the contemporary art writing scene in Russia; an interpretation and a portrait.

The first chapter in this book begins with the conspicuous opening line of "The Nomadic Theater of the Communist: A Manifesto" by the philosopher Keti Chukhrov: "Recently I understood clearly that art couldn't help but be communist." In this manifesto Chukhrov explores the possibility of reactualizing the notion of communism, if not as a politico-economic system, then as an ethical category based on compassion, emancipation and equality. Is it possible to bring communism back to its original meaning? And is art able to bear the mission?

Chapter 2, "The Center of Cosmic Energy" by Ilya and Emilia Kabakov, is an essay, written from the point of view of a character who develops his elaborate but naive "theory" outside the existing system of scientific knowledge and education. For this "theorist", the revolutionary claims for emancipation and domination over nature take a mystical twist, one borrowed from Russian Cosmism. Here, rising and falling utopias are manipulated by a technology that uses the hidden forces of nature – namely the energy of the Cosmos. This idea is an allusion to Nikolay Fedorov's theory of the "Philosophy of the Common Task"; this and Marxism were the dominant lenses for conceiving of social justice in the period preceding the Russian Revolution.

Communism and Cosmism as concepts are in fact deeply connected with regard to their attitudes to society and labor, and a number of authors in the anthology explore them. Russian Cosmism has a long history originating in the epoch of Enlightenment in Russia and was driven in part as a reaction to the suffocating, conservative and immensly oppressive regime of tsarism. For example, as George M. Young, scholar of Russian Cosmism notes in his book *The Russian Cosmists*, philosophy as a profession did not exist in Russia until the late nineteenth century because free thinking was of course a threat to the absolute power of the tsars (Young, 2012, p. 21).

Fedorov's theory did not constitute a philosophic system per se, not least because it was developed outside the existing Western philosophical tradition. Since the 1960s however, his writing and approach have influenced many Russian thinkers and revolutionaries who were grounded in the Russian Christian tradition and for whom the materialism of Marxism was a point of rupture.

> "I don't understand what you're troubling yourself about. After all, you won't be able to give those for whom you're troubling yourself anything except material well-being, since you don't admit to any other well-being; but meanwhile, working to obtain material well-being for others, you renounce it for yourself and indeed are prepared even to sacrifice your life for the sake of this. But what if material well-being is no more important to those for whom you're troubling yourself than it is for you? To what end is all your bother?" In the course of our conversation I heard from N. F. that the so-called great principles of the great French Revolution – freedom, equality, and brotherhood – are the product of extremely shallow thought, or even of thoughtlessness, since brotherhood cannot result from freedom to fulfill one's whims or from the envious desire for equality; only brotherhood leads to freedom, for brothers who love one another will not envy one brother who is elevated above others, and will not try to lower him to their own level;

and the brother who has raised himself above the others will try to bring all his brothers up to his level. For that reason, we must seek brotherhood first and not put it at the tail, after freedom and equality, as did the proponents of freedom, equality, and brotherhood – we must seek brotherhood first, and the rest will follow. (Young, 2011, p. 61)

This is a central problem that many Russian thinkers saw and see in communism. It can be argued that placing people's material needs at the core of political struggle demands unselfishness and an abnegation of material needs from those who conduct the struggle; these are qualities rooted in Christian tradition. Nikolay Fedorov's Cosmism attempted to solve this contradiction – and solve it with an understanding that accelerating technologies will reshape social life in the future. This was an insight rare for the nineteenth century. Many of Fedorov's pupils became scientists who did work of great importance in developing technologies for Soviet Russia; they included Vladimir Vernadsky, Alexander Chizhevsky and Konstantin Tsiolkovsky. The latter is the well-known creator of the scientific foundations of Soviet space exploration.

The space program was of course driven by state ideology and the Cold War (see the text by Vadim Zakharov in Chapter 13), but when we look at the stories and lives of people who participated in space exploration for Russia – Yury Gagarin for example – we witness strong collective ethics and unconcern with material goods (Danilkin, 2011). After his triumphant space journey Gagarin rejected the plan to build cottages for the cosmonauts in favor of building a block of flats where all cosmonauts and their families could conduct communal and collective life. Like most Russian constructivist buildings of the 1920s, the cosmonauts' block was built around communal service units, a canteen, a laundry, a kindergarten. The cosmonauts and their families were in fact the very "men from the future" for whom El Lissitsky and Iakov Chernikhov were creating their futuristic visionary projects.

Architecture of the Soviet period is the subject of Chapter 4, Andrey Monastyrsky's "VDNKh, the capital of the world". Here he explores the Soviet collective mentality as inscribed in the symbolism of the architecture of VDNKh, a large park in north Moscow purpose-built by the Soviet government to exhibit socialist economic achievements. Monastyrsky's piece takes on an ironic tone as the text's argument shifts between conflicting systems – different religions, dialectical materialism, post-Kantian critical philosophies and histories. The leitmotif of the text is an opposition between cosmos and chaos that unravels while the narrator moves around the park contemplating the perspectives that change in front of him. The narrative results in the conclusion that socialism built in the Soviet social and political order was "an embodiment of Classical German Philosophy in its romantic-shamanic-Hegelian version" and that socialism is simply "an abstraction of capitalism towards its own absolute." This conclusion brings us back again to the major dialectical contradiction of the concept of communism which, putting the material needs of people first, cannot be free from the consumerist mindset of capitalism.

It is no coincidence that one of the most influential philosophers of art, Boris Groys, emerged from the circles of Moscow conceptualism. Chapter 3, "The Truth of Art," raises a question that is fundamental for Russian art:

The central question to be asked about art is this one:
Is art capable of being a medium of truth? […]

Today I would, rather, like to ask the following question: To what degree and in what way can individuals hope to change the world they are living in? Let us look at art as a field in which attempts to change the world are regularly undertaken by artists and see how these attempts function.

In this chapter Groys reviews how art has responded to this quest since the Russian early modernism and then he projects his view onto the accelerating technologies of the present day that reshape not only the conditions of its mediation by art, but the very notion of truth.

"The Communist Revolution was caused by the sun" by Anton Vidokle concludes Part One. This chapter is a script for the second part of Vidokle's film trilogy on Russian Cosmism. The film is itself a collection of excerpts from poems, philosophical treatises, theological essays and historical studies, mostly written in the late nineteenth and early twentieth centuries, just prior to the Russian Revolution.

If the first part of this book examines communism and Cosmism as visionary utopias, Part Two is an exploration of contemporary aesthetics and ethics inherited from the Soviet period. It opens with Chapter 6, "History of Angels," by the curator Joseph Backstein in which he investigates connections between aesthetics and history (within Russian art in the Soviet period) in terms of autonomy, which he defines as "intellectual survival":

One should note that the principal topic in Moscow conceptualism, which determined its role as a pivotal axis of contemporary art in Russia, was the theme of "intellectual survival," the survival of a human being in circumstances

where it was impossible to do so without losing one's
individual human and predominantly moral character.

Artists who emerged after 1989 formed a generation of
action. At the beginning of their careers artists such as Anatoly
Osmolovsky, Alexander Brener, and Oleg Kulik loudly and
fiercely challenged Moscow conceptualism – and also negated the
legacy of socialism. In 1991 Osmolovsky led his peers to throw
their bodies onto the cobbles of Red Square to form the word
Х*Й ("dick") in front of Lenin's Mausoleum. Later in the same
decade he revisited the writings of Marx and Lenin and started
to promote them within the circles of young artists. Osmolovsky
organized a group, Radek, that was largely structured around
seminars and reading groups. Chapter 7, the second in this part,
is a discussion on abstraction led by two Marxist artists, Dmitry
Gutov and Anatoly Osmolovsky, a discussion held at a time when
Clement Greenberg's "Avant-garde and Kitsch" had not yet
been published in Russian. In fact, the first translation of it was
commissioned by Osmolovsky at around the same time.

An artist of the same generation, Olga Chernysheva
established her strategy through research into the methods
of the populist movement in Russian art of the nineteenth
century known as the Wanderers. Chapter 8 includes stills of
her "Screens" that incorporate video images with text. A row
of humble characters and overlooked objects, such as a plastic
bag, Moldavian builders in Moscow, a female worker on an
assembly line, a statue of a lion on the road from Aleppo to
Damascus, a flower on a windowsill, a passenger on a train,
evoke an acute feeling of sharing the world with others and the
fragility of every living and nonliving being.

Chapter 9 comprises two manifestos by Dmitry
Alexandrovich Prigov (1940–2007). Written in the late

1980s–early 1990s, they analyze the radical changes in the configuration of the world and look at the ways these changes reshape the concepts of "the West" and "the East." In the "Second Sacro-Cularization," Prigov predicts that following the collapse of the Socialist bloc, contemporary art will lose the very potentiality to be an avant-garde.

As if already in debate with Prigov's statement, Chapter 10, the recently written essay "The Form of Art as Mediation" by the theorist Maria Chekhonadskih, puts at the core of art the agenda "mediating the historical and political events of our time." She traces the development of storytelling in Russian art from the time of the revolutionary avant-garde through Moscow conceptualism to the works of the young artist Arseny Zhilyaev in a quest for a form of art that "can present the totality of an event in its relationship to lived human experience."

The differences in understanding of concept of communism between 'the West' and 'the East' are explored in Artemy Magun's essay "Soviet Communism and the Paradox of Alienation". His Chapter 11 addresses the ruptures (in understanding communism) between the Western left and the artists and writers of the post-Soviet domain who had a lived experience in the 'real' Utopia. For Magun, who grew up in the Soviet Union during the latest decade of Soviet socialism, lived experience lies at the core of the differences in understanding the concept of communism. He states that in Russia in place of collectivity lies the communality that causes alienation and distortion of the whole concept of communism. But the Western understanding of communism also has its distortions.

This narrative of alienation is probed in the poem "The Russian Avant-Garde as an Uncontrollable Beast" by Alexander Brener (Chapter 12) that concludes Part Two. Brener, one of the most radical actionists in Moscow in the 1990s, attacks

the art of today for its inability to face its mission to inherit
the historical impetus of the Russian avant-garde that was
concerned with the tasks of "planetary scale."

Part Three of this book considers the artists' archives as
a place of collision between the historical and the personal;
between the public and the private. It opens with Chapter 13
by Vadim Zakharov who for many years placed the archive at
the center of his work. In "Author, Cosmos, Archive" Zakharov
considers the cosmos and communism as equally constitutive
of the ideological machine of the Soviet state. Zakharov
gives an overview of the history of the archive of Moscow
conceptualism, in which he took one of the leading roles, and
which at the time was a form of collective publication in the
absence of any democratic infrastructure for art: "The archive
in the cage of the Soviet system, as a model of freedom, as the
defiance of enforced localization, sometimes through a
parody of it."

Chapter 14 by Bogdan Mamonov tells the story of his
grandfather whose archive he discovered. The story reveals how
temporalities of individual lives collide with the temporality
of historic events. In this case the revolution of 1917 and the
industrialization that followed were the cause of the most tragic
events in the artist's family life. Maria Kapajeva's Chapter 15
is based on a photographic archive belonging to her father,
and the time focus in this chapter is the comparatively quieter
years of the 1960s–1970s. This chapter is a reassembled
excerpt from Kapajeva's book project "Reading Apocrypha"
in which she created her own story out of found photographs.
Making sequences of chosen photos from the archive allows
one to assemble as many stories as one wants. The quotidian
life in these stories happens against the backdrop of images
of the exciting bigger world, represented by the pictures of

the TV screen (which remarkably was the subject of some photographs), and photos of the Western pop stars on the bookshelves.

The final two chapters in Part Three are constructed around the ways in which the history of art is intertwined with life experience. Andrey Kuzkin and Masha Sumnina are friends and both are children of Russian conceptual artists. In Chapter 17 Sumnina journeys into the past, when her father was a young artist who conducted a performance that is now one of the most recognizable works of twentieth-century Russian art. Sumnina revisits the venue of the performance in the woods near Moscow searching for material traces of that event, and her writing combines rigorous registering of facts and mysticism. In Chapter 16 Andrey Kuzkin revisits his own life during the time of his happy childhood symbolizing itself in places and humble objects.

Part Four formulates the cursed questions of Russian life, as seen by the current generation of artists working with the political agenda of today. The Russian artists who grew up after the collapse of the Soviet system and who emerged in the 2000s–2010s are rediscovering Marxism and anti-Stalinism and "putting political imagination at the core of the art agenda" (Dzewanska, Degot, and Budraitskis, 2013). In doing so, these young artists acknowledge and appreciate the fact that the vibrant contemporary art world in Russia today is a direct heir of the ethics and aesthetics of unofficial art of the Soviet period. It is no coincidence that four of the six chapters in Part Four explore the ethics of politics: in history (Budraitskis, Chapter 18), in art (Vilensky, Chapter 22), in the aesthetic (Venkov, Chapter 19) and in terms of the vulnerability of the subjects of socially engaged art (Gluklya [Natalia Pershina-Yakimanskaya], Chapter 21).

As is shown by Ilya Budraitskis in Chapter 18, the very existence of the Revolution disrupts the official populist narrative of the 'great historical Russia' whose identity was formed by the authoritarian rulers and religious orthodoxy. Budraitskis's text follows the paradoxical moral decisions made by the Bolsheviks in the process of seizing power and establishing the era of the proletariat and explores the ethics of revolutionary actions.

One of the myths about the Russian Revolution is that it was one pre-thought project conducted by a well-organized group of determined revolutionaries. In reality, revolutions are always a result of the conflicting activities of various political forces. Dmitry Venkov's Chapter 19, the script for the film *Krisis*, shows conflicting ethical choices engendered by a revolution. His focus is on recent events in Ukraine: the script is a reenactment of a dialogue between Russian and Ukranian contemporary artists during the early stages of the Maidan protests which occurred in Kiev in late 2013. The characters within the script belong to the same circles of the contemporary art community, but their opinions are irreconcilable and mutually exclusive.

Conflicting ethics as well as a conflict between ethics and aesthetics are the focus of Gleb Napreenko's Chapter 20, a closer look at activist art in Russia today. Napreenko interrogates the political forces which were put in motion by the radical performances of the 2010s and comes to a paradoxical conclusion: that it is the conservative ultra-right who might in the end gain from nonreflective artists' gestures.

The desire to change the world and at the same time the vulnerability of an artist who dares to put it at the core of her agenda are revealed in Chapter 21, "The Utopian Union of the Unemployed," by Gluklya (Natalia Pershina-Yakimanskaya), a co-founder of Chto Delat? (What Is to Be Done?). Her focus is the European migration crisis, and her essay is based on an extract from the diary she wrote while participating in an experimental project in Lecce, southern Italy, where artists attempted to build an immigrants' community around a local House of Arts. It was an attempt to create a utopian Island of Hope where art, economy and social transformations were to build a model for an improved society.

Chapter 22 by the founding member and a leader of the group Chto Delat? Dmitry Vilensky also looks on the ethics of resistance, but this time specifically within the field of politically engaged art. This chapter is an ironic polemic with the great artists of our time which reveals both the group's method and its place within international art practice and the politics of today's Russia.

Part Four closes with "Weakness" by Yevgeny Granilshchikov, a dialogue that is simultaneously a film script and a recording of the process of its own making. Granilshchikov's Chapter 23 utilizes this playful form to question the distribution of political agency in the filmmaking process: whose political will is enacted when the actor is reading the script? And does a film really start when it starts to play, or already when it is being conceived?

Finally Part Five addresses the reconfiguration of the subject and its relation to the future. The profound transformation we are undergoing as human beings by means of automation, digital technology, gene engineering and the anthropocene calls for a new, post-Cartesian ethical framework to describe ourselves and our place in the world. Part Five gathers the artists and theorists who share this need to reconsider the anthropocentric humanist conception of the world and to redefine our sense of attachment and connection to a planet shared with others: animals, minerals, objects, machines.

This concluding part opens with a contribution from another member of the Chto Delat? group, theorist Oxana Timofeeva. Her Chapter 24 examines the binary opposition of nature and the copious contradictions of contemporary philosophy. "My argument would be that this uncanny space or cosmos does not stand out or around the canny space of the oikos that we share with other natural creatures, but paradoxically emerges at the very heart of it." The last part of her text seamlessly drifts from rigorous theoretical argument into fiction, revealing the contradicting methods of philosophy today.

Chapter 26 comprises Alex Anikina's poem "How to Operate as a Human Artist, or the Antichton"; a short excerpt from a cyclical book – a recent artwork that addresses the materiality and kinetics of readership. The text is a meditation on the act of its own reading that attempts to criss-cross the border between the human and nonhuman bodies and temporalities. It reflects on the lifespans of the reader and the book, their mutual engagement in the slow revolution of both thought and the pages, and their common fragility in the face of large-scale events, emotions and responsibilities.

Arseny Zhilyaev's Chapter 25 enables a thought experiment on the possibility of the art process being completely replicated and automated by robots – a roboformalism inscribed within capitalist production. What new meanings would be possible then? Ivan Novikov's essay "I want to be afraid of the forest" in Chapter 27 raises the question of whether it is possible to perceive nature irrationally in the condition of materialist thinking of today. The metaphor of "fear of the forest" is used here as an artistic device to refresh perception of nature through the lenses of culture.

Part Five closes with a short story by Pavel Pepperstein, "The Skyscraper-Cleaner Pine Marten," which concludes both this part and the entire collection. The story addresses the radical changes that technology is bringing to subjectivity, blurring the line between the human, the nonhuman and the divine. The story's protagonist is a cloned pine marten, genetically engineered to perform a specific role – that of taking care of dirt and waste – in a very sophisticated structure that unites humans and other living creatures some 2,000 years from now. The element of contingency that accompanies complex and subtle technologies leads to an unpredictable chain of events that unexpectedly refer to the Russian religious discourse. This return to the religious at the end of this book is an ironic completion of the circle: a return to the contradicting dialectics of the material and the ideal within contemporary art thought.

Dedication

To Lora, Lilia and all who have believed in better futures

References

Adorno, W. Theodor, 1997. *Aesthetic Theory*, trans. R. Hullot-Kentor, Minneapolis: University of Minnesota Press.

Danilkin, Lev, 2011. *Yury Gagarin*, Moscow: Molodaya Gvardya. In Russian.

Dzewanska, Martha, Degot, Ekaterina, and Budraitskis, Ilya, 2013. *Post-Post-Soviet? Art, Politics and Society in Russia at the Turn of the Decade*, Warsaw: MBooks.

Kabakov, Ilya, and Groys, Boris, 2010. *Dialogues: 1990–1994*, Vologda: German Titov Library of Moscow conceptualism. In Russian.

Young, George, 2012. *The Russian Cosmists: The Esoteric Futurism of Nikolai Fedorov and His Followers*. Oxford: Oxford University Press

Zhilyaev, Arseny, editor, 2015. *Avant-Garde Museology*. NYC: e-flux

Part One

Past futures

During the Soviet era temporality was constructed as forward-facing. Everything from politics, technology, culture and science aspired to a better future. In particular, two systems of future-conceiving – cosmism and communism – were influential. The ripples of those past futures have permeated contemporary thought within and outside Russia. Although based on different predicates, one on Christianity, the other on sheer materialism, both cosmism and communism demand a collectivity and an abnegation of material needs.

While the quest for truth and an appeal to change the world have always been a strong impulse in Russian art, in what ways does it relate to the continental philosophical tradition as a framework for critical thinking?

Keti Chukhrov

THE NOMADIC THEATER OF THE COMMUNIST: A MANIFESTO

Recently I understood clearly that art couldn't help but be communist. This is not at all a manifestation of ideology, as it would seem to some. Nor is it dogma. It is just that suddenly it became obvious that all art – from Ancient Greece to the present day; that art which has overcome the egoism and conceit in itself – contained the potential to be communist. Regardless of its pessimism or optimism, such art is dedicated not to some social group but to one and all. This is not some kind of propaganda trick. That's what happens with an artist whose art is not afraid of people. Often art is either afraid of losing itself in the crowd or, the other extreme, it attempts to be artificially populist so it isn't suspected of being refined or subtle, or is addressed to an in-crowd of discerning connoisseurs and experts.

When I say communist of course I have in mind not membership in a party but a worldview. It is this breadth of worldview, which exceeds the boundaries of a single state, nation, class, artistic school, and the private or even spiritual interests of a specific individual, that predetermines the communist potential in a work of art.

This means that the artist has the strength to be not just one person, but many – the strength to not merely observe life and the multitude of living beings but to be or become them by means of art.

This mode of art where the artist can be "many" exists. Dostoevsky was able to be many people at once. Shakespeare, Beethoven, Vvedensky, Khlebnikov, Brecht, Mozart, Mayakovsky, Platonov and Beckett are other examples. The mode of art I'm speaking of is the so-called theater. I certainly don't mean repertory or genre theater. Ninety-nine percent of repertory theater is just cultural entertainment. What I call theater is a kind of anthropological and political mode that arises as the capacity to artistically *perform* the transformation itself.

For me, this inevitable shift to the theater occurred on the one hand from poetry and, on the other, from contemporary art. The limiting factor in poetry was its monologism, the fact that it condemned one in a way to acmeism and lyricism, i.e., to in the end being preoccupied all the time with oneself even when one speaks of the world, and often to castrating the heritage of both the avant-garde and modernism. Contemporary art is in a certain sense the direct opposite of poetry. It is not psychological nor is it subjective. By and large, it continues to operate according to the modernist canon of reducing the world to its own artistic idioms.

However, contemporary art's constant reference to its own territory and innovations in technique had already exhausted itself in the seventies and was forced to either dwell on the reproduction of languages, concepts and commentaries, or on eternally reproducing estranged spaces as modes of the optical unconscious. In any event, even when contemporary art attempts to come close to the event, it doesn't succeed in doing this because it immediately negates its attempt. Contemporary art's spaces of representation, exposition and commentary are organized in such a way that no matter what contemporary art concerns itself with, it is inevitably and in the final analysis concerned with itself and its own boundaries.

Even performance (or actions), despite its procedural nature and its unfolding in real time, is essentially the installation of a concept in space and time. It is a static, exhibited art object. It is forced to be this way.

Theater, on the contrary, is dynamic. It represents the experience of *performing*, not performance. In the mode of action that has not yet become but is becoming, it appeals to that which does not yet exist, whether in society, life or art. It not only lives through time, but *performs* time, i.e., it is capable of dealing with the present as if it were the future.

Exhibition spaces, even when they thematize certain social or political issues, remain bound by the politics of *things and spaces*. The theater presupposes politicization between *people*. The theater is experience that leaves things behind. It is the experience of consciousness becoming immaterial. If in contemporary-art performance the participant a priori conceptualizes themselves as a performer, then in the theatrical performance becoming-performer occurs thanks to the fact that the performer (actor) becomes a person and that person's political destiny. In other words, the performer becomes an artist thanks to the fact that he performs a human being in the play.

The theater is a space for humans, not a space for artists. But the paradox is that becoming-human needs to be performed, while the artist must naturalistically and physiologically inhabit the conceptual art-space of the performance while remaining an estranged individual. Even when it is a monologue, theater is a dialogue and starts with the number two.

The theater is capable of speaking and acting out an idea without reducing it to bare form or neutralized concept. This is because, in the theater, the idea is acted out as the living substance of relationships, in the mode of unreduced multi-humanity and polyphony.

In poetry, for example, it is difficult to overcome being fettered in the habitat of self. There's nothing bad about the habitat of self. There's also nothing bad in observing the subject beyond reality, beyond people, beyond society. But this is the perspective of a single point of view, a single consciousness.

Vsevolod Meyerhold coined the term *cabotinage,* which he considered one of the most important features of the theater. *Cabotains* are *nomadic* players who perform anywhere. In other words, they are not bound to a room, space or time, but create both space and time out of their *performance* of worlds, ideas, people, and so forth.

Theater is implicitly public, but often the concept of being public is identified with the audience who watches the spectacle, i.e., the contemplation of action as entertainment. But the fact that it is public means that the theater has the potential to be about everyone, about how the world is for everyone, about how to be with the world, if it is not for everyone; and what to do with those who for one reason or another have been left without a world. The theater assumes that it will no longer wait for money, prosperity, education or beauty, but it turns waiting itself into action, as in Beckett's *Waiting for Godot.*

In this sense, the theater's capacity to deal with politics exceeds the capacity of the idioms of contemporary art, no matter how numerous they may be, and even the capacity of poetry, no matter how existentially profound or socially critical it may be. This is because in the theater the political is not a theme or an issue, but *is clarified* between people when those people are not just documented objects or observed characters, but speaking political subjects. The essence of dramatization is that it is never reduced to the representation of a single idea; rather, many ideas or ideas/people come into conflict with one another in such a way that the solution or conclusion to that conflict flows from the action itself without being predetermined.

The voices and discourses of theater are not just the sounds, opinions and narratives typical of many video works and documentations within contemporary art. They are not interviews with victims who recount how they suffered or accounts of an event. The theater treats suffering differently than do the media, contemporary art, literature or poetry. It incorporates a *performance of this* role by the victim themselves or the so-called oppressed person (an awful word that is humiliating and degrading) that would be a (artistic) *performance* of their own victory over circumstances. Herein lie the political, aesthetic and communist potentialities of theater.

To be able to learn to speak not only for oneself but (as in the case of the author and the actor) to speak *instead* of many others: this has to be done if only to understand or clarify *what* happened or is happening among us, in our country, in our state, in the world; in order to understand how to go on living within it. (Isn't that Hamlet's purpose in launching his "theater"?).

The hardest thing is to imagine not only one's own development and self-improvement, even if it achieves great heights in viewing the world, but to discern the development and self-improvement of others. In other words, to understand the universal dynamically, multitudinously, as an action that happens "alongside" (one), rather than conically, spiritually.

I rely on one assumption: artistic achievements don't count, and the spiritual quest for the transcendental is not worth anything if they occur only because they don't take into account the great majority of people on this earth, who have neither time nor place nor elementary living conditions, the freedom of existence that makes it possible to think, create, love and live. No personal connection to the sublime counts if we do not understand that all people, no matter who they might be, are potentially artists, scientists, engineers, philosophers, interlocutors, comrades in arms, and just people. Without them it is impossible to achieve the fullness of the world and life. And potentially they are also capable of thinking the same way. Nothing more. This is the communist assumption in simple terms.

Actually, there is no communism and there never was, but there is the project of communism. It cannot help being just as humans can't help being as long as they are, as long as people exist in their multitude.

Many resist the communist in themselves, in reality, in art and in history. This is out of fear for oneself, for one's well-being, for what little power one has; for one's success, and, finally, for one's education and culture, acquired through such long, hard work. Everyone without exception has this fear. It is a bodily fear. But so what? It can be overcome. It is quite possible to think of oneself as if you were thinking about others, as if you were not thinking about yourself. This is very difficult, but it becomes easy when these thoughts take on flesh in the situation of artistic performance.

The nomadic theater of the communist is in a certain sense the opportunity to temporarily (artistic time is temporary, although it lays claim to immortality) create the relations of political Eros using the means available now, to introduce (albeit temporarily) this artistic communist space into the existing environment in spite of the circumstances. As many people as want and are able to do it right now do this, in the place they have found for it now and for those who are ready for such an encounter now.

In this case, the theater is not a genre but a method of emergence for the territory of the "artistic." Here the "artistic" borders on the poetic, and poetry emerges in the performance of an impossible situation, not in writing. The artistic becomes human and the human becomes artistic, because the entire person is engaged in the process of performance: her body, mind, thoughts, desire, and not just individual capacities or qualifications.

This doesn't at all mean that such "theater" presumes nothing more than creative improvisation, that it happens somewhere, somehow and is about something, in a spontaneous situation among spontaneous participants. It is also not an illustration of some story or plot on the theme of communism or the political struggle.

The nomadic theater of the communist is connected with a special type of metanoia that doesn't just beget a desire to create, but requires the world and other people in this world. This metanoia is an event and it presumes a desire for the universal and universality, making the person as it were a "communist" and an artist at one and the same time. It makes them an artist because it must repeat, "rehearse" this inescapable event of metanoia, which is realized in the repetitive practice of performance. And it makes them a communist because each time the performance makes it possible to experience, understand or create a co-presence with others, to examine the bases of such co-presence, and to perform the fulfillment of the universal.

Ilya and Emilia Kabakov

THE CENTER OF COSMIC ENERGY

I The principle and main structure of the "Center of Cosmic Energy"

Why is the "Center of Cosmic Energy" built in Essen, in the Kokerei region? (historical and archeological premises)

At the beginning of the twentieth century, some caves were discovered to the north of the city of Essen in the tall slopes on the right bank of the river Ruhr. These caves have not been preserved until our time. Some drawings that have been preliminarily dated as belonging to the beginning of the first century B.C. were discovered on the walls of the caves. These were executed with coal or etched onto the surface with some sharp instrument. A few photographs of these drawings were included in an album published in 1902 by Nordrhein Westfalen (scientific) society, and this album is kept in the Düsseldorf city library. Among other drawings, three strange depictions attracted the attention of scholars, but no explanation of them was offered at that time.

Interest in these strange depictions was reawakened in 1961 in connection with the construction of a ventilation complex in the region of Kokerei. In digging the foundations at a depth of 3.5 meters, semi-circular fragments made of a hard material and large in size (up to 40–50 cm in length) were discovered. Unfortunately, because of the construction of the factory, the archeological excavations that had begun in this place were halted, and were resumed only after 1991, when the entire complex here in Kokerei had stopped functioning.

Continued in 1993–94, these excavations led to unexpected, sensational results. Two groups of objects were found that still do not have any analogies in world archeological practice. Belonging in the first group of discoveries are three well-preserved reservoirs arranged at an angle, one above the other. Furthermore, these reservoirs are located in such a way that the mouth of the lower one enters into the bottom of the reservoir located above it. All the reservoirs are made of a dense rocky mass similar to concrete: the height of each is 2.6 meters; the thickness of the walls varies from 8 to 12 cm. Research has indicated that the walls and the bottom of the reservoir are completely clean, which attests to the fact that they did not serve as places for keeping reserves of some kind, but rather the intended purpose of these large, empty cavities was completely different.

The second group of discoveries, located at a distance of 40 meters away from the first group, consists of two objects: the same kind of bowl-like reservoir as in the first group, but of significantly larger size (more than 3 meters) and just as well preserved; and below this reservoir a complex of two arches connected to one another by their protruding sides. The size of each arch is 4.5 meters, and they are made of the exact same material as that used by the ancient builders for making the "reservoirs." Archeologists and other scholars immediately turned their attention to the close similarity of the discovered objects and the cave drawings. This similarity and the motives for making the former and the latter provoked great discussion in the scholarly press and prompted the emergence of a few versions describing the nature of the "Essen phenomenon" and the proposed hypotheses about the use of these objects and their depictions in antiquity.

Among such hypotheses, we can distinguish the following:

The presupposition that what we have are fragments of an ancient ritual, an "initiation," that was widespread among Celtic tribes. The date of the objects supports this version: 1–2 centuries B.C., a time when Celtic tribes densely populated this region. Another version associates the discoveries with the funeral rituals of the Druids. Cited as proof of this theory are the depictions of human figures on the drawings from the tunnels that also served, according to this theory, as burial places. The similarity of these figures to other cave-wall drawings in other places supports this meaning and purpose of these drawings. But still the genuine meaning of these "reservoirs" that do not resemble burial places remains unexplained.

Recently, the majority of scholars are offering a completely different explanation of these discoveries. This explanation appears rather convincing, and it has served as the basis not only for a scientific hypothesis addressing the past, but also as the reason for a large experiment that incorporates the necessity to build a special complex that will be called the "Center of Cosmic Energy".

Below we shall move on to a detailed description of this hypothesis. According to this version, the drawings in the caves, as well as the objects found on the territory of Kokerei, have one and the same *cosmic* purpose. In terms of meaning, they should be attributed to the same ancient kinds of proof of a connection with the cosmos, like Stonehenge in England or the slanted "ring" in the Ziggurat region in northern Mexico. Moreover, both in the drawings and in the objects, the presence of similar subjects that are connected to one another is very obvious: the schematic depiction of the two arches and the "real" arches in one case; the schematic depiction of three bowl-type reservoirs and the "real" reservoirs in another. In the first instance, we can thereby propose the presence of structures consisting of two arched antennas, one of which is aimed upward at an incline toward the cosmos, and the other one is aimed downward, in the direction of Earth. In the second instance, we can propose that all three reservoirs were intended for preserving in some special way the cosmic energy received here.

Such an interpretation of the discoveries served as the basis for the idea of verifying ancient practices and the proposal for such an "experiment": How and in what way can the energy of the Cosmos be received and processed, so that mastery over it would lead to the emergence of new, unlimited possibilities for mankind in the future.

Another stimulus for the benefits of continuing the ancient experiment was the ever expanding interest of modern science in the problem of so-called "subtle" energies that, up to this point, are still not received using highly accurate scientific instruments, but only by a specially oriented neuron system of the brain that under certain circumstances turns out to be many times more sensitive. This is precisely what is generally known and widespread under the understanding of "intuition," the cognitive capacities of which have attracted attention only very recently.

This capacity of human intuition is "set in motion" in the most serious way in the concept behind the creation of a

"Center," and will serve as one of the main methods to be used here, along with other scientific methodology conducted in the Center's experimental work.

II Four intuitions

Before enumerating these four intuitions and revealing the content of each of them, a few words should be said about the nature of "intuition" itself and how it differs from fantasy, even though the character of their emergence in the imagination is identical and the nature of both of them is rather similar.

The nature of fantasies, no matter how convincing these fantasies might appear for their author, is always transparent, ephemeral, it is always the result of the author's imagination and, as a rule, their images are born by the creative will of the author. In this sense, fantasy is always arbitrary and is obedient to the author's caprices.

Intuition, on the contrary, always has some real "ground" underlying it. In some way, intuition sees and reveals what "really does exist," and sometimes it is capable of foreseeing what will happen in the future. The presence of such "reality" emerges inside of consciousness like a signal, often without any anticipation or consent of the author. Consciousness in these instances turns out to be merely a conductor, a medium of these real forces and circumstances that in this way signal their existence and that subsequently will become known and accessible to each person.

Now a few words about the person in whom such "intuition" emerges. Often he, just like others, is surprised by what his intuition tells him. Moreover, it is merely a special strangely tranquil inner confidence that serves as a guarantee of the correctness and authenticity of this intuition, because there is nothing from the already existing "knowledge" that confirms it, and more often than not this existing knowledge contradicts what has been "revealed" to him by intuition. Often confirmation of such "correctness" requires significant time. And this occurs particularly often in those instances that involve intuitively discovered facts or knowledge.

1 Intuition of "place"

This intuition presumptively speaks about the fact that certain places on our planet for some reason are especially sensitive and perceptive to the reception of cosmic energy, at the same time that the majority of other places maintain their neutrality toward it. In these places it is as though a very high energy charge is present constantly, that most often does not coincide and is not connected with favorable climatic conditions in these regions. Moreover, these places are most often found in an especially "unfavorable" climate. In all probability, there is a sufficient quantity of such places on Earth, but they have not all been discovered yet. The human organism, his psyche, actively reacts when he winds up in such a place. His reaction, as a rule, is always the same: he feels a surge of strength, tranquility, confidence – being present in such a place is always a positive experience. In antiquity, and also relatively recently, such places were chosen as sites for erecting temples and other religious structures.

What is interesting in all this is the fact that such places may be entirely dissimilar topographically. They can be located in mountains or in valleys; you might say that they are indifferent to the geographical landscape, as well as to the climate. The cosmic energetics of these places is not connected with the change of seasons throughout the year, or with the rising and setting of the Sun and Moon – this cosmic energy is present here perpetually, without fluctuation.

Attempts have been made since long ago to discover the geometric regularities of the locations of such places on our planet. A few systems exist that establish a similar geometric network; moreover, in each such hypotheses, a proposed energetic (cosmic) center of the Earth is always indicated, from which "spokes" spread in all four directions. Energy points on the Earth are arranged along these "spokes." Various civilizations have indicated, as a rule, the presence of such a center on its own territory. (As in Ancient Greece in Delphi there existed such a center called the "bellybutton of the Earth" that was represented by an oval rock standing vertically near Apollo's temple.)

In conclusion, it must be repeated that we are always talking about a place on the surface of the Earth that was originally empty and not connected with those structures – forums, temples, altars, heathen places of worship – that were erected in these places one after another just because one civilization followed another. Just the opposite is true: they were erected here precisely thanks to the special favorable qualities of these places -- the cosmic chargedness that was perceived intuitively by the builders. In our case, intuition is affirmed to a great degree of certainty: the region of Kokerei possesses precisely those qualities indicated above.

2 Intuition of "60 degrees"

This intuition can be formulated briefly in the following way.

Cosmic energy flows toward the Earth to the indicated places not vertically downward, but at a 60 degree angle toward the plane of the horizon. This extraordinarily important and categorical maxim is confirmed by the most diverse methods from various epochs of countries and civilizations that existed independent of one another and that were separated not only by gigantic distances, but also by temporal intervals that were just as large. This permits us to assert the following regularity: As soon as some structure, willingly or not, includes in it an orientation toward the Cosmos, then the law of "60 degrees" is immediately activated.

An illustration of such an example is provided. In the lower part of the table there are examples of mythical or real structures of various ancient civilizations: Babylon, Egypt, Mexico. It can be seen on the sketch that the angle in all three cases – the Tower of Babel, the pyramids in Giza, and the Mexican Ziggurats is always identical – 60 degrees. Many artists of the Russian avant-garde of the beginning of the twentieth century also used this angle in numerous projects and sketches. The peculiar trait of these projects is their unbelievably active cosmic orientation, their conceptualization as such that was often unconscious even for some of the authors. This could have occurred because the revolutionary rupture that had been moving forward since the beginning of the century and then realized with the Russian Revolution, broke, if we might express it this way, the cultural and historical defense of the consciousness of a person and in this breach many sensed not only a world-wide catastrophe, but also an encounter with cosmic flows, with the "open cosmos." Many artists, on account of their special sensitivity, felt this "cosmic wind," they perceived a new cosmic energetics, they acquired, in the words of Matiushin, "expanded consciousness." New projects emerged that were cloaked in a new energy, projects that the authors perceived as visual images coming to them from the future. The following projects were created virtually simultaneously: Tatlin's Tower, "Lenin on the Tribunal," by El Lissitzky, Malevich's "Suprematism," A. Rodchenko's "Linearism," and many other works by various authors: Klutsis, Puni, Rozanova.

And works engendered by the "intuition of 60 degrees" (cosmic intuition) created by authors who were not at all similar, who were often separated by artistic orientations and methods that were contrary to one another – received common constructive elements all at once, such as diagonality, or the determination of the angle in relation to the vertical axis and horizon, moreover, as a rule this angle either approached or coincided entirely with (as in the case of Tatlin's "Tower), a 60 degree angle.

Subjecting such a "cosmic angle" to the analysis of archeological discoveries in the region of Kokerei demonstrated, as was anticipated, their precise coincidence: the angle of the axis of the slant of the reservoirs was a 60 degree angle (to 0.04 percent accuracy) in relation to the line of the horizon. This property became one of the leading ideas used in projecting the "Center of Cosmic Energy."

3 Intuition "The throne"

This intuition speaks about a means for perceiving the cosmic flow that is moving toward us. It is not intuition, but rather logic, that tells us that the optimal position for the reception of such a flow would be if the landscape were to be strictly perpendicular to this flow; that is, that itself was standing at a 30 degree angle to the level of the horizon. We shall return to such a layout of the landscape a bit later, but now let's turn our attention to the depiction of the human figure on the wall of the cave.

The slanted position of the figure is not accidental, and it is as though it is aimed in the direction of the axis that runs through all three "reservoirs." The thought automatically occurs that inside our body there are three main "arches of reception" for perceiving the cosmic flow that are constantly in a working state throughout our entire existence. These, as follows from sketch, are the back part of the skull, the lower part of the chest cavity in the back, and the pelvis. And these are those very places where, according to evidence provided by physiologists, the deepest unconscious impulses of our beings arise.

But let's return to the image of "The Throne." The very first explorers who went to so-called exotic places such as Altai, Tibet, Iceland, noticed that the local inhabitants were very familiar with special places in their landscapes, and that these places were profoundly honored. These places all have something in common, namely: each of them forms the shape of a "throne" -- a gigantic semi-circular hollow in the mountainside, where the "spine" turns out to be a tall, even slope, and the base departs vertically downward, revealing before it and far below an infinite valley or a view of the mountains all the way to the very horizon. And one other thing: inside of these "thrones" there is an extraordinarily strong presence of cosmic feeling, the presence of the same kind of cosmic flow that we spoke of earlier. In the northern Altai region, such a place is even called by an appropriate name: "The Throne of the Gods." The temple of Apollo in Delphi is also placed precisely on just such a "throne." The landscape in Iceland has similar structures, where the first parliament of this country was built at some point. The Tibetan capital of Lhasa and the ancient Mycenae in Greece are also laid out in such a fashion. All of these examples attest to the fact that the shape of a "throne" is optimal for the problem that interests us.

The horizontal, flat arrangement of the region of Kokerei it seems would not confirm what has been said above, but we must not forget that the configuration of the landscape in many cases is not a constant quality, but rather is subject to alteration. Samples of deep geological layers of the earth in this region

attest to another, more diagonal layout in the distant past.
A confirmation of the angle of the old relief is provided by the
angle of the clay layers of earth and the arrangement of gravel
around the three "reservoirs."

During the construction of the "Center of Cosmic Energy,"
the intuition of the "throne" as discussed above will find its
expression in the mechanism of the viewers' places in the
slanted hall.

4 Intuition "Close energy"

While thinking about the mutual arrangement of the two
"antennae" found during excavations where one was aimed
downward, the other upward, as well as about the configuration
of the "throne," the following questions emerge: from where,
from which point, does this energy flow toward us, how far
away is this place, and in general, can such a place actually exist
in the cosmos?

At first glance, such questions seem absurd. It is completely
obvious that, in the first place, the cosmos "envelops,"
surrounds, our planet on all sides evenly. The earth is
submerged, so to speak, in a cosmic ocean. In the second place,
if we imagine flows of cosmic energy, then they come to us
from the entire Cosmos as though from a unified whole, and
consequently, from such an unimaginable distance that we do
not have to speak about some specific point. All of this is logical
and obvious. But if we turn to an intuitive sensation that arises
when you find yourself on one of these "thrones" (in Iceland
or in Delphi), then a very strong feeling emerges of that energy
coming to this very spot, moving also from some specific place
in cosmic space, and what is most surprising, this point is
located not in the infinite, unimaginable distance, but relatively
close to the Earth. It is as though the irradiation from this one

point is aimed at a concrete place, and nearby, almost right next to it, it is not perceived at all, it is as though it doesn't exist.

This strange but real experience can be compared to the acoustic effect that is familiar in the amphitheater in the city of Epidaurus and in other amphitheaters in Ancient Greece. Ideal audibility exists only inside the space of such an amphitheater, but all you have to do is to step a meter or two away to the side, and the acoustic effect entirely disappears.

If we were to seek another comparison to convey the feeling of the energy flow coming toward you, then we might use the image of a shower and the specific spot where a person must stand in order to be under the flow of water. A step to the right or a step to the left, and you are outside the "shower."

If we accept what has been described above as admissible, then it becomes clear that the sphericity of the antennae aimed upward (we are talking about the "antennae" found in the excavations), is oriented toward the reception of just such "close" energy. But what does the antenna aimed downward signify? The very same intuition provides the answer: it is aimed at the flow of energy emanating from the depths of the Earth.

The most interesting thing is the adjoining of both antennae in the same spot. Does this mean that this is the meeting place of two energies that are aimed in opposite directions? What is their interaction? Do they transition from one to another?

5 E. Rozenfeld's Hypothesis

In an article dedicated to an analysis of the interconnection of such "split" antennae, the American physicist E. Rozenfeld put forth the following hypothesis: isn't it possible to make a connection between the diverse directions that the antennae are aimed, and at the same time, their interconnectedness with one another, by using the problem of "reversibility" in the movement of time, a problem that has attracted the attention of contemporary physicists for a long time. Moreover, Rozenfeld completely refused to interpret the significance of the antennae as sources of some sort of information from the Cosmos, confident that the antennae had a different purpose.

He focused his attention on the emergence of an uninterrupted line crossing over from the upper antenna to the lower one, as well as on the fact that the upper antenna was placed not symmetrically, but a bit higher than the lower one.

According to his hypothesis, the upper antenna, turned toward the Cosmos, is connected with future time. Consequently, the lower antenna, turned toward the Earth, is connected with past time.

The point of intersection of the two antennae, as a result, was the place where one time passes into the other. It is as though what takes place is a kind of transfer flow of the upper, future time, into the past. But, what is most interesting, is that time, according to this theory, flows not only from the future to the past, but also from the past to the future! This process is identified using the term "reversibility." The alternation of these two flows of time that are aimed in opposite directions occurs cyclically. In each cycle, during the first phase, time flows from the future to the past. The future in this case is active, and the energy of the Cosmos moves from top downward, from the upper to the lower antenna. But after a certain period, the energy of the Earth, which always acts as secondary, as perceptive, resists this movement and its energy begins to move from down to up. During this second phase, time begins to flow in the opposite direction, from the past to the future, to the very limit, until the action of the first phase begins again.

Such alternations profoundly affect, according to Rozenfeld's thoughts, the historical life of human civilizations.

The phase of the Cosmos's influence corresponds to positive, creative, active periods in their histories. The strong sensation of an approaching future evokes enthusiasm, positive emotions. During this period the attitude toward the past is indifferent, almost negative, and the desire to change it, to redo it, emerges. During the period of action of the second cycle, the future stops attracting us, and a period of stagnation begins; the past in all its forms seizes the social life, acts like an active, functioning beginning. But, since the energetics of the future and the past do not coincide in terms of their potential, the time of the future always begins with greater surprise and decisiveness than the past, which functions gradually and indecisively during its cycle.

In his hypothesis, E. Rozenfeld, in order to illustrate this cyclical nature, compared the first phase with a blustering approaching spring, and the second with a gradually approaching autumn. An indirect confirmation of this theory of "cycles" is provided by the history of the emergence of the construction of Kokerei and of this entire gigantic industrial region, and then dying out.

For verifying E. Rozenfeld's theory, a special observation camera that can register what processes occur at this point is installed at the intersection of the new antennae.

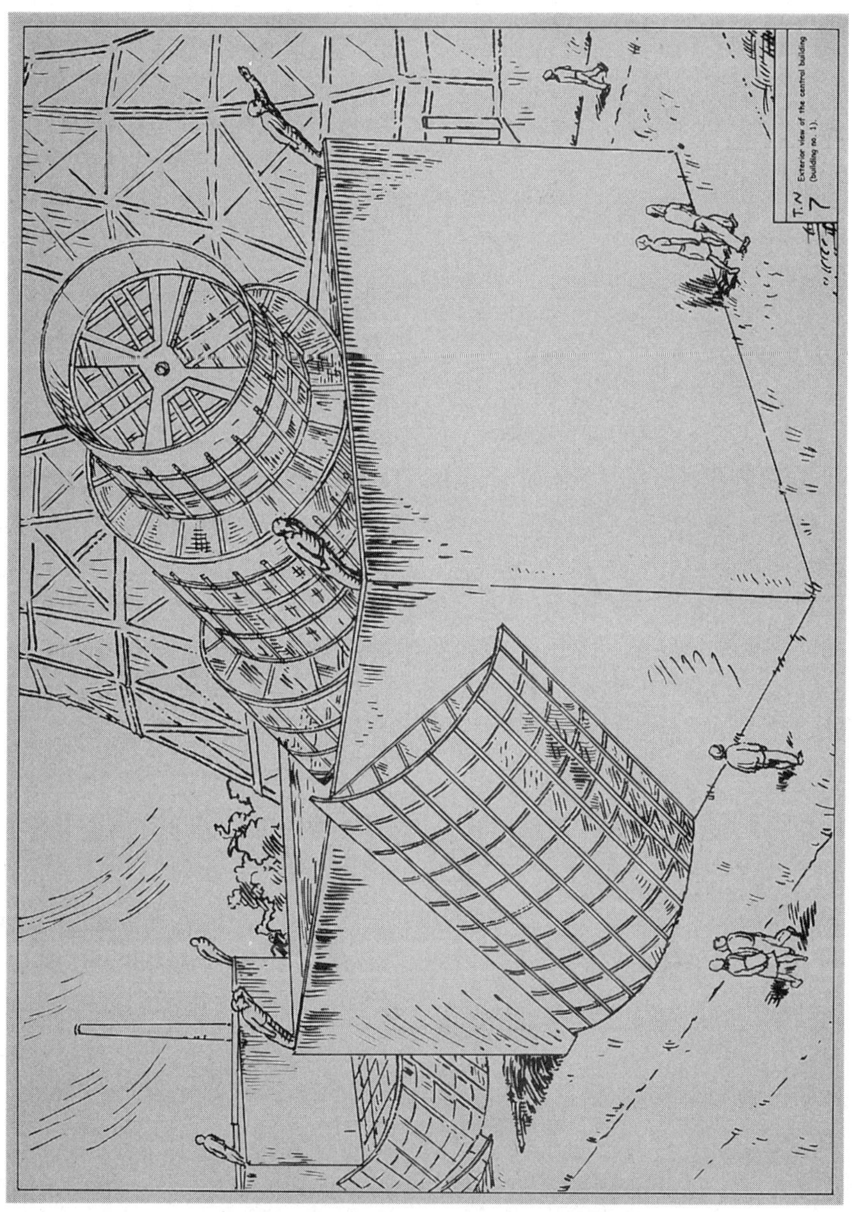

Exterior view of the central building (building no. 1). 2003

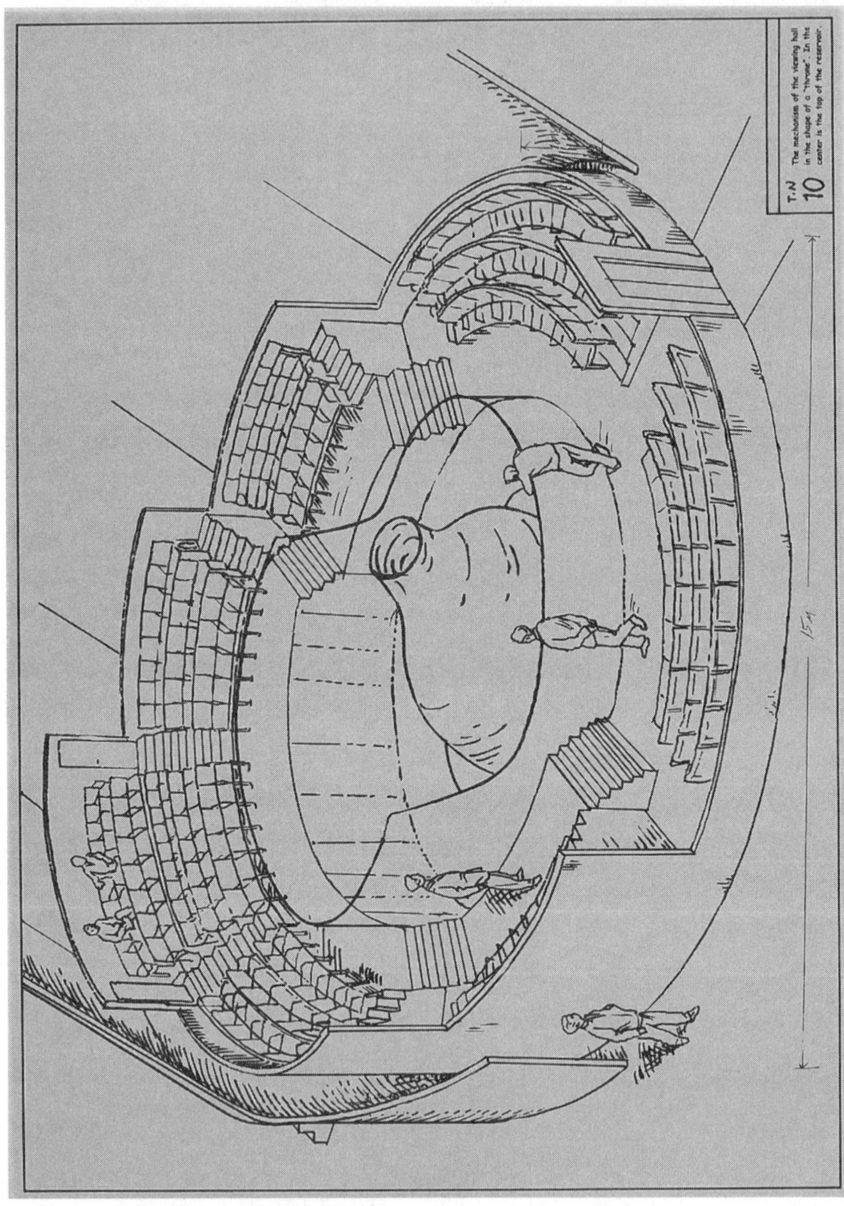

The mechanism of the viewing hall in the shape of a throne.
In the center is the top of the reservoir. 2003

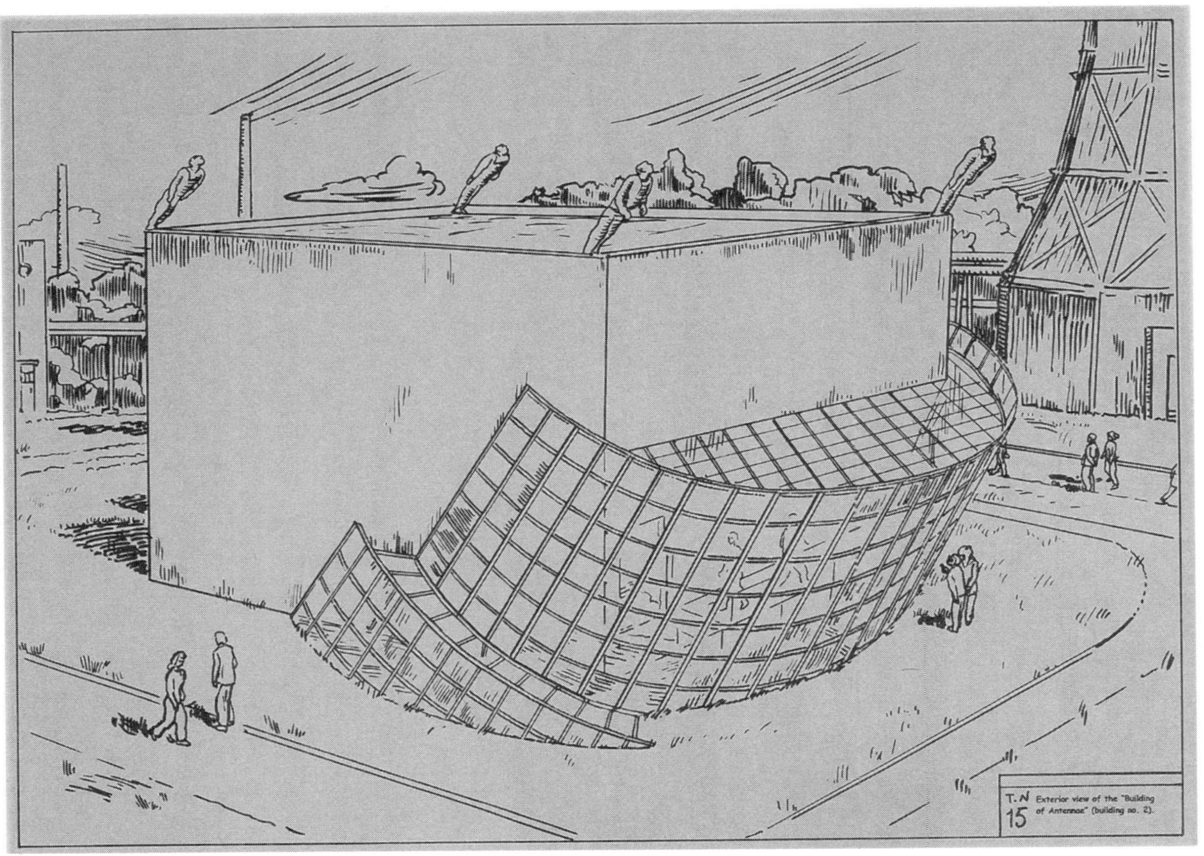

Exterior view of the "building of the antennae" (building no. 2). 2003

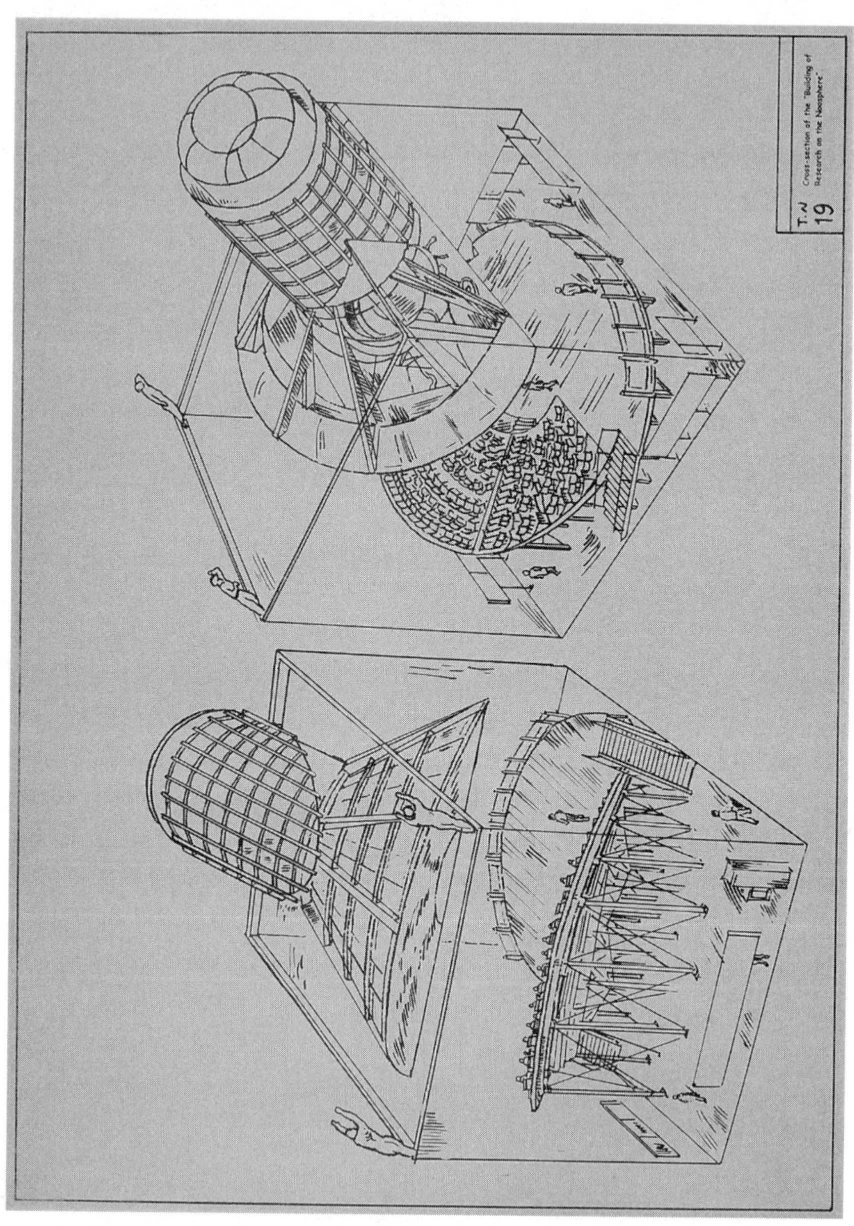

Cross-section of the building for research into the biosphere. 2003

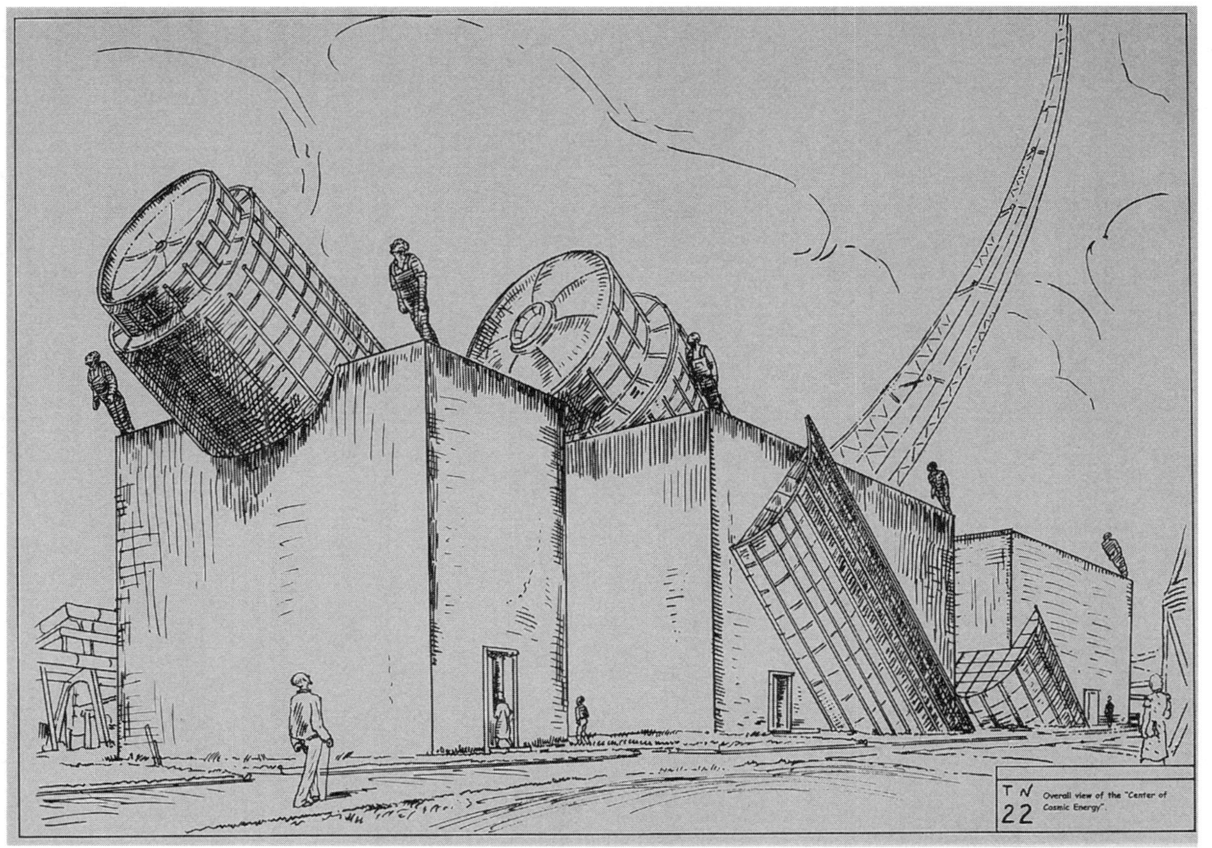

Overall view of the "Center of Cosmic Energy." 2003

Boris Groys

THE TRUTH OF ART

The central question to be asked about art is this one: Is art
capable of being a medium of truth? This question is central
to the existence and survival of art because if art cannot be
a medium of truth then art is only a matter of taste. One has
to accept the truth even if one does not like it. But if art is
only a matter of taste, then the art spectator becomes more
important than the art producer. In this case art can be treated
only sociologically or in terms of the art market – it has no
independence, no power. Art becomes identical to design.

Now, there are different ways in which we can speak about
art as a medium of truth. Let me take one of these ways. Our
world is dominated by big collectives: states, political parties,
corporations, scientific communities, and so forth. Inside these
collectives the individuals cannot experience the possibilities
and limitations of their own actions – these actions become
absorbed by the activities of the collective. However, our art
system is based on the presupposition that the responsibility

for producing this or that individual art object, or undertaking this or that artistic action, belongs to an individual artist alone. Thus, in our contemporary world art is the only recognized field of personal responsibility. There is, of course, an unrecognized field of personal responsibility – the field of criminal actions. The analogy between art and crime has a long history. I will not go into it. Today I would, rather, like to ask the following question: To what degree and in what way can individuals hope to change the world they are living in? Let us look at art as a field in which attempts to change the world are regularly undertaken by artists and see how these attempts function. In the framework of this text, I am not so much interested in the results of these attempts as the strategies that the artists use to realize them.

Indeed, if artists want to change the world the following question arises: In what way is art able to influence the world in which we live? There are basically two possible answers to this question. The first answer: art can capture the imagination and change the consciousness of people. If the consciousness of people changes, then the changed people will also change the world in which they live. Here art is understood as a kind of language that allows artists to send a message. And this message is supposed to enter the souls of the recipients, change their sensibility, their attitudes, their ethics. It is, let's say, an idealistic understanding of art – similar to our understanding of religion and its impact on the world.

However, to be able to send a message the artist has to share the language that his or her audience speaks. The statues in ancient temples were regarded as embodiments of the gods: they were revered, one kneeled down before them in prayer and supplication, one expected help from them and feared their wrath and threat of punishment. Similarly, the veneration of icons has a long history within Christianity – even if God is deemed to be invisible. Here the common language had its origin in the common religious tradition. However, no modern artist can expect anyone to kneel before his work in prayer, seek practical assistance from it, or use it to avert danger. At the beginning of the nineteenth century, Hegel diagnosed this loss of a common faith in embodied, visible divinities as the reason for art losing its truth: according to Hegel the truth of art became a thing of the past. (He speaks about pictures, thinking of the old religions vs. invisible law, reason, and science that rule the modern world.) Of course, in the course of modernity many modern and contemporary artists have tried to regain a common language with their audiences by the means of political or ideological engagement of one sort or another. The religious community was thus replaced by a political movement in which artists and their audiences both participated.

However, art, to be politically effective, to be able to be used as political propaganda, has to be liked by its public. But the community that is built on the basis of finding certain artistic projects good and likable is not necessarily a transformative community – a community that can truly change the world. We know that to be considered as really good (innovative, radical, forward looking), modern artworks are supposed to be rejected by their contemporaries – otherwise, these artworks come under suspicion of being conventional, banal, merely commercially oriented. (We know that politically progressive movements were often culturally conservative – and in the end it was this conservative dimension that prevailed.) That is why contemporary artists distrust the taste of the public. And the contemporary public, actually, also distrusts its own taste. We tend to think that the fact that we like an artwork could mean that this artwork is not good enough – and the fact that we do not like an artwork could mean that this artwork is really good. Kazimir Malevich believed that the greatest enemy of the artist is sincerity: artists should never do what they sincerely like because they probably like something that is banal and artistically irrelevant. Indeed, the artistic avant-gardes did not want to be liked. And – what is even more important – they did not want to be "understood," did not want to share the language which their audience spoke. Accordingly, the avant-gardes were extremely skeptical toward the possibility of influencing the souls of the public and building a community of which they would be a part.

At this point the second possibility to change the world by art comes into play. Here art is understood not as the production of messages, but rather as the production of things. Even if artists and their audience do not share a language, they share the material world in which they live. As a specific kind of technology art does not have a goal to change the soul of its spectators. Rather, it changes the world in which these spectators actually live – and by trying to accommodate themselves to the new conditions of their environment, they change their sensibilities and attitudes. Speaking in Marxist terms: art can be seen as a part of the superstructure or as a part of the material basis. Or, in other words, art can be understood as ideology or as technology. The radical artistic avant-gardes pursued this second, technological way of world transformation. They tried to create new environments that would change people through puttting them inside these new environments. In its most radical form this concept was pursued by the avant-garde movements of the 1920s: Russian constructivism, Bauhaus, De Stijl. The art of the avant-garde did not want to be liked by the public as it was. The avant-garde wanted to create a new public for its art. Indeed, if one is compelled to live in a new visual surrounding, one begins to accommodate one's own sensibility to it and learn to like it. (The Eiffel Tower is a good example.) Thus, the artists of the avant-garde also wanted to build a community – but they didn't see themselves as a part of this community. They shared with their audiences a world – but not a language.

Of course, the historical avant-garde itself was a reaction to the modern technology that permanently changed and still changes our environment. This reaction was ambiguous. The artists felt a certain affinity with the artificiality of the new, technological world. But at the same time they were irritated by the lack of direction and ultimate purpose that is characteristic of technological progress. (Marshall McLuhan: artists moved from the ivory tower to the control tower.) This goal was understood by the avant-garde as the politically and aesthetically perfect society – as utopia, if one is still ready to use this word. Here utopia is nothing else but the end stage of historical development – a society that is in no further need of change, that does not presuppose any further progress. In other words, artistic collaboration with technological progress had the goal of stopping this progress. This conservatism – it can also be a revolutionary conservatism – inherent to art is in no way accidental. What is art then? If art is a kind of technology, then the artistic use of technology is different from the nonartistic use of it. Technological progress is based on a permanent replacement of old, obsolete things by new (better) things. (Not innovation but improvement – innovation can only be in art: the black square.) Art technology, on the contrary, is not a technology of improvement and replacement, but rather of conservation and restoration – technology that brings the remnants of the past into the present and brings things of the present into the future. Martin Heidegger famously believed that in this way the truth of art is regained: by stopping technological progress at least for a moment, art can reveal the truth of the technologically defined world and the fate of the humans inside this world. However, Heidegger also believed that this revelation is only momentary: in the next moment, the world that was opened by the artwork closes again – and the artwork becomes an ordinary thing that is treated as such by our art institutions. Heidegger dismisses this profane aspect of the artwork as irrelevant for the essential, truly philosophical understanding of art – because for Heidegger it is the spectator who is the subject of such an essential understanding and not the art dealer or museum curator.

And, indeed, even if the museum visitor sees the artworks as isolated from profane, practical life, the museum staff never experiences the artworks in this sacralized way. The museum staff does not contemplate artworks but regulates the temperature and humidity level in the museum spaces, restores these artworks, removes the dust and dirt from them. In dealing with the artworks there is the perspective of the museum visitor – but there is also the perspective of the cleaning lady who cleans the museum space as she would clean any other space. The technology of conservation, restoration, and exhibition are profane technologies – even if they produce objects of aesthetic contemplation. There is a profane life inside the museum – and it is precisely this profane life and profane practice that allow the museum items to function as aesthetic objects. The museum does not need any additional profanation, any additional effort to bring art into life or life into art – the museum is already profane through and through. The museum, as well as the art market, treat artworks not as messages but as profane things.

Usually, this profane life of art is protected from the public view by the museum's walls. Of course, at least from the beginning of the twentieth century art of the historical avant-garde tried to thematize, to reveal the factual, material, profane dimension of art. However, the avant-garde never fully succeeded in its quest for the real because the reality of art, its material side that the avant-garde tried to thematize, was permanently re-aestheticized – these thematizations having been put under the standard conditions of art representation.

The same can be said of institutional critique, which also tried to thematize the profane, factual side of art institutions. Institutional critique also remained inside art institutions. Now, I would argue that this situation has changed in recent years – due to the internet and to the fact that the internet has replaced traditional art institutions as the main platform for the production and distribution of art. The internet thematizes precisely the profane dimension of art. Why? The answer to this question is simple enough: in our contemporary world the internet is the place of production and exposure of art at the same time.

This represents a significant departure from past modes of artistic production. As I've noted previously:

> Traditionally, the artist produced an artwork in his or her studio, hidden from public view, and then exhibited a result, a product – an artwork that accumulated and recuperated the time of absence. This time of temporary absence is constitutive for what we call the creative process – in fact, it is precisely what we call the creative process.
>
> André Breton tells a story about a French poet who, when he went to sleep, put on his door a sign that read: "Please, be

quiet – the poet is working." This anecdote summarizes the traditional understanding of creative work: creative work is creative because it takes place beyond public control – and even beyond the conscious control of the author. This time of absence could last days, months, years – even a whole lifetime. Only at the end of this period of absence was the author expected to present a work (maybe found in his papers posthumously) that would then be accepted as creative precisely because it seemed to emerge out of nothingness.[1]

In other words, creative work is work that presupposes the desynchronization of the time of work and the time of the exposure of the results of this work. The reason is not that the artist has committed a crime or has a dirty secret he or she wants to keep from the gaze of others. The gaze of others is experienced by us as an evil eye not when it wants to penetrate our secrets and make them transparent (such a penetrating gaze is rather flattering and exciting), but when it denies that we have any secrets, when it reduces us to what it sees and registers – when the gaze of others banalizes, trivializes us. (Sartre: the other is hell, the gaze of the other denies us our project. Lacan: the eye of the other is always an evil eye.)

Today the situation has changed. Contemporary artists work using the internet – and also put their work on the internet. Artworks by a particular artist can be found on the internet when I google the name of this artist – and they are shown to me in the context of other information that I find on the internet about this artist: biography, other works, political activities, critical reviews, details of the artist's personal life, and so forth. Here I mean not the fictional, authorial subject allegedly investing the artwork with his intentions and with meanings that should be hermeneutically deciphered and revealed. This authorial subject has already been deconstructed and proclaimed dead many times over. I mean the real person existing in the off-line reality to which the internet data refers. This author uses the internet not only to produce art, but also to buy tickets, make restaurant reservations, conduct business, and so forth. All these activities take place in the same integrated space of the internet – and all of them are potentially accessible to other internet users. Here the artwork becomes "real" and profane because it becomes integrated into the information about its author as a real, profane person. Art is presented on the internet as a specific kind of activity: as documentation of a real working process taking place in the real, off-line world. Indeed, on the internet art operates in the same space as military planning, tourist business, capital flows, and so forth: Google shows, among other things, that there are no walls in internet space. A user of the internet does not switch from the everyday use of things to their disinterested contemplation – the internet user uses the information about art in the same way in which he or she uses information about all other things in the world. It is as if we have all become the museum's or gallery's staff – art being documented explicitly as taking place in the unified space of profane activities.

The word "documentation" is crucial here. During recent decades the documentation of art has been more and more included in art exhibitions and art museums – alongside traditional artworks. But this arena has always seemed highly problematic. Artworks are art – they immediately demonstrate themselves as art. So they can be admired, emotionally experienced, and so forth. But art documentation is not art: it merely refers to an art event, or exhibition, or installation, or project which we assume has really taken place. Art documentation refers to art but it is not art. That is why art documentation can be reformatted, rewritten, extended, shortened, and so forth. One can subject art documentation to all these operations that are forbidden in the case of an artwork because these operations change the form of the artwork. And the form of the artwork is institutionally guaranteed because only the form guarantees the reproducibility and identity of this artwork. On the contrary, the documentation can be changed at will because its identity and reproducibility is guaranteed by its "real," external referent and not by its form. But even if the emergence of art documentation precedes the emergence of the internet as an art medium, only the introduction of the internet has given art documentation a legitimate place. (Here one can say like Benjamin noted: montage in art and cinema). Meanwhile, art institutions themselves have begun to use the internet as a primary space for their self-representation. Museums put their collections on display on the internet. And, of course, digital depositories of art images are much more compact and much cheaper to maintain than traditional art museums. Thus, museums are able to present the parts of their collections that are usually kept in storage. The same can be said about the websites of individual artists – one can find there the fullest representation of what they are doing. It is what artists usually show to visitors who come to their studios nowadays: if one comes to a studio to see a particular artist's work, this artist usually puts a laptop on the table and shows the documentation of his or her activities, including production of artworks but also his or her participation in long-term projects, temporary installations, urban interventions, political actions, and so forth. The actual work of the contemporary artist is his or her CV.

Today, artists, like other individuals and organizations, try to escape total visibility by creating sophisticated systems of passwords and data protection. As I've argued in the past, with regard to internet surveillance:

> Today, subjectivity has become a technical construction: the contemporary subject is defined as an owner of a set of passwords that he or she knows – and that other people do not know. The contemporary subject is primarily a keeper of a secret. In a certain sense, this is a very traditional definition of the subject: the subject was long defined as knowing something about itself that only God knew, something that other people could not know because they were ontologically prevented from "reading one's thoughts." Today, however, being a subject has less to do with ontological protection, and more to do with technically protected secrets. The internet is the place where the subject is originally constituted as a transparent, observable subject – and only afterwards begins to be technically protected in order to conceal the originally revealed secret. However, every technical protection can be broken. Today, the *hermeneutiker* has become a hacker. The contemporary internet is a place of cyber wars in which the prize is the secret. And to know the secret is to control the subject constituted by this secret – and the cyber wars are the wars of this subjectivation and desubjectivation. But these wars can take place only because the internet is originally the place of transparency …

The results of surveillance are sold by the corporations that control the internet because they own the means of production, the material-technical basis of the internet. One should not forget that the internet is owned privately. And its profit comes mostly from targeted advertisements. This leads to an interesting phenomenon: the monetization of hermeneutics. Classical hermeneutics, which searched for the author behind the work, was criticized by the theoreticians of structuralism, close reading, and so forth, who thought that it made no sense to chase ontological secrets that are inaccessible by definition. Today this old, traditional hermeneutics is reborn as a means of economically exploiting subjects operating on the internet, where all the secrets are supposedly revealed. The subject is here no longer concealed behind his or her work. The surplus value that such a subject produces and that is appropriated by internet corporations is the hermeneutic value: the subject not only does something on the internet, but also reveals him- or herself as a human being with certain interests, desires, and needs. The monetization of classical hermeneutics is one of the most interesting processes that has emerged in recent decades. The artist is interesting not as producer but as consumer. Artistic production by a content provider is only a means of anticipating this content provider's future consumption behavior – and it is this anticipation alone that is relevant here because it brings profit.[2]

But here the following question emerges: who is the spectator on the internet? The individual human being cannot be such a spectator. But the internet also does not need God as its spectator – the internet is big but finite. Actually, we know who the spectator is on the internet: it is the algorithm – like algorithms used by Google and the NSA.

But now let me return to the initial question concerning the truth of art – understood as a demonstration of the possibilities and limitations of the individual's actions in the world. Earlier I discussed artistic strategies designed to influence the world: by persuasion or by accommodation. Both of these strategies presuppose what can be named the surplus of vision on the part of the artist – in comparison to the horizon of his or her audience. Traditionally, the artist was considered to be an extraordinary person who was able to see what "average," "normal" people could not see. This surplus of vision was supposed to be communicated to the audience by the power of the image or by the force of technological change. However, under the conditions of the internet the surplus of vision is on the side of the algorithmic gaze – and no longer on the side of the artist. This gaze sees the artist, but remains invisible to him (at least insofar as the artist will not begin to create algorithms – which will change artistic activity because they are invisible – but will only create visibility). Perhaps artists can still see more than ordinary human beings – but they see less than the algorithm. Artists lose their extraordinary position – but this loss is compensated: instead of being extraordinary the artist becomes paradigmatic, exemplary, representative.

Indeed, the emergence of the internet leads to an explosion of mass artistic production. In recent decades artistic practice has become as widespread as, earlier, only religion and politics were. Today we live in times of mass art production, rather than in times of mass art consumption. Contemporary means of image production, such as photo and video cameras, are relatively cheap and universally accessible. Contemporary internet platforms and social networks like Facebook, YouTube, and Instagram allow populations around the global to make their photos, videos, and texts universally accessible – avoiding control and censorship by traditional institutions. At the same time, contemporary design makes it possible for the same populations to shape and experience their apartments or workplaces as artistic installations. And diet, fitness, and cosmetic surgery allow them to fashion their bodies into art objects. In our times almost everyone takes photographs, makes videos, write texts, documents their activities – and then puts the documentation on the internet. In earlier times we talked about mass cultural consumption, but today we have to speak about mass cultural production. Under the condition of modernity the artist was a rare, strange figure. Today there is nobody who is not involved in artistic activity of some kind. Thus, today everybody is involved in a complicated play with the gaze of the other. It is this play that is paradigmatic of our time, but we still don't know its rules. Professional art, though, has a long history of this play. The poets and artists of the Romantic period already began to see their own lives as their actual artworks. Nietzsche says in his *Birth of Tragedy* that to be an artwork is better than to be an artist. (To become an object is better than to become a subject – to be admired is better than to admire.) We can read Baudelaire's texts about the strategy of seduction, and we can read Roger Caillois and Jacques Lacan on the mimicry of the dangerous or on luring the evil gaze of the other into a trap by means of art. Of course, one can say that the algorithm cannot be seduced or frightened. However, this is not what is actually at stake here.

Artistic practice is usually understood as being individual and personal. But what does the individual or personal actually mean? The individual is often understood as being different from the others. (In a totalitarian society, everyone is alike. In a democratic, pluralistic society, everyone is different – and respected as being different.) However, here the point is not so much one's difference from others but one's difference from oneself – the refusal to be identified according to the general criteria of identification. Indeed, the parameters that define our socially codified, nominal identity are foreign to us. We have not chosen our names, we have not been consciously present at the date and place of our birth, we have not chosen our parents, our nationality, and so forth. All these external parameters of our personality do not correlate to any subjective evidence that we may have. They indicate only how others see us.

Already a long time ago modern artists practiced a revolt against the identities which were imposed on them by others – by society, the state, schools, parents. They affirmed the right of sovereign self-identification. They defied expectations related to the social role of art, artistic professionalism, and aesthetic quality. But they also undermined the national and cultural identities that were ascribed to them. Modern art understood itself as a search for the "true self." Here the question is not whether the true self is real or merely a metaphysical fiction. The question of identity is not a question of truth but a question of power: Who has the power over my own identity – I myself or society? And, more generally: Who exercises control and sovereignty over the social taxonomy, the social mechanisms of identification – state institutions or I myself? The struggle against my own public persona and nominal identity in the name of my sovereign persona or sovereign identity also has a public, political dimension because it is directed against the dominating mechanisms of identification – the dominating social taxonomy, with all its divisions and hierarchies. Later, these artists mostly gave up the search for the hidden, true self. Rather, they began to use their nominal identities as ready-mades – and to organize a complicated play with them. But this strategy still presupposes a disidentification from nominal, socially codified identities – with the goal of artistically reappropriating, transforming, and manipulating them. The politics of modern and contemporary art is the politics of nonidentity. Art says to its spectator: I am not what you think I am (in stark contrast to: I am what I am). The desire for nonidentity is, actually, a genuinely human desire – animals accept their identity but human animals do not.

It is in this sense that we can speak about the paradigmatic, representative function of art and artist.

The traditional museum system is ambivalent in relation to the desire for nonidentity. On the one hand, the museum offers to the artist a chance to transcend his or her own time, with all its taxonomies and nominal identities. The museum promises to carry the artist's work into the future. However, the museum betrays this promise at the same moment it fulfills it. The artist's work is carried into the future – but the nominal identity of the artist becomes reimposed on his or her work. In the museum catalog we still read the artist's name, date and place of birth, nationality, and so forth. (That is why modern art wanted to destroy the museum.)

Let me conclude by saying something good about the internet. The internet is organized in a less historicist way than traditional libraries and museums. The most interesting aspect of the internet as an archive is precisely the possibilities for decontextualization and recontextualization through the operations of cut and paste that the internet offers its users. Today we are more interested in the desire for nonidentity that leads artists out of their historical contexts than in these contexts themselves. And it seems to me that the internet gives us more chances to follow and understand the artistic strategies of nonidentity than traditional archives and institutions.

Notes

1   Boris Groys, "Art Workers: Between Utopia and the Archive," *e-flux journal* 45 (May 2013).
2   Boris Groys, "Art Workers: Between Utopia and the Archive," *e-flux journal* 45 (May 2013).

4

Andrey Monastyrsky

VDNKh, THE CAPITAL OF THE WORLD: A SCHIZOANALYSIS

"Are they balloons, too?" he asked.

Snowdrop and Cornflower laughed. "They're water-melons," they said. "Haven't you ever seen a water-melon before?"

N. Nosov, *The Adventures of Dunno and His Friends*, translated from the Russian by Margaret Wettlin.

The Bull on the Roof
ballet suite by Darius Milhaud

Balalaika, jangle gaily,
The housewife sits under the table,
On the table in furious fight
The devils put the wizard to flight.
children's folklore, 1986

As I strolled round VDNKh (the Exhibition of Achievements of the National Economy) with my child on a warm September day, we ended up in the rather deserted area of the exhibition where the Golden Ear of Wheat fountain stands. As it happened, although I had lived close to VDNKh and visited it quite often, ever since I became a responsible adult I had never entered this particular section of the exhibition. As I recall, the last time I had been there was as a child, with my own parents. Standing by the pond and gazing at the immense bull on the roof of one of the pavilions (at the age of about seventeen I was very fond of the music to *The Bull on the Roof* by Darius Milhaud, one of the composers of the French Group of Six) I was swept away by a torrent of nostalgic memories from those distant times when everything was experienced in its immediate sensuous and functional significance, when the world was still only an object of perception and experience and was therefore magical, new and magnificent … when my head was not yet cluttered with any gnostic grids and there was no frozen knowledge of the world, but only the process of its endless (as it seemed at the time) cognition, of getting to know it.

And so, having found myself in this wonderful nostalgic spot, I observed with horror my own present way of viewing everything surrounding me, that continuous schizophrenic scanning of nonexistent worlds. I discovered that I was not surrounded by amusing buildings and vistas, but by symbolic perspectives which immediately combined to form an integral, symbolic picture, the iconographical space of this zone of VDNKh. And this is what I came up with as a result.

The collective unconscious of the Russian-speaking region set out what one might call its "radical" and fundamental sacred essence, i.e. its collective consciousness, in the form of a mandala of government, not on Red Square, as might appear at first glance, but at VDNKh.

It is well known that the communists' fundamental ideologeme is heaven on earth, and entry to this heaven ('salvation') is only possible by means of social and economic transformations to the national economy, transformations in which the whole of society must be mobilized. But, after all, any idea is prone to acquire transcendent significance and metaphysical autonomy, and in conformity with the laws of transcendentalization, it immediately becomes manifested in signs and symbols. 'The National Economy' as an idea in the transcendentalization, symbolization and charismatization of Soviet society was arranged at VDNKh into a highly complex constellation of signifiers. This is a mandala of colossal dimensions, an open-air temple in which the place of the god is taken by collective consciousness itself (the communist collective), objectified in the symbol of the Golden Ear of Wheat fountain. This rises up at the very center of a large pond (if the plan of VDNKH is viewed 'vertically', it is located at the very highest level of the heavens and rests on cornucopias from which fruits, vegetables and so forth come cascading out). The fountain consists of eleven gold petals with a twelfth in the form of a trefoil. It is curious to note that the boons of heaven come tumbling out of it from below, into the water. But from what 'heavens' do they shower down, where are they produced?

The very largest building at VDNKh is the Cosmos pavilion. In general 'cosmos' (as order) is a rather complex concept. In polytheistic religions the cosmos is inhabited by gods and humans, while in monotheistic religions a god creates the cosmos while himself remaining unknown. In the sacred space of VDNKh the 'god' (as collective consciousness) dwells outside the 'cosmos', on the earth (or rather, on the water, but we will come to that a little later), since the 'cosmos' is objectified as a separate pavilion.

In the VDNKh mandala, the 'cosmos' is represented as the 'heavens', which are, moreover dialectical. And this is why. If you stand facing the Cosmos pavilion, to your right and slightly further back there is a complex of animal husbandry pavilions, where they display pigs, cows, horses, sheep and so forth. On top of one of these pavilions a bull of immense proportions has been installed, together with a plaster athlete, a titan, who appears to be subduing it. This is obviously a symbol of nature, which for the local ideology is a 'workshop' with which man must work, as he does with chaos, in order to discipline and order it, as he transforms it into cosmos.

Now let us move round to the left of the Cosmos pavilion again, where the Golden Ear of Wheat fountain is located, then stand facing it and look upwards. Directly in front of us we shall see the immense Cosmos dome, with the gigantic plaster bull on its left – they are at almost the same height and on the same scale. If we move along the left bank of the pond, rounding the Golden Ear of Wheat, we shall see the double figure of the Bull and the Titan gradually drifting onto the dome of Cosmos, as if immersing itself in it. In other words, this walk round the pond (the area around the pond is called the Georgian Park) is arranged to provide a visual demonstration of the process of ordering and mastering Chaos with Cosmos; it is itself sacred, symbolizing the path of 'ordering', the path of the Tao. It now becomes clear to us where the 'heavenly boons' come from as they tumble out below from the horns of plenty of the Golden Ear of Wheat fountain: they tumble out from the 'dialectical heavens' and the complex of these four elements – The Golden Ear of Wheat, 'The Bull on the Roof,' the Cosmos and the path itself, from which the entire process can be observed – embody the innermost hallowed impulse of the sacred topography of VDNKh – 'bringing the heavens down to the earth', that is, the construction of paradise here on earth.

The importance of the concept of 'cosmos', notably in the dynamic course of its 'earthing', is also emphasized by the fact that VDNKh is surrounded by a kind of diffusion zone, where the energy of this sacred 'cosmos' seems to weaken as it makes the transition to mundane everyday reality. For instance, located beside VDNKh are the Cosmos hotel, the Cosmos cinema and numerous streets with connection to the cosmos – Cosmonauts' Alley with the Rocket obelisk and the monument to Tsiolkovsky, Korolyov Avenue, Kibaldchik Street, Kondratiuk Street, Tsander Street and so on.

But let us return to the sacred pathway to the Georgian Park, which offers such a good view of the entire sacred center of VDNKh. As the observer moves further along it, if he makes a 180-degree turn – precisely at the point where the bull enters the dome of the Cosmos pavilion – he will see in front of him the small Domestic Services pavilion, which stands not far from the pond, on an elevated spot surrounded by trees. In a certain sense it represents the highest point of transcendence of the efforts of the collective unconscious – literally 'the next world.' Both the location of the pavilion and its amazing architecture (little houses like this can only be imagined in the land of Dunno and his titchy friends in Nosov's popular story), together with the fact that for some reason it is not marked on the guide-map of VDNKh, render it an entirely alien body, excluded from the grandiose panorama and topography of the general complex of exhibition pavilions. This feeling is reinforced by the fact that to the right of it, very close by, in the Water Management and Irrigation Works pavilion, the most sacred 'lower reaches',

so to speak, of the mandala are presented, i.e. the element of
water, in which everything arises, the force of Yin and also
in a certain sense, chaos, corresponding to the Bull on the
Roof. But whereas the Bull on the roof is superior chaos (the
force of Yang), Water Management is, as it were, 'inferior'
chaos (Yin). And the Golden Ear of Wheat fountain is located
precisely between these two unbridled forces. Incidentally, this
situation of 'double chaos' also demonstrates the 'economic
unviability' of this entire system of 'god' in the form of the
collective consciousness, which in itself manifests the same
shortcoming: for after all, the Golden Ear of Wheat fountain
stands in the middle of a pool of water and the 'boons of
heaven' tumble out of its horns of plenty straight into the
water, back into 'chaos.' But more about this below, when we
shall examine the links between the real sociopolitical system
and its mental 'guide-map'

And so, the Domestic Services pavilion peeps out of the
trees like some exceptionally beautiful, magical toy, in which
people (like Nosov's little titches) live eternally and joyfully,
performing the most ordinary of tasks: cutting hair, washing
laundry, mending things and so on, in short they realize their
eternal 'posthumous' existence or afterlife, which is symbolized
by this Domestic Services pavilion. That is, even though all
these dialectical, grandiose hardships of assimilating chaos to
cosmos are drowned in the water, in some magical fashion
they are finally resolved in this place of ultimate, paradisiacal,
toylike existence.

Moreover every element of the sacred complex described
here has its own figurative counterpart in one or another
religious tradition. The Bull on the roof is from the Zen series
of pictures 'In Search of the Bull,' the dome of the Cosmos
pavilion is built in the style of Catholic church architecture, the

Domestic Services pavilion is in the style of a Lamaistic shrine, where the heaven of Amitabha is located, and standing at the entrance to the Water Management pavilion are the immense wheels of an irrigation plant, seeming like the wheels of all-pulverizing samsara. The design of the Golden Ear of Wheat fountain is in the biblical tradition; after all, it is set at the center of a pool, it is, as it were, 'the spirit of God moving upon the face of the waters' before chaos has been cosmogonized, but it is presented here in the form of a collective (an ear in which there are many grains).

The guardians and custodians of this entire gigantic mandala are titans – the huge gilded figures of men and women on the Cosmos pavilion, on other pavilions and on the arch of the main entrance and the sculptural group 'The Worker and the Collective Farm Woman' (outside the territory of VDNKh, but very close by). As we know, in classical mythology the titans fought the gods of Olympus and one of them, Prometheus (a popular Soviet hero), gave fire to humans, that is, he participated in the act of 'bringing the heavens to the earth.'[1]

But the entire complex that I have described is, so to speak, sanctity in action, the transcendence of dialectical materialism as an ongoing process. But before entering this 'inner sanctum' of the world process, we first have to pass through the stable 'principles' (the Aeropagitical 'Principles', so to speak) that have been secured as a result of political and social struggle. In the VDNKh mandala they are represented by two sacred spaces – the central 'USSR' pavilion (absolute rule) and the Friendship of Peoples fountain (the unity of the mutual solidarity of the nations making up the USSR).

The back exit from VDNKh is very interesting (not the Northern exit, but the staff entrance, located to the north-east of the central entrance. Incidentally, it is interesting that on the

official map of VDNKh – which corresponds to the reality –
the southern and northern entrances are located on the same
horizontal line, almost on the same line as the central entrance,
which is indicative of the possibility of a 'vertical 'reading of the
space of VDNKh. Beside this western entrance there is a row
of enclosures containing various species of deer, and the last
of them contains reindeer. This is the edge of the world, the
edge of the universe, which coincides, as it were, with the real
topography of the Soviet Union (the far north). That is to say,
the sacred topography is tied to real geographical topography,
and defines very precisely the edges of the collective
consciousness of the region. It is obvious that the principle of
symbolization and 'objectification' of the collective unconscious
into consciousness is synergetic. The integrality and harmony
of its sacred meanings are built up and change gradually, not
at the will of a single person or group of people, but of their
own accord, as it were; that is, the schizophrenic guide map
(as mentioned in Carlos Castaneda's book *The Eagle's Gift*)
is objectified in the process of grafting the collective into
goal-oriented socioeconomic structures, the reality of which
subsequently unfolds, acting, so to speak, under the control of
this sacred 'guide-map', by the power of the symbol above the
free proliferation of life.

VDNKh is the 'Koschei's egg' of Russia, but unlike the
Egyptian pyramids and sphinxes, the ancient Roman temples
and similar stable symbols of the 'Foundations', under the
control of which those cultures stagnated and decomposed (a
process which did not occur in China, with its fluid, 'three-
line' sanctity), at VDNKh there is a Taoist–Buddhist, dynamic
sanctity (the complex around the Golden Ear of Wheat)
which presupposes a constant changing of structures and a
corresponding change in sacred objectness (the actual 'guide-

map' of the mandala). And so it would seem that in this way a completely closed society bears within it the potential for future changes. Having objectified the collective consciousness (the Golden Ear of Wheat) and presented 'the next world' in the form of a completely childish, fairytale little house of 'domestic services', the collective unconscious, which inevitably gives rise to the power of the symbol that is essential to stabilize society and preserve culture in a particular period of history, in this case finds itself in constant danger of self-destruction, self-liquidation. It grows weak, collapses into a symbol that indicates itself, gradually freeing up psychological spaces (entirely unknown) for the personal (and not collective) principle, literally casting the individual personality out into a void, where it can either perish or discover new structures and a new objectness. In a certain sense one can say that a society, the sacred dimension of which leaves a man free only in his breathing (although even in that there is a great deal of hyperbole) potentially nurtures a Prajapati (in a real sense – a schizophrenic) in every one of its members, and his breathing engenders reason, reason engenders gods, and gods engender worlds (his own, pathopsychological worlds).

In addition to everything else, the Soviet Union, as an objectified fruit of German classical philosophy, moreover in its Romantic-shamanistic version of Hegelianism, is, firstly, transcendental through and through and secondly (in accordance with the Romantic tradition of nostalgia) its transcendentality tends towards the most ancient, Vedic form, only instead of one Prajapati, as the ancient Hindus had, we have a potential 250 million of them and each one, in the innermost depths of his own soul, feels his own cosmic solitude and marginality and 'does not know joy.' He is surrounded by nothing but symbolic objects useless in everyday reality,

with no breath or life in them, like the stone women of the
Friendship of Nations fountain (who simultaneously express
the essential corporality of Soviet men and women) and
motionless, like the stalk of the Golden Ear of Wheat fountain
(which points out the position of existential manifestations
– only on the periphery!) When the ancient Prajapati saw a
picture like this surrounding him, he was not delighted (here
follows a quotation): "He decided: 'I shall enter into them, in
order to breathe life into them.' However, being one, he could
not do this. He divided himself into five parts, called prana,
apana, samana, udana and vyana …"[2]

After that History began. What will happen next to
our Prajapatis? At present almost all of them have split
personalities, a psychological illness. But perhaps they are in
danger of a five-way split? A perfect match for the number of
points on a five-pointed star and the types of breath according
to the Vedas? In the tradition of schizoanalysis, one can detect
in the Russian word *raspyaterenie* ('dividing into five') the word
raspyatie ('crucifixion') and draw the conclusion that Russia has
always been a sacrifice for the edification of other nations: 'one
commits a stupidity, so that many others will not.' On the other
hand there is complete uncertainty (after all, in the sacred sense
the Soviet Union always stands, as it were, at the beginning
of History) which can also lead to some kind of palliative
resolution, the emergence of new social structures, and the
well-worn rule of collective consciousness "social matters first,
then personal ones," which produces a situation in which all
the 'boons of heaven' somehow disappear (as the Golden Ear
of Wheat fountain demonstrates so clearly) or can suddenly
change into their opposites.

Having defined VDNKh as the central mandala of the
government of Soviet society by the collective unconscious,

it is possible to fantasize further on this subject in terms, for instance, of how the sacred and the real intersect in the general system of government of the Soviet Union and in the awareness of Soviet people.

It is no secret that the socioeconomic system of the USSR is absolute state capitalism (a monopoly) of the imperial type. What form does the leading role of the communists take in this system? First and foremost, they perform the ideological management of society, i.e. they are concerned with ideas, the medium for which is their own consciousness and the consciousness of the 'flock,' the consciousness of Soviet people. As shepherds and priests, their function consists of an adjusting mediation between the consciousness of the masses and a transcendent consciousness, which in this case is the economy, the reality of which, however, flows and is objectified (especially on the foreign market) in the forms of absolute state capitalism. After all, communism as a real system of socioeconomic relations does not exist. And socialism is simply the abstract generalization of capitalism to the point of absolutization, it is something like the Absolute Spirit of capitalism, which can also be called socialism (a purely linguistic problem). Consequently the communists, as people from 'out there,' from the future, communicate with the masses via a phantom, transcendent 'national economy,' objectified symbolically in the mandala of VDNKh; they are also under the power of their mandala and follow its 'guide-map' in carrying out their own purely conceptual performance. The thought-forms of this mandala also connect the masses and the communist leadership into the single psychological body of the collective consciousness.

For the collective consciousness of the Christian world a separate individual can become 'conscious' ('be saved') if he or she 'enters into the Mind of Christ' (Saint Paul). A special methodology has been developed for this 'entering in' or imitation of God, including the nine orders of Dionysius the Aeropagite, in which the human mind 'ascends,' as it were, through various psychological levels: angels, archangels, powers, etc. The Taoists have a similar system, and so do the Buddhists ('The Ten Stages of a Bodhisattva'). But how can a man imitate the collective consciousness? What is the psychological structure (not the structure by category and age, i.e. Little Octobrists, Pioneers, Komsomol members, Communists) of the Soviet collective consciousness, which has to be projected onto every individual personality, and does it contain a hierarchy of 'ascent'? We are talking here about the sacred 'orders' of Soviet consciousness. Probably they should be correlated and defined via the sacred thought-forms of the VDNKh mandala that we have described above. In that case the consciousness of every Soviet person should include five (basic) thought-forms: 'cosmonaut,' 'titan,' 'wheat ear,' 'titch,' and … 'Georgian.' What Georgian is this? Firstly, as it happens, the pool with the Golden Ear of Wheat is surrounded by a Georgian Garden, and the sacred path – the Tao which offers a view of this entire panorama – runs through this garden. Secondly, in geographical terms Georgia, which is part of our empire, is a land of the elements – sea and mountains – and therefore the 'Georgian' consciousness is most immediately and directly connected with reality, in particular with the socioeconomic system of absolute state capitalism. Let us recall Stalin's 'absolute statehood' and the market (i.e. capitalism), in which Georgians play the leading role. And finally the Georgians are the most active opponents of this system and at the same time they define it as an empire. They normally express opposition in their linguistic behavior (and after all, for schizoanalysis only this aspect is important): usually a Georgian traveling to the Russian markets to sell his fruit says that he is going 'to the USSR.' Indeed, there have been cases when the following announcement was made at a Georgian railway station: 'The Georgia–USSR train departs at such-and-such a time from such-and-such a platform.'

The communists are also concerned with these five 'bodiless orders' of the collective consciousness, both in themselves and in the people. In this system the order of 'titches' is the end product of society, in other words that self-same 'conscious' Soviet man that we desire, who seems already to be living 'in the next world' like Dunno, Doughnut, Dr Tablet, Tubey and other characters in Nosov's tale (in accordance with their professional orientation).

It seems that the other four 'orders' do not have any hierarchy in relation to each other, they somehow coexist chaotically and, moreover, in each individual one entity or another predominates. The Cosmonauts are the avant-gardists in all areas of science, technology and culture – from Lenin, Tsiolkovksy and Michurin to the contemporary avant-garde artists Sven Gundlach and Sergei Anufriev, who recently declared themselves 'cosmonauts.' The Titans are the various different heroes of war and labor and almost all Soviet women. The Wheat Ears are the opposite of the Titches, they are the upper Party leadership and the dissidents. This consciousness (in the individual personality unconscious) is inclined to self-destruction and oblivion, since this is where the actual collective consciousness (the local 'god') closes in on itself and collapses: the 'imitation' of this 'god' is impossible and therefore, in approaching it, the individual personality always feels like a black hole, which is endlessly falling into itself (this tendency to self-destruction is also manifested physically, especially vividly during the 1930s, when one section of the Party 'ate out' another section in immense chunks). The 'Georgians' are the people (not necessarily of Georgian nationality) who essentially hold everything up. Only they maintain real contact with the real system (people employed in the ministries, trade, communications and so on). Their activity is primarily criminal in nature and in the Soviet sacred order, by analogy with the Christian one, they play the role of 'devils,' who have constantly to be reeducated, driven out or actually annihilated. After all, for the Party leadership the national economy is an ideal, transcendental system and the ideal workers in it can only be 'Titans' (such as Stakhanov and so on).

Evidently this is the 'spiritual' topography of the Soviet five-way-split consciousness with which the communist leadership is concerned: it is not concerned with the real system. In various periods of history it activates one or another 'order,' which becomes the leading one. During the period of War Communism it was the 'Titans,', during the New Economic Policy it was the 'Georgians', at various intervals it has been the 'Cosmonauts'. The 'Wheat Ears' and the 'Titches' are beyond the scope of any changes, they are the alpha and omega of the entire sacred system. In the very 'highest' sense of sanctity, each Soviet person starts his or her life as a 'titch' (childhood) and ends it as a 'wheat ear' (old age). After the stage of the 'wheat ear,' the stage of the 'titch' begins again. The mechanism of Hinayana is clearly detectable here, but without its objectives: eternal existence in a 'titchy' paradise, metempsychosis and 'our immortality is our children' – the official choice is the final option, but in sacred terms it is the first. This unconscious choice explains in no small measure the lamentable state of the national economy of the USSR. After all, the giant watermelons, melons, grapes, apples – almost even including the pigs – which are displayed as the result, as the highest and targeted eidos of the national economy, come tumbling out of the Golden Ear of

Wheat fountain's horns of plenty and into the water. These are
the immense watermelons that Nosov describes in the towns
of the titches. In other words, it is the result that is sacralized
and not the technology. All the other pavilions display simply
technical means (they can be improved) for achieving the same
result – a watermelon as big as a house. That is, what should be
most important in the economic system – the technology – is
exported to the peripheral zone of sanctity, and a curiosity is set
at its center, the fruit of the labor of an individual 'Titan', not of
the activity of society.

In any case, that was how things stood during the
charismatic period of Soviet power – from Stalin to Brezhnev.
These immense fruits were displayed in the central 'USSR'
pavilion (while various sorts of ordinary potatoes were
displayed in the Agriculture pavilion. The 'USSR' pavilion is
closed now for a change of exhibition. There is at least some
hope that the changes will be in the direction of a national
economy that will not be the goal, but the means.

If it is possible to speak of the history of the collective
consciousness, of a line of succession of sacred mandalas of
government as ideologies and systems change, then we can say
that the appearance of the Soviets in an Orthodox Christian
region is a kind of 'revolt of the angels,' the very lowest 'bodiless
order' of the Orthodox collective consciousness (and since the
theme of this revolt was originally presented in the Christian
tradition, why should it not be realized in more palpable
forms?) Moreover, this 'revolt' was carried out supposedly with
'good intentions' (after all, communism in itself, as an abstract
idea, does seem like a good idea, although only in its most
popular, primitive interpretation, and in general it is also similar
to 'the kingdom of Christ, where there will be no churches,
for there is no one to worship' – also a well-known evangelical

topic.) And the fact that this 'revolt' could have taken place in Russia (apart from the real, objective causes) can be explained by the highly complex structure of the collective consciousness of the Russian Empire (which was constituted by Orthodox Christianity, which by the nineteenth century was completely 'museumified' and whose spirituality had become absolutely apophatic – founded on the complete incomprehension of divine providence). The structures of the collective consciousness were autonomized and the 'apophatic angels' – as the stratum of the collective consciousness farthest removed from its 'concealed center' ('God') and therefore completely free of any 'spiritual stuff' (in simple terms, the communists) – were able to carry through the October Revolution as a social experiment. It is interesting that the acronym formed from the surnames of the five major figures of the Land and Freedom party spells out the Russian word *PIZDA* ('CUNT'), and this group was actually called that in the nineteenth century, and in Orthodox iconography the apophatic symbol is sometimes depicted in the form of a black triangle above the head of the Lord of Hosts). The consistent realization of apophatic sanctity was also responsible for a distinctly necrophilic act which is rather strange for a 'materialist' society (that is, one would think, for a society of 'common sense') – the public display on Red Square of the corpse of its main leader. This exhibition is, as it were, the objectified 'node' of the connection between the old Orthodox (apophatic) mandala – 'The Ancient of Days Resting from All His Works' – and the new, communist, communal mandala – an incarnation of the queen bee in the communal hive. But, as in the case of the Golden Ear of Wheat, a symbolic 'failure' occurs – a dead queen bee is displayed, and its deadness and nonreality suffuse the entire structure of the communist leadership with the energy of nonreality and futility.

And so, in describing the collective consciousness of Soviet
society of the charismatic period we are essentially dealing
with the stratigraphy of the 'apophatic angel,' which in the
apocalyptic movement has become separated into layers – into
'Cosmonauts', 'Titans', 'Wheat Ears' (the bearers, by the way,
of apophatic nature), 'Georgians,' and 'Titches'. But each of
these layers, in its potential for rebirth, can easily be identified
with one of the five parts into which Prajapati divided: prana/
breath is the 'Titans', apana/exhaling is the 'Georgians',
samana/internal breathing, which unites all the other forms of
breathing, is the 'Wheat Ears,' udana/a sigh when dying or in
a dreamless sleep, is the 'Titches,' and vyana/the intermediate
moment between inhaling and exhaling, is the 'Cosmonauts.'

This hermeneutics translated eschatological spirituality into
the beginning of a new history.

Beside the Golden Ear of Wheat fountain, at the edge of the
pond, a new building has been constructed, but not opened yet:
the architecture is rather strange, perhaps a pavilion,[3] perhaps
a restaurant, or perhaps something else. It looks quite modern.
Attached to it on the pond side is something like an observation
tower with an external spiral staircase and viewing platform at
its summit. Quite possibly it is only intended for official use by
staff. I ought to go there and photograph all these places and
try to climb up that tower. From up there I might get a good
panoramic photo of the Botanical Gardens, located to the right
of this building, outside VDNKh. It might possibly be simply
a beautiful view, a landscape, and not a symbolic perspective.
Perhaps, through one little window of the gnoseological grid
of 'knowledge,' which destroys everything that is alive, it is
possible to find a loophole for a free view, even if it is free in
a specialized sense (like the outlook from the ancient Chinese

contemplation towers), deliberately cropped, but nonetheless with an 'empty,' desacralized center, where the most precious thing we have is always actually concealed – a recovered sense of the unknown.

September 1986

Notes

1   This perspective allows us to understand the phenomenon of Moscow's 'best metro in the world' and why, in the 1930s, the far from rich Soviet society went to the expense of such nonfunctional luxury as the Moscow metro system, with stations decorated in a style reminiscent of the internal design of Orthodox Christian churches. Most likely this is the result of a struggle between two mandalas of management – Orthodoxy's program of collective consciousness, which had not yet been completely eradicated, and the new, Soviet communality, with 'paradise on earth' (the basis of which is the Orthodox 'sobornost,' or 'togetherness,' while its summit and structural consummation is the GULAG system of camps, where communality is presented in its pure form). After all, if 'paradise' is realized (in the symbol) on earth, and not in 'heaven,' as it used to be, then naturally the 'places for prayer meetings have to be moved underground in order somehow to maintain the customary hierarchy. The marble facing of the Cathedral of Christ the Savior, which was blown up, also came in handy; it was used to decorate the Mayakovsky metro station, which during the Second World War was the place where Stalin and the Politburo led the celebration of one of the most important sacred rites of the Soviet regime – the anniversary of the revolution.

2   Types of breathing (the Maitreya Upanishad).

3   When I found out that this strange structure with the tower was the future Fish Industry pavilion, and that virtually the entire huge building was an aquarium, it became clear to me that all the architectural 'peculiarities' at VDNKh are primarily the result of the sanctity of this entire space, by the location of a given building in the VDNKh mandala. The Fish Industry pavilion (which, by the way, they started to build when Soviet charisma was approaching its final end, i.e. at the most dangerous moment for ideology) is a symbol of the Great Flood, the waters of the pond, where the Golden Ear of Wheat stands, have, so to speak, risen above the wheat ear – the pavilion stands right on the edge of that pond), and the lookout

tower is a symbol of Mount Ararat, where Noah found salvation. The line should be drawn under this 'eschatological ichthyology,' without taxing ourselves too greatly with the question of why (as in *Alice in Wonderland*) sacred spaces so easily merge into the realm of punning.

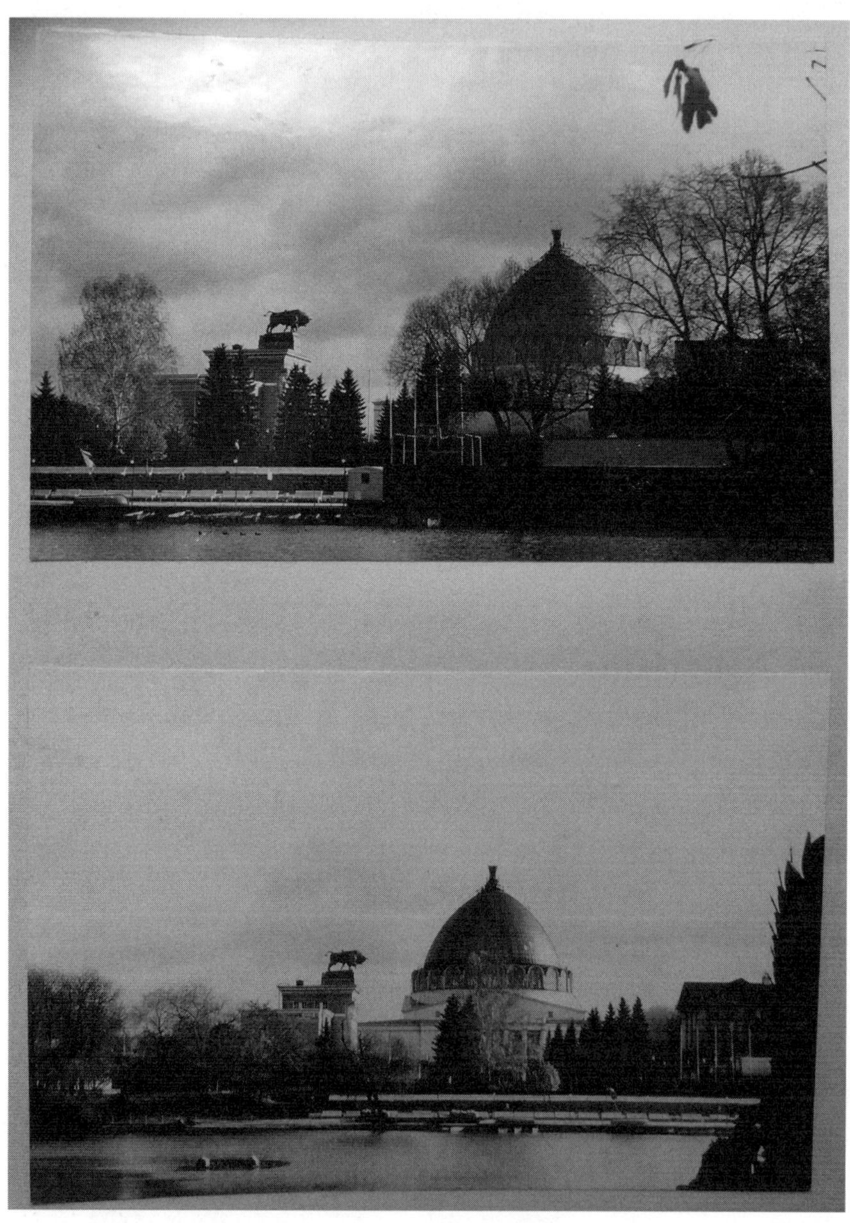

Andrey Monastyrsky. "The Bull on the Roof." 1986

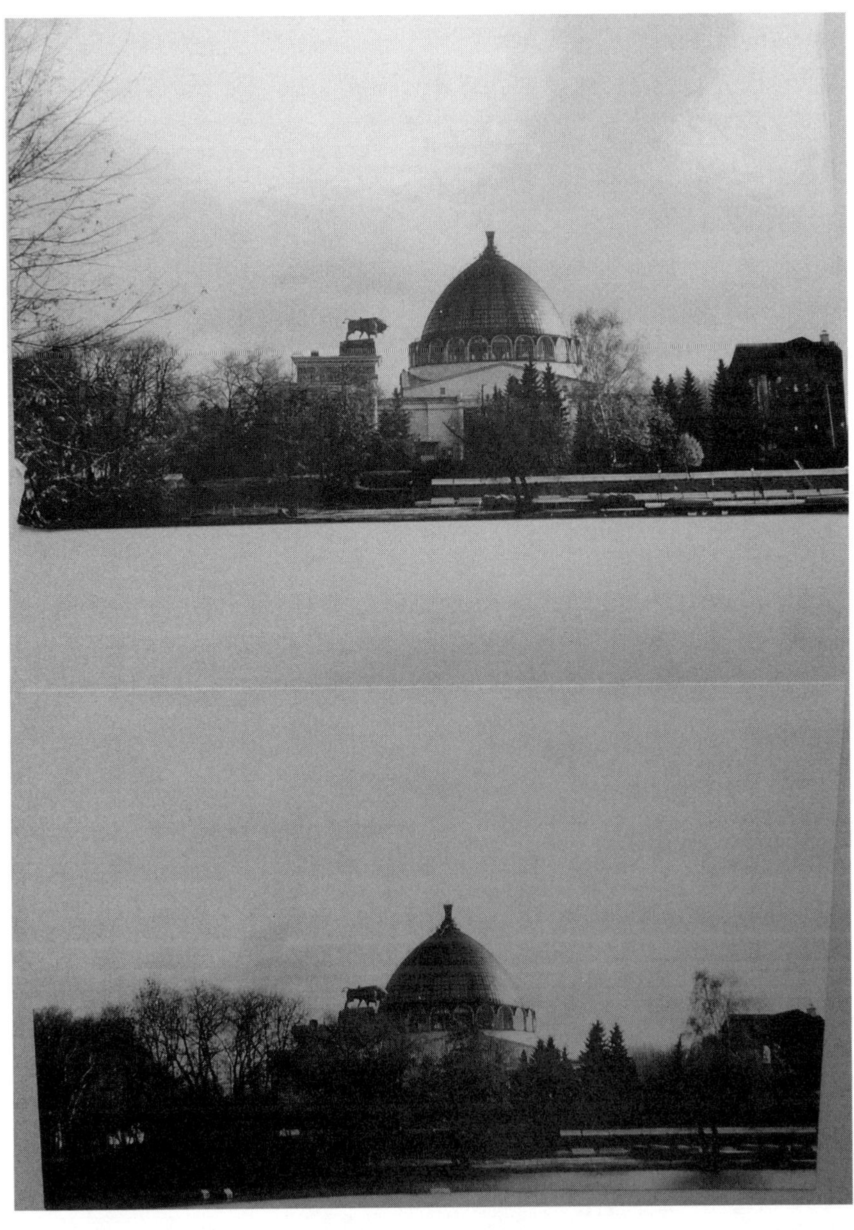

5

Anton Vidokle

THE COMMUNIST REVOLUTION WAS CAUSED BY THE SUN: A PARTIAL SCRIPT FOR A SHORT FILM

A FIELD OF WIND TURBINES.

Enormous white propeller blades fill the screen. They are rotating in slow motion and almost silently, except for a soft, rhythmic swish of air. The NARRATOR's voice has an echo.

NARRATOR
Make yourself comfortable.
Move around if you need to.
Like you do when you sleep.
It helps to relax.
As you begin to feel comfortable
Move your attention all the way down to your feet.
Imagine your feet starting to feel pleasantly warm.
Warm and relaxed.
Feel your feet relaxing.
Let this warmth grow and spread throughout your body.
And as you breathe in, this feeling of warmth

Will start to flow up into the muscles of your legs.

Feel the warmth and relaxation enter your muscles.

Notice that you are no longer aware of your feet

Because they are so relaxed.

Deeply relaxed.

Without any effort

Your breath starts to carry this feeling

Into the muscles of your lower body.

Your calves loosen up.

Your muscles are so very relaxed

That you can't be bothered to notice them at all.

Meanwhile, this relaxation is spreading upward

Like liquid absorbed into a sugar cube.

No need to notice your body as it relaxes all by itself.

The muscles of your neck and jaw,

Your tongue,

Your face,

Your scalp and ears,

All the way through from the tips of your toes

to the top of your head.

Warm and relaxed,

Deeply relaxed as you sit

Safe and comfortable

Breathing freely and easily.

You are no longer aware of your body.

You are barely aware of your mass.

Enjoy this feeling

This warm sensation

As your mind starts to feel at ease.

Without effort, your thoughts focus on what is important.

You are in control.

DESERT, A MOUNTAIN OF SAND.

It's windy. A man is walking in the foothills of the dune.
It's very hot: he walks slowly and with much effort. As he
approaches the camera, we realize that he is unusually large – a
giant with strong Asian features. He begins to speak very slowly,
taking long pauses between sentences.

KONSTANTIN

Lenin died during winter.
According to tradition, the body must be laid out for three days
    for mourners before being placed in a coffin and buried.
You can see the funeral on YouTube.
Heavily bundled people, snow, flowers, soldiers, and horses.
A river of people moving past the corpse
Looking strange, as if in a trance.
Many are crying.

NARRATOR

More than a hundred thousand people came to view the body
    during the three days. People kept coming and coming.
A decision was made to keep the body on public display in a
    wooden tomb.
After some months the whole thing started looking miraculous:
Flesh immune to decay.
Then the winter broke and the body began to decompose.
Something had to be done quickly.
Lenin's body was embalmed using a combination of glycerin and
formaldehyde: formaldehyde to kill bacteria, and glycerin
    to keep
the flesh moist. The brain was removed and given to a scientist.
Trotsky missed the funeral because Stalin gave him the wrong
    date.

A DRESSING ROOM OF A NIGHTCLUB

A young man is applying makeup, slowly transforming himself
into a woman slightly resembling Cleopatra. She uses glitter for
eye shadow.

NARRATOR

The ancient Egyptians believed that the soul would return to a
    preserved corpse.
Over three thousand years ago, their pharaoh invented a new
    religion of one god: the Sun.
This pharaoh worshiped solar energy, and called himself Son of
    the Sun.
He said:

CLEOPATRA

You are in my heart
There is no other who knows you
Only me, your Son
Whom you have taught your ways and your might.
Those on Earth come from your hand: you made them.
When you have dawned, they live.
When you set, they die.
You are lifetime, one lives by you.
All eyes are on your beauty until you set.
All labor ceases when you rest.
When you rise, you stir everyone.

A VILLAGE CEMETERY NEAR ALMATA.

Konstantin, Musa, and Svetlana are here. It's very dry and
dusty. Wheat fields stretch to the horizon in all directions. The
grain has already been harvested and farmers are burning chaff.
Black birds are circling plumes of smoke.

KONSTANTIN

It's not the Earth that feeds us but the Sun!
Solar energy is the source of life's exuberant development.

MUSA

The existence of life is not an accident:
Its very being reflects the radiance of the Sun.
The distribution of life on the planet
follows the intensity of solar energy.
The surface of this planet is shaped by living substance.
The biosphere hosts many manifestations of energy:
Energy of movement and energy of transformation.
This energy is amplified and nourished by the Sun.
Solar energy is collected and concentrated
through the living substance of the biosphere.
The biosphere transforms the Sun's radiance into oxygen
that envelops the entire surface of the planet.
It gives Earth its unique qualities.

KONSTANTIN

The origin and essence of our wealth comes to us
through the radiation of the Sun. It also comes
through the inhuman underground toil of miners.

MUSA

Solar radiation results in a superabundance of energy.
Its surplus needs to be spent.
The eating of other species is one such luxury.
Sexual reproduction is another: it ensures
the intense consumption of energy.

KONSTANTIN
Death is also a luxury: it's not necessary.

SVETLANA
Because the energy of cosmos is indestructible.
Because true religion is a cult of ancestors.
Because true social equality means immortality for all.
Because of love, we must resurrect our ancestors
From cosmic particles
As minerals, as animated plants.
Solar, self-feeding, collectively conscious
Immortal
Transsexual
On Earth, on space ships, on space stations
On other planets.

FIELDS ON THE OUTSKIRTS OF AN INDUSTRIAL CITY

We see coal mines, power lines, and graves.

NARRATOR
This is Karaganda.
We are here to build an aero-ionization dish:
An electric chandelier of invisible energy that
emits a field of negatively charged ion particles.
It will follow the designs of the Soviet
scientist who worshipped the Sun.
He lived in Karaganda for several decades.
First as a prisoner in a labor camp, where the
commandant allowed him to carry out
scientific experiments in a jail cell by night.
Then at the camp's coal mine, where he designed
an irradiation hall to prolong the life of prisoners.

A jailhouse sanatorium

And a resuscitation chamber.

A FACTORY WORKSHOP

A group of workers are constructing a large metal device: a
gridded dish with thousands of small needles soldered to the
intersections of the grid.

SVETLANA

The healthy movement of blood throughout our bodies is
    balanced by the negative electric charge of red blood cells.
This negative electrical charge is what enables the intricate
    movement of blood through sixty thousand miles of vessels
    in the human body, without getting stuck or clogged.
Red blood cells absorb oxygen in the lungs and transport it to
    the body's tissue and organs.
If electricity is applied to atoms of oxygen, it gives oxygen a
    negative charge.
Red blood cells transport these negatively charged ions of
    oxygen from the lungs to the rest of the living organism.
As a result, breathing should become noticeably easier.
Various aches and pains should disappear.

NARRATOR

These chandeliers were supposed to be installed
on all Soviet spaceships, to keep cosmonauts healthy.
Instead, they were installed in the offices of top government
    officials to keep them from going senile.

SVETLANA

We are building a very large version of this chandelier in a
    cemetery.

We want to know what it can do for:
    a. humans
    b. animals
    c. plants
    d. weather conditions

AERIAL VIEW OF A VAST CEMETERY

From a distance it looks like a strange city. As the camera gets closer, we can make out numerous graves and mausoleums. A group of workers arrives in a truck.

NARRATOR

The scientist who worshipped the Sun got in trouble because
    he wrote a book.
It was a study of the effect of the Sun on human history.
During the First World War, while observing sunspots through a
    telescope, the scientist noticed a remarkable coincidence.
Immediately following the passage of sunspots through the
    Sun's central meridian, fighting escalated on numerous
    fronts.
Fascinated by this observation, the scientist embarked on a
    comparative historical analysis of solar activity and the mass
    behavior of people.
He compared existing records of solar activity with key
    historical events recorded in different parts of the world
    over the course of the previous three hundred years.
The results appear to show that during peak periods in solar
    activity, the following tend to occur:
    a. social upheavals
    b. revolutions
    c. wars
    d. economic booms and collapses

e. epidemics

f. et cetera

In the cemetery, workers bring shovels to dig pits, into which
they pour cement. They are building foundations to install
towers, from which a giant dish will be hung about ten meters
above the ground. It's connected to an electrical generator.
When the power is turned on, the dish appears to produce wind.

NARRATOR

Solar activity is cyclical. Sunspots, flares, and coronal eruptions
pass through periods of minimum and maximum activity at
recurring intervals of about eleven years – nine times each
century.

Each solar cycle is also a cycle of historical events – a
historiometric cycle.

The scientist divided the historiometric cycle into four distinct
periods, each characterized by a degree of excitement in the
social psyche.

The first period, corresponding with minimal activity of the
Sun, is characterized by an apathetic, depressed state.

The dominant feelings and moods are those of:

a. resignation

b. passivity

c. tolerance

d. peacefulness

This psychosocial atmosphere creates the conditions for
conclusion of wars, peace treaties, capitulations. This is
the period most productive for arts and sciences, and for
creative activities in general.

The second period is characterized by an uplifted social mood
and increased activity, a crystallization of social positions

and opinions, an emergence of political alliances, and the
coalescence of the masses around certain ideas.

During the third period, the synchronization between solar
activity and human behavior reaches its peak.

The dominant social moods are those of:

d. enthusiasm

c. decisiveness

b. optimism

a. certainty

Societies enter a passionate state and are easily mobilized by
charismatic personalities: political and military leaders,
gifted speakers, and so forth.

Political unrest and uprisings, wars, conquests, and insurgencies
are the symptoms of this period.

The unity within social groups during this time enables them to
solve complex political and military questions.

The feeling of solidarity resolves most social contradictions and
disagreements.

Mystical, esoteric, and occult teachings, as well as maniacal
ideas, gain in circulation, and mass psychological delusions
or "psychotic epidemics" are common.

The fourth historiometric cycle is a time of lessened
psychosocial excitability.

The psychological unity of the masses starts to disintegrate.

Political and military alliances fray and fall apart.

Wars come to a standstill and separatist tendencies increase.

The lack of social unity inhibits mass action.

Gradually, the fall in excitability leads back to a depressed
social mood.

A number of animals are led under the dish by a shepherd: a
cow, a horse, sheep, and goats. There are also some plants and

several people who appear to be technicians or scientists. It's silent and animals don't move much. Nothing happens. This continues for a while. Eventually the animals fall asleep.

NARRATOR

Even though the Sun does not directly determine the outcome
of specific social or economic situations, it exerts an
influence on the biological life of the planet.
Therefore, it exerts an influence on the biological,
psychological, and social spheres of human activity.
Through this, the Sun influences the rhythm of all historical
processes.
The scientist who worshiped the Sun wrote:
A human is not only a terrestrial being,
but a cosmic one
connected by all his biology, all molecules,
all particles of the body
with its cosmic rays
its flows and fields.
Following the publication of his study, the scientist was
invited to lecture at Columbia University in New York, and
nominated for a Nobel Prize in science. Instead, he was
arrested and sent to a labor camp.
Because one possible interpretation of his work could lead to
the conclusion that: the Communist Revolution was caused
by the sun.

A TWO-LANE ROAD AFTER DARK

Through the car's windshield, the beams of car lights illuminate the white stripes of the lane divider. The car is moving at medium speed, making the flickering of white stripes hypnotic. The NARRATOR's voice has an echo.

NARRATOR

Focus.

Concentrate.

I want you to imagine that you are standing at a fork in a road.

As you look down the road that leads to the left,

you notice that it is a cold, barren, unfriendly, and dead road.

The sky is dreary and there is a cold drizzle of rain.

The trees are barren of leaves and the grass has long been
replaced with hard, cold rocks.

A cold wind blows.

This is a dead place.

This road leads to death.

As you turn from that road, and look down the road that leads
to the right, you see a beautiful path.

The Sun is shining brightly in a deep, clear, blue sky.

The trees are full of leaves and the grass is lush and green.

As you begin to walk down this path, you feel a warm, gentle
breeze playing in your hair.

With each step, you find yourself feeling healthier and healthier,
stronger and stronger.

This road leads to immortal life.

With each step, you feel more alive and more convinced that
nothing will ever again make you go back to that other cold,
dreary, deadly road.

You have chosen life. Infinite, healthy, strong life.

And nothing can ever change that.

Now, every positive change has been sealed into the deepest
part of your subconscious.

And every positive change reinforces itself in your mind, over
and over again, with every breath that you exhale.

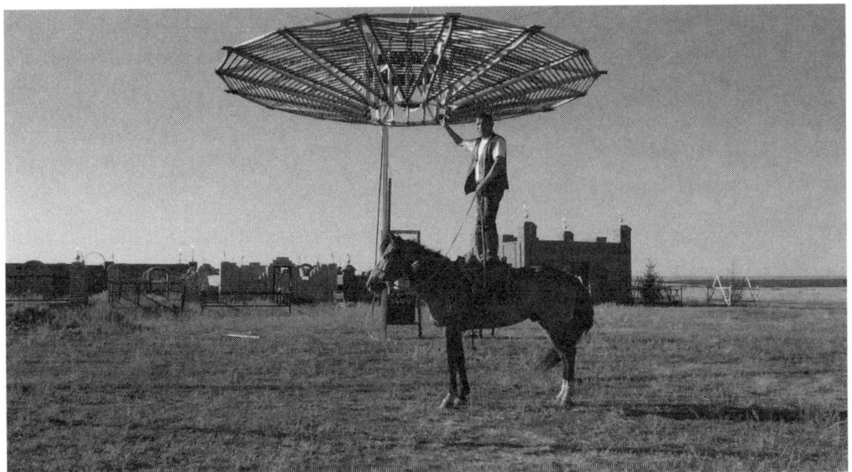

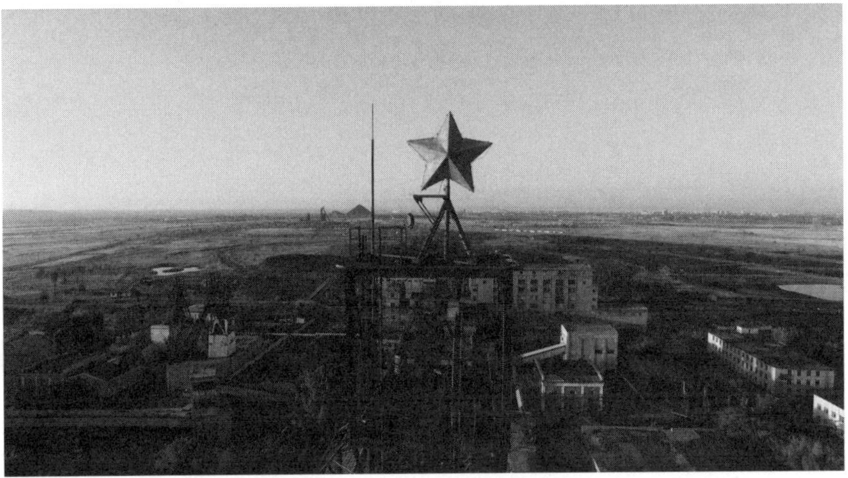

Anton Vidokle. "The Communist Revolution Was Caused By The Sun."
2015, film stills

Note

This script occasionally includes lines from the writings of Akhenaten, Georges Bataille, Nikolay Fedorov, Alexander Chizhevsky, and Vladimir Vernadsky, as well as paragraphs of clinical hypnosis script containing posthypnotic suggestions designed to help patients gain remission from addictions.

Part Two

Inherited aesthetics

The collapse of the Soviet Union in 1991 led to geopolitical shifts of immense proportions but it also caused fissures between the generations witnessing it.

What becomes inscribed in collective memory when its constituent parts are fragmented? What kind of inherited aesthetics and ethics become visible through these generational gaps?

6

Joseph Backstein

HISTORY OF ANGELS

A Klee drawing named "Angelus Novus" shows an angel looking as though he is about to move away from something he is fixedly contemplating. His eyes are staring, his mouth is open, his wings are spread. This is how one pictures the angel of history. His face is turned towards the past. Where we perceive a chain of events, he sees one single catastrophe that keeps piling ruin upon ruin, and hurls it in front of his feet. The angel would like to stay, awaken the dead and make whole what has been smashed. But a storm is blowing from Paradise; it has got caught in his wings with such violence that the angel can no longer close them. The storm inexorably propels him into the future to which his back is turned, while the pile of debris before him grows skyward. This storm is what we call progress.

WALTER BENJAMIN, THESIS IX, THESES ON THE PHILOSOPHY OF HISTORY

A tour of the philosophy of angels

Can an artist be appropriately compared to an angel, the visitor who sees this world with the eyes of God?

This identification works only when an artist combines the position of being inside the world with another in which they are also outside it; which is to say, only when he or she is able to reflect upon the world and create a permanent revision of its future outlook, conscious that people will then see the world again through his or her eyes.

In Russia, the artists from the circle of Moscow conceptualism became Angels of History par excellence due to their highly specific position as artists in Russia, where art has never been an autonomous social institution and artists frequently produced a localized form of aesthetic in a situation that was incapable of becoming aestheticized. The most rational historical explanation for the representation of power in Russian society was given by Boris Kagarlitsky, who said that "the peculiarity of Russia is in the fact that it lacks any developed form of popular representation in politics, so history is crucial for making power legitimate. Unable to confirm its legitimacy by honest elections and a proper mandate, the regimes and their governments that succeeded each other had to appeal to the past, to the roots" (Kagarlitsky 2008).

But why are these artists Angels of History?

There is an opinion that History is a temporal dimension where political forces struggle and that these forces become institutionalized in society; however, the time of History is the dimension that alone leads to the fair organization of a society ideally able to satisfy all people from all of its strata.

History in this sense is 'made' by a concrete individual only when this individual has been guaranteed his or her political rights, even – or at least – as an oppositional force. In the Soviet

Union, these Angels of History created their own world inside
the official world, a world that had its own institutions and
elements of civil society. Yet it wasn't Hermann Hesse's Castalia.

I thought it was significant to name the artists of Moscow
conceptualism as the Angels of History even if it is a rather
high-flown gesture, because I believe that they made a truly
historicizing revolution (or counterrevolution) within the space
of the Soviet metaphysics of their time: creating with their
actions a dimension of History inside the space of Bolshevism's
posthistoricism, in a manner similar to that which Vladimir
Nabokov once described as the "reversed transformation of
Bedlam into Bethlehem." Further, why do I believe that "Angels
of History" is a useful metaphor? From the traditional Christian
perspective, the angel is a herald, a herald of revelation, which
means truth. This revelation of truth can exist in different
forms. In the case of science, it exists as knowledge, as a kind
of concrete, if immaterial, substance. Unlike science, unlike
knowledge, however, the angel represents truth as a personality.
I also understand the angel as being a personal representation of
truth. That is why we can describe the artist as an angel.

While the angel is 'the truth' personified, it is not the
Absolute Truth of the Divine Revelation, yet it is not just
a partial truth. It is not simply a truth that holds enough
relevance so as to be heard as a public statement in a
democratic society – for then this truth would be nothing but a
personal opinion or conviction.

The metaphor of the Angel of History can also be projected
onto an analysis of the correlation between commercial and
noncommercial elements in the organization of any artistic
project. The New Testament motif of the expulsion of the
moneylenders from the Temple, when it is translated into
the language of present-day realities, reveals the limitation

of combining angelic (artistic) plans with market economy structures, not least because of the cultural and historical consequences (a succession of events and correspondences) connecting the Temple and the museum.

There is one sacramental question to ask: what happens to Angels of History when History comes to an end (as actually happened between 1989 and 1991)? Do they become fallen angels, or do they create new histories?

On succession in art

The succession of generations and some of the obvious links between them are evident in the works of the three groups and three generations that constitute the present exhibition ('Angels of History – Moscow Conceptualism and its Influence' that took place in M HKA in 2005). The first group comprises the founders of Moscow conceptualism who were active in the 1970s – the Brezhnev years of stagnation. The second, the immediate successors to the great Moscow conceptualist cause, were those who emerged in the limelight of the 1980s and were active in the years of perestroika. This second group was the winner of an ideological war against Soviet art. Its members were the founders of the legendary Club of Avantgardists (CLAVA), the perestroika branch or department of Moscow conceptualism, and they remained leaders of the Russian art scene until 1992. The third generation features some senior representatives, such as Oleg Kulik, Vladimir Dubossarsky and Alexander Vinogradov, Vlad Monroe and Anatoly Osmolovsky, who became the central figures of the 1990s, determining trends of aesthetic research during that period. It is important to note that many of them are performance artists, while such artists as Irina Korina and the BlueSoup Group brilliantly represent the tendencies of recent years, a period when the stabilization of political processes in post-Soviet Russia generated the opinion that political engagement does not guarantee the aesthetic relevance of art.

The main metaphor of this project, however, refers to all the groups of artists presented in the exhibition, although one might believe that the angelic view of History was, first and foremost, a characteristic of the senior generation of conceptualists and of Moscow conceptualism as a whole. On the other hand, the problem of succession in contemporary Russian art demands further investigation due to the fact that a gap does indeed divide the generation of Korina from that of the senior conceptualists. Today we live in a different country and in a different historical epoch, an epoch that is not the one in which Moscow conceptualism was formed. This historical change can only be compared to the change our ancestors experienced in 1917, but its direction has been reversed.

Here one should note an important fact: 2005 saw the fourth significant shift since the Second World War in the history of qualitative changes in the situation concerning the public function of contemporary art in Russia. The first change occurred in 1962, with Khrushchev's ideological clampdown on the first postwar exhibition of independent art at the Moscow Manezh. The second change came in 1974 with the Bulldozer exhibition, the famous show of independent art in the Moscow suburbs that was crushed by the authorities, using bulldozers to remove it. The third was in 1987, when perestroika brought about the emergence of new artists' associations and legalized the school of Moscow conceptualism. The fourth, meanwhile, was the opening of the first ever Moscow Biennale of Contemporary Art.

But doesn't this kind of contemporary figuring of succession reveal a similar model to that which characterized unofficial art of the 1970s? It was then that Komar & Melamid played a crucial part in the process of returning international art to Russia, when they based their creative work on Andy Warhol and not on Malevich – for the simple reason that there was no intellectual context in the early period capable of representing or discussing the meaning of art history in Russia itself, the value of this history or the fact that everything in the country had been ascribed historical meaning.

The future of the artist, the reality of his or her professional existence in a situation where any domestic career in art was impossible and where any future was thus associated with emigration and Western art, made Warhol more important than Malevich. The figures of influence shifted in their importance from the past to the future. As Michael Baxandall has suggested,

> influence is a curse of art criticism primarily because of its wrong-headed grammatical prejudice about who is the agent and who is the patient: it seems to reverse the active/passive relation the historical actor experiences and which the inferential beholder will want to take into account. If one says that X influenced Y, it does seem that one is saying that X did something to Y rather than Y did something to X. But in the consideration of good pictures and painters, the second is always the more lively reality. If we think of Y rather than X as the agent, our vocabulary is much richer and more diversified. (Baxandall 1985, pp. 58–9)

We copy the thing that propels us forward even if the copied object is in the past. Thus artists like Korina and the BlueSoup Group are in a generation inclined to pay greater attention to the international context rather than to the history of Russian art, which has not yet been written in any reliable form. They do it because they have already become, or are in the process of becoming, a part of the international context. It has nothing to do with their neglect of the history of their own country.

When I speak of the figure of succession, it is to explain what models of succession mean in the case of the Moscow conceptualists and not simply whether it was a case of the artist "not copying [a] predecessor, not caring about similarities, not matching himself against his model, but simply learning how something was done, miming the structure of art history itself in order to internalize and go beyond what came before" (Danto 1992, p. 121).

The generation of the Moscow conceptualists faced an important historical task: to abolish the Soviet government and its social systems. This task was successfully fulfilled. Yet one generation cannot have two or more historical tasks, or it would be a different history. Ilya Kabakov and Komar & Melamid may serve as examples for the younger artists, but this does not imply that the latter make any real attempts at understanding the older generation's aesthetics; for the younger generation, the older artists are principally an example of how to have a successful career, the career of a contemporary Russian artist in the West.

So what is the essence of Moscow conceptualism and why should so much attention be paid to it?

The objective of the current project is to demonstrate the logic underlying the development of contemporary art in Russia from the moment it was possible to make a sure enough diagnosis of its existence and which, if we rely upon our model of the historical and aesthetic processes, would again refer us back to the early 1970s.

We prefer to use the term *contemporary art in Russia* rather than *contemporary Russian art* because we believe it is important to detach ourselves from the local context and to emphasize the commonality of an international visual language.

It was the complete self-isolation of the Soviet Union that created the situation in which the artistic milieu of contemporary art became hermetic and concentrated on local topicality. Nevertheless, the parallels between what was happening in contemporary art in Russia and the processes happening in the West justify the use of an image of G. W. Leibniz – his idea of the "Monad," a structure that had no windows and yet was able to reflect on the world around it – as a means here to describe Moscow conceptualism. In the Soviet Union it was even more difficult to reflect upon the surrounding world, because the museums of art created there were not essentially artistic institutions dealing with art but rather social institutions that represented the "figures of power." The art museums were essentially transformed into historical and even ethnographic museums. So what was the meaning of everything that happened in the artistic milieu of Moscow in the 1970s? Why we do have grounds to call this period of postwar history in Russia (to use a term by Karl Jaspers) an "Achsenzeit" (Axis in Time)? Moreover, how can we position the Moscow conceptualism that emerged within this era, given that it is one of the major trends in the history of Russian art in the hundred years up to then, alongside the Wanderers, the Russian avant-garde and Socialist Realism? Only these four artistic movements had well-developed ideological programs as stated in their numerous manifestos. From the perspective of art history, Moscow conceptualism is often called the "second Russian avant-garde." This name emphasizes that it is a successor to the Russian modernist tradition, of the ideas and creations of Malevich and Tatlin. There is one essential reservation to be made, because

Suprematism was a radicalized, utopian idea of Western
modernism, whilst Moscow conceptualism was an anti-
utopian trend. Yet it is the very idea of political engagement
that unites both avant-garde trends. *History* as a term contains
within it one more meaning in the Russian language: it is not
just History, it is a Story. This circumstance is important in
our context because the historical nature of Russian pictorial
art also implies an inclination to base pictorial works of
art on narrative, to tell a story in pictures. And Moscow
conceptualism continued this tradition. In this sense, Russian
art has always been conceptual, and titles of paintings were as
important as their depictions, if not more so.

That is why Russian art often displays such a need for
commentary, which was precisely the reason Kabakov created
a new model of the work of art that incorporated comments on
each depiction into the structure of the representation proper.
This mania for commentary reflects a certain peculiarity of
political life in Russia, where commenting on and interpreting
the meaning of any event were often monopolized by official
culture. It is well known that the agencies of the Communist
Party edited and censored even the texts of Dostoevsky and
Gogol when they were prepared for adaptation on the stage.

Why did the group of Moscow artists that formed
the nucleus of 'unofficial art' in Russia call themselves
"conceptualist"? It wasn't just as an analogy to the objects
that Joseph Kosuth and other American and European
conceptualists had produced several years earlier. What was the
essence of their conceptualism? Was it simply their use of text
as an object of visual representation? Was it a radical review
of the essence underlying the plastic quality of their works –
as a continuation of the ready-made tradition – or was it the
description of a picture instead of the picture itself?

What did Moscow conceptualism add to this list of
conceptual art's characteristics? It created the institution of art
in a society where this institution was absent by creating works
that in themselves conceptually reproduced an institution, in its
meaningful structure; they reproduced an institution by the fact
of their very existence. It demonstrated the autonomous nature
of the aesthetic statement; it produced continuous commentary
and auto-commentary; it interpreted the uninterpreted, that
is to say, the social reality of Soviet Russia; it created new
objects of artistic imagination in a space where the objects of
representation and the forms of representation were strictly
fixed, even canonized, as had happened in icon painting; its
artists demonstrated the ability to 'live abroad' without ever
leaving the country and, on the other hand, 'remaining home
even when they lived abroad' (as Kabakov himself seemed to
point to in remarks made only this year).

On the correlation of the visual and the verbal in Russian art

Artists in Russia are traditionally obsessed with the content
of their visual statement, a content that can also be retold
verbally. The artist may not be totally convinced of a visual
statement's self-sufficiency; he or she believes that the complex
history of an event, which provided the reasons for the creation
of the 'picture,' is behind the picture itself. This justifies the
opinion that, in Russia, art has always been conceptual. Artists
working in Russia simply did not know that they "speak in
verse," as a famous character of the French dramatist Molière
once proclaimed. As a matter of fact, the content, narrative or
context of works of art could rarely be stated openly due to
censorship. This often made such factors even more important
than the plastic qualities of the artists' visual representation
alone. Thus in 1892 Isaac Levitan, a great Russian painter,

won fame for his landscape *Vladimirka* (The Vladimir Road)
not because of its particular style but due to the fact that
its title corresponded to the road used by Russian police to
transport political prisoners into exile, a fact well known to all
participants in the artistic life of that time.

The historical achievement of Moscow conceptualism
was in the fact that its followers realized the immanent
conceptual qualities of Russian art, its burden of content, its
inevitable lack of balance between form and content – and
they began to create works reflecting upon precisely this
Russian peculiarity. Unlike Kosuth's conceptualism, which
deconstructed the object of representation (a classic example
would be his combination of chair, photograph of chair and
reproduction of *chair*'s dictionary definition), the Moscow
conceptualism of its classic period deconstructed the gaps
inside the semantics of the Soviet – and Russian in the broader
sense of the word – aesthetic mainstream. Yet, from a Marxist
point of view, "reflecting upon the object does not imply its re-
objectification." Thus the reflection upon the ideological and
literary content conducted by Moscow conceptualism burdens
the aesthetic result of this reflection with this content and the
narrative surplus that is characteristic of it. In this sense the
works of the artists from the circles of Moscow conceptualism
always ran the risk of being nothing but another 'ethnic cliché.'
Continuing the tradition of modernism, Kabakov analyzed and
synthesized the various plastic forms of Soviet art to create his
own synthetic language of painting, conceptualizing the surface
of painting. Paradoxical as it may seem, the synthesism of his
method is visible not only through the lens of the 'Soviet eye'
but also through the unaided eye of the international viewer,
who has no knowledge of the stylistic peculiarities of the
methods combined in his work.

The concept of the "Total Installation" in Kabakov's work performs a similar function, reflecting upon a content that cannot be expressed in any other visual form. Here the content surplus is one of his most common methods as it is impossible to grasp the work in one glance and, of course, to interpret the variety of everything that is represented in the "Total Installation."

Methods of the same type were developed in the Sots Art of Komar & Melamid – the first attempt to produce a system of contemporary aesthetic thought registered in Russia in the postwar period. According to Komar & Melamid, Sots Art was an aesthetic phenomenon that emerged in a country suffering from overproduction of ideological content in any, but especially public, statements, whilst Pop Art emerged in those countries that had an overproduction of material things and where the consumerist mentality had triumphed.

Thus one could say that Kabakov regarded the book as a model of the work of pictorial art, it being no accident that he was one of the most famous book illustrators of the Soviet period, while for Komar & Melamid the political poster had the same function.

It is still necessary, however, to explain why art in Russia is so dependent on content and why it was only the Russian avant-garde who were able to break free from its embrace. When the content of a visual statement starts to dominate and when the visual sign demands an explanation, or when the sign itself turns into a simple decoration of the narrative given beforehand, then the depiction turns into an illustration.

An awareness of this idea made the text – as a source of content and something more important than visual representation (which is determined by and merely illustrates the text) – a basic object of depiction in Moscow conceptualism, uniting it with international conceptual art.

The early Russian avant-garde proved an exception to a certain degree because, during a short period of time (up to around 1929), artists who worked in Russia were driven by the supernatural energy of the Revolution. The artists themselves turned into independent aesthetic and political subjects, who implemented the metaphor of the phrase "in Russia, a poet is more than a poet" through their radical politicization of aesthetics and aestheticization of politics. The avant-garde determined the sphere of content on their own, something essential both for themselves and for life. Nevertheless the productivist aesthetic of the first Russian avant-garde, and the readiness of this aesthetic to be transformed into a form of applied art, testified to the fact that it was prepared to be dissolved into an elementary (external) content, be it one of everyday life or labor.

Yet while Kosuth, especially in his later works, used the transformation of text into decoration as his main method of presenting it as an object of representation, in Moscow conceptualism a text is not allowed to become self-sufficient as an end in itself; the text is only allowed to appear on the surface of paintings when they seem to depend on it – take, for instance, Kabakov's work *The Letter* (1983), where script from a love letter is dominated by an urban landscape in the background.

The ideas mentioned above imply that Moscow conceptualism is not just an aesthetic phenomenon, albeit a remarkable one, but one we also need to address as a deeply rooted and structured intellectual system, with its own philosophy, theory, and numerous aesthetic practices running through several generations of artists.

On the notion of the borderline in art

In the history of modernism, every remarkable work deals with a borderline that separates the ordinary objects of the

 Joseph Backstein **History of angels**

world from the things that are works of art; every time, in every artistic gesture, this borderline is drawn at some new place; and, every time, every remarkable work runs the risk of being refused the status of an art object.

The paradox of modernism lies in the fact that not every manufactured object produced as art becomes art proper. Unlike the situation in the West, where the borderlines of art were under constant revision and every serious work had a chance of being listed among other works of art, even if they were not regarded as such at the moment of their production, the borderlines between art and nonart in the Soviet Union had been determined once and for all, and Moscow conceptualism in Russia's official art history was doomed to be regarded as nonart.

The philosophy of Moscow conceptualism was not quite in line with the tradition in philosophy of 'art for art's sake' that constantly and with every moment of its existence emphasized its independence from the political institutions of Soviet society. Instead, it created simultaneously a tension with the dimension of History as it was brought to life by the political struggle going on 'along the vertical': a struggle with both the official art above ground and the independent art underground. This was quite different from the horizontal dimension of political struggle in a democratic society.

One should note that the principal topic in Moscow conceptualism, which determined its role as a pivotal axis of contemporary art in Russia, was the theme of "intellectual survival," the survival of an individual in circumstances where it was impossible to do so without losing one's individual human and predominantly moral character. The topic of survival gained an additional relevance in the changed circumstances of the 1990s and has done so to the present day – in so far as the theme of an artist's survival in the context of the market economy is now the crucial question, at a time when art increasingly runs the risk of being dissolved into the structures of the culture industry.

References

Baxandall, Michael, 1985. *Patterns of Intention*, New Haven, CT: Yale University Press.
Danto, Arthur C., 1992. *Beyond the Brillo Box: The Visual Arts in Post-Historical Perspective*, New York: Farrar Straus Giroux.
Kagarlitsky, Boris, 2008. *Peripheral Empire: Russia and a World System*, London: Pluto Press.

7

Dmitry Gutov and Anatoly Osmolovsky

CONCERNING ABSTRACTIONISM

In December 2003 Dmitry Gutov and I began a discussion on the internet. The occasion for the discussion was my reaction to reading several articles by Mikhail Lifshitz. I formulated my attitude to this kind of thinking in two letters and sent them to Gutov. This was the beginning of an exceptionally intense discussion that continued, with short breaks, for four months. At various stages the discussion was joined by Vladimir Salnikov, Igor Chubarov, Dmitry Vilensky, Keti Chukhrov and Bogdan Mamonov. This discussion falls into three sections, each complete within itself. The focus of attention in the first section is the thought of Mikhail Lifshitz. The major theme of this first section is the possibility of a return to realism. The second section is primarily devoted to contemporary abstract art and consists of a fierce debate between two participants: myself and Dmitry Gutov. The third section consists of a discussion of the problematics of contemporary art, with Mamonov, Vilensky, and Chukhrov joining the discussion in turn. The text which follows below is that of the second section of this discussion, which was published in the catalog of the exhibition "Art Without Justifications" in Moscow in 2004. The letters by Salnikov and Chubarov have been excluded.

Anatoly Osmolovsky

LETTER 1

From: Anatoly Osmolovsky
Date: Sunday, January 04, 2004, 3.24 p.m.

Subject: comments on the discussion

Greetings and a Happy New Year to all!

I've already told Dima that in my view the discussion project, in the format that has been used up to the present moment, has reached its end. Not because all the themes have been discussed or new frontiers of some kind have been reached, but because the perspective that was taken has somewhat exhausted itself (we need simply to take a rest for a while). I suggest starting a new discussion. To formulate it in elementary terms, about abstractionism. This is a different perspective on closely related problems, or even the same ones.

Take this for instance: in his last letter Dima raised the problem of content in visual art. The task of liberation from content (from narration) is one of the most important tasks of abstract art. The concept of content can be interpreted in an extensive sense – as the possession of any kind of meaning in general. But this interpretation blurs the problem, shifting it, as I have already written on several occasions, into a philosophical context, which has to be avoided, because it shifts the project into territory that is familiar to us, but in which it is difficult to work adequately.

In my view abstract art possesses very comprehensible
(and as yet unforgotten) artistic goals. It has a sufficiently long
history for generalizations to be made, and also includes an
endless sequence of distinctions.

Unfortunately, the abstract art that appeared in the Soviet
Union beginning from the late 1950s only conquered new
horizons in the isolated cases of individual artists (Zlotnikov,
Turetsky, Prokofiev, Slepyan). But even the newness that was
achieved was not thought through adequately. This entire
tendency, which originally developed as a trend towards
overcoming literariness, was crushed by conceptualism in the
late sixties and early seventies. For Soviet art, conceptualism
is a kind of eclipse of reason. No one, of course, denies its
achievements in the mass media and (in a number of cases)
in art, but then for several generations of artists it distorted
the perception of art in a most substantial manner. It replaced
the sensory perception of art with cerebral perception. One
of the most vivid and at the same time ineffectual attempts to
overcome cerebrality was the activity of the artist Leiderman
in the nineties. His invented installations, literally concocted
out of thin air, simulating insanity and a "resolute" rejection of
rationality, were a helpless attempt to overcome the rationality
of conceptualism through a rational rejection of rationality.
However, the true overcoming is to be found in completely
different areas.

Returning abstract art to the mainstream seems like
some kind of nonsense at the present moment. However,
in a situation where art has no right to exist, it is precisely
abstract art, liberated of content, of self-justification through
narrative and visible artisanal skill, which poses this problem
to society in the most radical fashion. In this sense realist art
is constantly justifying itself to society and to itself. Possibly,

if a new society should arise, free of alienation, realist art
will become the only possible form of artistic expression, but
in present conditions it is absurd even to contemplate this
hypothetical possibility. On the contrary, it is abstract art
that brings society face to face in the most clear-cut manner
with the central political problem of the last century: the
imperative need for a social revolution. It is not the expression
of some mythical freedom (as it was interpreted by the critics
of the fifties); on the contrary, abstract art (especially right
now) is a full-blown demonstration of individual unfreedom,
insofar as concepts such as art and freedom can be combined.
In other words, abstract art is fundamentally political (once
again, insofar as art can be political).

This is the first level of reasoning about the present-day
possibility of abstract art.

In hopes of an adequate response,
Tolya

LETTER 2

From: Dmitry Gutov
Undated

Hi, Tolik!

Here I share my initial considerations on abstraction
(January Theses).

1. The distinctive feature of this project is that it is
   being carried out by Osmolovsky. A master of social
   action. And consequently this initiative must also be
   read through that prism. If anybody else had begun this
   project here, nobody would even have noticed. None of
   the abstractionists themselves have any resources at all for
   mainstreaming their occupation.

2. The next specific feature of the project is linked to the preceding one: this is its temporal nature. It is obviously fast-moving. 2004 will be its peak. In 2005 it will reach even the most dimwitted. In 2006 it will withdraw into the realm of legends.

3. The special value of the initiative is its appeal to the basic characteristics of art. They have to be stated anew. Those who believe that in our times everything has already been elucidated are greatly mistaken. A clear example is our friend Vilensky. He boldly attaches labels: this is a backwards turn. What does he mean? (It's impossible to understand.) That the future belongs only to specific media, video, for example? Or only to acutely social problematics? For some reason that doesn't seem archaic to him. He thinks that he invented it.

4. A discussion of abstraction can (and should) move in two directions.

    A. A discussion about its morphological elements (color, texture, inclined, straight, effect on consciousness, the unconscious and so on *ad infinitum*).

    B. Abstraction in its opposition to imitation in art. The principled rejection of conveying a direct likeness of life.

5. An advantageous component of the project is its appeal to what has been thoroughly forgotten. To the age of pop art, that is, to prehistorically ancient times.

6. This project has a powerful commercial component. Like it or not, in dealing with such things, the problem of money and commodities cannot be avoided. Here there is already a direct exit to Marxist problematics.

7. Another extremely important theme is the elitism and democratism of art. The problem of refined and naive awareness. The problem of the viewer. For the naive

awareness, seeking in art something similar to life, abstraction is already something of a provocation. For a slightly more advanced awareness, it is a subtle thing that speaks to the professional in a professional language on professional themes. For the next level, it is a provocation within actual contemporary trends.

That's enough for the time being.

Hugs

Gutov

LETTER 3

From: Anatoly Osmolovsky
Date: Sunday, January 04, 2004, 10.46 p.m.

Hi, Dima!

Here is my response to your theses.

Osmolovsky and abstraction

I'm not so very confident of success. A large number of clichés of perception (including my own clichés) have to be overcome, as well as elementary organizational difficulties. Many of my initiatives have acquired a certain degree of fame but, after all, no one knows how many have met with absolutely no response whatever. The ratio here is 30–40% (well-known) to 70–60% (little-known or completely unsuccessful). In addition, in my view, the fame of any particular collective artistic project depends less on the PR abilities of the organizer than on its correspondence to 'the spirit of the time'. So I haven't attempted any special, particular, cunning dodges for the 'promotion' of a nonspectacular project, although it has been accepted across quite a wide range of artists. But I agree that the political (or, if you like, social) thrust of this project is very important.

The 'three-year' term of the project

In this assertion I sense a certain concealed negative attitude to the project. Dima sees it as "fast-acting" and "short-term," like pop music. I can't agree with that. Firstly, rapid projects require an industry, which does not exist in contemporary art (generally speaking, not even in the West). Secondly, the average length of any collective artistic project is indeed from three to seven years, but this project is only in part collective (and only in part a project). I have already written more than once that it is not the project structure that interests me, but the problematics of art that arise within abstractionism. And in addition to that, my current thinking is directly linked to nonspectacular popular art in a professional context two to three years ago.

Concerning the 'three-year' cycle of this project – this is already essentially incorrect. And Dima knows this better than anyone else. After all, I already spoke about my interest in abstract art almost two years ago, but it is only now that I feel ready to present my first labors. And I should say that during those two years I have conducted intensive analytical work. There is so much material that even two years will not be enough. In addition, very recently new, genuinely interesting artists have appeared, who can participate adequately in this project. How come? Surely one of the participants, Sigutin, was previously well known as an artist? Yes, he was well known, and even well known as an abstractionist, but only his new works disclose the aspect of contemporary abstract art that I'm seeking. I don't know how long contemporary abstraction will continue to retain its relevance, but there is certainly an entire untapped field of work here. And finally: the length of any particular phenomenon's life is not so important, the important thing is for the artistic results to be impressive.

The basic characteristics of art

Here Dima is absolutely right. This is precisely why I responded so simply and with such great interest to the "realist" project that Gutov is doing. Indeed, only one thing is clear – that nothing is clear (to paraphrase Socrates). And the most 'basic' characteristic of art, which has to be proved yet again, is art's right to exist. In his last letter Dima wrote very correctly about Kulik, continuing my discussion with Viktor Misiano just before the New Year: "inventing themes out of thin air, in order then to convince oneself that you-know-who has illustrated them best of all, is a senseless occupation. It has nothing to do with understanding (and what could be more interesting than understanding?). Understanding would show that Kulik illustrates a single theme: how an artist can survive in infinitely hostile conditions (but I don't remember that theme in Berlin)." During an exchange of opinions concerning the 'Moscow–Berlin' exhibition, Misiano asked the most intimate question: And who, in your opinion, was best suited as an illustration of the themes of this exhibition? Who had the most examples of all? And he answered himself (after our repeated failures to guess the name): Kulik. At the time I didn't grasp his train of thought very well (for instance, Viktor said that the artist Rothko could only have illustrated one of those themes), but in my view Gutov was the one who understood the heart of the problem. Kulik illustrates all of the curators' themes precisely because his fundamental task and goal is survival. But there is nothing more repellent and absurd than survival, demonstrated in art (in this sense Kulik's mummies are a metaphorical spectacle relating to himself).

And so: the right to exist as one of the basic characteristics of art. Dmitry Vilensky, for instance, denies art the right to exist. In his opinion, art must justify itself at least by participation in the present-day progressive political struggle. The very fact of art's existence is indeed an intolerable fact. For it asserts the existence of other values apart from capital: freedom in solidarity, altruistic concern, the gift without payment, the attainability of an ideal. Such apparently opposed concepts as 'revolution' and 'art' combine together very naturally. And during great social upheavals they somehow 'go together.' Perhaps the false conjunction of art and politics occurs because of the similarities of internal configuration between these two manifestations of human activity.

Abstraction in its opposition to imitation in art
What Dima writes about "endless" problems applies, of course, to practically any forms of art. But the important point here is which problems on this "endless" list become important in any particular social and artistic situation. Opposition to the imitation of life is hardly, unfortunately, the central problem – in large part because in the contemporary artistic situation there is practically no art that works with the category of lifelikeness. And all the versions of postmodernist art have more to do with media response and conceptual content, which can and must be criticized by contemporary abstraction as projects that are literary and dependent.

The commercial component and the problem of democratism
The commercial potential of the project is simultaneously its strong aspect and its weak aspect. But for me it is the discovery of an entire stratum of a different attitude to art. In the nineties the commodity value of art was not a serious artistic problem. And not so much because none of the

 Dmitry Gutov and Anatoly Osmolovsky   Concerning abstractionism potential buyers wanted the art of the nineties as because the main ambition of art at that time was power. And power is not exchanged for money.

The present situation is entirely different. The time of 'vulgar sociologism' and 'ultra-left deviations' has passed irrevocably. Art is ceasing to be the private activity of friends who know each other – the activity of an active radical minority. The time has arrived of interaction with the 'anonymous' viewer. But this is the problematics of the next text.

So long,

Tolya

LETTER 7

From: Dmitry Gutov

Date: Thursday, January 08, 2004, 2.29 a.m.

Hi, Tolik!

Remarks on abstractionism

I want to begin with one of Osmolovsky's ideas: "Possibly, if a new society should arise, free of alienation, realist art will become the only possible form of artistic expression, but in present conditions it is absurd even to contemplate this hypothetical possibility."

It is hard not to agree. But absurdity is not the kind of thing that should be shunned like fire.

It has given the world much that is remarkable. 2,000 years of Christianity (well perhaps, of course, less than that) have been tinted with it: I believe, because it is absurd. And for the 1930s those words meant a great deal. Lifshitz cites Tertullian in speaking of Lukács.

And for the founders of the avant-garde there was nothing better than the absurd. So we shall not be afraid to think absurdly. The problem is more to do with the difficulty of achieving the absurd.

And Osmolovsky himself actually writes, "Returning abstract art to the mainstream now seems like some kind of nonsense." But that does not bother him. It actually inspires him. And he also writes (about realism): "There are phenomena in history, a return to which, in a particular development of history, is simply impossible!" This is also undisputable. But then what do we do with the words: demand the impossible?

Does such a demand make any sense? Let me remind you of one of the remarkable ideas of Chernyshevsky (Tolik knows that I like to refer to him). In his dissertation he deciphers the saying "Even the wild beast runs to the stalker." An unrealistic demand can change a situation in such a way that it becomes realistic.

Osmolovsky continues, addressing the realists: "Precisely your failure, the impossibility of reincarnating realism, will be an argument in favor of the existence of history." He is right here as well. But the problem of failure is not simple. Lenin, analyzing the defeat of the 1905 revolution, wrote that taking up arms was required. Yes, the failure was fatal, but this experience proved a most valuable acquisition. One that was essential for the development of the revolution. Routed armies are good learners. You like to study the art of war, Tolik, and it is not for me to tell you about the value of defeat. (By the way, Giorgio Agamben believes that the very appearance of the human race was a result of evolutionary regression, a consequence of failure in the struggle for existence. So regress is not such an unambiguously bad thing.)

In these reproaches I actually perceive the weakness (or, more precisely, the strength) of the modernistic (in the sense of anti-realist) position. It always reckons with circumstances. It always calculates what will work and what won't. It doesn't contain any element of hopelessness and (genuine) nonsense. As such it belongs to our world of mercenary calculation. It contains no energy of despair (which Lenin also knew how to appreciate). That is, there's always a lingering aftertaste here of the fact that the artists have something to lose, and they don't allow themselves to take any genuine risks.

And what is the defeat of realism 'at the present stage of the development of history'? A sign that a world in which the human being is abased, unfree and deprived is celebrating yet another victory. But someone must remind us that human existence can and should look different.

From these, perhaps excessively general, considerations, I move on to abstraction itself.

From conceptualism via pop art to abstraction – that's really pretty good. Rather absurd. Osmolovsky has already elaborated everything here (the rejection of literariness and cheap kitsch, the acquisition of material, the absence of self-justification and so forth), and what he hasn't elaborated, he will. That is, it has to be done. But abstraction also has a different dimension, if it is viewed, not from ahead, but from behind. Over the course of many thousands of years, art depicted something. (Why would that be?) Everything that went into abstraction as pure artistic skill was well known before then, but it was achieved as a side effect. From a distance any work is an abstraction (and from very far away – a black square). In this sense the abstractionists have not greatly enriched art. On the contrary, by drawing out onto the surface what was concealed deep inside, they have weakened the power of art's impact. The harsh geometry of Dutch painting is less impressive in Mondrian. The force of the impression of the brush's movement is less in de Kooning, the energy of the patch of color is less in Rothko. They seem to warn you immediately: I'm about to punch you in the eye. It's not as overwhelming as in the late Titian or in Russian icon painting.

There also turn out to be not so many actually separated-out elements and combinations of elements. Here in fact there is no infinitude of distinctions. Precisely in this sense the project cannot run for long. The world of images is a different matter. Let me remind you that these subjects were already discussed in Pushkin's time. Here is his opinion: "If everything has already been said, why do you write? To say beautifully what has been said simply? A pitiful occupation! No, we shall not slander human reason, which is inexhaustible in its invention of concepts, as language is inexhaustible in inventing words."

It's the same story with self-justification. Abstractionism (and here Osmolovsky is again right), shouts right into society's ears: "The absence of content and subject matter means that I have no right to exist and my greatest value consists in that! Such is not the case with realist art. It is well aware of its own extreme disinterestedness, which none of its applied aspects are capable of canceling out. An icon is created as a sacred object, but for those who don't believe in signs or miracles, it is an absolute aesthetic value. Las Meninas plunges me into amazement, although who is Philip IV to me, and who am I to Philip IV?"

But overall it is impossible not to agree with Osmolovsky. In conditions of total cretinism, perhaps one should present society with questions, as he puts it, "in the most radical manner."

And many more of Osmolovsky's observations also strike me as being valuable.

Here are some: "Abstraction's opposition to the imitation of life is hardly, unfortunately, the central problem – in large part because in the contemporary artistic situation there is practically no art that works with the category of lifelikeness." Good.

Or again: "And all the versions of postmodernist art have more to do with media response and conceptual content, which can and must be criticized by contemporary abstraction as projects that are literary and dependent."

Or: "In realism there is too much of the conceptual, only not in a distilled, separated-out, reduced, demonstrative form, as in conceptualism, but in a concealed manner, as standard." Only here I see this as a strong aspect (conceptualism is not my enemy), and especially strong in that it is concealed, given as standard.

And so, although the opposition of abstraction and the imitation of life is not a pressing practical problem, it is at the very least a theoretical one. The essence of abstraction, its concept (in Hegelian terminology), consists in a rejection of the imitation of life. Just try to ignore that fact. As I have already written once, the historical content of this phenomenon is that the forms of real life had already become so hostile to the human being that human beings gave up representing them. While the revolutionaries struggled unsuccessfully with the task of humanizing those forms and changing their condition so that they would be worth reflecting, the abstractionists testified that the revolutionaries were not really getting anywhere.

Perhaps this is what Osmolovsky has in mind when he writes, "It is abstract art that brings society face to face in the most clear-cut manner with the central political problem of the last century: the imperative need for a social revolution."

But there is one idea of his that I didn't understand (can you clarify?): "Abstract art is not the expression of some mythical freedom (as it was interpreted by the critics of the fifties); on the contrary, abstract art (especially right now) is a full-blown demonstration of individual unfreedom."

Hugs to everyone

Gutov

LETTER 12

From: Anatoly Osmolovsky
Date: Tuesday, January 13, 2004, 12.07 p.m.

Hi to everyone!

The abiding weakness of any demagogy is its absolute focus on achieving power. Demagogy takes nothing into account – neither historical facts nor common sense – but most importantly, it cannot discard anything: everything that is convincing and historically verified, that can be used one way or another in the struggle for power, has to be integrated, swallowed, appropriated. Demagogy's unbridled appetite eventually devours itself: it frees any historical facts from their historicity, and artistic or social phenomena are adduced as positive examples of any manifestations of negativity (contradictions), thus depriving them of precise boundaries.

The conception and historiography of socialist realism, as developed by Soviet art history, is a glaring example of demagogic manipulation. Singling out the essence, without going into the details, the idea is simple: everything in the history of art that is a generally acknowledged achievement is claimed as an attainment of the realist school. In one of his latest articles, Boris Groys expresses the incisive thought that the spokesmen of orthodox Marxism regarded with suspicion all philosophical and artistic phenomena that had arisen after Marxism, precisely because they had arisen *after* it. After Marxism nothing serious could arise in principle, by definition. In my view this suspiciousness can be explained more simply: orthodox Marxism, having been transformed from a scientific method into a faith, can only work exclusively with verified artistic phenomena that are not subject to doubt. The only claim made by such a true-believing Marxism is a totalitarian assertion, in which there is no place for experiment, discussion or error.

All these considerations are of direct relevance for the arguments expressed by Gutov. According to Gutov, the realist project involves everything that is most correct, kind, intelligent, true, genuine, authentic and so on, like in the Russian folktales: the positive hero possesses only positive characteristics and the negative hero possesses only negative characteristics. In this way, so it seems to Gutov (and to Soviet art history), 'two birds' are killed with a single stone: arguments are historically confirmed, the position becomes as hard as steel, and there is no need to take responsibility for anything or justify oneself.

However, this 'steel-hard' position has an absolutely fundamental defect – the artistic phenomenon that had to be defended loses its defining features, effectively becoming transformed into an equivalent of divine providence. In actual fact an elementary mistake is made, one that was already known to the positivists. One of the positivist axioms (the axiom of the falsifiability of knowledge) says that if a phenomenon aspires to the status of a scientific fact, it can be disputed. Everything that cannot be disputed is a matter of faith and not science.

Appealing exclusively to positive examples, the present-day defenders of the realist project, educated by Soviet art history, cast themselves out of the historical process and out of scientific discussion. Here is a typical example of such an assertion: "I wish to remind you of several ideas of the Wanderers group which are almost forgotten today. For the Wanderers a superfluity of expressive means, 'painting,' was specifically regarded as a flaw, and it was the idea, the meaning, the life, the typicality, the truth, the historicity that were valued. And the question is whether a picture has these qualities. It is only their presence, and not at all a formal resemblance to the original, that makes a representation realistic. And so there are various kinds of realism. That is on the question of Shilov …"

Dima! I want to remind you once again that we are not discussing realism as one of the equivalents of truth, but as a real historical style, with its own positive and negative instances. If realism is understood as *truth* in art, then there is nothing to talk about. Truth becomes 'truth' through the arbitrary will of the one who pronounces it *first*. And contrariwise, an understanding of realism as an artistic phenomenon will allow us to give serious consideration to historical errors, and also to its present-day exploitation. Gutov, reluctant to note the negative aspects of his reply to a question about the use of realism by those in power for purposes of manipulating consciousness, writes: "Of what importance is this? Artists who have managed to do something worthwhile were clearly not inspired by this desire." But no, it is important. And although, without the slightest doubt, every individual artist "who has managed to do something worthwhile" is justified by his art, there are also thousands and thousands who employ the very same method to brainwash people, to cast them into the meat grinder of war, to stultify them and oppress them intellectually. It is precisely the realist method that has been exploited by the bloodiest regimes as an effective instrument for the mass manipulation of people. Realist representation lacks 'a filter for protecting the mind,' it does not possess enough *relativity*. And it makes no difference whether viewers identify themselves with Dionisii's Christ or the Christ of a run-of-the-mill twentieth-century hack, since what is necessary is to liberate any viewer from the very habit of identification, which allows him or her to be manipulated, and which is testimony to the viewer's infantility and naivity. Furthermore, liberation from this habit is a real step towards overcoming the passivity of the masses, towards awakening in them the necessary abilities to defend their own rights.

All of this actually exists in Western Europe (not, by the way, in the USA, where contemporary art is extremely localized) – and there contemporary culture long ago became a straightforward fact of everyday life, from which the average citizen draws the strength and justification for demonstrating his or her own particular protest. They protest because it is relatively hard to get them caught up in the vortex of identification. They know and defend their own boundaries: the boundaries of their bodies, of their thinking, of their civil rights. And if we extract from the archives concepts such as 'the revolutionary class' or 'the political avant-garde,' then it is precisely these citizens, educated by contemporary art, who are the best material for their live content. There is only one 'little thing' lacking – real economic problems. However, the prospect of these is already visible: social welfare payments are shrinking, the pension age is increasing, cultural processes are running out of control. Western art becomes more leftist with every passing year. Hearst, Muik, the Chapman brothers – these are all yesterday. But the most important thing is that the pressure of the Third World is growing stronger and stronger. And no atomic weapons will save the dying elitist regime of western capitalism.

But somehow in modern-day Russia there is no sign of any achievements in the area of educating the masses after socialist realism has existed for more than fifty years. On the contrary, now icons are peeping out from behind every realist image. Dima, have you been to the Cathedral of Christ the Savior? All the frescoes there are in realism, you know. And not Shilov, by the way, but entirely professional work (although I admit that I didn't look closely). I know for certain that there are new churches where genuine professionals work. Possibly religious obscurantism will acquire a 'high artistic' form for itself. Is that possible? Entirely. Only all this is not consumed artistically, but religiously.

These questions are exclusively political, but art cannot be outside politics. Its true political significance is manifested in a refusal to participate in politics – regardless of whether one paints red banners or Christs and the apostles. There is no refusal without rejection, Adorno wrote, and precisely because of this a responsible artist must now repulse any attempts to impose any kind of function on art, even if that function is politically progressive. This rejection also applies to classical art. The avant-gardist rejects the classical, not because it is bad, untrue or mendacious, he rejects it out of the immanent logic of working with his material. This is the path of the artist; the art critic cannot permit himself such an error. Precisely in this sense the artist must be naive, his naivety is transformed into radicalism, which in turn leads to real artistic achievements.

Your final question about the elite nature of abstractionism can once again be answered in Adorno's words: "art shows respect for the masses in opposing them and knowing what they could be, and not in accommodating itself to them in their degrading image that is an insult to human dignity," and also: "he who shouts about art's supposedly innate formalism and about art being art – such an individual is acting as an advocate for that inhumaneness, that very same inhumaneness of which he accuses formalism – in the name of the cliques who, in order to keep the enslaved on a tighter rein, command art to accommodate itself to them, to take the road of opportunism."

And finally, let me explain myself with regard to the unfreedom of the contemporary abstract image. Of course, here I am using the concept of freedom in a very narrow, instrumental sense of the word. In art, unfreedom in the sense of surviving is intolerable, it contradicts the very concept of art. When I personally see 'works' of this kind, I almost always feel slightly nauseous (in an entirely real sense). I meant a different kind of unfreedom. I'll come at this from a slight distance. When, as a youngster, I decided to work in art, my choice was conditioned by the apparent freedom of art. It seemed that in art everything was possible! And this feeling, brimming over with energy, simply sucked me into creating art (which would certainly not have existed if I had not known the art of the avant-garde). However, fairly soon I realized that art has its own *logic*, its own development. I understood more and more clearly the difference between freedom and arbitrary will. It is precisely in this sense that I wrote about the unfreedom of the abstract image. Art must be abstract, otherwise it is not art. But as I have already written, now there is no longer any place for genuine abstraction, the subjective gesture without any justifications is no longer possible. However, we can achieve the *effect* of abstraction by making the mimetic or conceptual essence of any particular image unimportant in the process of production.

Wishing everyone new prospects for creative work and development!

Osmolovsky

LETTER 14 (extract)

From: Anatoly Osmolovsky
Date: Tuesday, January 20, 2004, 7.02 a.m.

[…]

Finally, a few thoughts about 'communist society' and about the idea, constantly repeated by Igor, of the impossibility of achieving the communist condition. In my view, Igor's

letter draws an entirely incorrect comparison between the
'communist ideal' and the Stalinist regime of 'real socialism.'
And although the idea that there is no need for any kind of
revolution (or, therefore, for art) is very incisive and just, it still
has to be admitted that this was an *organized* lack of any need.
In objective terms Soviet people were under the monstrous
yoke of a repressive regime, and to assert that 'This was,
admittedly temporarily, but nonetheless a realized communist
utopia' is incorrect.

Is a communist utopia realizable? It seems to me that it is
entirely realizable. In what way does the organization of specific
socioeconomic relations actually differ, for instance, from the
organization of a tractor factory? Only in terms of scale and
the need to possess more profound and precise knowledge. But
the description of communist society as 'heavenly paradise'
is rather naive. This is a question that concerned the Marxist
theoreticians of the early twentieth century – they argued about
whether the communist phase of society's development is final
and free of contradictions or whether there would be certain
limitations and contradictions in that society. The question is
absolutely meaningless.

The prospect described by Marx is achievable. More
than that, it will necessarily be achieved. The denial of this
prospect's achievability is a denial of progress and of any
development at all. But, after all, society is not in a motionless
condition. And in Western Europe we can observe for
ourselves the results of progress (not only in the scientific, but
even in the moral sphere).

May you all live to see the embodiment of the communist
ideal.

Osmolovsky

LETTER 17

From: Dmitry Gutov
Date: Thursday, January 22, 2004, 5.33 a.m.

Dear Friends,

I reply, although belatedly, to Osmolovsky's letter of 13.01.2004.

In it he subjects me to a harsh attack, direct, consistent and uncompromising. Really trying to smash open my irrational head with a club.

What can one oppose to such an onslaught? Only calm defense, deft dodges away from the blows so that they will slide off, if not actually miss. Something like aikido. Perhaps the attacker will trip himself up.

I must admit that Tolik understands my meaning and reproduces it rather accurately, even accentuating it to the limit. He formulates one of my ideas, which is **'an example of glaring demagogic manipulation'** in this way: **'Everything in the history of art that is a generally acknowledged achievement is claimed as an attainment of the realist socialist realism."** If "socialist realism" is replaced by "realism," then I am prepared to accept this reproach. I do not like the term 'socialist realism' and never use it, since I very much doubt that any phenomenon exists in the world that could be signified by it. It is usually employed to embrace a complex of the most varied phenomena that existed in Soviet art and had little in common with each other. Or rather, phenomena which were directly opposed to each other.

This formula of realism, which discloses its link with all the great achievements of the past, may seem to Osmolovsky to be a **simple idea** and may not correspond to generally accepted word usage, but it suits me. And let modernism appeal to the ages of decadence. No one is preventing Bonita

Olivier, whom Tolik has criticized so thoroughly, from seeking kinship with mannerism.

Tolik also accuses me under a point of law formulated by Groys; **"the representatives of orthodox Marxism regarded with suspicion all philosophical and artistic phenomena that had arisen after Marxism, precisely because they arose *after* it."** I accept this reproach too. I see a grain of sanity in this suspiciousness. There are some achievements that are very difficult to restrain. It's no accident that Lifshitz called his studies "ordinary Marxism," and saw convulsive creative work as a great threat to it. Look at the bold accuser of Marxism Vilensky. He knows no fear, which is the beginning of all wisdom.

Osmolovsky does not stop there, going on to lambaste me with the following argument: **"Orthodox Marxism, Marxism that has been transformed from a scientific method into a faith, can only work exclusively with verified artistic phenomena that are not subject to doubt."** This too is rather well formulated. Only a couple of clarifications. What does *to work* mean? Fortunately Chubarov's letter – that encyclopedia of trivialities – is close at hand, I'll use an example from there. Concerning Soviet times he writes: **"In these conditions the development of art could not happen, all that was possible was a repetition of the same old canon."** It is possible to work with classical phenomena in this way, but it can also be done differently. That is, to take **verified artistic phenomena that are not subject to doubt** in order to understand what made them such. Let me remind you that this is where Marx saw the most important and most difficult question. This is no longer a question of a faith or a canon. Furthermore, one of the lessons to be drawn from paying attention to the monuments of classic art is that they were not created mechanically, following

a recipe. As Goethe put it: we should learn from the ancients
that which they could not have learned from anyone. Where an
attack on this respect for **phenomena that are not subject
to doubt** is most correct is that this is the point at which it is
easier to deviate into faith and a canon than anywhere else. And
it happens across the board. But (and I am not tired of repeating
this) there is no fatality about this.

Now here Osmolovsky is wrong in saying: **"such a
position is as hard as steel, and there is no need to take
responsibility for anything or to justify oneself."**

The essence of the matter is that by realism Tolik means
any imitation of life. This takes in the frescoes of the Cathedral
of Christ the Savior and Shilov and the devil only knows
what else. He calls this the **"realist artistic style, with its
positive and negative examples**." This can't turn into an
argument, so I'll ask Osmolovsky himself. In abstractionism
do you distinguish a wall stained by a building worker from
museum exhibits? Tell me, how do you do it? Or is all this
simply another **"artistic style"**? Is there any boundary at all
that separates art from not-art?

Since I have been forbidden on pain of the death penalty
from using the concept of 'truth,' I am prepared to explain
myself in the language of nominalism

What has been called art *is* art. OK, although I don't
really like it all that much. But the question remains. We are
surrounded by surfaces that have been stained and scribbled
on, no less than by images in imitation of life. Nonetheless,
not all of them have been deemed worthy of being called
abstractionism. If you puzzle this out, then there will be fewer
problems, with Shilov too.

I hope there will be also be fewer of them in connection
with the subject of manipulation, using the realist method of

classical art. The **"thousands and thousands who use the very same method for brainwashing people"** will still be there of course. But it will become clear that their method is somewhat different. More than that, it will become clear that their methods (externally so similar) are separated from each other by cosmic distances. As Lifshitz appealed to us: let us distinguish things, and not jumble them together.

For all the similarity between the methods of kitsch and realism, it is not so very difficult to formulate the difference. I could do it myself, but I'll adduce the testimony of Greenberg – perhaps Osmolovsky will listen to him. (All the emphases in bold type are mine.) "A new commodity was invented – the **ersatz culture** of kitsch, intended for those who, while remaining indifferent and insensitive to the values of **genuine culture**, nonetheless experienced a spiritual hunger."

"Exploiting as its raw material **cheapened, corrupted** and academicized simulacra of **genuine culture**, kitsch welcomes this insensitivity and cultivates it."

"Kitsch **is mechanical and acts according to formulae. Kitsch is substitute experience and fake feelings.**"

"Kitsch is the embodiment of everything **inessential** in modern life."

"Kitsch borrows from the cultural tradition its methods, tricks, artifices, basic rules and themes, it transforms all this into a certain system and discards the rest. One can say that kitsch draws its own blood out of this reservoir of accumulated experience."

"Today in the country that is supposedly ours, it is not enough to have a propensity for **real culture**; a person has to feel **a true passion for real culture,** a passion that will give him the strength to resist the **fakes** that surround him and exert pressure on him."

Tolik, note that Greenberg boldly uses the words "genuine culture," "real culture," and "true culture," or, on the contrary: cheapened, substitute, fake, inessential, mechanical. What is this if not working with the concept of truth? Or the use of antonyms of those concepts (idea, meaning, life, typicality, factual truth, historicity) that the Wanderers group used to characterize what moved them in art? Tolik! Explain why only Greenberg can do this? What kind of discrimination is this? I want to do it too.

And another extremely important question, about the elite nature of the avant-garde. Here Osmolovsky refers to the authority of Adorno: **"art shows respect for the masses in opposing them and in knowing what they could be."** This is a very important assertion and it is worth paying attention to it. It is in the same line as Greenberg's idea of the opposition between the avant-garde and kitsch. There is no doubt that the phenomenon of the avant-garde is more advanced, more refined and richer in meaning than kitsch. There is an element of respect for the viewer present in it. The artist does not pander to bad taste, but says as it were: develop culturally and you will see that this is not a daub, but a phenomenon that requires refined taste, a well-honed eye and educated aesthetic feeling.

There is no denying the logic of this approach. But there is another line of argument in support of the avant-garde, from the other direction one might say. On one side it is opposed to kitsch, but on the other, to the classical. In the early twentieth century this aspect was developed by Russian intellectuals. Take, for example, the ideas of Andrei Bely. According to his way of thinking, classical, realist art was precisely highly elitist and aristocratic. Take Pushkin. Everything seems so simple and clear that the unsophisticated reader, contenting himself with this superficial diamond shell, does not even make any effort to penetrate the depths of these texts. He does not even suspect that concealed behind this shell there lie treasure troves of thought. The avant-garde, on the contrary, smashes open this protective shell and the reader is acquainted willy-nilly with the secrets concealed behind it. Thus the avant-garde is defended as a more democratic phenomenon than the classics. (Bely, of course, is writing about symbolism, but the essence is the same.)

And so here, as in any matter, everything depends on the position from which one views things. In this perspective the avant-garde does not raise the masses, as Adorno puts it, to the condition of what they could be, but **"accommodates itself to them in their degrading image that is an insult to human dignity."**

There is a difference between raising an individual to an understanding of (let us take the maximum), say, Mark Rothko or of the Ghent Altarpiece.

As Greenberg correctly writes, today **"the alternative to Picasso is not Michelangelo, but kitsch."** That is how things are in real life, but from the viewpoint of what should be or, as Adorno remarks, of what **could be**, the alternative should be precisely Michelangelo. And that, in effect, is Lifshitz.

There is another extremely important aspect to this discussion about elitism. There are different elitisms. What is their essential difference in our case? Not only that, according to Andrei Bely's witty observation, realism (Tolik, the other realism, not the one that you thought of! Well, if you don't like the word, put in 'classical' if you like) is hyper-elitist. Yes the simplicity of the language, the elevation of the subject, and the recognizability of the details satisfy the naive mind. They give an illusion of understanding. But the possibility of gradually moving farther, to the strata that follow, is always preserved here. Whether a person will want to take advantage of it is a different matter. It is precisely the absence of an element of compulsion in the classics that is not to Bely's liking.

The avant-garde does not exist in conditions (here I shall call on Greenberg for help again, since Osmolovsky is hardly likely to listen to anyone except him in the near future) where **"on the one side there is constantly a minority of those who hold power (and are therefore cultured) and on the other, a huge mass of the exploited and poor (and consequently ignorant)."**

This is a different type of elitism. It is built entirely on disjuncture. Here the possibility of rising higher is excluded. It is a frank culture of a minority that possesses the privilege of education and leisure. It is possible to love Levitan because he painted birch trees so convincingly; it is possible, proceeding from this starting point and studying art, to discover many more things of interest in his painting. Avant-garde art excludes this approach. Here one already begins from a certain cultural level. (And if you have started from the fact that here the colors have been applied beautifully, then you have wandered into different territory altogether.) And the bourgeois world cultivates this distance. It is one of the fundamental negative features of our time. A defect of culture. This division is growing and it will not lead to anything good. Of course, it is accepted that the artist does not accommodate himself to the masses' lack of taste (here Adorno is not in error) but is it not possible to find another way of respecting them? Without demonstratively pointing out their uncivilized state, but also without any pandering to bad taste?

Both theory and practice tell us that it is not possible. Greenberg himself testifies that today **the avant-garde is the only living culture**. And sixty-five years later Osmolovsky says:

Don't even bother to try. Even Lifshitz said that it is hard to transform fish soup into an aquarium. But is it possible at least not to take delight in these circumstances?

Hugs to everyone

Dima

Note

This version of the text is abbreviated from D. Gutov and A. Osmolovsky. *Three Debates*. Moscow: Grundrisse, 2012. In Russian.

8

Olga Chernysheva

SCREENS

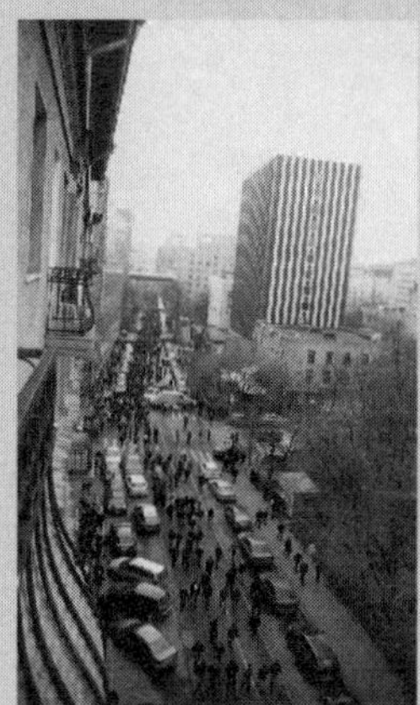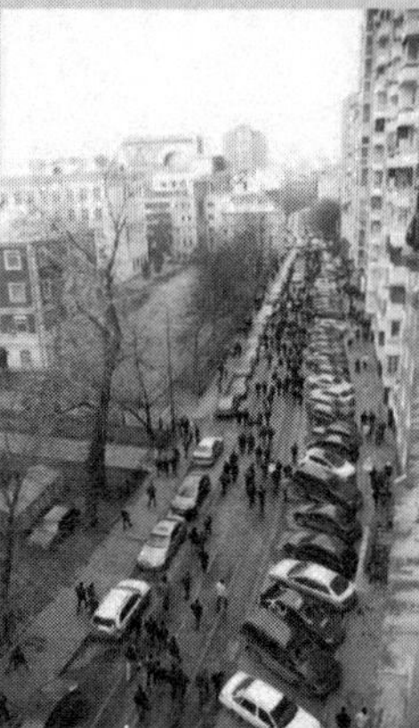

A holiday in the absence of the usual trimmings.
One fall morning, the usual regime of sounds vanished, the usual traffic noise, the clamor from the nearby school yard. None of these things could be heard. Only a sound of rustling, of shuffling, came from the street. It turned out that the unusual sound was made by soles slapping against asphalt in silence. Down below, men in dark clothing streamed by.
Kurban Bayram, a holiday we have not managed to get used to, was underway.
Moldavian repairmen watched all this with interest from the next balcony over. They played the role of spectators in this new situation, which resembled, in reverse, the demonstrations that Rodchenko had shot from high above.
Everything special about Rodchenko's photographs, everything expressive in the specifically photographic sense was missing: the sun, the orchestras, the splendor and the festive decor. Women and children were discretely missing. All the usual trappings were missing.
But then again, Rochenko's gaze has been missing for a long time as well.

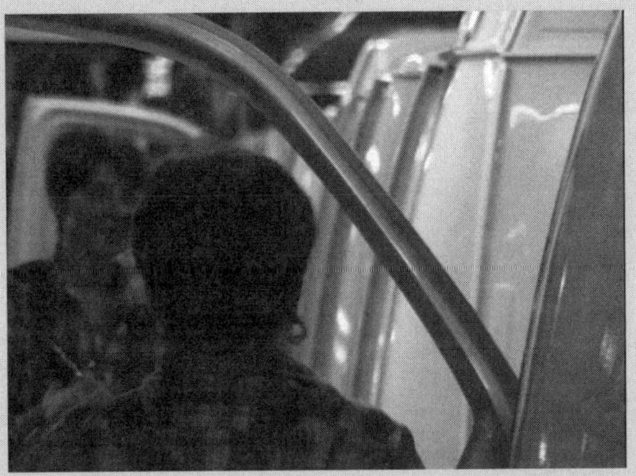

Assembly Line
The feeling of things not working out is familiar to me. Hence my
fascination, once, with a particular assembly line or, rather, the perfect
anti-assembly line, where everything was dictated by human, rather than
mechanical, rhythms. Next to the assembly line, a piece of paper wide as a
column and covered in writing was taped up. It listed the reasons why
something or other had not worked out. The assembly line was more like a
motorists club, its members dressed in neat overalls. Everyone was making
an effort. Cleanly, calmly and quietly. Things were moving along the
assembly line like clockwork, invisible to the eye.

Black Dot
It is very unusual and refreshing to be a black dot for a common cause.
There's a chopper in the sky and the cause is the same.
Black figures are milling around, independently as it were.
But they too are part of the cause.
This is how black dots come together on Sakharov Square.
Just like Hokusai: lots of emptiness and magnetized essentiality.
But on the square it turns out the cause is not common.
Causes become interests,
and there you stand, playing a little black dot.
And dots all look the same, no matter whether they agree or disagree on the inside.
And again you regret that nobody ever taught you how to whistle.
A whistling black dot. We had one of those on our kettle, from where the steam would billow out.

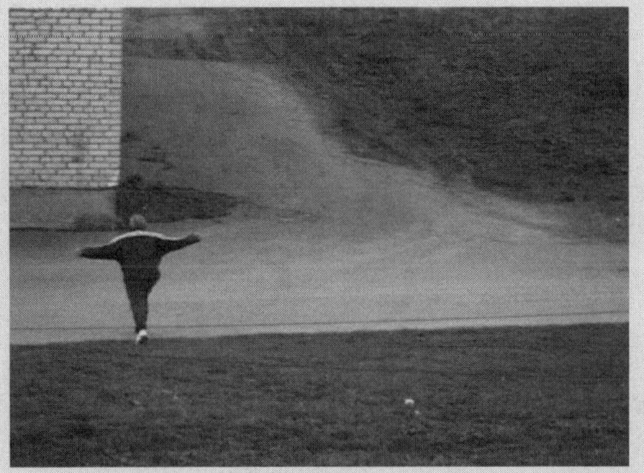

Exercises

Every day is like life on the whole. Who will you meet and what will you have to deal with? You can never tell in advance. This is why people do their exercises. They want to keep in shape to be ready for any changes that might come. Exercise is like an inoculation, an advance experience of all the day's efforts in a light form. Thus we play out the script of our meetings and travels in our heads. What if the train breaks down in the metro? What if they turn off the internet? What if you can't be human anymore? Will you have to become a bird?

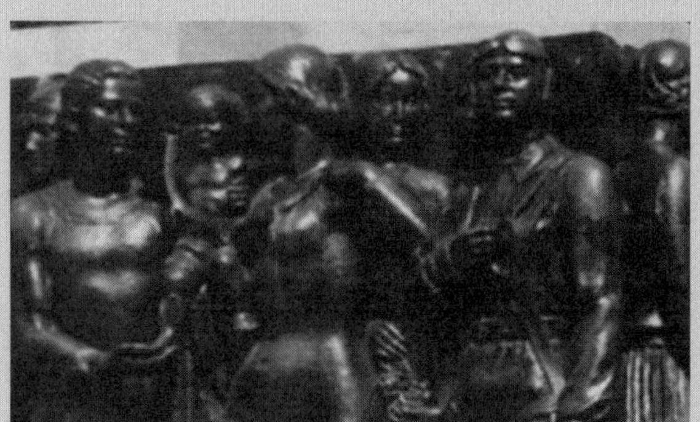

It is said that there is a sense of vitality in Moscow. It is more like tenacity, survival.

There is a pushiness and carelessness in tenacity. It is an amorphous vitality. The bygone bronze Soviet pagan gods, brilliantly sculpted by Vera Mukhina for the bas-relief of the Soviet Pavilion at the 1937 Paris International Expo, are animated and vital in this way.

Now, after a so-called restoration, their overall aspect is stagnant. They are pointless, sluggish and somehow mediocrely mundane. As if it were not the sculptures that had been smashed to pieces (the pedestal with the original bas-relief was destroyed in France) but the spirit of each character, its will, faith and intellect pierced and demolished. They say that people dug up after premature burial are like this. They do not survive for long and live amorphously. True, these sculptural survivors are funny as well, apparently made of clay, but in fact fashioned from bronze.

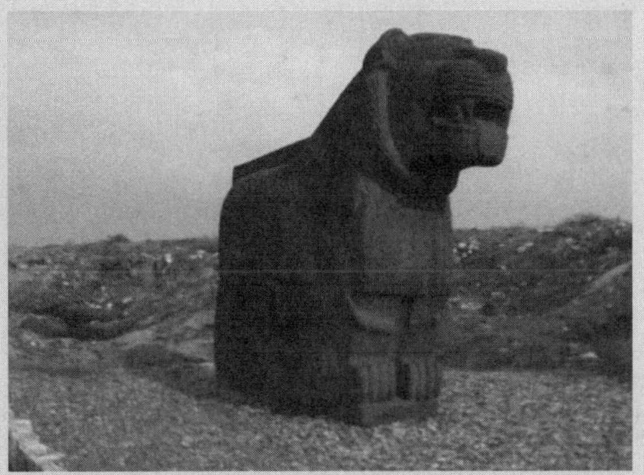

Lion
How is the Basalt Lion doing?
It stood on a hill in the open air on the road from Aleppo to Damascus.
Below, a peasant was plowing terra cotta land under gray olives. The lion
was perfection. It would be the pride of any museum today, and around
four thousand years ago it graced a Hittite temple.
It was magical. From far way, it looked ferocious, but when you got close
to it, the lion turned out to be one-eared and smiling. No one really
looked after it, although there was an empty guard box at a distance from
it. Clearly, the lion itself stood guard over those parts. I wouldn't want
for its life, which is measured by millennia, to be over.
No video camera is trained on the lion. I'm unable to click a button in the
Internet and find out whether it is still intact.

Plastic Bags
Once upon a time, when modern life emerged, it seemed that humanity had produced tons of masterpieces, and like folks born by some fluke during a harvest, we would now get done to dealing with all this stuff. It looks, in fact, like we'll just skim past, lightly pressing against this mass of creations, and vanish. And in this sense, the plastic bags nuzzling up against the pyramids in Giza seemed to me kindred spirits. Over the years, you begin to realize that the world does not exist for you, and that you yourself exist for something else. (This is what I was shooting when the sand-filled wind made my video camera go haywire and break down.)

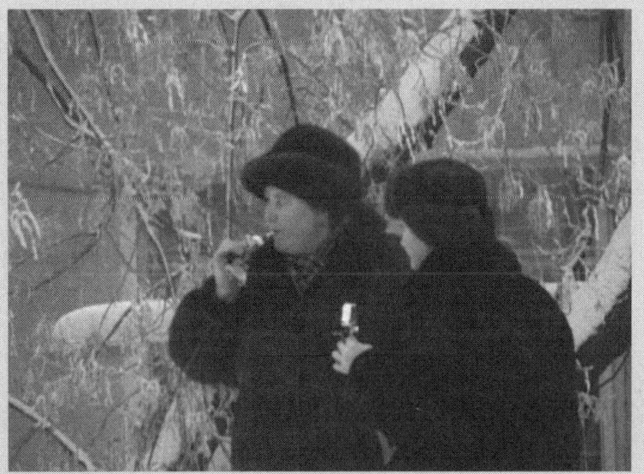

Platform

One way of reconciling yourself to your surroundings is to imagine something not as part of the hodgepodge of real facts, but, for example, as a disappearing core of a certain crystalline system, now receding into the past. As this principle grows smaller, all the strings start to tighten, tangle, and droop. Snowy platforms are always generous like blank sheets of paper.

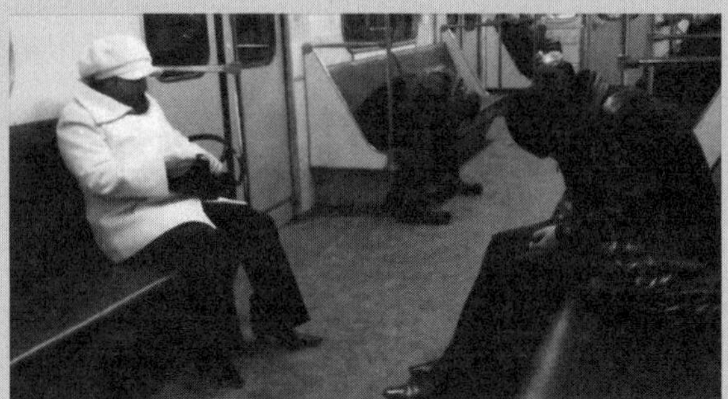

Private Spaces

In the Russian language, spatial characteristics often stand for moral ones. For example, there was a key word in the 1990s that characterized senseless, unmotivated acts of violence: беспредел, literally: boundlessness.

This is like if you ask what Doctors Without Borders is doing, and the answer is "without borders." Such local notions don't just include big themes like Russian "boundlessness" (i.e. violence) and that touching tiny little private sphere that a person organizes the first chance they get. It's also a dog-sized towel on the beach, temporarily but clearly marking the border of a spontaneous private space, or seats in the metro, those charged, resistant millimeters surrounding the other passengers.

Some time ago, spatial voids started popping up in the wagons of Moscow's metro. If you stand on the platform and look through the glass, you might see that part of the car is crowded while part of it is suspiciously empty. And this tells you of the presence of a social outcast sprawled out over the benches.

In the little situation I am describing, this sleeper was just some normal drunk guy. A wave of passengers would flood in, bump into the benches and step back in disappointment. The train moved. Everything took on a rhythmic quality. The train stopped abruptly and started again. The "king of the bums" appeared in the doors. Everyone stepped aside and the airspace around him had a concentrated density and power of smell. He moved toward the bench with the drunk guy on it, which the other passengers considered occupied, swayed back and forth a little, and sunk down onto it as well. And this new human unity rode on.

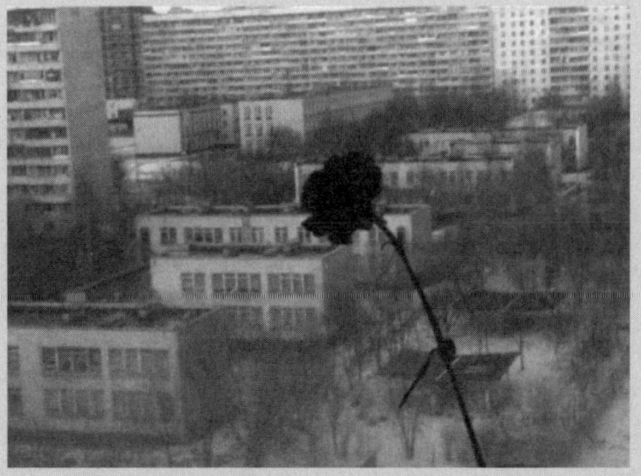

The Sound
Once I went to visit my parents. They seemed very busy, restlessly wandering all over the apartment. I went into the room that we call the "big room": everything was the same as always.
But somewhere in the distance, there was a subtle sound, a muted whine, as though a mosquito had begun to sing a melody more complex than its regular monotonous hum.
I started to look for the source of this sound. When I opened an old German cupboard, the sound got louder, and I recognized the melody of the old Soviet song "Victory Day." After searching through a pile of junk, I finally found a postcard wrapped in a piece of cloth that kept playing the same tune over and over again: taam-tam-tam..., tam-ta-ra-ra ta-tam-tam...
I brought the postcard to my parents.
Oh no, they cried in unison, why did you take that thing out again? It's a card we got from the president on May 9th. For veterans. From Putin to Papa, that is. It came a couple of days ago, we opened it, and now it won't stop playing, so we hid it as best we could. It'll run out of juice and stop playing some day, won't it?

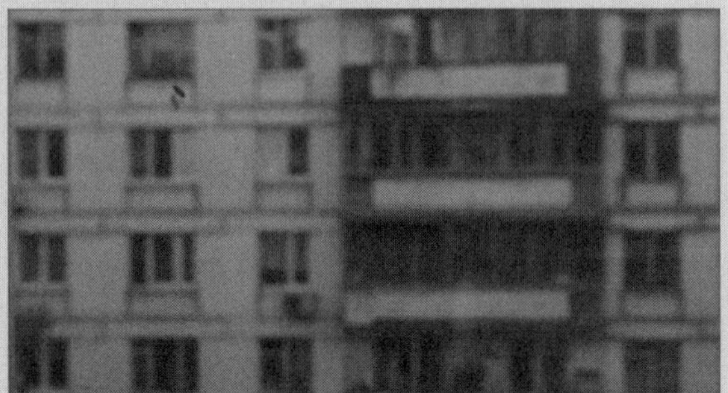

Windowpanes have an Inside Out
From the topographical point of view, one side of the windowpane shows a more important picture than the other at any given moment. Sometimes one side of the windowpane is turned off, as if there is fog on the other side. This side of the pane already exists and doesn't seem all that attractive. It would be a stretch to interpret this video as the irresistible gravity of half-rotten Moscow real estate, with its out-of-reach prices. To get a den for docking in Moscow means to gain your freedom, according to the law of the unity of opposites.

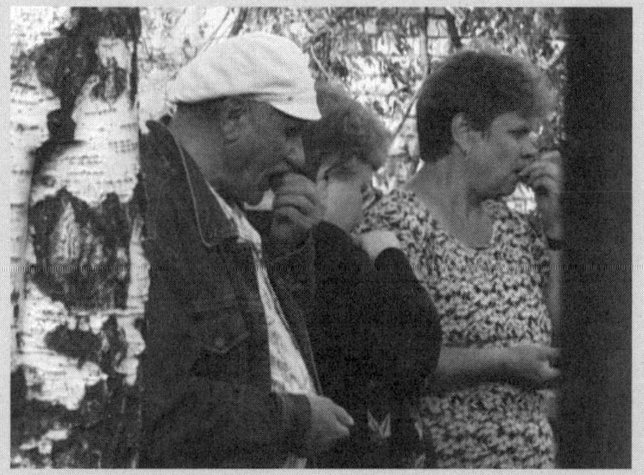

Words
There are some days in spring and autumn when you cannot say whether it is autumn or spring.
They look the same.
But autumn and spring smell very different.
Looking at a person, it is often difficult to tell whether he or she is developing or regressing until he or she speaks. Words can be as dense as the smell of human bodies.

9

Dmitry Prigov

TWO MANIFESTOS

Where are our hands, in which our future lies?

The specific cultural situation, with its dramaturgical interweaving of fragments of previous situations and embryonic elements of those still to come, shapes the dominant and concomitant models for the behavior of artists.

In order to understand the essential nature of the present cultural situation, one must understand how it differs from the preceding one and put forward possible suggestions concerning its dynamics, duration, and location.

In effect, there are three conjectures that can be proposed: (1) The current process will develop and the current moment, together with the forms of its sociocultural organization, are temporary; while the previous period's forms of sociocultural organization have become obsolete and are no more than an apologetic rudiment, if not a retarding encumbrance; (2) the present situation will continue interminably, with small-scale fluctuations, sometimes backwards and sometimes forwards, so one should not be in any hurry to bury the past; (3) everything will come full circle and the former channels of association and socialization should therefore be scrupulously and lovingly preserved, without indulging vain hopes in an enticing future.

What, then, did we have in the past that we are currently in the process of rejecting and in relation to which we are structuring our current strategy of behavior and suppositions concerning the future?

The previous cultural situation was constructed on the principle of a rigid binary opposition: 'official/unofficial', which, like the two poles of a magnet, was repeated at every point of the structure. In the Union of Writers, let's say, (as in the other unions of the creative professions) an opposition of 'left/right' emerged, followed by an opposition of 'Union of Writers/milieu around the Union,' and then an opposition of 'milieu around the Union/unofficial literature.' In the milieu of unofficial literature the articulations followed the principle 'can be published/can't be published.' A form of insult even appeared: you could get published! This scale of derivatives from a single basic principle of oppositions formed the entire unsophisticated spectrum of variety.

If one set out all these positions on some single scale, then noncongruence with the starting point of official recognition offered compensation in the form of an entitlement to artistic truth and moral judgement, a right augmented by an increase in the distance from that point. The significance of this law is interesting, not in those cases when it coincided with the real right of a gifted writer and highly moral individual, but when it was mechanically extended to anyone who came under the given system of calculation. By the way, even officially recognized and freedom-loving masters of the official art could not avoid, if not acknowledging this law openly, then at least feeling it with their not completely hardened hearts and developing an inferiority complex about it.

At the present moment, in about twenty years of functioning the unofficial culture has developed into a rather formalized organism with its own hierarchy, means of socialization, and rules of acceptance into it. Incidentally, this very formalization creates difficulties for the active representatives of unofficial culture which, if not the same in essence, are probably just as complicated as those faced by representatives of the official culture in terms of depth of psychological restructuring and adjustment to a new cultural mentality.

In the unofficial culture (in the milieu of artists and writers) two basic structures have taken shape – the milieu around the Union and the strictly unofficial milieu. The appearance of the structure around the Union was facilitated by the way that established masters and clans disrupted the natural means for the younger generation to enter official circles, with the result that a horizontal, generational cross-section was formed, united by a desire to be included in the official culture and the impossibility of this happening, a circle of people of extremely varied poetic and artistic predilections, who at any other time would have been unlikely to come together on a single platform. By the very necessity of life this 'overcooking' in the official sphere engendered in many of them distinct features of unofficial consciousness.

The unofficial culture was established on the basis of a principled rejection of the official culture. It consists of several, so to say, vertical and parallel threads of an alliance of individuals of various ages, but with closely similar aesthetic leanings.

Such a cultural situation also rigidly codemarked locations: on the one hand journals, exhibition halls, and stages; and on the other hand apartments, basements, and typed manuscripts, engendering a corresponding, instantaneously engaged mechanism of orientation and perception. Moreover, this rigid codemarking meant that the appearance of unofficial artists and writers in official places always bore features either of a scandalous event or a travesty, which prevented artists and writers from identifying with them.

All these appearances had the significance of events that exceeded their literary or artistic significance, and their infrequency generated a frenzied commotion around them that bunched together people with rather different professions and interests in the sphere of culture and art. Accordingly there crystallized out a certain type of artist-poet-performer-tribune, standing in at every specific point for all of these positions, being their plenipotentiary deputy and at the same time champion, martyr, and teacher. In fact such an image of the artist-poet arose here very long ago and has simply varied, depending on the times.

The present cultural situation is characterized by an erosion of the oppositional structure (by which I mean the sociocultural structure, and not the simply cultural one, which will evidently always exist – and incidentally this very moment is the hardest of all at which to determine precisely the position of purely cultural opponency). There also seems to be emerging an imprecisely articulated third zone of culture, emerging as it were unclearly, virtually.

This leads to a reconfiguration of the groups that have emerged in an unofficial culture, of which the vertical structure is rapidly being eroded by horizontal age-related trends. And meanwhile the circle of the milieu around the Union is undergoing intensive differentiation according to degree of ideological and aesthetic identification with the official culture.

Incidentally, whereas previously fellows in art and fate were primarily fellows in their fate, nowadays the art is beginning to dominate as the criterion of fellowship.

Literally only yesterday a conversation at home was more than a conversation, it was a cultural event. Over the course of time, the intonation of domestic confidentiality, the significance of intragroup events, and the appeal to a narrow circle of those who had accepted this fate had become features of the poetic (and this did not represent any decline, since fresh springs of culture welled up at precisely those points, the sore spots of culture gaped open at precisely those points). But now it is as if one of the walls is collapsing, revealing those seated there in almost defenseless nakedness, and the force lines of culture are being rearranged, so that former merits are unfortunately no guarantee of the genuineness of present actions and utterances.

In going public, the a priori rights of the unacknowledged and persecuted are lost, the right to unappealable moral judgement is lost, the advantage of trust that was automatically advanced is lost. And this, by the way, can be seen from several free poetic readings, from the collected volume of the Leningrad club Krug and from the experience of socializing rock groups.

The formation of certain new associations, refashioning the boundaries of past articulations in culture, and the socialization of small domestic groups dictate a new ethics of cultural behavior, replacing all-round mutual support and ideological kinship with principles that are close to a corporate code. Many judgements, pronouncements, and maxims that were formerly based on the pardonable, noncommittal nature of table-talk and friendly trust, and sometimes simply on sympathy, are now revealed as simply expressions of weakness and inadequacy. This, by the way, is the same time when there occurs a

fundamental cultural and stylistic break, which can be detected
in all forms of art and also facilitates a reconstruction of the
hierarchy that has taken shape in both the official and unofficial
spheres, as well as rearrangements of the hierarchy of actual
types of art within culture.

It is clear that poetry's age-long role of pop-heroism is
slipping away from it to the rapidly expanding rock movement
and the pop sphere. Because of this, an event in literature is
shrinking to the true dimensions of a literary event, a poetic
event, an event in visual art … If everything continues in the
same vein, then the present status of literature, say, may persist
by inertia for another two years or so, but then it will assume a
form familiar to us from western examples: normal commercial
literature and literature as such, which circulates in narrow
academic circles. With twenty or thirty years of honest and
selfless service a writer will attract the benevolent attention
of some award-granting foundation or some prestigious prize
or other, and they will appoint him a celebrity, without any
subsequent necessity for anyone to read him. If everything
moves in this direction and does not return to the past, or if
no local means for the existence of culture is found, then it is
entirely possible that the prevalent form of writer will be the
philologist, the well-balanced individual capable of calmly and
honestly dividing his time between business and literature,
whereas the ideal type of local poet is a tramp, genius, favorite
of the masses, and hysterical prattler; the poet who is a national
hero retreats into history, like the storytellers, Slavic bards, and
rhapsodists no longer known to us. In addition, before our very
eyes the press is taking away from literature perhaps its most
fundamental reader – the lover of social wit, moral problems,
an instantaneous, on-the-spot response to instantaneous events,
and a certain kind of ambiguity. Perhaps the press, along with

the spheres of philosophy, sociology, psychology, and the institution of religion, which have been engendered by the current social awakening, will become the people's teachers, relieving literature of the backbreaking burden but also, of course, stripping away its aura of exclusivity.

And so literature will be left to be literature.

Therefore it is pointless for the Poetry club, let's say, to place its reliance on events like a festival in the Dukat club in its cultural and community activity. One must become accustomed to reading in a narrow circle of staunch lovers of this activity (which, by external necessity, was effectively the case previously, but the invisible yet palpable external groundswell of suffering readers and listeners who were not admitted created the impression of a major event and gave rise to illusions); now it will all happen without any added value, be what it is, according to the natural course of things in culture. The same thing will happen with passionately anticipated publications. While literally a year and a half ago a book by Zhdanov, say, was an event even for writers far removed from him, now it would pass off unnoticed except by a narrow circle of lovers of poetry.

It is obvious that the processes occurring in visual art are moving in the same direction. The syncretism of the event is being removed from exhibitions and they will be, or rather at this point wish in the future to be, subject to the laws of the market.

I would like to remark that I am describing all the changes, assuming the uninterrupted development of the present process, that is, understanding everything that is happening now as temporary formations, since this process in my view can only be described with a dynamic model, although of course a change of vector is possible.

Therefore I regard such strange emanations as the Poetry club, with its 180 members, as mutational formations. In the sphere of culture, as I see things, only one functional structure is possible: pluralism. Therefore, if some conscious effort is to be invested, it should be in the direction of pluralism, and the creation of huge alternative formations. As a start it would be good to have numerous clubs and associations, the existence of which could later be regulated, for instance, by an institute of free cooperative publishing houses or journals. In visual art I see a solution in the fragmentation of the single channel of resources that dictates a single artistic and stylistic policy. Possibly this will be facilitated by the self-employed labor activity that is now emerging, which will make possible the accumulation of sufficient resources in private hands and revive the glorious institution of patronage of the arts.

The question arises, of course, of participation in this process. Naturally, the basic precondition making it possible to involve oneself in this process is a certain internal confidence in the possibility of a result. At this stage, of course, it is a matter of purely personal intuition and risk. But on condition that the process is taking place and is irreversible, nonparticipation in it, which was formerly a merit, a cross and an inalienable part of poetics, now becomes simply a matter of personal choice, a personal preference. In exactly the same way, preferring a private apartment to a public hall ceases to be a cultural-moral act and is merely a personal one.

And the final thing: if, as I mentioned above, the harsh codemarking of places and binary nature of culture previously made it possible (as Boehme put it, an angel in the midst of hell flies in his own little cloud of heaven) to fly onto other people's territory and depart unsullied, now, with boundaries blurred, one is simply identified with the point at which one presents oneself, as happened with the actions at the Manège, the appearance of heroes of the underground on the television screen and so forth, in other words, untainted places are required, which will have to create their own image. I therefore hope that this hall, despite its plain homeliness, will become one such place.

1987

The second sacro-cularization

In the period of time (and for these days it is quite a long one – about two years) between declaring my theme – "the second sacralization" – and receiving the theses of this conference, somewhere a mutation has occurred in the title, to "The second secularization." However, having briefly considered the matter, I realized that everything that happens of its own accord (as things usually do) has much more meaning, at least it reflects far more accurately what is happening to me, as a participant and character in a 'big' cultural process. (Something like Freudian slips of the tongue, slips of the tongue in the process of cultural dialogue.) That is, the very process of transformation and ease of any vectorial conversion (which has unwittingly been summed up in the typologically similar process of transformation of the name) is far more adequate to the present, suspended, pseudo-unarchivized condition of culture and art bereft of both evaluative and axiological preferences. For this reason, the contamination of names, in reflecting the general condition, also indicates two possible (entirely and completely heuristic and nonobligatory) routes to resolving the situation (which is perceived as one of crisis), two possibilities which can be extrapolated into the future as equally possible. The equal possibility and indefiniteness of the proposals (as distinct from the imprecise articulation of recurrent features) are testimony to an attempt to guess at a fundamentally different structure from within the limits of the old cultural mentality that is coming to an end. And it is the attempt to describe this very mentality as already achieved and approaching its conclusion, with its specific parameters, history of formation and signs of exhaustion, that will manifest at this moment the possibility of understanding at least what should not be expected.

The term "second sacralization" arose as a certain metaphorical definition of the entire sum of vague attempts to make sense of the current situation in art within my own artistic experience, and correspondingly through means far removed from terminological and experimental purity and correctness. But of course, taking into account the history of such ancient relations as those between religion and art, bearing in mind the dynamics of social and ideological processes, it hardly makes sense to expect a sharp shift of balance towards religion in their interrelations – just as there are no grounds for counting on the appearance of a new, big religion or significant denomination that would advance a fundamentally different cosmology and anthropology. Exactly to the contrary, it is, rather, precisely within the confines of culture that any substantial ideas might arise (well, of course within the framework of the fundamental basis of Christian culture, which is culture as such in the aspect we are considering here, that of historical development). Precisely these ideas, postulates, and maxims can become the extra-aesthetic limit of artistic aspirations and activity, a limit which, while not transcendental, is factored out beyond the boundaries of purely artistic problems – and I actually wished to designate them metaphorically as "the second sacralization."

At the same time, the identification, deconstruction and objectivization of the inner spirit of contemporary art and its ambitions to be a quasi-religion could be called a "second sacralization."

But all this is something like a finale, a summation or conclusions, obliged, owing to the mishap with the title, to outstrip the natural course of the account of the event and therefore possessing a perfectly real chance of appearing a second time at the end of this text.

And so now there will rightfully follow the totally and absolutely real beginning.

Right then.

Round historical dates, especially the end of a millennium, are always experienced psychologically as catastrophic frontiers. Their thresholds always abound in apocalyptic anticipations expressed, if not in the terms of religious dogma, then at least in eschatologically tinged terms. This is all the more evident within the limits of the former Soviet Union, where the end of the millennium coincided with the end of the Soviet period of Russian history and, possibly, with the end of the great Russian messianic, logocentric mentality. If such a situation does not itself give rise to a crisis in art, it does at least create and facilitate the growth of fine cracks and gaps into rifts and almost terrifying abysses, ready to smash to splinters the edifice of culture that was erected above chaos with such long, laborious effort. The crisis of the eastern, communist component of the intricately arranged mechanism of global equilibrium cannot help but affect the West too, if not in its economic and state organization, then at least in its system of cultural notions and world outlook. Western leftist thinking that identified itself with communism (perhaps not the real thing, but the powerful myth) and Soviet oppositionist dissident thinking, orientated towards western democracy (in its absolute terms and ideologemes also possessing all the features of myth) have lost their relevance and in their collapse are provoking and presaging the reconfiguration of elements of ideology, political thinking and culture. It is also obvious that hitherto stable western society, coming up against the sharp increase in volume of the economically backward world, into which all the former socialist countries have tumbled, will find itself face to face with an eternally breathing abyss, ready to gape open in front of it at some unexpected and therefore unprotected place.

Of course, something similar has occurred more than once in history. But every time it has been resolved by rather earthly means, so far without vindicating the expectations of the apologists of apocalyptical thinking. Let us hope that this time also everything will be resolved in a similar fashion.

The entire complex of problems enumerated above, which are more a subject for politological and social research, is of interest to us as a background, a complex of events that have coincided with an extremely important and painful phenomenon in the sphere of art as such – the end of the avant-garde type of artist and work in art. It should be said that the definition 'avant-garde' works within the limits of a large historical period, overlaying all other definitions and closing off stylistic divisions, in accordance with a stable and dominant strategy of artistic behavior that is characteristic of all the actual tendencies of this time.

In fact, the basic drama of the avant-garde type of behavior in culture and the appearance of basic problems in culture was manifested in the constant resolution of the fundamental opposition between art and not-art, in the sense of a constant expansion of the zone of art until a condition was reached when no zone of art remained. That is, the zone of art became all possible spheres for the manifestation of the artist with a dominating, designatory gesture.

This process proceeded slowly but uninterruptedly and insistently throughout the whole twentieth century. Every time

an artist emerged into public sight, dragging something out
and declaring: This is art! No! No! they shouted to him, but
they got used to it and the next time, at the sight of something
else, they again shouted No! No! and Yes! Yes! said the artist.
And it really did turn out to be Yes! And again they got used
to it. And so on, until at any gesture, at a mere single assertive
attempt by a cunning artist to take something out from under
his shirt, everybody shouts in advance: Art! Art! – just hang
on, will you! – no, no. Art! Art! – just hang on, will you! the
disheartened artist shouts in reply (I mean the artist who has
thought and worked in the categories of a strategy, and not
simply the producer of its material byproducts, the tracks of
this dramaturgical activity.) And so, the problem is solved. In
exactly the same way, as it happens, as a different dramaturgy
was exhausted previously: the beautiful and the ugly.
Duchamp's urinal made its appearance in culture as the symbol
of its end and resolution.

So we now find ourselves in that congealed, suspended
time that is the only concentrated embodiment of what is
customarily called postmodernism. Usually this concept is
blurred to the extent of losing any specific features, by using
it to cover any and all tendencies that don't fall within the
classical definitions. But the present-day condition of culture
(by no means a tendency or a style), in which eclecticism,
intimacy and the absence of a preferential axiology, position,
or language are the consequence of a discarded dramaturgy,
of nondramaticality – precisely this could be preferentially
and specifically termed postmodernism (of course, these
are strictly my own preferences, not prompted by anyone
and not constraining anyone to anything). Existence in this
rather enervated culturo-dramatical condition, an excellent
understanding of it (a profoundly considered position, if not

personally, then by groups, communities or simply the large artistic process), a reluctance to overcome it, and even the fostering of such a situation, are typical for the majority of artists who determine the present-day artistic situation. This reflects not only or even so much the wager made by certain artists on a certain hedonism, as the general dead-end state of large sociocultural processes.

This dearth of strategy and inertness in artists' behavior is reminiscent of existence in a culture of traditional craftsmen, who lack any idea of the affirmation of any particular artistic or poetic stance, that is, the articulation in culture of some actual image of the artist (logically preceding the generation of texts or objects). The crisis is precisely of the immediate relevance of the strategy that is set and, through the inertia of direct inheritance, is continued in the reproduction of certain, almost ritual gestures of the supposed conquest of new territories against the background of an all-accepting culture, since the way it runs through all the paradigmatic possibilities of the given model of behavior creates the impression of a certain automatic, a certain robotlike deadness.

Obviously, when bounded by the horizon of the old dominant cultural mentality, it is extremely difficult to forecast the mentality of the future. As a rule, the overcoming of the present-day situation is habitually conceived as overcoming the canon of the dominant way of thinking through an intensification of the existing means. The ease and rapidity of a change in directions, styles, stances and artistic positions in recent decades, especially in the sphere of the visual arts, gives rise to the illusion of the ease of overcoming the crisis that has now emerged. But all previous innovations have proceeded within the limits of a full-blown, unified dramaturgy of avant-garde artistic practice, as distinct from the end and crisis of this self-same dramaturgy, in the history of the development, consolidation and consummation of which we can distinguish, as it were, its three 'ages.'

The first is the futuristic-constructivist age (of course, by this we do not intend a description of a period or movement in its completeness, but a certain ideologeme and extreme) the basic objective of which was separating out the ultimate ontological units of the text (geometrical figures, textures, and pure color in painting – Malevich, Tatlin, etc.) and using the genuine laws so distinguished to construct genuine things. Already manifested in this pure, abstract construction is the implicitly inherent idea of certain universal units, fragments or quarks of the world, and general, universal laws that can be extrapolated into any sphere of human activity. For this reason it was highly typical for artists to move into the sphere of practical and social activity and a huge number of utopian-projectural, philosophical, and esoteric texts were produced by the authors of this generation. Through the inertia of this intention to define the human being as a certain extremely simple, unequivocal, pure unit of the social text, in many ways, both ideologically and psychologically, they predetermined and facilitated the totalitarian mentality of the mid-twentieth century. The proponents of totalitarian culture, having taken this mechanistic utopianism, made an extremely interesting and fundamental addition to, or interpretation of, a linguistic strategy of such a kind: they discovered and promulgated 'large' ontological units of text, macromolecules as it were, that can be manipulated as an indestructible and genuine ultimate unity with the same ease: for instance, the classical tradition, humanist philosophy, magical practice. (This should be distinguished from the conceptual and postmodernist manipulation of others' practice and citation of their texts as nongenuine and not possessing any self-sufficient value, coherence or comprehensibility out of context.)

The second age of the avant-garde (we do not have in mind, of course, the tangled chronology of the multinational art of that time, with heterogeneous elements moving at discrepant speeds, but a certain logically discriminable, ideal progression) was, naturally, one of reactions against the mechanicity and projectural euphoria of the first. Proclaimed in opposition to it was the absurdity of all levels of language, which is not determined either by any general regularities or general memory or generally applicable operational laws with conventional optionality in the choice of units of a text. Being a romantic, more vitally oriented movement (as distinct from the first, constructivist-projectural stage) within the bounds of totalitarian cultures, absurdism was a negative reaction in the sphere of social awareness against the state's claims of being a simple mechanism embodying pure projectural ambitions. It should be noted that within the bounds of big culture, alongside the marked avant-gardist trends there were also found traditional, inertial tendencies that were not an articulation of a new type of artist or a new type of cultural dramaturgy. Essentially they were the direct outcome of an official, depersonalized culture (in this case I have in mind the specific features of Soviet culture) and as a result they were vague, unreflecting perpetuators of the ideology of the avant-garde's first age. It was precisely from them that the most recent Soviet avant-garde was able to read off and recode elements of linguistic tactics into strategies, coinciding in time as they did so with the new western avant-garde, a result of the direct inheritance of the tradition.

And finally, the third age (this is the most recent avant-garde mentioned several lines previously), the beginning of which

is identified with the appearance of the pop art/conceptual
movement (as the notorious and odious, classical, dialectical,
Hegelian-Marxian consummation of the dynamic triad within
our Soviet bounds) which attempted to resolve the contrarily-
mutually orientated linguistic positions of the first two ages. The
thrust of the third period was the affirmation of the genuineness
of every language within the bounds of its axiomatics (identified
with an adequate degree of probability and self-evidentiality)
and the declaration of its falseness and totalitarian ambitions
in its attempts to break through these bounds and cover the
entire world with itself. In this case there arises a huge, almost
incalculable cluster of possible variations that originates from
the center of the problem: the interrelations between object and
language and languages, the mutual ambitions of languages
behind the back of the world of objects, the substitution
of language, the contamination of languages, the hierarchy
of languages, the world of objects used as a language, the
objectification of language and so on, and so on, and so on. And
in this sense art and the artist in this kind of manipulative and
mediatory activity find themselves in the metalinguistic zone of
the operational level. This kind of metalinguistic position, having
invalidated the tactile and formal features of visual art, drew into
its sphere such types of artistic activity as the performance, the
happening, the action and also text, videos, and audio effects,
which in terms of their generic and specific features were in
former times qualified rather as types of theatrical, literary,
musical and cinematic activity. All these difference are canceled
out at the level of the artist's linguistic-behavioral model. In fact,
very often, only the authorial, volitional gesture of designation
can determine, even *post factum* (after the primary artistic act of
the material production of a text or an object) the role a work is
meant to play – designate it as literature or as an object of visual

 Dmitry Prigov **Two manifestos**

art. And incidentally, precisely this media-oriented, operational model of behavior has entirely prepared the ground for a possible move in the near future to working with technogenic, virtual, computer-based pseudospaces.

Correspondingly, even modern-day museums of contemporary art, in organizing their own space, image and model of museological behavior, have been converted into the temples of a kind of religion – their huge, beautiful buildings occupy the finest sites in cities. The prestige of visiting them coincides with the fundamental incomprehensibility, almost transcendentality, of both their exhibition of work and their policy agenda, their embeddedness in the specific problematics of contemporary art, their involvement in the immanent processes of intracultural self-awareness and profound, concealed, almost sacral dialogues between those who belong to the narrow circle of the initiated. For the outsider this process is sometimes revealed only in the form of some kind of kitschy, mass-media enticements (by no means providing access to the inner, immanent laws and motivating causes of the emergence of things of this kind).

In addition, with the proliferation in the practice of modern art of the intensity of the installation, the performance, the image, and media process in general and the activity of artists, the museums accumulate a huge number of certain objects produced by this activity (or even the life) of the artists, as the material bearers of their phantasmal activity, which are impossible to understand without a knowledge of the work of the specific artist as a context, as well as of the broad context of art as a whole. In other words, the items presented are, as it were, sacred objects or, figuratively speaking, the relics of the 'saints' of modern art, which demand worship, but not understanding and empathy.

This overview of the completed and exhausted state of both the immanent-dramaturgical, sociocultural level and the strategy of cultural behavior prompts the suspicion that the specific cultural type and mentality are exhausted, which, after a certain period of inertial reproduction of the basic, habitual features of this manner of thinking and existing, creates the impression of an end and a crisis, if it proves impossible to discern the clear, visible features of a breakthrough and the appearance of something new.

Actually, this is the point in the text at which there could appear once again the beginning that was promised as the end and was conceived as the end, but showed up at the beginning simply as an explanation of a certain confusion with the title as declared and as unveiled, remember: The second sacro-cularization.

Actually, there is not even any need to reproduce it, it is quite enough to refer the reader to it.

And having lost the space required to reproduce it, I can conclude all this only with the assumption that the sacro-cularization is already in operation, i.e. that its features are sufficiently visible. However, it is, after all, proceeding within the bounding horizon of an avant-garde art that is exhausting itself, while something new that is already complete (although it will be to some extent subject to our present abilities to identify and evaluate it) could be described as either one thing or another: accomplished secularization or simply secularization.

1990

10

Maria Chehonadskih

THE FORM OF ART AS MEDIATION: A HISTORY AND STORYTELLING BEFORE AND AFTER MOSCOW CONCEPTUALISM

In place of an introduction: A ≠ A, or dialectical doubt

The basic problem of art today is the search for a form that is capable of mediating the historical and political events of our time. In a wider sense the question of a new form abuts on classic discussions about how art can present the totality of an event in its relationship to lived human experience. By the mediation of historical and political events we do not mean the goal of a simple representation of an event; the modern mass media cope successfully with that goal. In presenting an event, a journalist first of all gives it a name. In a certain sense the profession of journalist is actually based on the successful search for a name that can serve as a ubiquitous explanatory mechanism for a historical reality. Thus, the protests and demonstrations in the Arab world were quickly labeled the 'Arab Spring,' and this brandmark became a symbol of the struggle against dictatorship. The events in East Ukraine are called the Russian intervention or the American intervention

– the interpretation depends on the geopolitical stance of the
interpreter. In other words, the interpretation of contemporary
events is correlated with the global political situation, and at the
basis of this interpretation lies the positivistic language of naked
facts and their skillful manipulation: empirical accounts from
the scenes of events are supposedly an expression of objectivity,
they are a certain given, behind which the deft manipulation
of the name is concealed. In the last three years, names like
this have taken over the ambient living space, so that we think
and reason about what is happening on the basis of a formal
logic of names. However, thoughtful observers, and especially
participants in events, remain silent, flabbergasted by the
incoherence of the geopolitical linguistic operators who take
the fortress of an event by storm. These false names bury the
meaning of history beneath themselves and paralyze the faculty
of critical judgement. The substitution of signifier-names for
events turns us into consumers of ready-made interpretations.

The mediation that we have in mind is the inherent
materiality of art, which lays bare the complexity of an event
in a critical and dialectical manner. In other words, art should
begin with doubt and negation, it should undermine the
absolute identity of any given X and Z, whether they are the
'fascism' and 'antifascism' of the Maidan/Antimaidan or even
the binary ideology of *pro and contra* itself. Unlike journalism,
art is not obliged to provide ready-made names and clichés, its
fundamental task is to establish a special position at the center
of an event, from where it can reveal the event's dialectical
logic: 'A' is simultaneously 'not-A,' night is not night, because
night presupposes day, and day alternates with night. As a rule,
art takes its beginning from such doubts concerning the sense
certainty of our experience and it abjures the mimetic function
of simply denoting its subject.[1] 'This is not a pipe' in Magritte's

work, this is not a bed in Rauschenberg's, and this is not a urinal, as a urinal, in Duchamp's. In Kosuth's work a chair is not simply a piece of furniture on which we sit, while the works of Yuri Albert are radically 'not' those of all the other artists in whose manner he paints.[2] In order to say that a thing is always something else, which repudiates its mute givenness, one must be able to tell the story of this thing, and this requires a special scrutiny of the object from all sides. Unlike journalism, art is able to speak from the viewpoint of the specific thing, taken in the totality of its relationships. However, telling the story of this thing also requires a storyteller, i.e. someone who can articulate this story in some given form.

For Peter Osborne the storyteller presents the articulation of absent otherness – in our terminology, he is the 'not' that was mentioned above. A storyteller is a narrator of the past, which is in itself the absent other in the present, the story of the otherness of other people's lives. That is to say, art can present history through storytelling when the object of art becomes the speech of people. Osborne emphasizes that telling the story cannot be reduced to the perfunctory narration of a case study or the implementation of a research project. To tell the story means to find communicative forms for presenting historical time in a fragment of that time (or of the present, of an event).[3] Here Osborne is revisiting Walter Benjamin's essay "The Storyteller." And indeed, according to this text, the storyteller is a figure who sees a fragment (a story) as the totality of history.[4]

However, Benjamin also cast doubt on this ability of art to tell the history of a thing. In "The Storyteller" he remarks that after the First World War men came back from the front struck dumb, they couldn't tell the history of that war. A war, like any other forms of capitalist shock – economic or social – leads to the erosion of speech, a kind of aphasia that is expressed in a deprivation of experience and inability to speak.[5] Benjamin, however, has something else in mind. In his opinion the appearance of cultural information – newsreels, newspapers and radio – removes the very need to tell the story of history, since henceforth all explanations are delegated to the mass media. Information, not storytelling, becomes their prerogative.[6] Even experience is privatized by the media machines and subordinated to the logic of empirical life: to the statistics of dead and wounded, of ruined and restored cities. What story can anyone really tell about modern-day wars? Isn't any authentic story today a ready-made spoken or scripted godsend for the television propagandists? Hence the mistrust of any forms of discourse and criticism, definitions and concepts. This kind of reaction is generated by postshock aphasia: the right words to explain things simply don't come to mind.

In an age of information and media, in what way can the form of art mediate historical and political events? We think that the experience of Moscow conceptualism is crucial here. However, in order to understand this role more clearly, it is essential to take a retrospective glance at its practices, i.e. from the position of the past in its relationship to the present. The present text is rather preliminary and only sketches out possible lines of analysis, symptomatically and genealogically rereading the storylines of Soviet conceptual art.

Benjamin's "Storyteller" and the Land of Soviets

For Benjamin, telling a story is related above all to the function of exchanging experience. A reminder is required that by experience, he means something like an existentialist narrative of life, its *formatting*, the imparting of *form* to it. Experience is the biography of a life, its molding. Experience as an empirical category – a record of sense certainty – has nothing in common with this. However, empiricism of this kind meets with an uncritical reception in certain practices of contemporary art, which can be reminiscent of the above-mentioned journalism or positivism of the pure givenness of sensations and emotions.[7]

In order to clarify this idea further, we need to turn to the writings of György Lukács, who distinguishes between empirical experience as the flow of lived impressions and the experience of life as form. In his early work *Soul and Form*, Lukács separates *life as such* from *essential life*. Life is a negative category as long as we mean *life as such*, because *life as such* is the current of the formless, negative movement of empirical life, full of nondifferentiation: the indifference of sensory data and their perception. Life becomes *essential* only when it is singular, separated out and opposed to empirical experience – to the biology of pure survival and politically unaware social life.[8] "There is no system," writes Lukács. *Life as such* is accidental and it can only acquire its essence in the concrete and singular: "In life there is only the separate and individual, the concrete. To exist is to be different. And only the concrete, the individual phenomenon is the unambiguous, the absolute which is without nu-ance … [The] individual thing is the only thing that is; the individual is the real man."[9] The young Lukács links this romantic idea of life as *essential life* with the goals of art and philosophy. The artist's job, as he sees it, is to purge life of its indifference, while at the same time not transforming life itself into a pure aesthetic form. To put this differently, the goal of art does not lie in the aestheticization of life, but in molding it dialectically: in life's becoming form, subject to the proviso that it does not ultimately presuppose any ideal form.[10]

For Benjamin, storytelling is the practical molding of life into a narrative of life. Storytelling articulates and molds life when people pass on information by word of mouth, giving each other advice. According to Benjamin, modern capitalist society is characterized precisely by the absence of the institution of 'advice,' which is replaced by a technology of informing.[11] The gradual disappearance of storytelling begins in the age of the novel, when the very experience of the written word becomes individual and isolated from people's lives, whereas the phenomenon of the storyteller is always linked with the exchange of experience and the act of living speech. The novelist "himself lacks counsel and can give none."[12] Storytelling molds a narrative of life in the experience of life, while information and the novel, as its harbinger, construct the plan of life artificially – its invented biography, creating something like ready-made variations of life, its absolute patterns.[13]

However, as we know, at the time when Benjamin's "Storyteller" was being written, there existed an entire Land of Soviets – the literal meaning of the Russian word "soviet" is precisely an advice – where the exchange of information was anchored, in formal terms at least, at the level of the state and politics. Notwithstanding this, the Soviets lent meaning to the phenomenon of the storyteller at a level very far from that of the state. In 1919 the literary theoretician Boris Eichenbaum turns his attention for the first time to the phenomenon of "skaz," demonstrating the importance of the 'audial' and oral principle in classical Russian literature.[14] Skaz signifies a special genre of the oral form of narration in which the plot is less important than the stylistic devices used to convey the living speech of the storyteller. Here the authorial voice and intonation become an integral part of the storyline, and this creates the illusion of live storytelling. In skaz the reader's attention is focused on the expressions, gestures and sounds or physiognomy of the language, and the storyteller and his own story are at the center of events. In Eichenbaum's opinion, in modern prose – the works of Andrei Bely and Boris Pilnyak – the reader is not dealing with oral narrative as such, but with an imitation or stylization of skaz: instead of the storyteller, the focus is shifted to the word itself, its sound, smell or even taste.[15] As we can note, the skaz of Eichenbaum's time corresponds to what replaced Benjamin's authentic storyteller, who was an individual of an epic, oral culture.

We should also note what Eichenbaum failed to notice. In postrevolutionary Russia, skaz in general becomes the basic form of the chronicling of the revolution, and the Soviet avant-garde constantly has recourse to the forms of skaz, the fragment, the Russian folk epic, and the fable in order to convey the experience of the participation of the masses of peasants and workers in the revolution through the figure of a storyteller from among the people. Such are the prose of Andrey Platonov, the verse of Velimir Khlebnikov, the painting of Pavel Filonov, and the cinematic experiments of Alexander Medvedkin; even the satirical opuses of the 'ROSTA Windows' propaganda posters can be regarded as an appropriation of the form of skaz. Svetlana Krasovskaya notes that skaz acquired immense significance for the artistic culture of the 1920s because the experience of the revolution needed a new historical narrative. No genre could describe the battle of the proletariat and the transformation of the world better than skaz, based on legends, folklore, the living speech of the streets and dialects.[16]

It might seem that the fragmentary character of works from the 1920s, with their leaning towards the forms of essay, reportage, documentation, chronicle and memoir, is entirely inappropriate for the task of describing the sheer scale of revolutionary events, but according to Benjamin, it is precisely the fragment that can express the totality of history. Dziga Vertov's 'Kino-Eye' works on precisely this principle: it glides

over reality, capturing, observing and seizing fragments of
it from a viewpoint of socialism and a totality of new social
relationships. Platonov's prose is also structured in a similar
way.[17] And all because the artists assemble their works like
a mosaic: situated in the thick of events, they convey the
experience of participating in a revolution of the masses by
grabbing fragments of the sweeping social landscape. Precisely
in this way, by the artist deliberating on what he sees around
him, an event does not become objectified and freeze in a naked
abstraction of fact, but is conveyed as the lived experience of
people. In point of fact, Platonov's works and Vertov's films
recount the story of revolutionary events in a way that no
documentary film or history textbook can do. And all because
we can share the experience of the revolution with them, while
the dry logic of facts leaves to us only their interpretation.

The storyteller after the storyteller: the experience of Soviet conceptualism

The tradition of skaz outlived the revolution and Stalinism,
to be revived in the new narrative strategies of the Moscow
conceptualism of the 1970s. However, the artists of this circle
were not engaged in creating an epic saga of the proletarians'
struggle in an age of great revolutionary events, but in
chronicling the experience of the anonymous Soviet man.
This chronicling was narrated by the artist-storyteller, who
was himself a fictional, nonexistent figure of 'western art' in
a Soviet context that was hostile to him. In his article "Ilya
Kabakov. The artist as storyteller," Boris Groys notes that the
very genre of Kabakov's albums "presupposes that the viewer
is dealing with a story" and the subject of this story is "the
evolution of certain artistic systems" of western art, represented
however, in the spirit of an allegorical epic of the life and death

of invented characters who are not living on the scale of the historical time of realism and surrealism, but of the cycle of the human journey of life (the album "Ten Characters," 1972–5).[18] As in a novel, the meaning of a character's journey, which is a metonymy for art in general and for a specific form of life in art in particular, is only revealed after his death – at the end of the narrative of the entire album.[19] However, the album does not specify a 'model of life' in the same way as, according to Benjamin, a novel produces one. Instead of this, Kabakov creates a kind of double fiction: an imaginary model of western art and the historical living-through of this model in a singular manner, like a 'character,' as if Kabakov himself is nothing other than a Soviet modification of this western history of art. In his characters, art always develops within the limits of the subjective time of one life, and this life is the life of a solitary Soviet artist. The albums pit the typical little man of classic Russian literature against big history. The dialectic of these two entities is mediated by textual commentaries that express the banality of everyday routine.

Victor Pivovarov's album series and cycles lay bare this conflict between big history and an unattractive little Soviet life even more powerfully, accentuating to the limit the existential ennui of the anonymous biography of the statistically average individual. Such is his cycle "Projects for a Lonely Man" (1975), which frugally spells out the bio-political regimen of the life of a typical member of the intelligentsia in the typical circumstances of the time: a nondescript view from the window, ascetic furniture in a Khrushchev-era, five-storey, panel-built apartment block, work until six in the evening, lots of free time and a daily routine that doesn't change for years. Pivovarov's project of a life can be understood as the romantic ideal of an artist's life in the conditions of the Soviet period, but the paradox is that the banality of this life is typical, that it actually expresses the materiality of late-Soviet life in general. The dry, perfunctory language seems to be a comment on the impervious ennui of social stagnation, frozen in the subjects, objects and urban landscapes. In the Soviet conceptual art the anonymous language of everyday speech is a narrative of the banality of existence in general. The prose of this language permeates every corner of life, and an artist's life is no exception here, because this life in no way differs from a million other Soviet lives. The artist is just as banal as the municipal housing maintenance office, with all its dramas. This is an expression of the Soviet, classless principle of life, as declared by the October Revolution and mangled somewhat by Stalinism. The tacky anonymity of 'Anna Petrovna,' trying to identify the owner of a grater that has gone missing (Ilya Kabakov, "Olga Ilichnina Zuiko: Whose grater is this?" 1982) is an integral image of the entire late-Soviet experience, concisely expressed in one single phrase, written in neat handwriting on a board that is painted the green color of a Soviet entrance hall. 'Anna Petrovna' is not merely communal speech and discourse (in the poststructuralist sense),[20] she is facticity, grasped in language, but possessing an extralinguistic, material substantiality. Her image, impossible to grasp entirely, was nonetheless probably best grasped by the 1920s writer Leonid Dobychin in another, similarly brief phrase, mentioned in passing, in the way that he does, in the story "Konopatchikova": "Polushalchikha came in from the kitchen and stood there, priding herself."[21] 'Anna Petrovna' is not simply a phrase, she's not even a woman, she's an entire story, perhaps even an entire world, which prides itself as it displays its monolithic solidity to the view of everyone who has arrived too late to see more than its ruins. What is she? She is the

Soviet form of life, with its patriarchal order and authoritarian husbands, festive tables at New Year in kitchens crammed to bursting point, apartment building lobbies and squeaking swings in children's play areas. She is a kind of fragment of the Soviet world, through which its totality is grasped. The same function is performed by Mikhail Roginsky's unexpressive objects – a stove, an iron, a door, matches. This is the reincarnation of the "comrade-thing,'"[22] which has ended up in an adventure epic of the Brezhnev period. Behind it, too, stands the bewildered 'Anna Petrovna'.

In the age of the internet, it is hard for us to imagine the live, oral, transmission of experience, but we can recall those not-too-distant times when a provincial would make his or her way up to Moscow and then, when he or she came back, gather a circle of friends to tell them stories from the life of the capital. In late Soviet times, this was the exact way in which information was passed on about forbidden exhibitions, books, film screenings and other events, because the 'grapevine' merges to some extent into the epic genre: any inaccessible information becomes a storytelling, since the object of desire is imagined more than presented as something real. As a result, the information itself is transformed into a mythological narrative. This is why Kabakov accompanies a showing of his albums with a kind of poetic performance: he reads the textual commentaries of the albums in a monotonous and methodical voice, transforming the work itself into a genre of oral history, and himself into a storyteller rendered wise by experience, inviting only a circle of the chosen to listen to his story. To some extent the same thing occurs in the actions of the Collective Actions group, which are essentially an exchange of experience. As we know, the actual activity of the group's actions is often accompanied by the wearisome anticipation of a certain event,

   Maria Chehonadskih   The form of art as mediation

and this event becomes the subject of the commentaries to "Trips to the Countryside" – the collections of documentation on the actions. The exchange of impressions between the participants lends meaning and form to the action itself. The self-mythologization of the milieu of Moscow conceptualism is similar in nature, with its special esoteric language, dictionary of terms, hierarchies and various ritual objects such as, for instance, the famous cigarette holder of Andrey Monastyrsky, the leader of the group. The artists of this circle created not only imaginary characters, but also their own imaginary group identity. By an irony of history, this storytelling eventually led to the journalistic mythologization of their own name and the appearance of the "false name" of "Moscow conceptualism,"[23] which in its time startled the western public and perplexed the conceptualists themselves.

As we can see, Moscow conceptualism's turn to the figure of the storyteller is the result of a deficit of public artistic life, as well as a deficit of information, which is replaced here by narrative strategies of various kinds (within the limits of this essay we have limited ourselves to only the most obvious examples). But have not information and technology, and the activities of analysts and journalists become the dominant forms of culture and art today, just as Benjamin anticipated?

This is precisely why, in Russian art of the 1990s, and then of the 2000s, discursive conceptual art was displaced by actionism – the art of pure action. If we analyze the key actions of Alexander Brener or Oleg Kulik, we can come to a curious conclusion, in the given context, 'action' should be understood as a nondiscursive act, such as throwing a boxing glove at Yeltsin on the platform of the *Lobnoye mesto* in Red Square (Alexander Brener, "The First Glove," 1995), or turning into a dog (a series of performances by Oleg Kulik, given in

1994–8). We can regard as an intermediate link between Soviet discursiveness and post-Soviet aphasia an action by the ETI (Expropriation of the Territory of Art) movement, who depicted an obscene word with their own bodies on Red Square several months before the collapse of the USSR (ETI, "KhUI," 1991). Having begun with poetry readings, ETI ended the Soviet era of their activity with a gesture that transformed the 'Soviet logos' (of poetry and literature) into the abusive invective of the streets, while Brener and Kulik pushed the 'muteness' of post-Soviet actionism to the limit. According to Lev Vygotsky, in an individual's development, action always precedes speech, and even when speech arises, for instance, at the age of three, action and thinking are logically at variance rather than in agreement, or they run parallel to each other. The same situation is characteristic of several aspects of adult human life, in which an image of an action does not necessarily precede the action itself. The nonalignment of act and speech is specifically characteristic of actionism, which expresses the impossibility of saying anything, since the reality of original accumulation outstrips any speech, for after all, an utterance that has not yet arisen already no longer corresponds to the logic of events of the historical moment. In our opinion the dialectical struggle between act and speech is expressed literally here.[24] And this is precisely why the mass media occupy a key role in action art – they mediate naked acts and impart form to the action, illuminating and disseminating the scandalous image of the dog-man or the boxer-man in their various outlets. While storytelling itself actually *mediates* lived experience and history, information is all about the direct mimetic reflection of the veracity of the fact and the empiricism of the case study. Action art is anti-storytelling.

Does this mean that the figure of the storyteller finally disappears, together with the Soviet Union? In point of fact, the album arises as a specifically Soviet form of art, which is impossible to reproduce in an institutional context, even if Kabakov were to agree to repeat the performance of his page-turning in front of a group of outsiders, although this is to some extent what is done today by artists like Walid Raad and Hito Steyerl: they often accompany a showing of their works with a performative action, cladding political commentaries on one or another set of political events in the genre of oral history.[25] In this sense the narrative methods of these artists come close to the figure and function of the storyteller in Moscow conceptualism. Of course, in the practices of Raad and Steyerl the storyteller often acts as a mediator between the form of a work and its political context. Consequently, storytelling in the age of information is the reworking of information as such through the means of storytelling. Arseny Zhilyaev develops the traditions of total installation and literary narration in his works. The form of total installation, which emerged during the international period of Kabakov's work, can also be understood as a narrational technology. It replaces the intimacy of the albums and the friendly exchange of experience with a subjectless narrative about the past from the position of the present (of an internationally recognized Soviet artist). It is a story that objectifies Soviet and Kabakov's experience, or an *informational story*. It informs the western public about the recent and exotic Soviet past. Zhilyaev complicates this gesture. His imaginary characters become epistemes of Soviet artistic culture and history as such: he goes back to an interpretation of museology, the practices of the Proletkult and the avant-garde, using the actual medium of the museum for narrativizing ideas of the Soviet past, so that these ideas are personified and transformed into the storyline of a tangled story, expressed in dry, expository language. His anthology of the museum avant-garde – a collection of texts by prerevolutionary and Soviet philosophers, artists, art historians and writers – can be regarded as a kind of conceptual object that blurs the boundaries between a real historical document and the invented narrative fervour of his 'museological' utopianism.[26] In this sense Zhilyaev's projects are a critical development of the *informational story*, located conceptually and aesthetically between the projects of Raad and Steyerl and those of Kabakov himself.

In the 1990s, Moscow conceptualism was criticized as asocial and autistic, and for its dependence on its own subculture and ethic of escapism. For this reason the attitudes of contemporary post-Soviet artists have been based on the rejection or transcendence of conceptualism. However, invented characters, along with invented collectives, activities or even historical events and the ability to tell a story – in other words, the notorious literocentricity – are exactly what was lacking in mute actionism, which could not find the words to express what was happening and preferred to act. Words, discourses and stories lost all their authority and meaning in a situation of shock therapy and the original accumulation of capital. However, the time arrives when the ability to speak returns, and consequently the individual who wants to and has to tell his story appears. And this story must be, among other things, the story of the reinterpretation of conceptual art in its actual interaction with the context of art today

Notes

The author thanks Arseny Zhilyaev for his valuable remarks and commentaries on the text.

1   Here we paraphrase the critique of the immediacy and the given experience in Hegel's *Phenomenology of Spirit*. See: Georg Wilhelm Friedrich Hegel *The Phenomenology of Spiri*, translated by A. V. Miller, with a foreword by J. N. Findlay, Oxford University Press, 1977, pp. 58–66.

2   Here we refer to the following works: Rene Magritte, "The Treachery of
     Images" ("La Trahison des images"), 1929; Marcel Duchamp, "Fountain"
     ("Fontaine"), 1917; Robert Rauschenberg, "Bed," 1955; Joseph Kosuth,
     "One and Three Chairs," 1965; and a series of works by Yuri Albert "I am
     not ..." (1980-2006). Robert Rauschenberg's "Bed" consists of a pillow
     and a padded quilt, attached to a wooden frame and hung on the wall,
     so that the bed is transformed into a painterly object. In the context of a
     consideration of dialectics and mimesis, it is appropriate here to adduce
     Arthur Danto's comment on this work. He writes that we can easily
     imagine a situation in which a layman, examining Rauschenberg's "Bed,"
     imagines that it is an object for sleeping on. And all because the layman
     imagines that art is a copy of reality, so all the artist is doing is trying to
     get us to buy this futuristic bed. However, the world of mimesis is a thing
     of the past, a bed is no longer a bed, as a real object it becomes a piece of
     art. See: A. Danto, "The Artworld" in *Journal of Philosophy*, 1964, vol. 16,
     no. 19, pp. 575–80. It should be added that art has always been a luxury
     item and, as we can see from the example of "Bed," the theory of mimesis
     can only support commodity fetishism and empower the consumerist
     imagination with regard to art.

3   Peter Osborne, *What Makes Contemporary Art contemporary? Or, Other
     Peoples' Lives* (an electronic resource) in *Art & Education*. Available
     at www.artandeducation.net/videos/peter-osborne-what-makes-
     contemporary-art-contemporary-or-other-peoples-lives (accessed on:
     05.05.2016). This is a lecture, given in 2014 at the Centre for Critical
     Theory of the University of Nottingham in Great Britain.

4   Walter Benjamin, "The Storyteller" in *Selected Writings*, ed. Howard
     Eiland and Michael W. Jennings, translated by Harry Zohn, Cambridge:
     Massachusetts, London: The Belknap Press, 2002, pp. 143-166.

5   Ibid., pp. 143–4.

6   Ibid., pp. 147–8.

7   Just as Hollywood orchestrates the physiological economy of soap operas,
     provoking the viewer into hysterical tears or laughter, the performance
     artist Tino Segal believes that a collective emotional experience can
     be encoded in exactly the same way by means of recurring rhythmical
     patterns and specially organized aesthetic space – darkness, strident,
     rhythmically recurring sounds and choreographed movement (in this
     respect his performance "This Variation" is indicative. It was given
     at the exhibition "dOCUMENTA (13)" in Kassel in 2014.) The
     positivist reliance on the authenticity of experience reduces affective
     states, emotions and other manifestations of feelings to physiological
     reactions of the organism. Belief in the sensory veracity of experience

and the possibility of undergoing it collectively and directly and the economy of affective states that accompany this given logic are a big aesthetic problem. See my analysis of a performance by Tino Segal: Maria Chehonadskih, "'dOCUMENTA (13)' and the Blind Horror of the Meteorite's Point of View," *Moscow Art Magazine (Khudozhestvenny zhurnal)*, 2014, Digest 2007–2014, pp. 198–208.

8 György Lukács, *Soul and Form*, trans. by Anna Bostock, Cambridge, Massachusetts: The MIT Press, 1974.

9 Ibid., p.32.

10 On essential life and form in this sense, see ibid., pp. 28–41.

11 Benjamin, "The Storyteller," p. 149.

12 Ibid., p. 146.

13 Ibid., p. 156.

14 Boris Mikhailovich Eichenbaum, "How Gogol's 'Overcoat' Is Made," in *On Prose: Collected Articles*. Leningrad: Khudozhestvennaya Literatura, 1969, pp. 306–26 (in Russian). See English translation in: Boris Mikhailovich Eikhenbaum, *Russian Prose*, Ardis, August 28, 1985. Translated by Ray Parrott.

15 Boris Mikhailovich Eichenbaum, "Leskov and Contemporary Prose," in *On Literature. Works from Various Years.* Moscow: Sovietsky Pisatel, 1987, pp. 409–24 (in Russian). See English translation in: Boris Mikhailovich Eikhenbaum, *Russian Prose*, Ardis, August 28, 1985. Translated by Ray Parrott.

16 Svetlana Krasovskaya, *The Prose of A. P. Platonov: Genres and Genre Processes*. Blagoveshchensk: VGPU Press, 2005, pp. 67–70 (in Russian).

17 See Valery Podoroga's comparison of Vertov's cine-eye and the "eunuch of the soul" in Valery Podoroga, "The Eunuch of the Soul: Positions of Reading and the World of Platonov," *The South Atlantic Quarterly*, vol. 90, no. 2 (1991), pp. 357–408 (pp. 379-380).

18 Boris Groys, "Ilya Kabakov: the Artist as Storyteller," in: *History Becomes Form: Moscow conceptualism*. Cambridge, MA: MIT Press, 2010, pp. 88–9.

19 Ibid., p. 89.

20 Here we have in mind the poststructuralist interpretations of conceptual art that were popular in the 1980s and 1990s, the most well-known of which was written by Victor Tupitsyn. See a recent English version of his work in: Victor Tupitsyn, *The Museological Unconscious. Communal (Post) Modernism in Russia*, Cambridge, London: The MIT Press, 2009.

21 Leonid Dobychin, "Konopatchikova," in: *The Town of N. Stories*. Moscow, Khudozhestvennaya Literatura, 1989, p. 176 (in Russian). See English edition: *Leonid Dobychin, The Town of N*, Northwestern University Press' July 22, 1998. Translated by Richard C. Borden.

22 On the concept of 'comrade-thing' see: Ekaterina Degot, "Performing Objects, Narrating Installations: Moscow Conceptualism and the Rediscovery of the Art Object," in *e-flux journal*, #29, November 2011 (a digital resource). Available at www.e-flux.com/journal/29/68067/performing-objects-narrating-installations-moscow-conceptualism-and-the-rediscovery-of-the-art-object (accessed on 05.05.2016).

23 For criticism of the term 'Moscow conceptualism' see Peter Osborne, "The Kabakov Effect: 'Moscow Conceptualism' in the History of Contemporary Art," in *Afterall*, 42 (Autumn/Winter 2016), pp. 108–15.

24 See: Lev Vygotsky, "Thinking and Speech" in *The Collected Works of L. S. Vygotsky*, trans. by N. Minick, R. W. Rieber and A. S. Carton, vol. 1, New York, London: Plenum Press, 1987, pp. 39–285; see also my article with a critique of Russian action art of the 2000s: M. Chekhonadskikh, "What is Pussy Riot's 'Idea'?" in *Radical Philosophy*, 2012, no. 176, pp. 2–7.

25 This is precisely why Raad's performances, which often include objects and installations, are nonetheless easily translated into the form of a written narrative. See: Walid Raad, "Walkthrough, Part 1" (a digital resource) in *e-flux journal*. Available at www.e-flux.com/journal/walkthrough-part-i (accessed on 05.05.2016)

26 See Arseny Zhilyaev, ed., *Avant-Garde Museology*, Minneapolis: University of Minnesota Press, 2015; see his text: Arseny Zhilyaev, *Conceptual Realism: The Vulgar Freedom of Avant-Garde Museum Work* (a digital resource) in *e-flux journal*. Available at www.e-flux.com/journal/conceptual-realism-the-vulgar-freedom-of-avant-garde-museology (accessed on 05.05.2016).

11

Artemy Magun

SOVIET COMMUNISM AND THE PARADOX OF ALIENATION

In departing from its initial revolutionary impulses, Soviet "communism" made its state and economy ultra-alienated. By the 1970s, its system brought on the atomization of society and the victory of an ideology of individualism and consumerism, comparable to the situation in bourgeois societies. But the Soviet experience also had another side: the "common" or the "collective" was really not appropriated; in the bureaucratic system of collective irresponsibility, it turned out to be unneeded, belonging to no-one.

The Soviet landscape, a landscape that is only slowly disappearing and still very much surviving in provincial Russia, is a landscape of abandoned construction sites, empty lots, or the open street-doors, where one could easily urinate or drink a little bottle of vodka … In many senses, the common remained vacant and free. In spite of itself, through a "trick of history", the Soviet regime achieved a free common where it was not looking for it … Of course, all of this was

uncomfortable and ineffective, and the new bourgeois prophets
of the Perestroika began by pointing at this scandalous trait
of Soviet "communism", suggesting to privatize it in order
to tie humanity more closely to the material "base" of its
surroundings. But for now, none of this has worked: the new
private owners have little respect for the world of things, which
is why they have subjected this world to predatory exploitation
(based on the same disrespect), while disrespect for the public
sphere is so much of a part of our very existences that we still
hardly worry about the environment in our everyday lives; we
never fix up our hallways and are rarely capable of uniting for
any action in protest.

The common, however, belongs to no one. In their total
worldliness, empty lots play the role of sacral spaces, segregated
"zones." The sacrality of the profane is perhaps an alternative
formula of democracy or, more precisely, *communism* in its true
unrevealed meaning. The real common, the common aside
from exchange, the common without the universal, lies beneath
our feet at the exact place where it is nobody's. The question
is actually, on the one hand, how to preclude the usurping of
this common (through bureaucracy or capitalism), and on the
other hand, how to preserve a relationship to it: once one is
deeply involved in their private lives, s/he hardly notices the
common void that chases their particular little worlds. And the
unconscious communism turns into its opposite, the realm of
universal privateness/deprivation.

Therefore today: does this mean a regime of the grand
collective appropriation of everything by humanity, or on the
contrary a project of a sacral denial of property (compare the
same dilemma in the definition of democracy: a representation
of people by government, or, as in Claude Lefort, a taboo on the
embodiment of people). To achieve in alienation, this prevented

them from exploring the concrete content of communism
at all. Today, to reconsider this, we may need to get back to
Marx' definition of alienation and recall that the early Soviet
aestheticians, and later Brecht, used a synonym of alienation as a
positive category describing new revolutionary art. If alienation
looked suspect to Marx from the economical point of view, it
turned to be essential for new communist state in the aesthetic
sphere. If, following Schiller, we perceive "an aesthetic state" in
the no man's land between the public and the private, we may
say that the Soviet communism built such an aesthetic state of
alienation in the midst of its repressive ideological state.

Communism as idea

"Communism" is a concept that, from the very emergence of
its present meaning during the period of the French revolution
was meant to be a radical and down-to-earth alternative to the
idealistic slogans of the Jacobins (liberty, equality, fraternity,
etc.).[1] Unlike the former, "communism" includes a reference
to economy and, more precisely, to a society without private
property. This materialist content was later reaffirmed by
Marx who, after first having rejected the concept altogether,[2]
expressed allegiance to a "communism" that is for him and
Engels "not a *state of affairs* which is to be established, an
ideal to which reality [will] have to adjust itself" but "the
real movement which abolished the present state of things."[3]
Communists, with their "criticism of the Earth,"[4] belong to the
revolutionary branch of the Romantic movement that aspired to
reverse the usual spiritualist orientation of humanity away from
the Earth to Heaven, to redirect it into the depths of Earth, and
towards the depth of matter and the prose of life.

In France, this tradition was followed for example by Jules
Michelet, the romantic left-wing historian. He writes in his

The same tendency was continued a hundred years later during the Bolshevik revolution in Russia. One of its early supporters, the poet Alexey Gastev, wrote: "We will not aspire to these heights that are called 'heaven.' Heaven is a creation of the idle, lazy, and timid people. Let us rush down! Together with fire, metal, and gas, and steam, let us dig mines, let us drill the largest tunnels in the world, let us empty in the bowels of the earth the untouched old layers."[6]

All of this is important to argue against the dominant liberal-conservative perception of Soviet communism as yet another ideocratic dictatorship.[7] If it was an Enlightenment educational regime, it was such only for the reason that it emerged out of a materialist struggle against idealism – the only properly idealistic philosophical state is, of course, a liberal state.

Nevertheless, the ambiguity of the concept of communism, the one between a vision and an ontological statement, remained even for Marx himself who certainly had a vision, although vague, of a future communist society, "where nobody has one exclusive sphere of activity but each can become accomplished in any branch he wishes, society regulates the general production and thus makes it possible for me … to hunt in the morning, fish in the afternoon, rear cattle in the evening, criticize after dinner,"[8] and where "the free development of each" would be "the condition for the free development of all."[9] Communism would be a society of abundant free ("available") time used by the subjects for self-education. From here we may see that in his positive program of communism, Marx remains an aesthetic Romantic thinker. And this suggests that communism is somehow possible as a way of life *beyond labor* or remaining in its shadow.

Therefore, by the time that the Soviet and pro-Soviet Marxism died "in itself", serious attempts have emerged to conceive "communism" at the level of contemporary philosophy and of the existing political–economic condition. Indeed, after the victory of the liberal vision of society, communism sounded once again as the only viable alternative to the idealistic models of human togetherness, whether understood as the representative state, the rule of law, or a social contract combining individuals into a whole. This idealistic liberal unity remains relative; it hypostasizes an individual who originally exists by itself and only then enters a society. Excesses of this model are the melancholic and moralistic individualism of the bourgeois subject, the crushing of the "general will" in the Rousseauist republic, and especially *nationalism* as a collective egoism which unites individualism and collectivism.

There should be a way to conceive a stronger totality, which would not involve a transcendent principle of unity (like God), but would nevertheless allow for an infinite relationship of a member to the whole, which it would "run through." When Marx described the effects of the bourgeois revolution, he noted that this "political revolution dissolves civil society into its elements without revolutionizing these elements themselves."[10] The goal of a new revolution would thus be a chemical or even nuclear *dissolution* of the social fabric which would allow it setting off from the fixed opposition of egoism and idealism, and which would strive for a new kind of unity.

In such a totality, elements would interweave and interpenetrate, and would be free in the aesthetic sense of a "virtuosity" (Virno),[11] and free play, instead of the liberal freedom within pre-set boundaries. Hegel had already expressed something like this with his concept of "absolute" (i.e., "the bacchanalian revel, where not a member is sober; and … [at the same time] the revel is just as much a state of transparent unbroken calm"). However, Hegel thought that the revolution had been superseded by the organic state and was rightly accused of conservative tendencies. His followers, the young Hegelians and primarily Marx, looked for such an absolute from the side of the *substance* (underestimated by Hegel, in their view), and emphasized its negative, dissolving force which they reoriented against Hegel's own philosophy.

It is important to note that, unlike the recurrent bourgeois apologies of solidarity (communitarianism in USA, "civil society" in the recent sociological and political discourse), communism, even if aimed against private property, is not a univocal "collectivism". Both Marx and recent theorists of communism actually emphasize its *negative* predicates, oriented at least at the dissolution of already existing social units. Communism is a vision of society, which justifies the forces of social dissolution acting in every society, while liberalism uses these same forces as an argument for its dualism of individual and state.[12] But, in the context of communism, these forces are seen as revolutionary, to wit, as *social* forces of auto-dissolution that bear energies of collective liberation. The totality/commonality that "communism" promises proceeds not only from the positively defined goal of an activity (here, a unitary collective subject would suffice) but rather as a negative unity of the suspended, dissolved multitude who are co-ordinating among themselves, so to speak, "by default."

However, Negri and Virno both explicitly deny that exodus is important because of its negativity;[13] they follow Deleuze in insisting on the inherent positivity of any event, which leads them to think that the task of a revolution consists in giving full freedom to the already-existing creative force of the multitude. Against this claim, we should perhaps look for the revolutionary resources in the social negativity itself, as in the unconscious collective form of dissolution. Communism is revolutionary not as a supposedly positive form of society that must be affirmed against all others, but as a condition intimately tied up with the destruction of the status quo.

These ideas revive the old Marxian dilemmas of communism. If Soviet communism was wrong, if communism is a "hypothesis,"[14] as Badiou suggests, or a theorem yet to be proven (realized in practice), then it risks to be viewed as one more ideal. If communism is an ontological condition of humanity (even an "ecstatic" one), then it escapes historical determination and does not inspire much insurrectional activity. Finally, if there is a progressive tendency within capitalism, then how can it destroy its own presuppositions (namely, that of capitalism)? To escape this dilemma, we have to find a *political* definition of communism, and then to find something in actual reality that would "destroy the present condition" – precisely something that we do not see in the current philosophical discussions of communism.

"Communism" of the past and communism of the future

This leads us straight to the more specific historical condition of Central/Eastern European communism. If this was not communism, then (so liberals say), communism remains a utopian fantasy. If this was actually "historical communism," then it is predominantly presented, if not as "totalitarianism," then as an unpleasant, outdated sociopolitical regime in a poor and authoritarian country with an excessive push for collectiveness, which "goes against human nature." The latter opinion is more widespread, and one normally speaks of the state of contemporary East and Central European societies as "postcommunism," assuming that communism had already taken place. Ironically, for citizens of the Soviet Union and other socialist countries, communism had always remained a utopia or a project to realize in the future. Thus, strangely, communism, at least in Soviet Union, was first in the future, then in the past, but never making it into the present.

Thus, there are two common-sense perspectives; the first, that communism was an unrealistic utopia never achieved, and second, that the only possible realization of communism *was* a Soviet-style socialism, that is to say, "totalitarianism."

However, there is a third perspective, and it is shared by several authors who have written on communism in the recent years. From this perspective, communism did really exist (and perhaps still exists), but it did not equal the Soviet-style state socialism at all. On the one hand, there is an argument of Paolo Virno that there is a "communism" that is inherent in the capitalism but is subdued by its logic. On the other hand, some analysts of "really existing socialism" also believed that communism existed under this regime, although it did not coincide with the official ideology or the accepted form of property. In Russia, it was Alexander Zinoviev, a Soviet dissident philosopher and émigré, and an author of an important treatise on Marx's dialectics who then turned to formal logic and, at the same time, to the violent critique of the Soviet regime expressed in semi-fictional satiric essays, who held this view.

In his essay "Communism as a Reality" (1980),[15] Zinoviev stated that communism really existed in Soviet Union, although it was not a politico-economic regime alternative to capitalism but a more profound *societal* regime of what

he called "communality" – an excessively collective life of
man which, he claimed, had been normally reduced in the
West by "civilization." The rest was a violent critique of the
"communism" which vividly reminded the reader of the Western
conservative theory of "masses" in the spirit of Le Bon, Tarde,
and McDougal. Zinoviev, logically enough, was skeptical about
the perspectives of positively transforming Soviet communism,
and this may explain his spectacular ideological U-turn in
the 1990s, when he sided with the reactionary and chauvinist
"Communist Party of the Russian Federation" in its critique
of perestroika and of the liberal-democratic reforms. Then, he
became an apologist of the Soviet society, emphasizing that "it
made the historical being of the people meaningful", and that in
it, "citizens are guaranteed jobs, free medicine, retirement and
other social goods", along with "powerful police forces and the
military power to protect the country from a foreign attack." At
that time, Zinoviev tentatively called the new Russian regime
"communist capitalism."[16]

A view partly similar to that of early Zinoviev was held
by yet another soviet dissident philosopher and émigré,
Boris Groys. From his works of the Soviet period up to the
recent *Communist Post-Script*,[17] Groys has emphasized the
substantively peculiar character of the Soviet regime, which
did not coincide with socialism per se, but consisted, according
to him, in the ideocratic and mythopoetic power of this
state, which was thus different from the more down-to-earth
materialist western societies. For Groys, the communist regime
was "dialectical," by which he (idiosyncratically) understands
the ability to incorporate any reality into one's ideological
outlook and to behave in an entirely unprincipled way.

The earlier work of Groys, as it is known, takes a more
critical stance vis-à-vis communism and speaks of Stalin's

USSR as a sui generis aesthetical project that inherits in the footsteps of Soviet avant-garde.

In a similar line of argument but with a more positive attitude, Oleg Aronson claims that Soviet cinema (as well as western mass cinema) created a certain "sensible" communism, which consisted in the making-common of image, not of material things. Aronson thinks that a poetic of "cliché," which is characteristic of mass culture, is paradoxically more "communist" than the authorial techniques of many art house films. Thus, "perception of cinema becomes immanent to the type of commonality where it remains not word and not silence but a communication (relationship to the other that proceeds from the insufficiency of Ego)" (Aronson, 1993: 86–7).

I think that both Groys and Aronson are up to something when they emphasize the *aesthetic* (sensuous, autonomous, unproductive) nature of Soviet communism. It was indeed a sort of Schillerian *Aesthetische Staat*. But why? It is the argument of this paper that the aesthetic communism did not coincide with the conscious ideological project of the state but formed an autonomous sphere within the regime, and this sphere was characterized by *negativity*. The civil society in Soviet Union was *negated by* the state and party, and thus sublated -- relegated to the aesthetic (neutralized) level. Therefore, as we will see below, the negativity did not just consist in the Benjaminian mass imagery, but also in the constant process of subjectivization and in a vacuous intersubjectivity.

While all of the described theories of communism are certainly more interesting than Soviet official philosophy or the Western theory of "totalitarianism," they may and must be criticized from the Left. However, all of these theories dismiss the emancipatory sociopolitical nature of the regime

that achieved what it did, not by setting free some age-old
chaotic energies of the masses, but through a wide-range
destruction of the institutions of private property, and through
a democratic revolutionary mobilization of the society. Many
of the phenomena that are deemed to be "communist" in the
aforementioned "real communism" tradition are in fact the
results of the large-scale destruction of the social link, which
allowed a communistic questioning of traditional forms. Some
admire this situation as a purely aesthetical massified sensuality,
but in fact aesthetics is here inseparable from a political
revolutionary project, from the negativity which is a virus of a
negative, and therefore politically active, communism.

Desert communism

To understand the "communism" of Soviet society, we need to
be attentive to its peculiar melancholic character and, moreover,
to the *negative condition* of the ecstatic "communality" which
ultimately led to the regime's destruction. Moreover, at the
background of a motion, be it a collective purposeful activity,
an expectation, or mourning, humans become apparent as
ground and not figures.

Paradoxically, any talk of the "communality" or
"communism" of Soviet society should start from the
consideration of the most noncommunist phenomena possible.
The Russian people *today* are among the most atomized and
egoist in their values and attitudes. They value individual
happiness above all, they do not care about charity, they are
apolitical, and the majority abstains from collective action.[18]
Everyday communication among strangers is extremely
alienated: a contemporary Russian will rarely excuse oneself if s/
he kicked you in the crowd, would not say "hi" if s/he leaves next
door in your stairwell, etc. If one is in the way of another person,

s/he would silently push you or your body part away without saying a word. As a recent American visitor, the writer Jack Milestone, shrewdly remarked: "It appears that Russians made a secret agreement to treat each other like a piece of shit … How did these people manage to get together and to shoot the Tzar with his whole family, while they never even say 'good morning' if they are not introduced to each other, I will never learn this."[19] Russians live in cozy apartments, but usually their stairwells are rotten and in a state of disrepair. Against an obvious objection that this situation is a product of the rogue capitalism of the 1990s, one must immediately rejoin that these traits have existed throughout the conscious life of the generation born in 1970s and appear as rigid behavioral patterns that the new western-oriented culture politic tries in vain to revert. However, in the late Soviet society, these traits coexisted with some intensely communal elements (living in communal apartments, relying on friends for services, career advances, and unofficial entrepreneurship) which were subsequently denigrated and now, while still existent, are regarded as an obstacle and residue of the past, while in fact, ultra-individualist values are a residue of the past to an even larger degree.

Realistically, the anti-communality of today's Russians may be explained by the extreme zeal with which the Soviet state, starting in the 1930s, placed families into packed "communal apartments" without permission of the existing tenants, and by the fact that it subsequently moved many of these families into private apartments in the 1960s and 1970s, creating conditions for a modest but zealous embourgeoisement. Communism seen as a unilateral collectivism reinforced, with time, its suppressed side of atomistic competitiveness. *Thus, the postcommunist Russian middle class is a mirror-image of the Western educated class; the latter are atomized by law but strive for some idealistic solidarity,*

*while the former, more united and interdependent physically,
consciously defend and institute the newly-acquired individualism.*

Is the ubiquity of social alienation a proof that Soviet socialism was "totalitarian," but not truly communist? Perhaps this excessive alienation points to something else, and hides a "positive," more attractive side. Indeed, in the Soviet Union, the existing public space was a space of anarchic freedom, and complete alienation was a guarantee of nonappropriation. The attractively deserted character of Soviet space is well shown in Soviet art, most famously in Andrey Tarkovsky's film *The Stalker*, with its estranged but mystically utopian industrial ruins as a space where a deep communication becomes possible. However, long before Tarkovsky, the same poetic was elaborated by Andrey Platonov (1899–1951), the greatest Soviet prose writer of the revolutionary generation. There were other theorists and writers before Tarkovsky, such as Lev Vygotsky and Mikhail Bakhtin who, under the Soviet regime, produced apologies of communism as an ecstatic utopian force that destroyed identities and deliberately created chaos. We can even speak of a *communist anti-communist* canon of people who in their thought and imagination preserved the constituent (or more precisely, *destituent*) power of communist revolution.

In many of Platonov's allegories of communism (including the builders of a foundation pit, a premature attempt to build "communism" in a small town called *Tchevengur*, or the emancipation of a small Turk tribe called the *"Dzhan"* wandering in a Central Asian desert), people are shown in alien deserted spaces, in extreme poverty, fatigue, and solitude. In opposition to Marx, communism for Platonov is the regime of poverty and negativity. At the same time, as is clear biographically and textually, he was a staunch supporter and participant of the Soviet project.

Tchevengur, in accordance with Badiou's doctrine, is a town where communism is organized by the *"prochie"*, or the unaccounted "rest" of society. The wandering of the *Dzhan* people ends in their dissolution, when they depart one by one in all directions. Platonov sees communism as both solitude and community,[20] but these two are presented not as an organic development from one to another (as conceived by Virno in the concept of individuation), but as a dialectical tension. For instance, a very characteristic diary note from 1931 reads: "The mystery of prostitution: union of bodies implies a unity of souls, but in prostitution the unity of souls is so absent, and it is so apparent and terrible, that there is no love, that from surprise, from the fall, from fear – 'unity of souls' starts to emerge."[21] At the same time, Platonov presents human sociability on the basis of a literary trope which Olga Meerson called the "re-familiarization" (opposite to Shklovsky's "estrangement" or "de-familiarization"):[22] the presentation (and perception by characters) of weird and surprising events (such as a bear working as a blacksmith) as *normal occurrences* not accentuated or marked within the otherwise realistically looking narrative. It is a special kind of sociability which grows from universal alienation (strangeness) and social dissolution and which takes others for granted.

Platonov's universe of a collective solitude where humans relate to each other nonthematically, as to ground rather than to figure, appears as a utopian communism of senses. However, it is clear that for Platonov, such communism is not just aesthetic sensuality (as Aronson attributes to him in the aforementioned reading), but that it exists in the framework of radical subjectivization, which implies the questioning of traditional, fixed subjectivity. Platonov's characters are obsessed with finding out *who* is doing what they are doing. One of them says, in a latent polemic reminiscent of Descartes, "I don't exist here … I only think here."[23] Another says, "In spite of my self-consciousness as a right-winger, left-winger, and a reconciliatory quietist, I am still sad, and consider this statement of mine to be insufficient, to be a typical démarche of a class enemy."[24] This latter phrase is a parody of the "self-criticism" which was required at that time for Soviet citizens. But for Platonov, it is a genuine movement of subjectivization; a performative self-refutation manifesting the existence of the revolutionary subject. It is nevertheless clear that this subject, in its suspended and unstable nature, belongs to the aesthetical and educational rather than purely political or scientific spheres.

All of this is indicative of the meaning of sadness and solitude in Platonov; they are affects of self-destruction, which is needed in order to retroactively create a subjectivity for the ongoing Soviet project. A revolution conceived by intelligentsia for the sake of the "proletariat" then had to build this proletariat and to grow its own roots, requiring a regressive, destructive approach. This is the meaning of the metaphor of the "foundation pit"; the joyful optimistic construction of the future means nothing without all the mourning, which it redeems, and which needs to be constantly reconstructed.

The inattention and aggression in late Soviet/new Russian streets and apartment buildings may simply mean that Russian citizens take other people *for granted*, as a ground not as a figure. It is completely opposite from the behavior vis-à-vis strangers typical of contemporary US and Western Europe, where an encounter produces a shock of almost disbelief, and the exaggerated rituals of politeness are meant to hide the embarrassment of the encounter itself. Russia and the "West" thus display the same value components of social attraction and repulsion, but they are structured differently, even inversely

to one another, which makes one be cautious against any
nondialectical "pluralism" of "alternative modernities."

Paolo Virno suggests that communism is a way from the
assumed collectivity to "individuation".[25] This is an organic
version of the coexistence and passage between these two
opposites. Alas, a gloomier scenario exists in Russia with the
move from an assumed commonality to egoism and cynicism.
It still serves as a manifest proof of the preexisting being-in-
common. But, as elsewhere, the newly formed "subjects" do
everything to suppress and destroy the ground sociability, the
premise of their existence.

Thus, the presumably «totalitarian» Soviet party-state in fact
did produce a common space by virtue of its very alienating
force: the state property was informally considered "ownerless."
This did not help economic development, but did maintain
a paradoxical sense of belonging and commonality via the
relationship to this ruined state property. This, in a strict sense,
is associated with what "common" really means; "*res communis
omnium*" in Roman law was distinct from the "*res publica*"
or "*res nullius,*" because it was a good, which belonged to no
one (including the Roman people, etc.), and could not be
appropriated (as res nullius could be).[26] One may say that *res
communis* is a mediator between *res nullius* and *res publica;* in a
sense, it also belongs to no one, and this very nonbelonging is
protected by the public.

In the Middle Ages,[27] common land could belong to a
feudal lord, but he did not have complete sovereignty over it;
property, in such cases, did not exclude the right of usage by
others. This is also the case with public property in today's
western countries. But, the fact that this is property of the
people makes it necessary to police it: prohibit starting fires
drinking, or smoking, install cameras, etc. In contrast, in the

case of the *res communis omnium,* the legal rule was rather closer to the Schmittean right of exception; law excluded a territory from the regime of property.

Now, how do we understand this *communist anti-communism* in the Soviet Union? There are at least two obvious explanations.

The first explanation is that Soviet socialism was a weird way to block the modernization of social relations in the spirit of bourgeois Enlightenment and, being unable to suggest anything new, managed to freeze a certain pre-Modern sociability of a mutually suspicious crowd and family-like networks of kinship and friendship, using clientelist networks for economic activity and living in a perpetual communion of feast and alcohol. This version is close to Zinoviev's "communality," except that the features in question are not collectivist. In fact, the late Soviet society on an everyday basis was *less* "communal" (in the sense of communitarian) than the contemporary western society (where, for instance, the regular co-habitation of "roommates" or other previously not acquainted individuals exists as a normal institution for young people and does not cause a large social problem or generate a dissident discourse, as in the case of Soviet communal apartments).

The second explanation, paradoxical in nature, is that the cunning of history made the quasi-theocratic Soviet party-state a placeholder for the profane sacrality of a *terra* and *res nullius,* which was strangely at the same time a *res communis.* This version would be close to Groys's theological parallels, except that it is the negative, apophatic elements of religion that are emphasized.

In both cases, there is a danger of taking these situations for granted, ignoring their eventful, catastrophic coordinates, or dismissing them as archaic.

In fact, communism is not necessarily anything "nice," and even not necessarily anything "collectivist." Both its utopian force and its force of a real movement build on the potential of immediate solidarity *and* on the power of disrupting and dissolving the social body, exposing humans to each other in their extreme solitude. It is this power that makes communism a threat and a hope for the status quo. It is a potential of revolution and subversion, and at the same time, is an *idea* of a society, which would not correspond to any model or idealist definition. In fact, communism would actively destroy any such model, building instead both the structures of social dissolution and the structures of aleatoric sociability. The current nonbeing of solidarity in postcommunist countries may well correspond to a temporal mode of communist existence which remains a "specter", having passed away without having ever been there. This is quite natural for the phenomenon of *negativity* as such, which is always unstable and fleeting but which, at the same time, returns in its very repression.[28] The culture of the collective solitude formed in the authoritarian environment may also be used, in an inverted way, to invent an alternative to bourgeois sociability.

Negativity in communism

It is important to treat communism politically and subjectively, and to maintain it as an alternative and a liberating abolition of the existing state of affairs. We can admit that in some sense we are all already communists. But without political subjectivization, communism remains an ethically neutral and ambivalent process, which can lead, politically, not only to self-management, but sometimes to the authoritarian destruction of the social link, or even to the fascist-like hyper-identification of a collective. The political institutions of communism should somehow be themselves "negative" and foster the destruction of identities and the invention of new unclassifiable entities.

As mentioned in the beginning, a parallel may be drawn between the concept of communism and the concept of "democracy." Claude Lefort famously argued that democracy is a regime where the place of supreme power is temporarily left empty, and special care is taken to regularly empty it out (Lefort). It is analogous with communism, at least in some crucial spheres; private property should not just be forbidden, but should be actively resisted as an informal social institution. The partiality and ideality of the concept of democracy, which subordinates life to law, covers up for authoritarianism in a corporation or in dealing with noncitizens, as well as serves to demobilize people and consider them only as passive bearers of interest, may be criticized. However, we see that in today's world there are democratic states (like France or Italy) with numerous mass illegal or informal protests led by a nonsystemic opposition and directed against the existing regime. These states certainly do not encourage their citizens to do so, but there is something about these states' liberal "democracy" that provokes some individuals to go against it in a "democratic" way.

Jacques Rancière, an influential apologist for Western democracy, uses the argument that democracy starts where there are new unrecognized subjects (the "sans-parts") emerging to contest the status quo. In this sense, what we mean by communism is a more radical and less formal version of the same thing that the left-wing understanding of democracy entails, that is, a regime which is constantly capable of self-overcoming.

There must be ways to preserve the subversive, ecstatic character of communist constituent power, even at the price of its potential destructiveness. The current sociopolitical situation shows, furthermore, that there is a Schillerian need for constantly *educating* and reuniting its citizens into *subjects*. The negative dissolving force of communism itself risks producing apathetic "last men" at the moment when the ideology vanishes. Thus, an effort must be made to make the communist background of the current atomization and apathy evident. But, any educational posture could produce a countereffect of overturning of the educators. So, perhaps a communist government should be truly dialectical (as opposed to the pseudo-dialectical liberal state, as well as to the ideocratic dogmatism of the Soviet state to which Groys attributes a dialectic for false reasons). Such a government should be dialectical in its rationality and aesthetical in its virtuosity: harsh, but plastic at the same time, constantly preparing its own downfall and rescuing itself from it.

Notes

1   By Restif de la Bretonne, then by German Jacobins: see Jacques Grandjonc, "Quelques dates a propos des termes communiste et communisme," in *Mots*, October 1983, no. 7. "Cadrage des sujets et dérive des mots dans l'enchainement de l'énoncé," pp. 143–8.

2   Karl Marx, Communism and the *Augsburg Allgemeine Zeitung*, in: Marx and Engels, *Collected Works* Volume 1, pp. 215–21.

3   Marx and Engels, "German Ideology," in *Collected Works* Volume 5, p. 37.

4   Marx and Engels, "Contribution to the critique of Hegel's *Philosophy of Right*," in *Collected Works* Volume 3, p. 177.

5   Jules Michelet, *Histoire de la Révolution française*. P.: Robert Laffont, 1979. T. 1, P. 67.

6   Alexey Gastev, *Poezia rabochego udara*. M.: Khudozhestvennaya literatura, 1971, p. 138.

7   Such as represent, in (post-)Soviet studies, B. Groys, M. Ryklin, E. Dobrenko, and others.

8   "German Ideology," p. 37.

9   Marx and Engels, "Manifesto of the Communist Party," in *Collected Works*, Vol. 6, p. 506.

10 "On the Jewish Question," *Collected Works*, vol. 3, p. 160.

11 P. Virno, *A Grammar of the Multitude*, New York: Semiotext, 2004.

12 See Kant's notion of "asocial sociability" in: "Idea For A Universal History With A Cosmopolitan Purpose," in *Cambridge Texts in the History of Political Thought* (2nd edn) (Cambridge: Cambridge University Press, 1991), pp. 41–53.

13 See for instance Antonio Negri and Michael Hardt, *Empire* (New York and London: Harvard University Press, 2000), p. 131–2. See also an important critical article by Ernesto Laclau criticizing Negri and Hardt for inattention to the negativity of history: E. Laclau, "Can immanence explain social struggles," in P. Passavant and J. Dean, eds., *Empire's New Clothes: Reading Hardt and Negri*, New York and London: Routledge, 2004, pp. 21–30.

14 A. Badiou, L'hypothèse communiste, Paris: Lignes, 2009.

15 Alexandr Zinoviev, *Communism kak realnost'* (1980). Translated into French as *Communisme comme réalité*, Paris: Juillard/Age d'Homme, 1981), pp. 56–9].

16 Alexander Zinoviev, *Perestroika in Partygrad*, New York: Peter Owen, 1992.

17 See reference above.

18 Atomization and extreme individualism of the Russian citizens, on the level of conscious values, are demonstrated in quantitative sociological data; see for instance Vladimir Magun and Maxim Rudnev, "The Life Values of the Russian Population," in: *Sociological Research* (2010), Vol. 49, No. 4, pp. 3–57. (There is a difference of Russia against other European countries, in the higher value of individual achievement and self-affirmation, as opposed to the values that "transcend the individual self.")

19 http://fishki.net/1697319-vpechatlenija-amerikanca-vpervye-pobyvavshego-v-rossii.html Last visit 11.02.2016

20 See Jonathan Flatley, *Affective Mapping*, Cambridge, MA: Harvard University Press, 2008.

21 Andrey Platonov, *Zapisnye knizhki*, Moscow: IMLI RAN, 2006, p. 185.

22 Olga Meerson, *Svobodnaya Vesch: Poetika neostraneniya u Andreya Platonova*, Berkeley, CA: Berkeley Slavic Specialties, 1997.

23 Andrey Platonov, *Kotlovan* Moscow: Gudyal Press, 1999, p. 7. *The Foundation Pit*, trans. M. Ginzburg, Evanston, IL: Northwestern University Press, 1994, p. 13.

24 "Zabluzhdenie na rodine kompota." Arkhiv Platonova. Moscow: IMLI, 2009, p. 254.

25 P. Virno, *A Grammar of the Multitude*, New York: Semiotext, 2004, pp. 64–9.

26 Inst. 2.1, 2.1.1, Dig. 1.8.2 pr.-1 (Marcianus), in: *Corpus Iuris Civilis*, http://web.upmf-grenoble.fr/Haiti/Cours/Ak/. Last visit 5.10.2010.

27 Cf. Yann Moulier Boutang, "Les nouvelles clôtures: technologies de l'information et de la communication ou la révolution rampante des droits de propriété," www.ulb.ac.be, Last visit 5.10.2010.
28 On these and other features of negativity in politics, see my *Negative Revolution*, London: Bloomsbury 2013.

12

Alexander Brener

THE RUSSIAN AVANT-GARDE AS AN UNCONTROLLABLE BEAST

Dedicated to Barbara

I visited Kiev recently.

And there I ran into the Black Malevich Square!

Kiev is a totally gutted and pillaged city.

Like all the other cities in the world, in fact.

But Kiev looks like it has been bombed.

The government cliques and oligarchs have robbed the people blind.

The populace are like wraiths, rummaging about in the ruins.

The streets have been captured by corpulent automobiles, which maneuver like tanks.

They drive up onto pavements and prevent pedestrians from passing.

They barge along the highways, polluting the air and honking their horns.

They carry bandits, bankers and beauty queens.

And ordinary people move aside and shrink away, squealing.

They drink in nauseating cafés in order to forget their own negligibility.

It is as if the city has been occupied by a hostile army.

Nonetheless, I did meet one living, rebellious creature there.

And it was Black Malevich Square!

That was what I called the black cat with little white socks on its four paws.

Black Malevich Square is the cat's first name, patronymic and surname.

This cat hid under the cars.

It was leading some kind of secret life there.

Possibly it was damaging these cars, putting them out of action.

Or perhaps it was sniffing the petrol to trigger its hallucinations.

It was using the petrol to stimulate its imagination!

In any case, it was clearly not knuckling under to the occupying authorities.

The occupying authorities wish to eradicate imagination.

The occupying authorities wish to control people's thought and visions.

And neither does the Russian avant-garde knuckle under to history or museums.

The Russian avant-garde is a cat that defies any attempt to train it.

I think the avant-garde wanted to leave the human race and become a beast.

According to Nikolai Aseev, Kruchenykh turned into a jackal.

A jackal is an animal that cleanses the world of carrion.

And Igor Terentiev could leap like a cat, from standing, straight up onto the table.

Without the slightest effort!

Tatlin created the Letatlin flying machine in order to fly like an owl or a magpie.

Tatlin built the Letatlin in order to fly away from people.

And he was right!

Gilles Deleuze thought about that – about becoming a beast.

Mankind! It isn't descended from a monkey, but from an ant.

That's what Malevich said.

Mankind, according to the suprematist, had got mired down in labor and objectness.

"Objects are the concupiscence of the human kind," Malevich noted down.

The goal of mankind is to transform forests into furniture.

Malevich despised labor.

He loved nature.

The Black Square is nature, it's a beast!

Malevich wrote the treatise "Idleness as the real truth of mankind."

Giorgio Agamben is very fond of this treatise.

It states that idleness is the highest condition of man.

It attacks both capitalism and socialism, which constrain man to labor.

Malevich says in this treatise that even machines should be as indolent as donkeys.

One day Malevich saw a book by Schopenhauer in a bookshop window.

The book was called *The World as Will and Representation*.

Malevich burst out laughing.

"Where there is will and representation, there is no world," he said.

Malevich did not like the human will.

Will is directed towards the control of objects, he believed.

Will creates objectness.

But cats and buffaloes live in a state of objectlessness.

And Malevich had no respect for any kind of representation either.

To representations he counterposed cosmic objectlessness.

To representations he counterposed nothingness.

Malevich regarded all the "isms" of art as limited representations.

Malevich regarded "isms" as illnesses.

He wanted to organize the academy of art like a medical school.

Where all the "isms" would be studied as ailments.

In 1928 Malevich went to Kiev.

Where he wanted to teach the "isms" as sicknesses.

But he wasn't allowed to do it.

Malevich also said that there is no conscious mind in suprematism.

Suprematism is free from reason. Like an animal!

In suprematism there is no constant pursuit of perfection.

Suprematism not only lies beyond the bounds of objectness, but beyond the bounds of invention.

Suprematism is based on excitement and excitation, like nature!

On excitation and sensation.

The world is objectless and only man wishes to objectify it.

That was what Kazimir Malevich thought.

And he also hated the state.

Moles and sparrows loathe it too.

And giraffes, and butterflies …

The mole, by the way, was Marx's favorite animal.

And Malevich liked to keep away from human settlements, like a hedgehog or a moose.

He liked to sit under a solitary oak tree and gaze at the horizon.

Birds would come and perch in the tree.

Malevich said that people would eventually be the end of this "little ball."

The "little ball," of course, is the globe of the Earth.

Velimir Khlebnikov called himself Chairman of the Globe.

One day Khlebnikov retreated from mankind into the steppe, like a saiga antelope.

Or did he withdraw into the wilderness, like Jesus?

Like Khlebnikov, Jesus loved flowers and animals.

But mankind is bogged down in the mire of internecine war and slaughter.

Mankind has built prisons and put living creatures in them.

Khlebnikov hated zoos, where animals are incarcerated.

He wrote a poem about this – "The Menagerie."

All the futurists wanted to become fish and swim away into the ocean.

Terentiev once composed a fish-poem.

There were no words in it, only bubbles.

As well as the stirring of gills.

And Khlebnikov wrote a poem consisting of nothing but punctuation marks.

The Russian futurists were not enthusiastic admirers of machines, like Marinetti.

Khlebnikov attacked Marinetti when the Italian came to Russia.

He though Marinetti was a swaggerer.

Khlebnikov was interest in water nymphs, not automobiles.

Water nymphs are girls who are turning into fish.

Khlebnikov himself wanted to turn into a constellation.

Walter Benjamin considered constellations to be the source of inspiration.

The Russian transrational poets used zaum, they didn't want to speak in human language.

The Russian human language was wallowing in banality and bygonality.

That was what Kruchenykh thought.

Zaum is nonhuman Russian language: jaunty and objectless.

In zaum the words don't descend on your head like axes.

Zaum has no need of oaths and vows.

Zaum is words flying like gnats.

Sometimes they bite, and sometimes they simply drone.

Zaum is words flying like fireflies, leaping like grasshoppers.

Zaum is words devoid of meaning, because meaning has become botchery.

The zaum poets didn't want to write and publish literary compositions.

They constructed decompositions.

Ilya Zdanievich believed that all literature had been transformed into botchery.

All art is botchery.

Botchery is words intended for sugary goo-gooing and agitation.

Botchery is the whole of modern literature that caters to the needs of society.

Society, by the way, is also botchery. That is what the Tikkun thinks.

Instead of literature, we need droning, said Kruchenykh.

The droning must irritate men of letters and show them that they are fools.

Kruchenykh called himself a dronejurer.

He was not only a jackal, but also a mosquito.

And Mikhail Larionov invented the movement of rayonism in painting.

"Rayonism is almost the same as a mirage," said Larionov.

A mirage appears in the scorching hot air of the desert.

Rayonism is what a camel sees in the desert.

It is not the objects that are important, but the rays of the sun as they are refracted.

And by the way, Pavel Florensky also pondered over mirages in *Iconostasis*.

Serge Sharshun considered octopuses to be more interesting than people.

Sharshun's painting is the painting of an axolotl.

And Pavel Filonov cultivated his paintings like crystals

In the way that a leaf grows out of the bud.

Filonov also wanted to be a proletarian.

A proletarian is a new being growing out of the old mankind.

A proletarian is not a worker, but a thinker.

That is what Marx thought.

The Russian avant-gardists wanted to think!

In short, the avant-gardists were sick of mankind and all its works.

Jacques Camatte, by the way, also believed that mankind had lost its way.

That is why the avant-gardists loved geometry and wild animals.

The geometry of the Russian avant-garde is the right pathway to wild animals.

Long live the world, but not objects.

Long live the black cat with the little white socks!

Long live the cosmos!

To sense the cosmos – that is what the avant-gardists wanted to do.

To sense the cosmos means to be in a poetic state on Earth.

Long live idleness!

Idleness – the kind that cats have, or three-toed sloths, hanging from the trees?

Or is Malevich's idleness something different?

Is it clear to you what idleness is?

If not, then read Malevich's treatise.

Go to the primary sources.

Part Three

From the archive

Archives, as lost and recovered collections of humble objects, are the material evidence of the weight and flow of history. They reveal ruptures between different types of time – historical, psychological and collective.

Can archives then be the site of social change, as arguably was the case with the archive of Moscow conceptualism?

Vadim Zakharov

AUTHOR, COSMOS, ARCHIVE

The subject of this book could have been formulated in various ways: "The Author in the Cosmos of Ideology" or "The Cosmos as a Symptom of the Neurotic Condition of Totalitarian Society" or simply "The Author as Archive." But anyway, in this case the three elements – Author, Cosmos and Archive – are crucial to an understanding of social utopias and philosophical, aesthetic and psychoanalytical theories.

The artists, poets and philosophers of the early twentieth century vaguely envisioned the cosmos as a vector of escape into the bright future. As a general rule, however, the fuel used for takeoff was an ideology of one kind or another, together with all its nuances. The Cosmos as an obsessional idea for society as a whole, and in particular for the Author. Malevich, Kandinsky, Filonov, Labas, Williams, and many others are the cosmonauts of their own utopias and concomitant ideologies. The theories of Fedorov, for instance. All these utopias ceased to exist in the 1930s, when the flames of personal utopias gave way to the infernal communist conflagration. Authors who launched themselves into a cosmos turned out to be ideologists of individualism, and therefore enemies of the socialist society that was being built. A society that aspired in its totality towards the 'heavens' of a collective world order that had tossed the individual into the combustion chamber of the booster rocket.

Every author actively structures the utopia of his own individual personality and realizes himself in this utopia, expanding its boundaries in all manner of diverse spaces, including the cosmos which, in the final analysis, is the goal towards which his primary ambitions are directed. Of course, the very concept 'cosmos' often changes. When the cosmos becomes the real objective of a collective author, ideologies become actively engaged – socialism, communism, Maoism. In contrast with the individual methods and practices for mastering a different space, or religious and psychological methods, the collective methods and practices resemble posters or slogans. Everything about them is sham. From the very beginning real flights into cosmic space were accompanied by a battle of ideologies with banners displayed on both sides. But when the cosmos becomes exclusively an object of scientific research, most people forget about it.

Today there is a notable upsurge of interest in the cosmos both in the West and in modern Russia, which is once again dashing into the abyss of totalitarianism. How many official declarations there have been recently in Russia about flights to Mars and the construction of stations on the moon. The cosmos is again being transformed into an ideological vector, an arena for confrontations between Western and post-Soviet ideologies and the battle between new technologies, a field of military domination.

It is interesting to follow this change in the attitude to the
cosmos and the individual as exemplified by Russian artists. The
artists of the sixties – Vladimir Nemukhin, Dmitry Plavinsky,
Vladimir Weisberg, Mikhail Roginsky and many others – based
their work on a personal, existential position, counterposing
themselves to the inhuman machine of totalitarian society and
the 'cosmos' as a collective project. Ilya Kabakov's albums
are already a subtly ironic comment concerning existential
problems. Nonetheless in these albums too, people fly and break
out into the cosmos. The beginning of Sots Art – the work *Laika*
(1972) by Vitaly Komar and Alexander Melamid – is directly
linked with the theme of the cosmos. The absolute irony here
is obvious, the emphasis is placed on the dog, not on the first
man to fly beyond the bounds of the earth. I think this is a result
of Russia's having lost the space race with the USA, which put
the first man on the moon in 1969. After that Cosmos and
Author came together on the territory of postmodernism, in the
space of self-irony. And they continued to exist in this capacity
until very recently. Until one country (Russia again) set course
for a return to the homeland of victorious socialism. In short,
touchdown has been made in the past, where cosmos and
author once again occupy the positions of antagonists.

The first work that I authored, in 1978, the only one on the
subject of the cosmos, was called "An Exchange of Information
with the Sun." I was nineteen, I set my thumbprint (a portrait
of the Author in-the-making) on a little mirror and directed the
reflection towards the sun. The moment the Author appears in
the world, the very first thing he does is to assert his presence in
the cosmos. Later my authorial ambitions became burdensome
to me and led me directly to the archive.

It seems to me that the archive is always an alternative
to 'flights into the cosmos'. It's not by chance that the first

action taken by dictators who are befuddled by one ideology or another and their sidekicks is to close and burn the archives. They annihilate the memory of the past, while constructing the cosmodrome of the future for more zombified subjects. People, as individual archives, are then annihilated ruthlessly. The Cosmos and the Archive are antipodes.

Escape into the archive was no accident for me. The concept of the *archive* took shape on the Moscow scene in the early 1980s, with the publication of the MANI Files (MANI – Moscow Archive of New Art). The most important element in this title was not the hint at 'manifesto', but precisely the archive – the Moscow *Archive* of New Art. In 1981 Victor Skersis and I compiled the second of the four collections of MANI Files.[1] And so at the age of twenty-two I had already accepted the archive as my basic form of activity.

In Russia the early 1980s saw the beginning of a new stage of self-appraisal in a small circle of Moscow artists – a distance appeared that made it obvious who was doing what. The MANI Files are one of the important collective publications of that period, they were a natural form for preserving and at the same time disseminating information in Moscow's artistic community. This publication could only have come into being in a vacuum, in a setting where Russia completely lacked any institutions of modern art. And it is important that its originators and editors were artists themselves – Andrey Monastyrsky, Victor Skersis and Vadim Zakharov, Elena Elagina and Igor Makarevich, Natalya Abalakova and Anatoly Zhigalov. As a result of this initiative the archive became a distinct genre in modern Russian art. That is my personal opinion. The archive, bookkeeping (see MANI Album No. 5 – *Buchgalterium*), numerous hierarchies – these all relate to an attempt at a universal accounting of Everything, both serious

and otherwise. The archive in the cage of the Soviet system, as
a model of freedom, as the defiance of enforced localization,
sometimes through a parody of it. The artists themselves
created archives and collections. The official Soviet institutions
didn't do that. Moreover, the MANI Files included more than
just archive materials. In actual fact a lot of the material dated
from the same year in which the files were created. In this sense
the concept of an *archive* signified freedom of action against
the background of a totalitarian system. A group of artists from
three generations preserved and developed its history in the
face of multitudinous prohibitions. The editors asked artists
to prepare five copies of their material (at that time any more
than five copies of a typewritten text came under the terms of
an article of the criminal law – for the distribution of samizdat)
and put them in five identical envelopes. The files assembled
in this fashion were circulated in artistic circles, including
the groups of Kabakov, Monastyrsky, Natalya Abalakova
and Anatoly Zhigalov, our group of a younger generation of
artists and, if I'm not mistaken, I think one copy was given
to the Sots artists, the circle of Prigov, Orlov and Lebedev.
Consequently the files made the rounds of the artists and
became the information media of that time, and they were
called the Archive of New Art. I see no contradiction in this
– back then an archive was a more relevant, provocative, far-
reaching concept than the manifesto of any group. In effect
the archive *was* a manifesto. The MANI Files were followed by
the MANI Albums. Andrey Monastyrsky was the originator
and editor of this publication. Six editions were published
from 1986 to 1991. Each issue had its own title. For instance,
the first was called *Ding an Sich*, and the second was *Rooms*.
Three issues were compiled together with Joseph Backstein,
and one together with Sabina Khensgen. The final editor was

Yury Leiderman. The number of copies produced of each of the MANI Albums varied from 3 to 5. It is important here to emphasize the various phases of the archive's existence in the Moscow circle in pre-perestroika Russia – from collective to personal. I started publishing the journal *Pastor* in 1992 when I was already in Cologne, continuing the line of small-circulation publications, and it included the same set of names. Unlike the preceding publications, *Pastor* was an attempt to present the Moscow conceptual discourse in the West. As the publisher, at this important moment – the beginning of the dialogue with western culture – I tried to preserve the context of the methodology and terminology of Moscow conceptualism, which had been developed and established over the years. *Pastor* became the center of my archive – it published complete lists of the MANI Files and Albums for the first time. The "Dictionary of Terms of Moscow conceptualism," compiled by Andrey Monastyrsky, was first printed in *Pastor*. The first issue of the journal appeared in 1992 and the final issue, the eighth, in 2001. The print runs of the issues varied from 30 to 100 copies.

A lot of people collected archives, and some exhibited them later. In 1993 Ilya Kabakov put on an exhibition entitled "The Big Archive" at the Stedelijk Museum in Amsterdam. In 1995 I put on an exhibition, one title of which was "The Park, the Archive et al." And later I exhibited my archive very often, actually defining it in conflicting terms: "The Living Archive" and "The Killer Archive." Over time the archive had killed the artist in me: I was constantly required to collect new materials and process them, spending my time, money and energy on this. I teetered on the brink of this contradiction for a long time.

After finding myself in the West in 1989, I actively pursued the archival line of work, giving it prominence among the others – publisher, collector, artist. It was obvious that, with

the promotion of Russian conceptual art in the West after
perestroika, western culture, with its system of archives,
required material to fill the niche that had appeared (although
no one actually asked me in person to do this). In this instance
the initiative of the artist was a natural gesture for me. I found
myself at the center of a current being channelled from Russia
to the West and I started actively recording what was happening
around me: the numerous trips by Russian artists, friends and
colleagues to solo and group exhibitions in Germany, Italy,
Switzerland, Austria, America, etc. Unique video material was
shot. So my archival obsession turned out to last until 2014.
Two hundred and twenty-eight exhibitions by Russian artists
(including my own, of course) were captured on video, plus 330
exhibitions recorded in photographs, as well as the numerous
movements of artists across countries and continents, readings,
drinking sessions, and conversations. And in addition to this,
the hundreds of catalogs, posters and invitation tickets that
were collected. It is important to mention that I collected a
'real archive' – unlike many other artists, who merely dealt
with the subject of the archive. Processing the archive and
preserving it (digitizing the video and photo materials) required
a tremendous effort from me as an artist, and so eventually I
had to stop collecting the archive. In this sense I consider 2014
to be the final year. It coincided with an exhibition of my video
archive in the Garage Museum of Contemporary Art, under the
appropriate title "Postscriptum after RIP."

My activities as archivist, collector and publisher became
for me an important platform for reaching an awareness of
myself as an artist with expanded opportunities. *This* is where
my understanding of the artist today has found its expression –
the artist as institution, the artist functioning freely in culture,[2]
the author as a multi-faceted figure, who shapes open territory

through his activity. I have in mind the position of an artist who takes upon himself the functions of institutions, without being afraid of losing himself as an artist. In my opinion, it is precisely this position, and not simply the production of yet more individual works, that expresses the modern artist's *freedom of activity*. In the final analysis, it is a matter of the balance between the parts of this activity. Sooner or later this is disrupted – there is simply no energy left to maintain the balance. An author cannot escape from the cosmos of his or her utopias. He/she is the only cosmonaut on his ship. But when strength departs and it becomes impossible to launch the ship every day, he/she starts raising up a monument to himself. Man, as we know, is weak. In the final reckoning an author is the monument to his own utopia. In 2006 I made a work called "The Author – Monument to Utopia," dedicated to Pavel Filonov. I took a child's toy – a lion that moved if you pressed a button on its underside. I increased the length of the lion to almost four meters and used a complicated mechanism to make it move and assume various positions. In this case the lion symbolized the author, or rather, his numerous guises: from a position with the head held high in pride – "I'm a genius" – to the stage of depression and doubts – "I'm shit." Filonov's world view is a cosmic image shattered into millions of little pieces. He tried to assemble the little pieces into a jigsaw, his picture of the world. In my work the lion also consisted of large and small pieces trying to assemble themselves into the image of an author of genius, but with every new second the author kept losing the sense of his purpose.

Author, Cosmos, Archive – these are categories, constantly attempting to correlate with each other. A balance between them is only rarely established. For millennia this trinity has been urging humankind on to endless efforts to soar aloft, break away from its material burden, escape, in the final analysis, from the archive of its own ego, but this never happens.

Additional terms used by Vadim Zakharov from The Dictionary of Terms of the Moscow conceptual School[3]

SKY

(a) Something for which there is no explanation. Its meaning is unknown, its content is incalculable, the causes of its occurrence are inconceivable, its volume defies measurement, it has no boundaries at all, the individual who invented it all has not been found. It arouses indeterminate feelings: inclusion, dissolution, reconnection, fading, suspension. It arouses the following states: mundanity, melancholy, despondence, loneliness, fear, death, happiness, euphoria. It always gives rise to the same questions: How? What for? Why? In what way? Who's the boss? And it always provokes the same answers: I don't know! I don't understand! I can't explain! I've never come across it! Methods for imitating the sky's absence are: taking no notice, pretending that you already know everything, wearing a cap, pretending to be a fool, complaining of a pain in your back, blaming everything on the imperfection of society, drunkenness, and the depravity of the apparatchiks, and also blanking out your own thoughts and superfluous questions with wine, tobacco, drugs, and obstinacy and by reading literature;

(b) an abiding point of discord between consciousness, the unconscious and the unknown.

SUN

(a) Something small, clever and punctual (sometimes replies to questions it is asked). It helps to overcome depression, but sometimes encourages it and other psychological disorders.

During its stage of rising, in combination with lighting effects and the singing of birds, it creates a state of trance, happiness, lambent nuances, cultured conversation, and amatory intrigue, frequently accompanied by tears, sobbing, and a desire for nothing. At the stage of its highest ascent it evokes a feeling of exhaustion, extreme irritation, lust, and desire for a quick death, it encourages migraines, cancer, skin conditions, and infectious diseases. At the stage of its departure it evokes a sense of measure and time, cozy family happiness and impunity, anticipation of evening-time relaxation and tranquility, and desires for indeterminacy;

(b) a heater that torments the memory.

FULL MOON

(a) Something incredible. It is reminiscent of plenitude of power, full flood, full-blooded. It stimulates an upsurge of unequivocal strength in men, animals, seas, oceans, and poets. In man it provokes the following: somnambulism, stupidity, idiocy, ignorance, and vulgarity, making him take the visions, dreams, and phantoms inspired by classic literature for reality.

In animals it provokes a human feeling of exhaustion and serene self-confidence.

It provokes seas and oceans to splash out their ambitions and subconscious into the constraints of the poetic.

It provokes poets to eat the following:

> *Why or not – I don't know*
> To the Moon or to a star
> But I tried the Moon with my tongue
> In forty-one in Kazan.
> (V. NEKRASOV)

(b) A certain lighting device that appears by chance and illuminates sections of the unconscious which consciousness defines as absolutely known.

STARRY NIGHT SKY

(a) This is one hell of a thing. It almost always arouses a feeling of total insignificance, abandonment, idiocy and stupidity, and I think that somewhere deep inside your body and soul the realization emerges that life is not all beer and skittles;

(b) a screen on which your own neuroses are lit up (sometimes in the following forms: objects, pictures, installations, and also major international exhibition spaces).

CRESCENT MOON

I can't understand or explain. Something very funny and dangerous – "the crescent moon emerged from the mist, clutching a little knife in its fist."

Notes

1   The Mukhomor group began collecting the fifth MANI File in 1983, but it was never completed. Later Georgy Kizevalter became involved in compiling the file but, having failed to appear in its own time, it was never completely assembled. Extracted from the past and presented today, it cannot rank in importance with the first four publications. In its own time it did not convey the uniqueness of collective creative work and did not become a rare form of information exchange in culture. Today it can only be regarded as an unsuccessful attempt to publish a fifth issue, dealing with the political victimization of the Mukhomor group. As a result, three of the five members of the group were crudely and forcefully recruited into the army.
2   Functioning in culture is activity that influences an already formed cultural and conceptual space at any of its points with using the following methods: probing, rocking, simulation, substitution, surpassing, restraining, stagnation, and others. The term appeared in 1979 during the period of Vadim Zakharov and Igor Lutz's co-authorship, was developed

by the group SZ in 1980–84 and used in part by Vadim Zakharov and Sergei Anufriev in considering methods of throwing up ideas and total repetitions – in connection with the theme of 'The Zone' (1986).(*The Dictionary of Terms of the Moscow conceptual School*, 1999)

3   Compiled by Andrey Monastyrsky, and first published in the journal *Pastor*, No. 7, 1999.

14

Bogdan Mamonov

A BINARY SYSTEM

I'm writing this text at a desk with scuffed red baize, three lateral drawers and six side-column drawers. The lid of my laptop conceals from my sight an old paperweight, a brass beaker for quill pens and a cast-metal bust of a girl with naked shoulders. They probably didn't come as accessories to the desk when it was bought, but for me these items are an inherent part of its landscape.

The desk is my entire meager legacy from my great-grandfather, Grigory Karlovich Speier.

The desk and also, of course, the Taxiphote – my greatest treasure.

Grigory Karlovich Speier was a principal engineer at Kolomna and a builder of railway bridges. The bridge over the Moskva River that connects Kolomna with the capital was his work. And that bridge is still standing to this day.

Grigory Karlovich's father, Karl Speier, came to Russia from Germany at the very beginning of the last tsar's reign.

His trade is unknown to me, as are the details of his biography. A photograph of Karl has, however, been preserved in Grigory's archive: it shows my great-great-grandfather in front of a house in Rechki – a village near Kolomna, where the Speiers used to spend the summer.

It is no longer possible to locate the building but, judging from the photographs, it was a two-storey, detached, wooden house with a carved paling fence, decorative window surrounds, a large park, and a pond.

In addition to his primary occupation, Speier Jr was an outstanding amateur photographer. And being a man of some means, in 1910 Grigory Karlovich ordered a stereoscopic camera from France, together with a special device to accompany it – a Taxiphote: a strange apparatus equipped with a highly complex system of lenses and a special mechanism that allowed the images displayed to be changed. These images were applied to extremely thin plates of glass that were stored in special cassettes, concealed in the Taxiphote's spacious, wooden-clad entrails. I know that a similar device was owned by the Russian royal family (it is now kept at the Alexander Palace) and Viktor Misiano told me that he saw one exactly like it in the Goldenweiser Museum. Furthermore, it is generally believed that in France the apparatus was used for certain distinctive, titillating purposes. The contention is that in the dens of iniquity which prefigured the peep shows of modern times, the Taxiphote served for the display of seductive pictures – naturally, not free of charge. Allegedly that is where it got its name – Taxiphote, i.e. photographs for money. I don't know whether this is true or not, but the idea that the proto-virtual aesthetic of stereoscopics might prompt thoughts of pornography does not appear exaggerated to me. There are two circumstances that suggest such a conclusion. Firstly, the space

of a stereoscopic image does not appear simply realistic, but
super-realistic, I would even say perversely realistic, and this
is an intrinsic feature of pictures of a certain kind. Secondly,
the very process of viewing the photographs smacks of blatant
voyeurism. Pressing one's eyes to the viewing lenses of the
Taxiphote one feels as if one were peeping through a keyhole.

My friend Anna Kuznetsova, who appreciated the merits
of my great-grandfather's archive, remarked that the position
of her own body while she was viewing a picture (the viewer
is usually obliged to bend over in order to glance into the
eyepieces), in combination with the hyperrealistic quality of the
image, aroused her sensuality.

Of course, the subjects chosen by Grigorii Karlovich were
very far removed from even the slightest hint of impropriety.
Picnics, strolls along shady, tree-lined alleys, tennis, a game
of leapfrog and other summer-retreat amusements – such
was the basic repertoire of his themes. Essentially they were
typically bourgeois bucolic idylls, and if not for an exceptional
compositional flair and camera angles that were quite surprising
for those times, these experiments would not transcend the
limits of a banal family album. It was not by chance, however,
that I touched upon the theme of eroticism, since as an
adolescent I had first-hand experience of the equivocal magic of
my great-grandfather's stereoscopic images. But first I should l
tell you how the Taxiphote came into my possession.

Speier the son took the main body of his stereoscopic
photographs in 1913. This was evidently the family's last happy
year. An air of lightheartedness and unblighted happiness
permeates the fragile, wafer-thin glass plates created during
these pre-war months.

In 1914 the First World War began. Karl managed to leave
for Germany in good time. Grigory Karlovich, his wife Nina

Gustavovna and their three daughters – Faina, Margarita and Lidochka – remained in Russia. At this stage it is hard to understand what could have induced the German engineer to take a step that would prove so fateful for the Speiers.

Whether he was overtaken by events or he suddenly felt loath to leave the apartment in Kolomna and the little house in Rechki, or whether some part was played by the historical attachment of the German nature to Russia – none of that makes any difference now. At first, it must be said, things didn't go too badly. Strangely enough, even the sudden, overwhelming calamity of the revolution had no impact on the family's well-being. Speier's authority as an engineer became their passport into the new life. The Soviets were in need of specialists, and the problem of nationality had not yet become acute. I don't know what Grigory's political views were but, positing his nature as an artist, I have no doubt that he shared the conformism which is inherent to our caste.

To be sure, the archive did yield several photographs recording an anti-German demonstration in Kolomna, but for Grigory Karlovich these were probably merely historical documents and nothing more.

The family's life in the late 1920s is concealed behind an impenetrable veil. The reserves of glass plates had evidently been exhausted, and it was pointless even to dream of acquiring more – all contact with Paris had been lost. In 1932 my great-grandfather was finally overtaken by the fate from which he had been granted such a long respite. The authorities launched the so-called Engineers' Case, nowadays almost completely forgotten. Grigory Speier found himself one of the suspects and was arrested. He hanged himself in prison. Such, at least, is the official version. Whether it is true or whether the suicide was staged remains unknown. His youngest daughter,

Lydia, unable to endure her father's death, died herself as a result of a mental illness that flared up. Grigory's property was confiscated. Only the Taxiphote, the archive of stereoscopic photographs, and the desk survived by some miracle. The two oldest daughters, Faina and Margarita, kept these relics at their home in Kolomna and in 1972, sensing that death was already close, they passed them on to my father, Kirill Mamonov. I saw the sisters a couple of times in my childhood – they were very wrinkled, little old ladies, but the image of young Faina, created by my great-grandfather at Rechki in 1913, was already pervading my first erotic dreams. At that time I was not yet able to appreciate fully the ambiguity of the inscription made by Speier on the glass plate:

'Faina eating strawberries and cream.'

I don't believe in the transmigration of souls, but today, when I look at my wife in profile, I discern the distinctive configuration of sharply delineated cheekbones (where could the German girl Faina have acquired that?) and the piercing glance that overwhelmed me in my childhood in that stereoscopic photograph of 1913. Since that time my own life has been confounded by the magic of duality.

As Vasilie Uršič remarked, in the East two plus two does not give the same result as in Europe.

In his opinion, the difference in understanding arose because in China they arrived at the concept of 'two' at a different time and by a different route from in the European languages, when their concept of duality was formed. Uršič goes on to remark that the number two resolves itself into a singularity, because it merely reflects the dual, paired nature of our eyes. From out of singularity there arises multiplicity.

'For, not being capable of perceiving the potent actuality that is presented to it as a singularity, the spirit fragments it, breaks it

up, transforming singularity into multiplicity in order to be able
to accept it and carry it away piece by piece.' (V. Uršič)

This quotation bears the most immediate possible
relevance to my investigation, because for me the duality of the
stereoscopic image is not simply an optical trick, but a metaphor
for the understanding of history. Let me explain. As we know,
the traditional view of the historical process assumes the past to
be linear in nature, as opposed to the multiplicity of the future.
Thus, in his book *Culture and Explosion*, Yuri Lotman regards
history as a straight line in the situation when we are looking
back, and as a bundle of possibilities from out of which we
choose our future. In fixing on one of these, we are obliged to
reject everything else, which engenders trauma. And it is here,
according to Lotman, that we find ourselves in need of art,
which allows us to experience that which was never actualized.

It seems to me, however, that this picture is incorrect, first
and foremost in its evaluation of the past as linear. Experience,
and in particular our own immediate post-Soviet experience,
tells us that the past is not unidimensional. It consists of a
multitude of versions, which are frequently mutually exclusive.

But this method of considering history is by no means new.

The individual who must be acknowledged as the founding
father of this type of historical analysis is the Roman writer
Gaius Suetonius Tranquillus, the author of the famous work
The Lives of the Twelve Caesars. Suetonius employs a simple
but ingenious method, especially effective in the conditions
of political instability that were so typical of Rome in its age
of decadence. In a situation when the outcome of even the
most immediate political conjuncture was hard to predict, and
therefore the political demands made on an author could change
at any moment, in each case Suetonius gives two versions of the
biography of the Caesar concerned, clearly in the hope that at

least one of these versions will suit the powers that be. I believe, however, that this method, engendered by the constraints of circumstance, is extremely effective for the analysis of history in general. Those who, like me, were born in the 1960s in the capital of a great empire and today find themselves eking out a meager existence on the boundaries of the wild steppes, under attack by barbarian hordes, are only too familiar with the procedure of manipulating the past. But where is the Taxiphote that is capable of focusing our double vision and rendering it unitary?

P.S. When this text was already being written, I phoned my father in order to clarify certain details of the biography of Grigory Speier. I should explain that at the end of the last century I had already taken my historical queries to him and received quite comprehensive replies. I used many of the facts communicated to me by my father in the film *Caligula 2*, the one that Barbara Vanderlinden selected for Manifesta-98. My father had seen this film several times and never once said a word about any inaccuracies. Imagine my amazement when, nine years later, he informed me that Karl was not Speier's father after all, that his surname was Ermter and he was the father of Nina, Speier's wife, which means that Nina's patronymic was not Gustavovna, but Karlovna. And therefore Grigory Speier had a different patronymic, which my father could no longer recall. I didn't know which version of the story I should abide by. After all, my father had expounded the first version to me when he was sixty-one, and the final version nine years later. At first I was saddened by this. But then I realized that this fact is nothing else but a confirmation of my conjectures concerning the nature of history. Possibly this was the very moment at which the reality of life fused with the reality of the project to form a unitary space in which truth and invention have become indistinguishable.

The city outside there has no name yet, we
don't know if it will remain outside the novel
or whether the whole story will be contained
within its inky blackness.

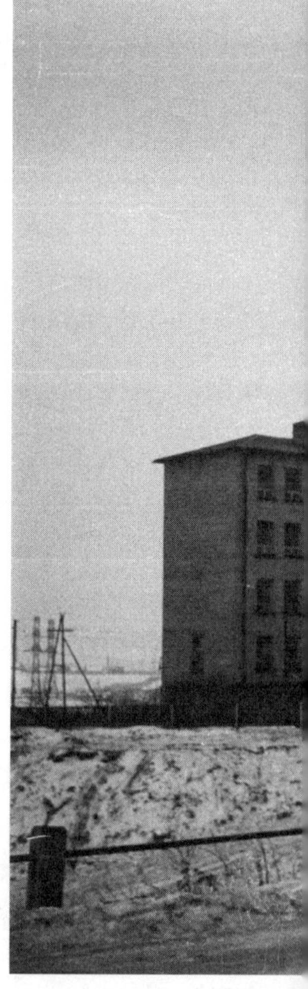

Maria Kapajeva

YOU CAN CALL HIM ANOTHER MAN (2015–2017)

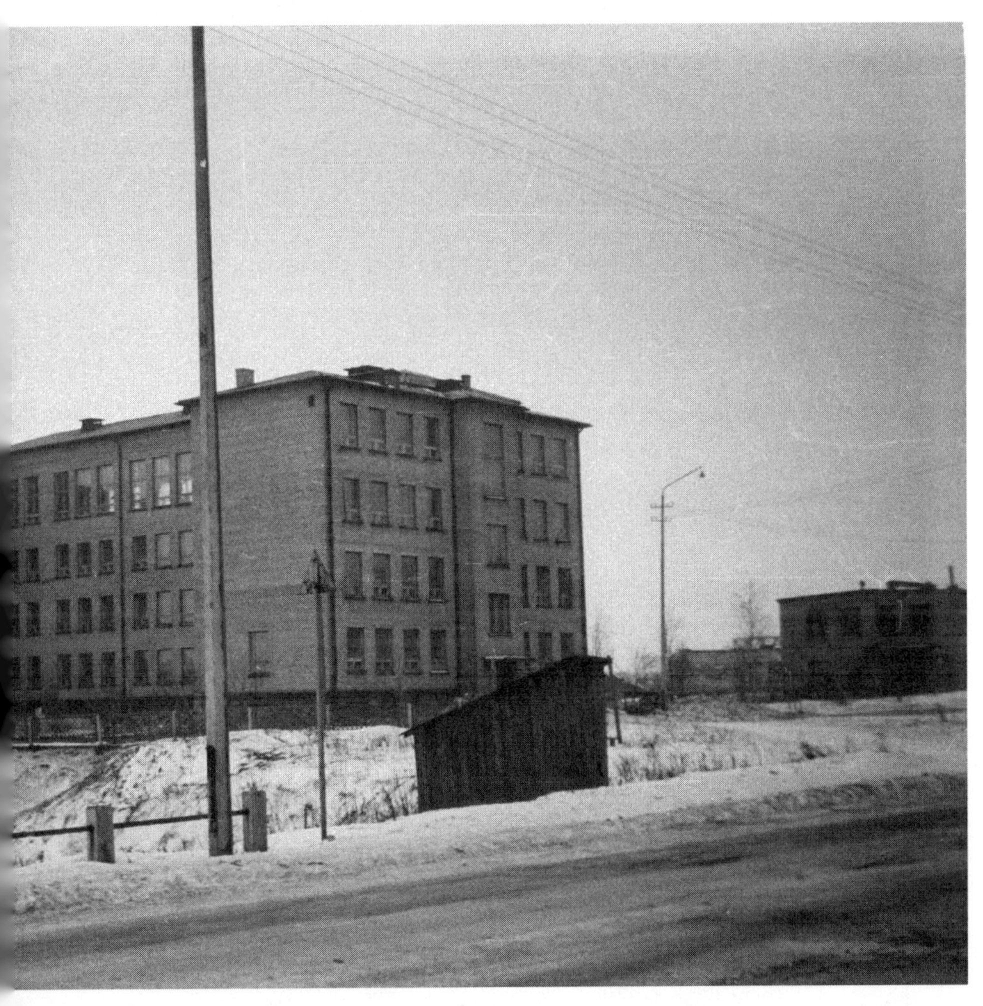

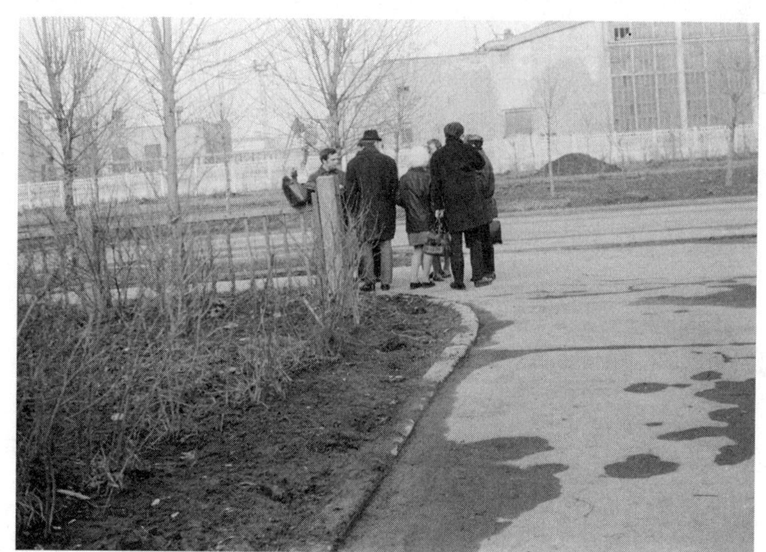

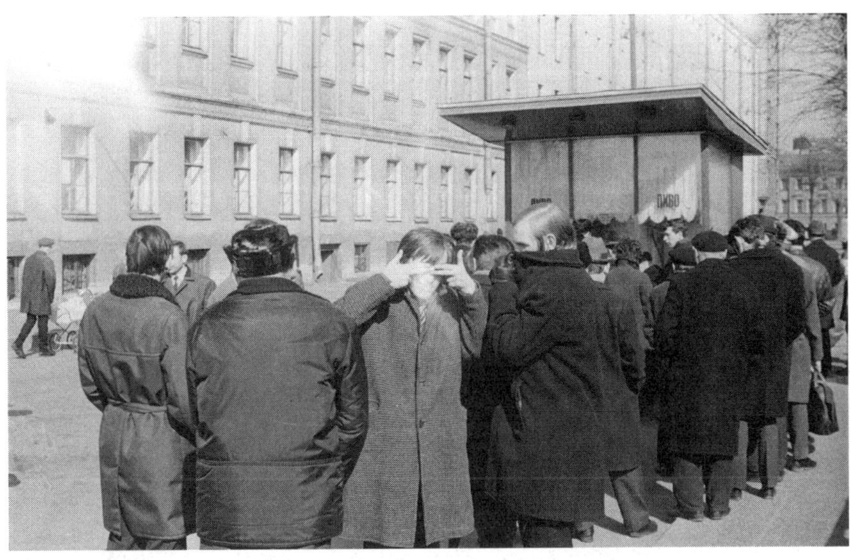

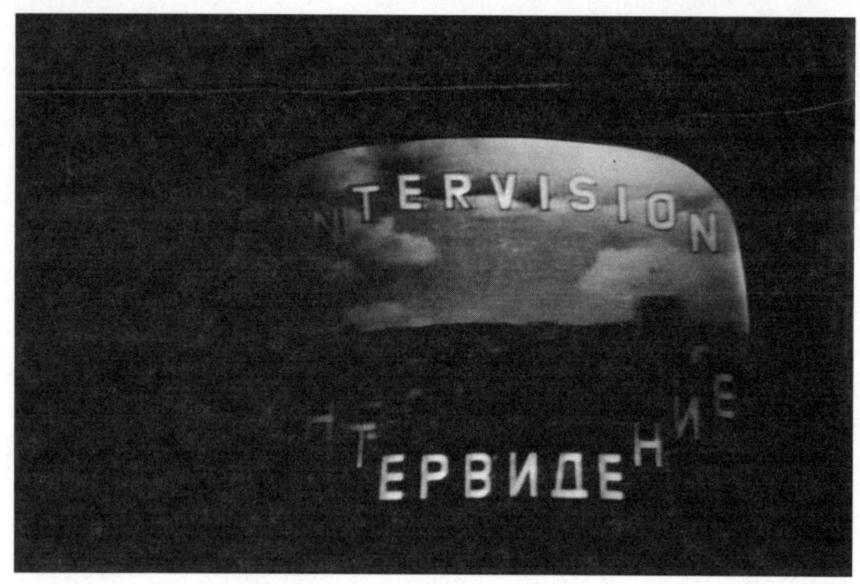
TERVISION
ТЕРВИДЕНИЕ

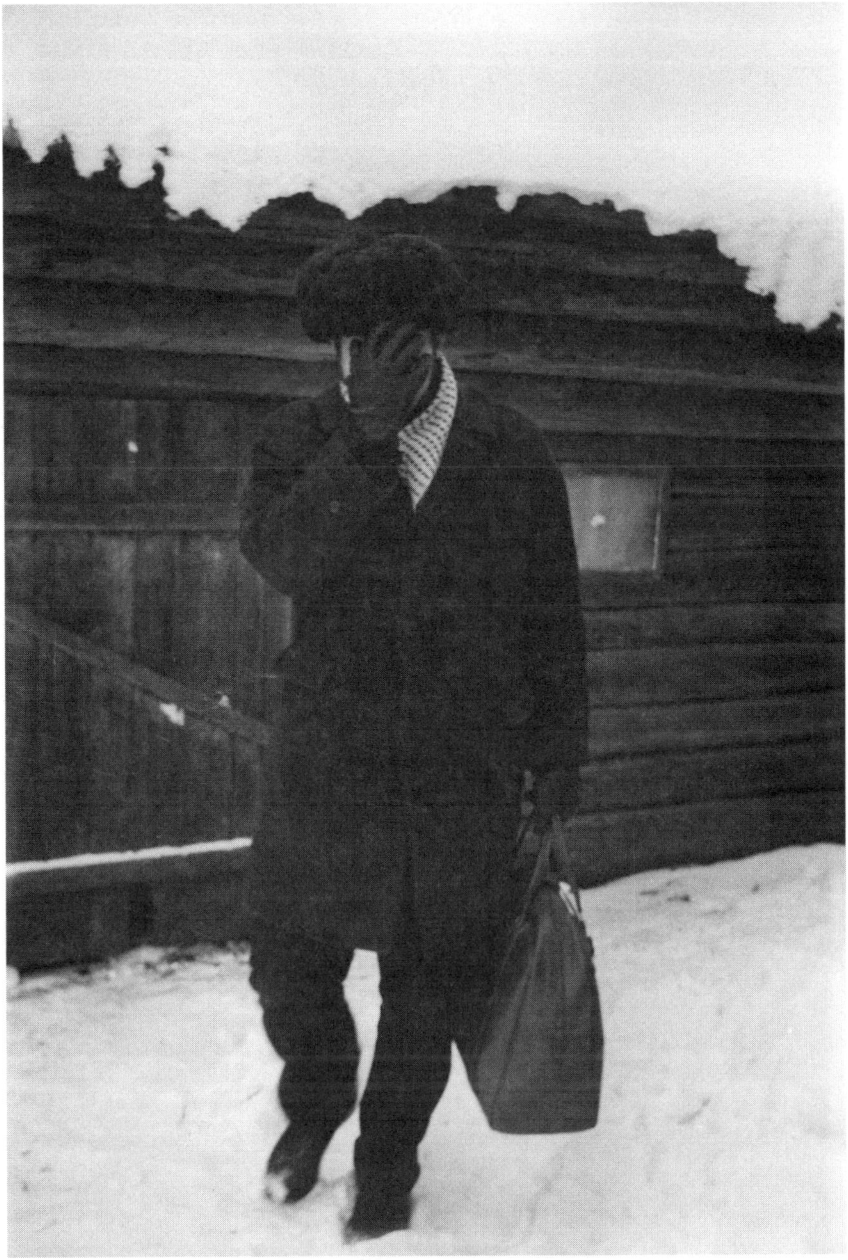

271   Maria Kapajeva   **You can call him another man**

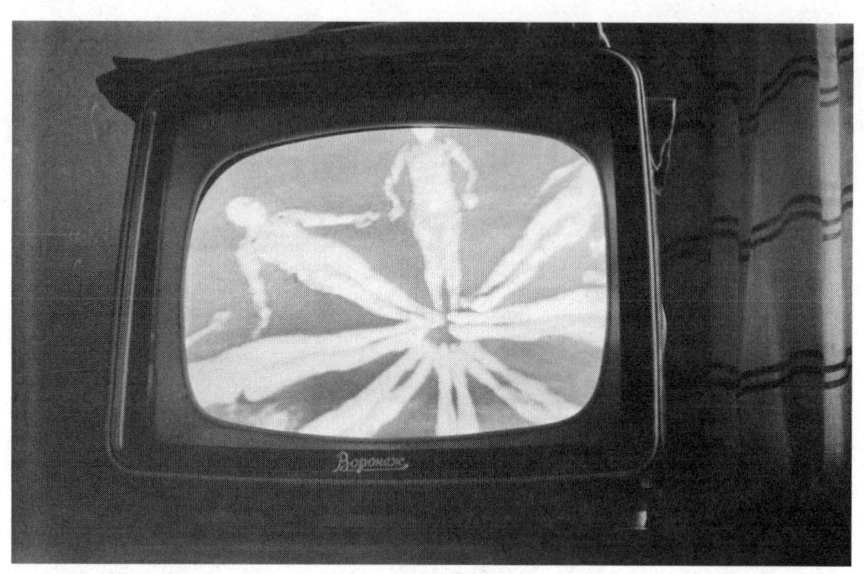

Воронеж

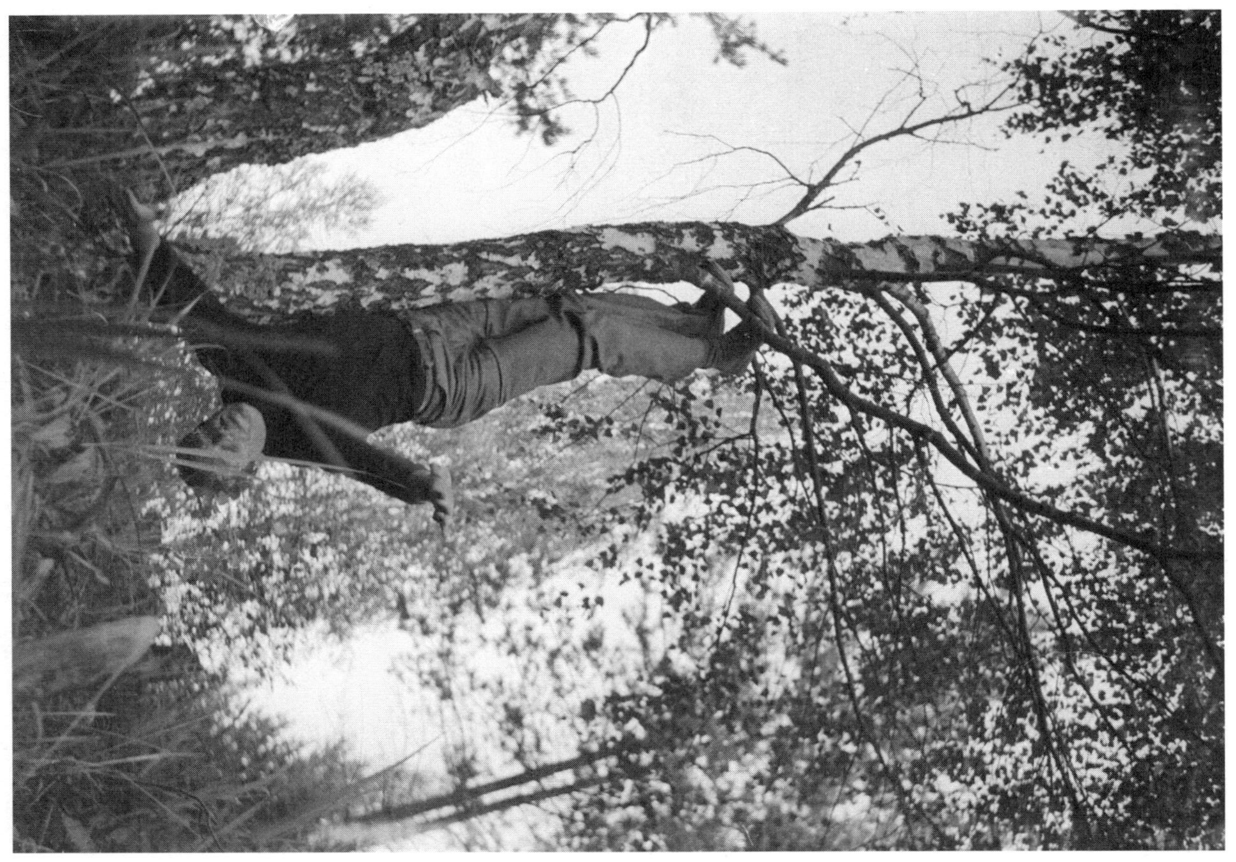

   Maria Kapajeva   **You can call him another man**

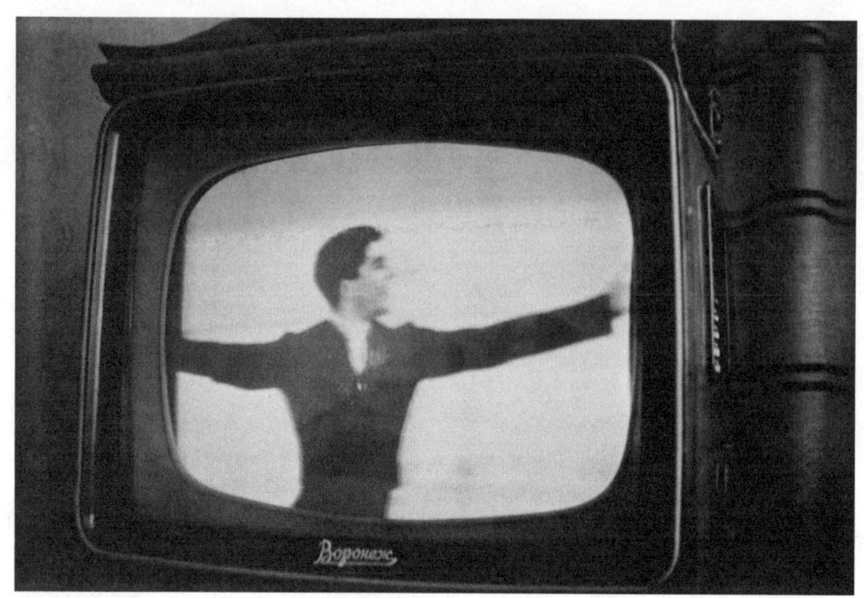

Воронеж

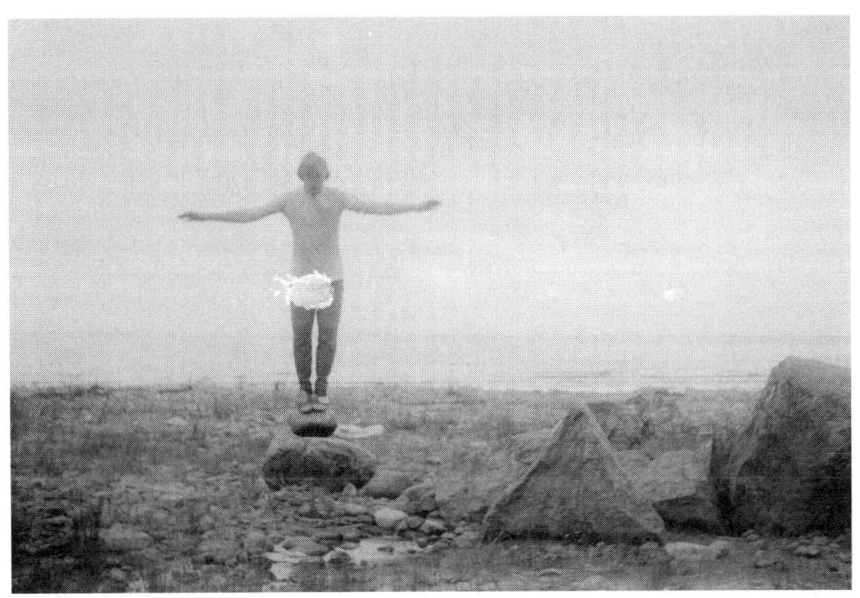

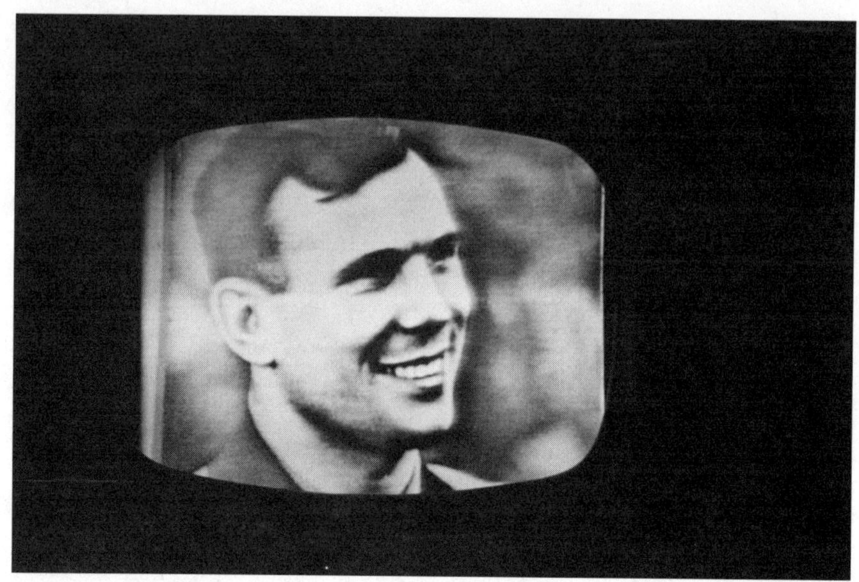

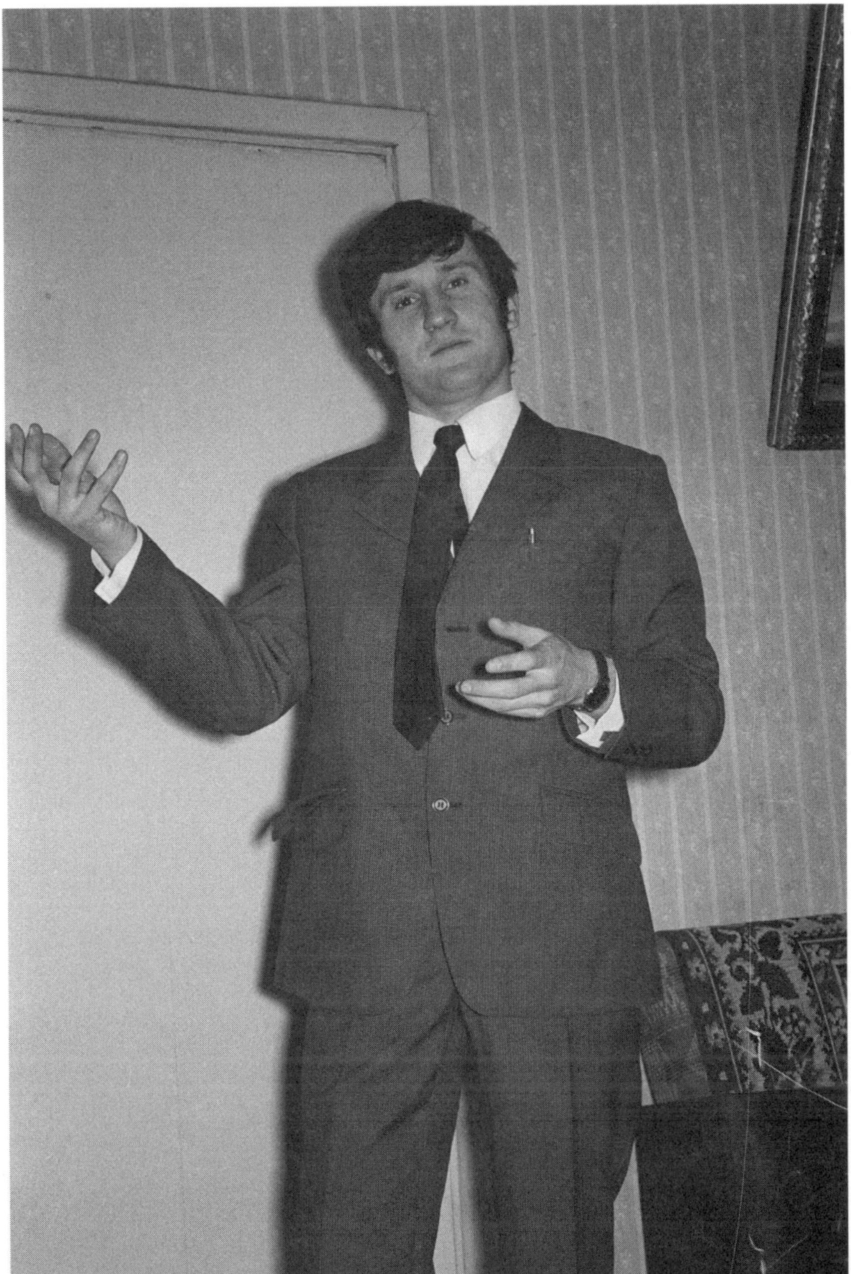

277   Maria Kapajeva   **You can call him another man**

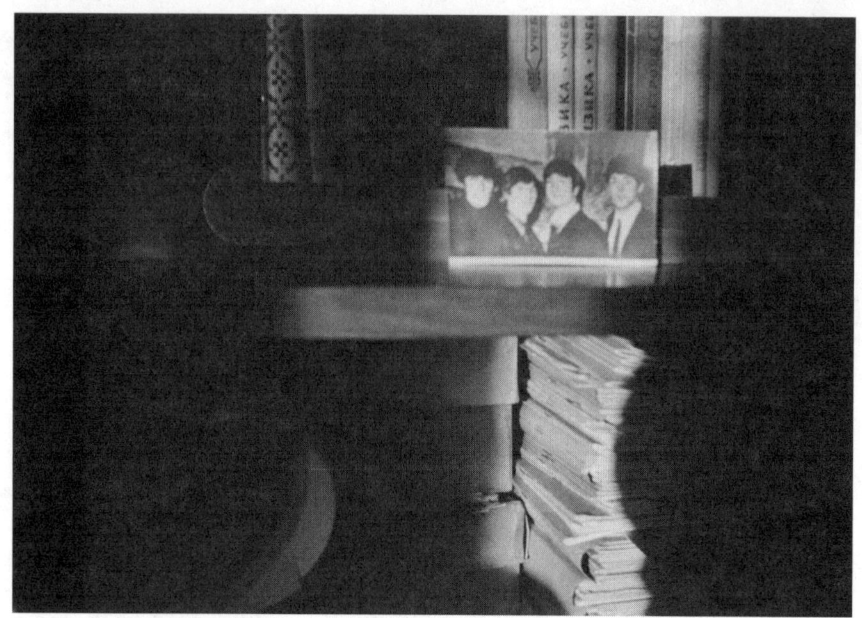

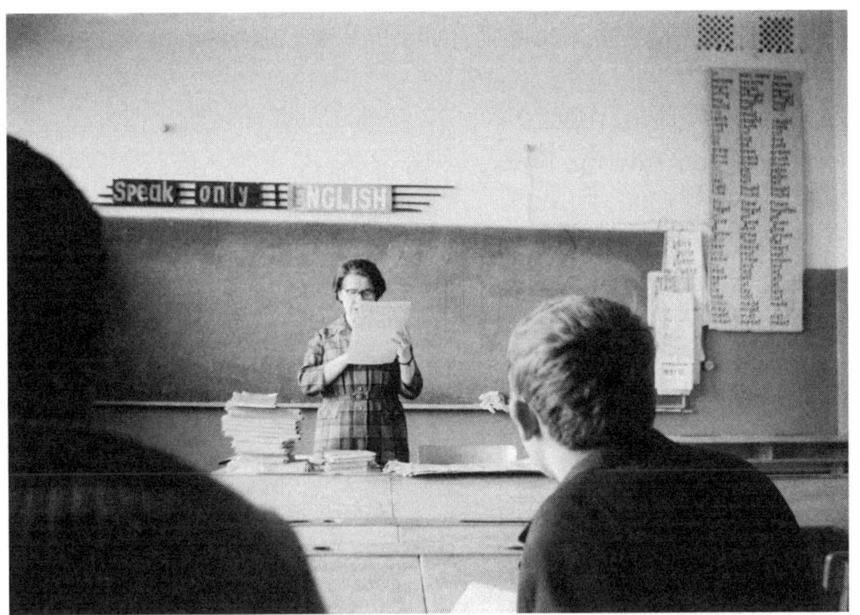

279   Maria Kapajeva   **You can call him another man**

But how to establish the exact moment in which a story begins?
Everything has already begun before, the first line of the
first page of every novel refers to something that has already
happened outside the book.

Note

The images were selected from my father's archive without his involvement.
The words above were borrowed from Italo Calvino's novel *If on a Winter's
Night a Traveller* (1998, London: Vintage, pp. 14 and 153).

The project was developed during the FATHOM residency at Four
Corners Film, London, in 2015 and it will be published as a book in 2018.

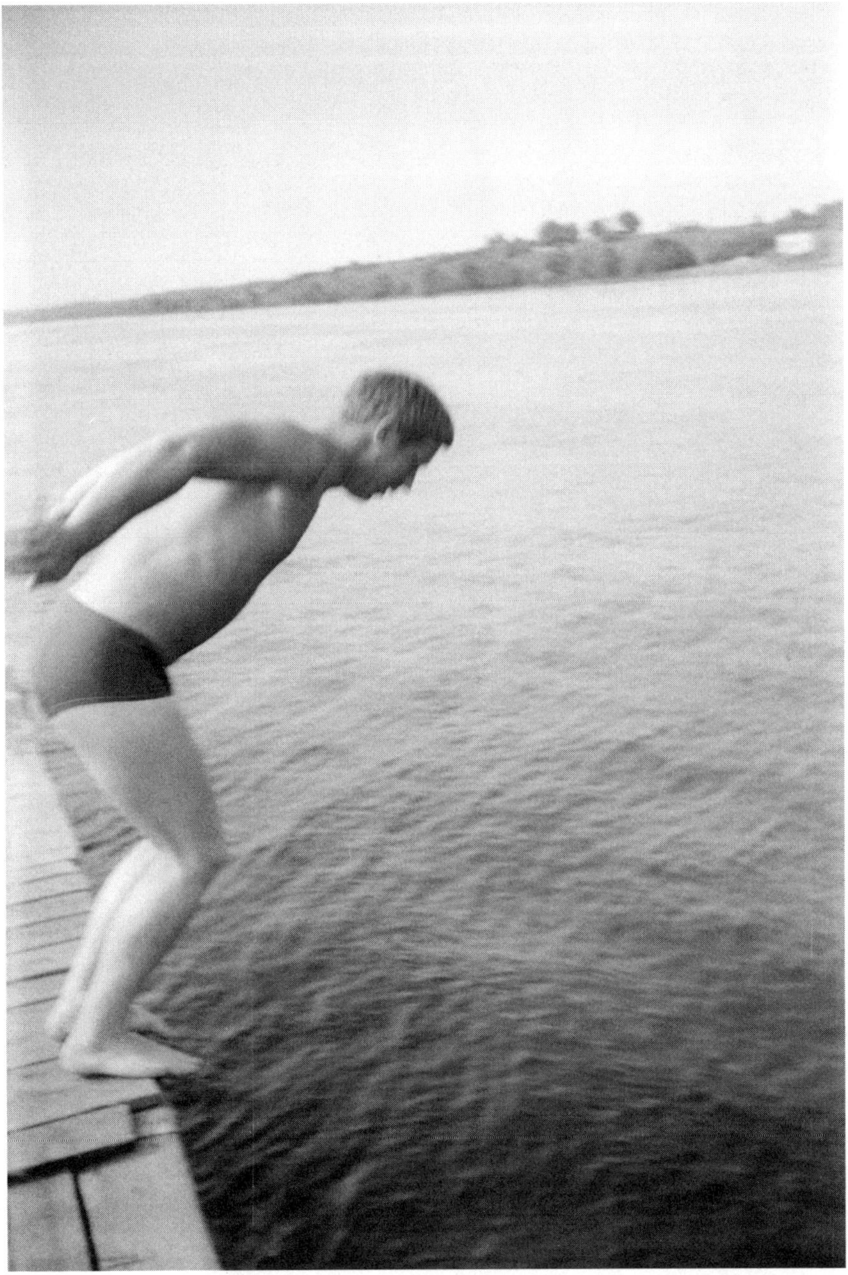

16

Andrey Kuzkin

RUNNING TO THE NEST

Nakhabino
03.06.2013

Foreword

I'm running. Where can I be running to? What am I running away from? I'm running away from everything. I could say I like everything, I could say I don't like anything – it's exactly the same. A lie. If anything, I don't like anything; if anything, it all frightens and alienates me. I struggle with it somehow, learn to tolerate it, not to notice it. Only then, I start not noticing anything and even ending up in places where I ought to feel good, but feeling the same nothing anyway. "Well, so what?" – that's the feeling.

But by force of habit my legs take me back to where I came from – back into the c**t, into the egg, into the place I saw first, and I took a good look at it and remembered it and, without even realizing, fell in love with it. It's as if it can say to me: this is you, and all the rest is not you – it can identify me with myself. Yes, this is you … and these are fir trees … and these are wild strawberries … and this is an asphalt road, reflecting the sun.

But they hurtle along the road – aliens, gleaming and glittering. They build houses here, they sell and buy, they know how to do that, they know how to live, they know how to travel around, they know how to make deals and earn profit. They're alien and there are lots of them. I'm surrounded by them and I feel uncomfortable.

They have different speeds and different interests.

But I was here before them.

I was born here.

I first saw the sun here, I saw the high, blue sky, cloudless and serene, I wallowed in the droning of dragonflies here, I examined the leaves and noticed the behavior of the birds. To this day I tremble when I hear the shriek of a swift, I used to be able to observe their flight for hours. Now something has happened. To them? To me? I can barely hear them.

Yasha, raven from my childhood, I saw you today, although not up there on top of the pylon, but still with your 'girlfriend,' you've got bigger, doubled in size. I've grown too, I called you, but you flew away. If you're lucky, you'll live your raven's life for 300 years. You watch what's happening from the outside, the way I used to know how to watch … But it's easier for you, because you're a bird. I'm on the inside, so I can't make out the whole of it. That's why it's hard, that's why I thrash about, searching for the way out, and I can't find it …

I've come here again. Have I found what I was looking for? I don't know …

Everything has molded itself into some kind of quest.

Not-very-odd oddnesses that I'm now going to try to mold into some kind of whole. What for? So as not to forget. So that I won't forget, apparently, that's all it's for.

Why is it important not to forget? I don't know … And what else do I have to remember, what else do I need to know? Oh Lord.

Forgive me and all of them. Help me and my nearest and dearest. Preserve us as human beings, the way we're supposed to be, and not empty shells with glassy, staring eyes. Don't let us become self-satisfied, stupid swine, it's so easy to become like that, allow us to preserve our souls, to preserve the genuine feelings in them, teach us to cry again …

The journey

I set out from home at about 10 in the morning. At approximately half past eleven I was at the Tushinskaya metro station. I walked out onto the railway station platform, went across to the ticket office, and asked for a return ticket to Anikeevka.

"There aren't any trains!"

Bewildered, I asked:

"Where have they all got to?"

"There's a gap!"

"So when's the next one?"

"At 13.10."

I go to look for a bus …

I walk out into the square and read the names of the stops on the schedules in the minibus shuttles – bold, red, stencilled letters – I need to ask someone.

Suddenly I hear familiar words – "Nakhabino, Anikeevka …" – and I turn round … A young girl in the same situation as me, she's missed the train and is asking a red-necked shuttle driver how to get to Nakhabino or Anikeevka … I say: "That's where I'm going too."

The driver explains where the bus stop is – we go there. We walk into the ticket office, the time is about 12 o'clock. The biddy there says the bus should have come at 11.35, but it hasn't arrived yet. We buy tickets for it. We walk outside and the bus immediately drives up. People crowd around. Eventually we clamber in too. We sit on different double seats, almost all the places are taken. Off we go. The bus's air conditioning is working, but it hardly cools the air at all, the women sitting in front of me ask the driver to open the ventilation hatch in the roof. After a bit of bickering, he agrees, turns off the air conditioning and opens the hatch. It gets significantly hotter (at least, that's how I feel), but the women are happy – they got what they wanted. For the rest of the way after that they discuss vegetable-plot business – tomatoes, onions, etc. For instance, about how you have to sprinkle salt on the soil to stop the weeds from growing. A woman who looks like the mother of the only girl I ever managed to pick up in the metro in my youthful days says that somewhere, either Krasnodar or Ukraine, she saw boundless fields of incredibly green, hardy onions, and they really do water them with salt water there. Although the next year they use a different field and the first one rests and rids itself of the salt. I think about my own 'bread-and-salt' figures. Levashov had the idea of calling the exhibition they were in 'Salt of the Earth.' I catch myself thinking how stupid it is to spend your time on a vegetable plot in the modern world. But I immediately pull myself up short: what isn't it stupid to spend your time on, working out crosswords? There is evidently some kind of urge towards a primeval state in this. The women spend time on the vegetable plot, and the men go fishing …

The girl going my way tries to find out if the bus stops in Nakhabino. I say it pretty certainly does. She's going to the hospital to see her granddad, and she has to meet up with her granny somewhere on the way. She talks to her granny on the phone. It turns out that her granddad has been moved to an ordinary ward. My grandfather died in the Krasnogorsk hospital when I was about the same age as she is now (the end of school and the start of college). I think about that. I say I'm getting off at Anikeevka myself and if she likes, I can see her to the station. But apparently she's afraid of me (my head is shaved and I have stubble sprouting on my chin) and she declines. I get out at the turn for Anikeevka and the bus drives away with the girl.

I cross the Volokolamsk Highway at a traffic light and walk towards the Anikeevka railway station. For about half a kilometer. I imagine that if the girl had agreed to walk with me and I turned out to be a psycho, I really could have dragged her into the woods here, after putting my hand over her mouth first. But she declined, and I'm not a psycho, so I stop thinking about it.

I get to the station. The place is deserted apart from an elderly man standing by the steps with a winter fishing-tackle box, summer rods in a case and a stick. I ask him: "What's up, no trains?" He says: "I don't know, what time is it?" I take out my phone and look – it's 12.50. "Yes," I say, "the first one won't set out from Tushino until 13.10." He says regretfully: "I should have stayed and done a bit more fishing …" I say: "That's for sure" – and I smile.

I ask what he caught and where.

He says in classic style: "Not much, sod it …"

"Roach?"

"No, little carp …"

"But where?"

"Right here."

And he points to the woods.

"But I didn't know there was a pond here, I only know the Nikolo-Uryupino ponds …"

He smiles.

And with that we say goodbye …

The man hobbles along the railways tracks in the direction of Nakhabino and I walk towards the village of Anikeevka.

There

Immediately after Anikeevka there used to be a stream that flowed from the Nikolo-Uryupino ponds, but it ran into a bog here and ended in another little pond. Now they're filling it in, forming new land for building dachas on. But the water's breaking through somewhere from under the layer of clay and sand and flowing along the gutter beside the road. Concerned-looking men, apparently from the construction office, are squatting on their haunches, watching the water, making notes about something and photographing the stream with a mobile phone. Apparently they have to eliminate this leakage.

I walk on. I look at the blue sky and the tops of the fir trees, I have a good, calm feeling. I walk as far as the way into the woods, where we left our shoes a year earlier (*Manipulator, a shifting of values*, 1,2). I force my way through the raspberry bushes, as I did a year ago. Only this time I'm alone. And that sense of elation is missing. My mother calls. I say I'm taking a walk; when she asks: "Where?" I answer "It's not important."

I find a few pairs of shoes and the tree stumps we sat on to watch videos a year ago.

The shoes look fairly fresh, they've just grown a bit deeper into the moss. But then most of the fir trees have dried up and are standing there dead. I'd noticed that earlier, when my mother and I went to the cemetery close by to visit my father. They've been attacked by some kind of blight. It's sad.

Event number one – the manipulator mirror

I walk back out of the woods onto the road and walk on, and then the first unusual event occurs.

I see a 'Manipulator' sign on a tree, exactly the same as the one I saw the first time in the winter of 2012 opposite the spot where it was later decided to perform the action with the shoes, and later, during the second part of that action, in June 2012, it disappeared.

Afterwards Masha and Volodya [M. Sumnina and V. Machinsky – *editor's note*] and I saw it when we were performing the "Green Swing" action, but in a different spot, closer to the swing. I still remember Masha saying then that it had moved.

This time I decided to take it away with me. I took out the lower nail and then I saw that the reverse side of the manipulator was a MIRROR. That astounded me. It was genuinely amazing. I started photographing and videoing the sign, from different angles, trying to catch my reflection in its reverse-surface mirror. But on one nail it started spinning in the wind and dodging away all the time, reflecting bits of the woods from behind me. Yes of course, they had some pieces of mirror-surface plastic they didn't need, and they printed their sign on the reverse side, but that's really not important, is it? … The important thing is that the manipulator acts like a mirror, it reflects everything, basically, that's really cool.

Event number two – the green swing

I took down the sign, attached it to my backpack with the mirror side outwards and moved on, feeling pleased. Now I was walking towards the swing.

The route we followed to get there the first time in winter proved impassable, there was standing water everywhere … The alphabet of hollow green letters, nailed to a fir tree to indicate the entrance to the zone of the action, had disappeared. I walked round to the left of a ditch filled with water and moved straight towards a break in the trees on the opposite side of the clearing. It was a bit drier here, I only occasionally had to jump over puddles that were deep, but not very wide.

AND THEN I SAW IT. An involuntary gasp burst out of my chest – "Ah!"

The swing was hanging exactly where we had left it.

That means it wasn't a dream, that means it was all real.

That means something does exist and something continues to preserve memory.

I cannot describe the extent of the joy and astonishment that I felt at the sight of the green swing.

In addition to the swing, almost everything else had survived – the mirror cap, the glasses, the raincoat (it had simply fallen off the knot on the tree onto the ground), the auction figures on little legs in the tin can were standing in the same place. They had got soaked and faded, but they were still there. The book *Psychology* [author unknown – *editor's note*] was lying under the swing. In the damp, some of the pages had crept out of it a bit, but the text was perfectly readable. I picked up one of the pages that was lying in a conspicuous place and read what it said. The text dealt with decision making and implementation – about intentions and actions, will and infirmity of will. For some reason, the example adduced was a tenth-form schoolboy, or rather "a pupil of X class" (and the figure 10 really was given as a Roman numeral), planning a trek in the Altai Mountains for his school holidays. The text considered how he would prepare and train before his trip.

(By the way, my five-year-old son has developed a very strange trait: he wants to plan everything and know everything that is going to happen to him in advance, and then follow the plan that has been drawn up precisely and undeviatingly. He's always irritating everyone by asking "And what are we going to do after that, and tomorrow, and the day after tomorrow …" etc.)

The article on decision making concluded by saying that people should be judged by their actions and not their intentions. Naturally, I decided this text was addressed to me. That it was rebuking and scolding me. Saying I plan a lot, but don't do much, and don't do it very competently …

I phoned Masha and, without saying hello, read her the text and hung up …

"The volition of desire:
I was riding along the beautiful embankment on my bike
and I stuck my hand in my pocket – to take out my phone and call you and tell you about it –
and the phone rang in my hand."

Then I hung about under the swing for a bit longer, took some photos and shot some video. I only managed to find two of the groups of objects: one with the 'attention' notice, the other with the metal objects No. 16. And something had been added to the metal objects – a dilapidated penknife that wasn't there to begin with. They were all lying on a big tree stump. And in addition, under the pine tree on the right I discovered a little toy rubber galosh from a doll, one of the items rejected by Masha. It rhymed quite excellently with the real shoes I'd seen earlier that day.

And that set me thinking that while, in the action with the shoes (*Manipulator, a shifting of values* – 1,2) the drama of death and oblivion was real, here it had become toylike; that play, if it hadn't actually defeated this horror of death, had reduced it exponentially.

Missing items included: the explanatory note (a printed insert from the book *Psychology*) that had been torn off the tree, and also the instructions from the fire brigade. I also didn't find the book *Problems of Psychological Health in Children* [author unknown – *editor's note*].

As I was leaving, I photographed the swing again from a distance.

On emerging into the sunny clearing, out of the corner of my eye I spotted something yellow fluttering about. I thought it was a butterfly and turned towards it, but it immediately slipped out of my field of view, and then, as soon as I started walking forward, it appeared again, I spun round again, and it disappeared again. This was repeated several times before I realized that it wasn't a butterfly, but a spot of sunlight cast by the manipulator mirror fastened to my backpack. And naturally the spot disappeared when I turned away from the sun. I took off the backpack and spent quite a long time admiring the bright spot of light, shining it into the grassy shade.

That concluded the visit to the swing and I decided to go to the place where the wooden pylon with the ravens' nest on the top stood in 1985 – the pylon above which, as testified in the diary of spring kept by my grandfather and me, "the raven Yasha performed his mating display."

…

The journey to that place was filled with various events.

I now find myself thinking that I want to give these places new names of their own. "The shoes," "the swing," "the corner of three," "Yasha," or "Yasha's Pylon." Everything really is turning into a quest. Space is being mythologized. A kind of fairytale world is being created, an exclusion zone that protects me and preserves my soul.

At the beginning of the journey – from "the corner of three" (the action "The Three") – I thought about a big, red letter A that I had wanted to install on the left of the road, but I felt that the letter A's time was over or, perhaps, on the contrary, it hadn't arrived yet. On the right of the road, closer to the turn for Nakhabino, I had wanted to perform an action in honor of Gudym Alpeev, but he actually hadn't found his place here either.

When I'd almost reached the turn for Nakhabino, on the left of the road I saw a fallen wooden pylon like Yasha's, only smaller. It reminded me once again of the goal of my journey. The pylon was lying there, draped across an old electric transformer booth, and I took several photographs of it. I remember my grandfather warned me about a boy who was playing hide and seek and hid in a transformer booth and got burnt to death. I don't know if it was that particular booth or another one, but in my mind it was precisely that one.

The booth's interior was empty now, and I could look at the woods through it. Here I turned off towards the sign that said NAKHABINO at the entrance to the village and photographed it. Now in my own mind I dubbed it "the sign of the shout." Beside this sign, on 1 March 2012, after the action with the shoes (*Manipulator-1*) I tried to yell over the roaring of the cars "YOU ARE ONLY WHAT IS THERE BESIDE YOU!" and Kostya recorded a video of it that didn't go into anything afterwards.

After visiting the sign, I turned round and walked in the opposite direction – towards the spot where "Yasha's Pylon" used to be. At the beginning of the road I came across a children's board game with some kind of alphabetical puzzles that had been dumped. I photographed it thoroughly in the hope of making sense of this later.

Event number three – the red-dotted wood

AND THEN THE NEXT EVENT OCCURRED: on the left of the road I noticed red dots on the trees, made with spraycan paint. They were on almost all the trees. This phenomenon intrigued me greatly and put me on my guard

The first version of the machine action "You Are Here" involved hanging signs with red dots on them on the trees. This was a direct reference to that action. It looked rather frightening and mystical. I wandered through the red-dotted wood and on the half-rotted support of a telegraph pole I suddenly saw the Russian word НЕГР ('negro'); because it was written vertically, at first I read it as *HELP*. I don't know exactly what the author of the inscription and the dots had in mind, but it all looked terrifying. I walked on deep into the wood, but the dots still didn't come to an end. The trees marked with dots were alive and dead, thick and thin.

On one tree I came across the inscription "V 5" and an arrow pointing downwards. I walked on further and the dots started becoming faded, they had clearly been made earlier, and then they gradually disappeared. In that red-dotted wood I also came across a rubber boot standing all alone, the packaging from a condom and a broken baby carriage.

I went back to the road. I was all tensed up inside. Further on along the road the trees had the same kind of dots on them, on one I counted 26, and on another I saw the inscription "Vis 13" and an arrow pointing down.

Event number four – the triang

When I reached the clearing where the pylon used to be, I calmed down a bit. Especially since the trees with the dots were on the left of the road, and the clearing was on the right. There was an old, improvised boom blocking off the entrance to the clearing – two low pillars with a log laid across their tops. This is a classical gate, or an American Indian altar, I thought, and no danger lies beyond it. I took a deep breath and walked in behind the 'gate.'

(When I was performing the action "To Be an Artist is to Be an Indian" near Samara, I studied Amerindian life a bit. Inside the tepee an altar is placed in front of the fire opposite the entrance. This is two forked sticks, across which a third stick is placed to form a gate. The altar has to be sprinkled with ashes from the fire and may be decorated with feathers and all sorts of other stuff. After living in a tepee for a week, I experienced for myself how the altar inside it organizes the space and has a calming effect. Without it, it feels as if there is disorder in the dwelling; with it everything immediately becomes snug and cozy.)

And so, I went in behind the gate. Here there was bright sunshine, peace and quiet. I knew that the pylon, which happened to resemble the framework of a teepee, had been gone for a long time. But I decided to scramble through the bushes anyway, to the place where it used to be, to see if I could find the remains of the wooden piles. So there I am, clambering through the osiers … and the second involuntary "Ah!" of the day bursts out of my chest. At the spot where the large wooden pylon used to stand, THERE IS A RUSTY, PYRAMIDAL METAL STRUCTURE ABOUT SIX METERS HIGH.

It is completely concealed from all sides by bushes and cannot be seen from either the road or the clearing at the side of it. My joy knows no bounds. I examine it from all sides. I photograph it. Precisely at its center there is a short concrete pillar driven into the ground, with a round metal medallion set into its top, and the raised letters on the medallion read: *TRIANG USSR 26769*. Now everything is clear to me. This is a triangulation point. Nikolai Lvovich Pobyl, the traveler, geodesist, geographer, historian and archivist, told me about them. (He died last year.) He used to install points like this right across the USSR. Mostly at its extreme points. In principle they are set in high places, and from each pylon it should be possible to see all the others; in that way it is possible to identify and locate on the map any point within the triangle that is formed – this is the science of triangulation, a part of geodesy. With the invention of GPRS navigation, the pylons became unnecessary. Apparently the little metal pylon deputized for a big one, and it had been preserved.

I pull myself up onto the lowest beam, dangle upside down for
a moment and scramble to the summit of the pylon. I sit on
it and smoke for about half an hour. I call Slava and tell him
about where I am right now. "Yasha's Pylon" is mentioned
in the action text "Glory for Slava." So the commemorative
symbol-sign has still not rotted away yet, it's still standing
here in the bushes, as if nothing has happened. I'm very glad.
I rise to my full height, grasp the rusty, protruding metal pipe
between my legs and stand there in silence, towering up above
the bushes for a while.

When I get down, I decide to hang the manipulator sign inside
the pylon. And I proceed to do that. I don't need to drag the
manipulator mirror home, what is this passion for dragging
everything back home, what good is it to me at home, who can
I show it to, what story can it tell to the uninitiated? My home
is here. And the manipulator should remain here. The sign
swings about elegantly inside the pylon, displaying the text and
the mirror side by turns. I photograph the pylon again, with the
manipulator in it, and go back to the road.

....

I decide to carry on and visit the sand quarry on the left at
the end of the road. At the point where the asphalted road
used to end, there is now a fence and a boom – a new dacha
colony – but the dirt track on the left has been preserved. I
walk along it. On the right are the new dachas and fences, on
the left are the woods. The manipulator has been left in the
pylon and apparently my primary mission for today has been
accomplished. There is no more mystery, no more of this tricky
action art stuff. Here and there in the wood I can still see red

dots, but they don't produce a terrifying impression on me. I reach the quarry. It is completely overgrown and has turned into a swamp. I can't see any sand. Grass and bushes are everywhere. There's no way through to the center of it. I clamber up onto the cliff and walk round the quarry to the left. This used to be a sand quarry, there used to be big puddles on its bottom, with frogs, tadpoles, leeches and even some kind of little fish living in them. They could be seen clearly on the sandy bottom. It was as if the quarry had a microcosmos of its own inside it. The wild strawberries ripened fastest of all on its slopes. Now it had been turned into swamp, I only managed to find a scattering of sand and stones on the furthest slope. It seems as if Gudym Alpeev must be lying somewhere around here.

From the quarry I decide to walk through the woods in the direction of Nikolo-Uryupino. I don't know this route, I simply imagine the approximate direction and hope to bypass any military bases lying along the way. For a long time I stubbornly force my way through the wet woods. I get my feet soaked through, jumping across the latest watery obstacle. I reach the military bases and try not to go out onto the roads; I walk through the wood. Like playing at spies. I come across a lot of moose tracks and dung. On an open area I see two gigantic ravens by an army rubbish dump. I shout out –'Yasha, Yasha' – and they fly off into the pine trees. I walk on. Beside a field fenced off with barbed wire that has a sign saying "Underground explosion work area" I find three Aspen bolete mushrooms with plastic explosive detonators for mines beside them. I walk on, get tired and scratched all over, my trainers are squelching and covered in mud. I hear the noise of a main road gradually getting louder. Shit knows where I actually am. About twenty-five minutes after I hear the noise, I finally emerge onto the

embankment of the road. It's a place I don't know. I'm thirsty.
The road is very busy (the Novorizhskoye Highway, I checked
the map afterwards), I see a signpost – a turn for Nakhabino and
Ilyinskoe in 400 meters. In the other direction, a kilometer away,
is a village and a pedestrian bridge over the highway. I go that
way. On the way I ask the guards at the Little Fir Tree dacha
colony for a drink of water. I cross the road via an underground
tunnel still under construction and climb back up. This is
Buzlanovo village. The last bus to Moscow left at 17.30. It's
seven o'clock now. I find a shop, buy an ice cream, two half-litre
colas and cigarettes. I rest. I find out from a man what buses
go from Ilyinskoe and how to walk there. I walk to Ilyinskoe
in about twenty minutes, get into a bus, and ride through the
traffic jams for a long time, periodically falling asleep, to the
Pavshino railway station. There I buy a ticket to Dmitrovskaya
metro station and keep traveling on and on and on …

……………………

I'm writing this text. What will it tell anyone? What can it
convey? Does the person reading it not get that painfully
familiar feeling – "well, so what?" And do I need this reader?
Do I need to try? To mangle and pervert language, borrow
turns of speech, put together words and jiggle my balls, which,
as everyone knows, are what actually get in a bad dancer's way.
To try to run a thread along the only possible correct path
through these doggone-blasted words. To create something
very far from resembling the original. Maybe I should start
everything again from the beginning? And shorter, faster, point
by point, syllable by syllable, in leaps and bounds?

Man, fishing rods, shoes in grass, mirror sign, manipulator,
green swing, woods, woods, woods. Red dots, help negro, rusty

pylon, scattering of sand, woods, woods, woods … Video clip consciousness, flickering pictures. Memory.

And once more and again from the beginning, from the beginning, from the beginning …

I remember … in school … maths homework … some kind of complicated example … I start solving it … and the moment comes when I realize I'm on the wrong track; the numbers acquire eight-figure tails after the full stop, I've already covered three pages with them, and it's absolutely clear that I've made a mistake somewhere, but I carry on struggling doggedly with them, trying to make the answer fit the one in the textbook, feeling a morbid kind of excitement rising.

Eventually, of course, I give up …

I take a fresh sheet of paper … and it turns out that everything is solved in only two moves, three at the most.

But that pile of pages lying on the table, covered in incorrect calculations, is still exciting somehow.

There seems to me to be some mystery concealed in this deluded raving, the jittery scrawl looks a lot more interesting than the neatly traced-out correct answer.

Let it be the way it is. Let it be. For the time being let it be.

17

Masha Sumnina

BRINK, KERBSIDE, FENCE, MARGIN

13 June 2016. The search for the site of Slogan-1977

"I DON'T COMPLAIN ABOUT ANYTHING AND I
LIKE EVERYTHING, EVEN THOUGH I'VE NEVER
BEEN HERE AND I DON'T KNOW ANYTHING
ABOUT THESE PARTS."
Slogan-77, Collective Actions Group, 1977

Because I'm really smart, I decided to forestall any possible
pre-journey insomnia and I took a sleeping pill.

As I sank into a sweet sleep, I came to a sudden halt at the
kerbside between consciousness and the bottomless gulf of the
unconscious. The gulf of the irrational gaping open on one side;
systemic consciousness pressing up against me from the other.
I froze, dumbfounded by the mechanism that had been revealed
to me in all its might.

"And what if something like this can happen without any
pill, simply in ordinary daily life, and then suddenly you're
not watching this from the *kerbside*, but you get sucked in

immediately, like a waterfall falling from a dam. That's how people go insane, isn't it," I thought. And I couldn't fall asleep any longer. All night until morning. Because I'm really smart.

(When Shura and I tried mushrooms in our young days, I thought: "The little hedgehog was walking along, forgot how to breathe and died" – and I instantly forgot how to breathe. It was a good thing that just then Shura spoke up and I was distracted by her idea that the ambulance crew would find us and realize what we'd died of and we'd be ashamed.)

Anyway, I took another pill, and then some sedative drops, it was getting light and I was still observing oneiroidal pictures, balancing on the *kerbside* and finally and absolutely not getting to sleep.

In the morning I switched on the television and there was a program about dolphins, who, as we know, sleep with half their brain.

I put on the red dress and took my white dress and a red ribbon.

At last everyone has gathered. Shura's laughing and waving a shapeless red robe, Volka is concerned about the signs falling, Kuzkin was hammering in a nail at four in the morning.

Misha drives us there out of coerced compassion, because I can't take the wheel.

The road to the lake by car is blocked off by fences. There are fences everywhere here, but between them there are very nice people, who showed us the right gap, which we sneaked through and reached the lake.

We took photographs on the *brink*, looking at the gulf of the *waterfall*, imitating the 1977 photo:

We made camp at the lake on Artyom Beach, where it was not recommended to swim but, of course, we took no notice. Shura covered herself in the loose red robe and started flitting about, and I pressed the button on the camera. Shura flitted about on land, and then in the water, then with the light shining through. Very beautiful.

But then not one of the 100 shots came out. Because the camera had to make two clicks – sort of before the event and after it. Kerbside.

Easily overcoming this debacle, we walked up to the top of the hill and set off along a path. The path led us to yet another fence. We went back to a clearing on the hill and I, full of determination, not giving a damn for the nettles and my bare legs under my special red action dress, dashed into the thickets, trying to spot the open spaces of 1977 through the branches. They weren't there.

I was scurrying up and down the slope, comparing the view with the photograph, when Kuzkin overtook me and set off friskily along the river bank. We found a couple of places that could have been the same ones, but the number of fir trees was different from what it was then.

We decided to start all over again and went back to the pond. An elderly couple in white greeted us politely. I asked them if they had been here in 1977.

No.

We ran into another fence, climbed over it, puffing and panting, and immediately found a hole in it. But we didn't find the right place.

We decided to come in winter, when the riotous foliage had subsided.

We went back to the beach. Shura won't give up – she put the loose robe on again, altered the settings in the camera and handed it to me.

I pressed the button, Shura fluttered her red wings, sent up sprays of water, floated and flitted.

Very beautiful.

But then not one of the 100 shots came out. Because the camera had to make two clicks – sort of before the event and after it. Kerbside.

At this point I started getting the feeling that I had somehow, somewhat, kind of got snagged on a fence, dangling by my trousers.

The time came to wind up the expedition. We set off back to where we'd come from, and suddenly came across the same elderly couple, walking towards us. The old guy was in white, with a red bag and playing a mouth organ. Shura, Volka and Misha walked on past them.

"Did you find 1977?" the old lady asked.

And the old guy suddenly turned towards Kuzkin and me and started reciting his own poetry – the beginning was about how the past can't be brought back, but I videoed the rest of it anyway.

What I had intended to do there concerned my borderline presence/absence in these parts. I was present at the hanging of Slogan-77 as an embryo. Even then I probably didn't complain about anything.

In total:

2 photographs conceived, but not shot, about my presence/absence.

200 photographs shot, but not taken, with Shura in her robe.

1 photograph shot from a precisely identified 1977 spot, but which the participants forbade me to show in public.

A golden pencil found.

Half of the old guy's poem recorded.

https://www.youtube.com/watch?v=2lHn10K1lXE

And that night an incredible thunderstorm gaped wide open.

Truenottruenottruenottrueskyblue

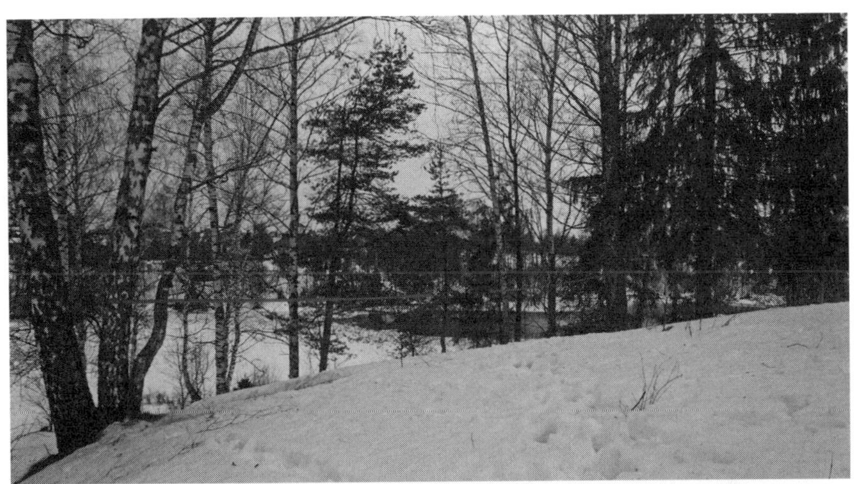

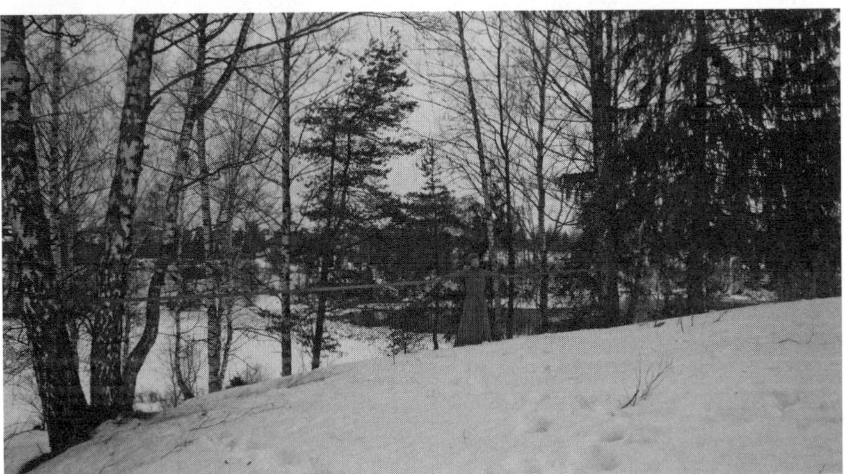

Photographs taken in March, when everything worked. 2017:
photo 1 "I am not here"; photo 2 "I am here"

Part Four

Russia, today

The work of any contemporary artist is always immediately inscribed in politics.

What choice is there for the artist to make between political and activist work, and making work 'politically' in Russia? Is the artist purely a subject of cognitive labour, or is she a part of a collective with an ability to open up new political dimensions?

18

Ilya Budraitskis

A HERITAGE WITHOUT AN HEIR

It would seem that the hundredth anniversary of the revolution could not have come at a more inopportune moment for Russia. The colossal scale and universalist ambitions of that event are fatefully at odds with the present-day condition of a society that is wallowing in apathy and mired in a state of continuous, mounting crisis. And the more steadily Russian post-Soviet capitalism continues moving in this direction, the more aggressively its propaganda apparatus carries on rehearsing, over and over, the rhetorical figure of an 'eternal present,' presenting itself as a synthesis of all of Russia's previous national history.

The 'eternal present': the Russian version

The Kremlin's vigorous historical policy (which takes the place of actual political life) is based on the idea of a struggle to preserve a heritage that is under constant attack by external competitors and internal enemies. This is an artificially created version of national history as 'empty,' mythological time, in which everything is repeated and people's actions are deprived of all autonomy. The only history that exists is the history of our forebears – of rulers and their faithful subjects. This is a Russia that is reproduced in every one of their heroic feats or crimes, a Russia that demands only devotion to itself. This kind of devotion is capable of justifying any action at all and it leaves no room for choice.

In this schema the year 1917 does not contain anything that is principally new and it is reduced to an already known pattern: here also we have the devious machinations of neighboring countries, the moral forces of internal resistance, a thousand-year-old state imperilled. And it is from this precise combination that the genuine spiritual 'meaning' of the conflicts of the revolution can and must be extracted, a meaning that was beyond the comprehension of the actual participants in events, but is well known to every present-day employee of the Minister of Culture. It is important to grasp this meaning, not only as part of a heritage, but also as practical guidance on how to avert revolutionary excesses in the future. The revolution is a legitimate part of our history, which must never be repeated. This is the practical truth that the government recommends us to grasp in this new year of 2017. This, precisely, is the 'objective assessment' of the Russian Revolution for which Vladimir Putin appealed to the participants in the Congress of Russian Historians a year ago.[1]

Such an appeal for 'objective assessment' accords with the most universal function of ideology, which is intended to justify the existing state of affairs as the only one that is possible. Ideology is rigid, devoid of dynamism, it does not have a history of its own – since its very significance is to secure hard and fast the point of 'here and now' from which this 'objective assessment' becomes possible.

While for the Kremlin's official narrative the fact of the revolution is transcended through the completeness of the present, which asserts its right of historical succession, for the liberal opposition intellectuals, on the contrary, the specter of communism remains the curse of an incomplete modernity. According to the anti-communist narrative that is widespread among a significant part of the intelligentsia, Russia cannot rid itself of its criminal past by becoming a 'normal country' – i.e. by sharing unreservedly in the principles of the ideological consensus of global capitalism. It is proposed to exorcise the specter by means of a radical purge – both on the symbolic level (so-called 'decommunization' on the model of other postsocialist countries) and through moral 'repentance' (the collective acknowledgement of responsibility for the sins of previous generations).

Today, a hundred years on, the two attitudes to the revolution that exist in the public space of Russia – the official conservative approach and the liberal, anticommunist one – look like two different versions of farce. The official formula of an 'historical Russia' substitutes a false spectacle of 'national reconciliation' for the genuine drama of a revolution, the victory of which ultimately led to the re-creation of a repressive state. As for the appeals for repentance and 'decommunization,' they look like a charade of moral purity. While the authorities propose setting up new false monuments, their opponents propose removing the old false ones. In this form the proposed purging of the falsehood and ambiguity of the past is no more than an ambiguous attempt to lend the present day the character of authenticity.

Of what, then, does this heritage consist? How can we describe and accept the entire volume of its internal contradictions – when a flat, unhistorical approach to them can easily lead to the simple absorption of one or other of the currently dominant ideological positions?

A revolution against circumstances

The course of events in 1917 was a challenge, not only to the old world, but also to the revolutionary social-democratic movement in its previous form – a movement which saw itself as no more and no less than an instrument for the realization of the laws of history. From the moment it was established, the Second International, which had proclaimed Marxism to be its official doctrine, based itself on a clear teleology of progress, in which the socialist character of a revolution was determined by necessary and inevitable preconditions. A social revolution had to be prepared by objective circumstances and it had to be the resolution of the contradictions that are inherent in the capitalist mode of production.

Thus a revolution, as an inevitability, was the direct opposite of any voluntaristic, individual impulse or chance event lying outside the major contradiction of the age (i.e. the classic antagonism between workers and capitalists). The factor of unpredictability, a kind of Machiavellian 'fortuna,' which would create the space for political choice, has been completely expunged from this concept of history. The entire sequence of events in the revolutionary process of 1917, from the spontaneous uprising in Petrograd in February to the Bolshevik coup in October, included, in addition to a combination of 'objectively' given factors – poverty, despotism, a devastating world war – another variable: the despair and determination of the masses, together with the radical, aggressive strategy of the Bolshevik Party. A strategy which included something more than sober analysis and a pure, passionate desire to seize political power.

In this sense the Russian Revolution was the direct and deadly negation of the entire preceding tradition of Marxist politics: it was a revolution in an unexpected place, with an unexpected result. This aspect of 'defiance' runs through the entire history of 1917, engendering hope and surprise in European radical dissidents within social-democracy. Thus, in April Rosa Luxemburg writes exultantly that the revolution is taking place "despite the treason and the universal decline of the working masses and the disintegration of the Socialist International."[2]

Six months later Antonio Gramsci hails the October coup in Russia as such, calling it a "revolution against *Das Kapital*."[3] For Gramsci, Russia became a place where "events have defeated ideology," and the Bolsheviks had opted for events. The unique combination of these events, which preceded the coup, repudiated the absolute determinism of the "laws of historical materialism" by giving the masses, who had liberated themselves from the dictatorship of external circumstances, an opportunity to make their own history. "Death from starvation could overtake anyone, it could strike down tens of millions simultaneously … a multitude of wills were first united by this general cause, and then acquired an active, spiritual unity." According to Gramsci, this liberating act also signified the beginning of the liberation of Marxism itself, which had previously been "corrupted by the emptiness of positivism and naturalism."[4] Gramsci concluded his text with an open appeal to return to the sources of Marxist thought, which lay in "German idealist philosophy."

One could say that in this practical appeal to classical German philosophy the revolutionaries of 1917 drew on Kant no less than they did on Hegel. Having liberated themselves from the 'dictatorship of circumstances' and refused to accept

 Ilya Budraitskis **A heritage without an heir**

circumstances as the pure and indisputable expression of historical reason, the Bolsheviks made the moral question the central one, both for the fate of the Russian revolution and for the entire dramatic history of the socialist movement in the twentieth century.

Despite the fact that class-conscious workers, organized into Soviets, were the main driving force throughout 1917,[5] the goals of the revolution and its socialist character resulted from moral and political decisions taken by the Bolsheviks. Just as the Russian revolution was not predetermined by a simple combination of circumstances that added up to a crisis, the goal of the transition to socialism did not in itself grow out of the dynamics of the class struggle. On the contrary, it was a kind of new, autonomous circumstance, a genuine moment of Kantian 'practice' – of a moral action that was based only on an inner conviction of the correctness of the decision taken. The party of Lenin accepted this moral burden of making the transition to socialism in a country which, according to all the definitions, was not ready for such a transition. The dead weight of this decision would assert itself throughout the whole of Soviet history, and without any doubt the moral responsibility for all the events of that history runs back to the crucial decision taken by the Bolsheviks to seize power in October 1917. And what is more, the question of this responsibility is legitimate only to the extent that the Bolsheviks themselves were fully aware of it. The choice made by Lenin's supporters was initially based on a tragic acceptance of the risks involved in a contradiction between goal and means that was implicit in the decision to seize state power.

This contradiction was expressed most precisely and profoundly by György Lukács as early as 1918, at the very dawn of Soviet history. In his programmatic text "Bolshevism as a Moral Problem,"[6] Lukács, a scion of a bourgeois family and recent disciple of Weber, anticipated his own later transition to Marxist positions as a consequence of the moral challenge of the Russian revolution. According to Lukács, the goal of this revolution is not determined by the revolution itself, but lies outside its specific social content. It is directed not simply towards the victory of the lower classes, but to surpassing class society as such. This is a path from the 'great disorder' of capitalism, alienation and the splintered condition of human life to universal good. Such a goal is universal, global and transcendental in relation to the circumstances of the specific historical situation in Russia. As Lukács wrote: "The final goal of socialism is utopian is the same sense in which it transcends the economic, legal and social framework of present-day society and can only be realized by destroying this society."[7]

But while the general good as the unattainable, supreme goal had always been bracketed out of the arguments for making a moral choice (for Kant the morality of the means is determined by their indifference to the goal), the Bolshevik coup brought back the problem of a just society as an inalienable element of the moral question. The goal of the Bolsheviks' conscious action in throwing down a challenge to the circumstances resulted from the materialization of the concept of the common good, which, from being an exalted, constantly elusive ideal, had to become an achievable reality, a 'real utopia.'[8]

Lukács reformulates this alternative approximately as follows: either remain 'good people,' autonomous in one's morality in relation to immoral, unjust circumstances, and wait until the conceptual general good becomes real 'through the will of all' or seize power and impose your will on these irrational circumstances. Inevitably the state becomes the instrument of this volition towards the common good, although

historically it was founded for a diametrically opposed goal.
In this way the moral problem is transformed from a personal
one into a substantial one. The state is acknowledged as an
evil which is nonetheless necessary. To use the state, which
was designed to assert inequality and injustice, for the
triumph of equality and justice, entails consciously accepting
the destruction of one's own moral integrity, deliberately
attempting, as Lukács put it, "to drive out Satan with the hands
of Beelzebub."[9] In "Bolshevism as a Moral Problem," Lukács
is still not able to identify himself completely with Russian
Leninism, while accepting the possibility of a positive answer
to the dilemma that it has posed ('Can good come from evil?')
exclusively as a consequence of 'faith'.

In effect, Lukács explains in the terms of Kant's moral
philosophy the contradiction of a workers' state, which was
formulated in the terms of Marxist theory by Lenin in *State and
Revolution*. This text was written by the leader of the Bolsheviks
in August 1917, on the eve of the seizure of power. Lenin
assumed that the state which the revolutionaries were about to
seize would cease to be a continuation of the state of the old
type, i.e. an instrument of one class's domination of the others.

On the contrary, Lenin's 'dictatorship of the proletariat'
is a 'withering state', a state with a goal that is anti-state, a
dictatorship for the sake of ending all dictatorships. This is
a force that Walter Benjamin would later define as 'divine
violence', i.e. violence that removes the conditions for the
replication of violence as such.[10] For Lenin the mission of the
new proletarian state lay in proving itself unnecessary to a
victorious class, the true class interest of which lay in dissolving
both its own domination and itself in a consciously 'organized
society'. The task of the Bolsheviks is not to reinforce the state
apparatus they have inherited from previous overlords, but to

"smash and break" it.[11] According to Lenin's thinking, such a state should not attempt to present itself as a moral force, an educator of the masses: on the contrary, it must convince these masses that they no longer need any educators.

However, while accepting responsibility for the creation of such a historically unprecedented, negative, self-negating state, the Marxists are aware of the immense danger implicit in it. Having become the stewards of the proletarian state, the revolutionaries must not cease to be aware that it as an evil (although an inevitable one for a brief transitional period). The moment this state starts believing in itself and starts seriously playing the role of a teacher of morals for a people that is not yet class-conscious, the significance of its existence will change radically. Once such a state starts perceiving itself as the good, not only will it not 'disappear', it will consume society and be transformed into a totalitarian apparatus of oppression, exploiting the argument of the common good as the basis for its own monopoly on violence.

Not only do these conclusions, which follow directly from the reasoning of Lenin and Lukács, contain a prophecy of the Stalinist dictatorship, but also – and most importantly of all – they are founded on an awareness of responsibility for its very possibility. And therefore the Bolshevik coup was not the consequence of that old, familiar, unreflecting political instinct to seize the power that has fallen out of the hands of the previous government (as the coup is often explained by banal anti-communists). On the contrary, it was a moral choice that opposed itself to the previous laws of power and politics. A choice which also incorporated an understanding of the low chances of success.

Stalinism – this victory of 'the ethical state' over the striving for an 'organized society', to use Gramsci's terms[12] – was the primary proof of this state's practical failure. However, even in the harshest conditions of totalitarian dictatorship, the moral basis of Bolshevism, its will to struggle against overwhelming circumstances, remained the reverse side of the reality of a revolution that had suffered defeat. This can be seen in the tragic struggle of the Left Opposition between 1920 and 1930, and in the interpretation of the experience of the GULAG by writers such as Varlam Shalamov. Forty years after "Bolshevism as a Moral Problem" György Lukács himself, having himself endured trials and tribulations and suffered persecution, wrote that Solzhenitsyn's *One Day in the Life of Ivan Denisovich* was the finest example of genuine "socialist realism," since the true question of "real socialism" was still the moral question.[13]

However, it is Lenin's book *State and Revolution* that must be regarded as the fundamental text of the Soviet age, and the key to the mystery of its origins. It was always something like the ghost of Hamlet's father in Shakespeare's play, hovering over the Soviet state throughout its entire history. Packed into the canon of official ideology, this book was a constant reminder of the arbitrary nature of this ideology, substantially placing in doubt, over and over again, the very right of the bureaucracy to hold power. It is no accident that on the cusp of the 1950s and 1960s many dissident youth groups were born out of a close joint reading of this book.[14]

This dual nature of Bolshevism – as moral choice and actual historical experience, as conscious practice and the overwhelming force of circumstances – constitutes its heritage in an essential, undivided form. Historical Bolshevism was an attempted answer to an irresolvable moral contradiction – the question of correct action by the individual in an incorrect, distorted reality. Admittedly, this attempt was not conclusive and it ended in defeat, but to date it is perhaps the only such attempt in modern history to have been undertaken so seriously and on such a vast scale.

Order and disorder

While the negative aspect of the heritage of the revolution, its ability to place in question any completed figures of ideology, has today been left without any obvious heirs, this heritage as a completed page of national history that has already been turned is comprehensively expressed in the actual policy of the state. For instance, in 2017 there lies in wait for us the unveiling of a monument to "reconciliation in the Civil War." The place where it will make its appearance is the Crimean peninsula, which was 'reunited' with Russia in 2014. In the words of the minister of culture Vladimir Medinsky, the future monument, "a powerful visual symbol, erected where the Civil War ended, will be the best possible proof that it really is over."[15]

However, the genuine result of the reconciliation between the revolution and its opponents, which took place a long time ago, was the Russian state itself. It was a "third power," which didn't take part in this war – "historical Russia, which has been reborn from the ashes." According to Medinsky the Bolsheviks, despite their own anti-state attitudes, "were obliged to deal with the restoration of the ruined institutions of the state and the struggle against regional separatism. Owing to their desire to organize the state, there were more strong personalities on their side than on the side of the Whites. The unified Russian state became known as the USSR and maintained almost exactly the same borders. And thirty years after the death of the Russian Empire, Russia unexpectedly found itself at the pinnacle of its military triumph in 1945.[16]

This declaration, I think, reproduces the basic conservative thesis regarding revolution, which was first proclaimed more than two hundred years ago – concerning the lack of correspondence between a revolution's awareness of itself and its true significance. Conservative thinkers were convinced of their own ability to perceive the true content of a revolution, which was concealed from the revolution's actual participants, a content determined by Divine Providence, a metaphysical national destiny or historical inevitability. This ability, as Joseph de Maistre expressed it, "to delight in the order in disorder," allowed them to perceive in every victorious revolution its ineluctable self-negation.

De Maistre wrote with satisfaction: "All the monsters begotten by the Revolution have evidently only labored for the sake of royal power. Thanks to them the brilliance of victories has caused the whole world to be filled with admiration and has surrounded the name of France with a glory that the crimes of the revolution have not been able to eclipse completely; thanks to them the King will once again ascend the throne in all the splendor of his power and, perhaps, even mightier than before."[17] While de Maistre regarded the "order of disorder" as part of a divine providence yet to be manifested, Alexis de Tocqueville discovered this providence in the reproduction by the revolution of the forms of organization against which it was supposedly directed. The French revolution "begot a new power, or rather, this power emerged of its own volition, as it were, from the ruins heaped up by the Revolution."[18] According to de Tocqueville, after clearing away everything that had outlived its time, the revolution completed the work of creating a centralized bureaucratic state that had been begun by Bourbon absolutism.

Following this logic of de Tocqueville's, one can say that via the right of succession and the development of forms of the state, the French Republic existing today is the heir, to an equal degree, of both the *ancien regime* and the revolution that overthrew it: the gulf between them is no more than an element of a revolutionary mythology that divides the nation: this mythology is a quasi-religious, millenarian faith in the ability of people to overthrow the old, sinful world through their own conscious effort and create a Kingdom of God on earth that lives according to completely different laws. A nation split apart by revolution can become aware of its continuing common history and overcome its own internal division only when it buries the destructive revolutionary religion conjointly. In this spirit, on the eve of the 200th anniversary of the Revolution, the historian François Furet, a follower of de Tocqueville, called for the completion of the French Revolution by taking a final leave of the illusions to which it gave rise. The history of the revolution has not been completed as long as the political tradition that it created, based on myth, is still alive.[19]

Entirely in keeping with this conservative approach, in present-day Russia the final completion of the Civil War and the revolution in people's minds is only possible through the total rejection of the illusions that motivated the participants in these events. The rejection of the revolutionary ambition to create a new world is capable of revealing to us the true meaning of the events of a hundred years ago and allowing us to discern the outline form of an eternal state organism that is hidden in the mist.

On the path to the "historical Russia"

Medinsky's thesis concerning a "third party" to the revolutionary conflict – "historical Russia," whose victory was eventually embodied in the postrevolutionary Soviet state – is the present-day inheritor, although in a vulgarly bureaucratic, simplified form, of the ideas of the Change of Signposts movement of the 1920s. Its ideologues, such as Nikolai Ustryalov and Yury Kliuchnikov, also saw Soviet Russia as the continuation and development of a thousand-years-old Russian state, the logic of which has proved more profound and more powerful than the internationalist perspective of the Bolsheviks.

Sergei Chakhotkin, in his article "To Canossa" in the programmatic compendium *A Change of Signposts* (which was published in Prague in 1921), wrote: "history has forced the Russian 'communistic' republic, contrary to its official dogma, to take up the national cause of gathering together a Russia that had almost fallen apart and at the same time restoring and increasing Russia's relative weight internationally."[20] Furthermore, in the opinion of the 'signpost-changers', the very victory of the revolution had realized an internal necessity of Russian history, by overcoming 'the gulf between the people and power'. In Ustryalov's opinion, the tragically high cost of the revolution was the price "paid for the rehabilitation of the state organism, for curing it of the prolonged, chronic malady that led the St Petersburg period of our history to its grave."[21]

Through the zigzags of Bolshevik policy, determined by the contradiction between communist ideology and reality, Ustryalov glimpsed the triumph of the "reason of the state," manifested outside the law. In effect closely approximating the well-known concept of a "state of emergency" as formulated by Karl Schmitt, Ustryalov regarded the Russian revolution as a triumph of the spirit of the state through the flouting of its letter.[22]

Every step that the Bolsheviks tried to view as taken under compulsion – the limited recognition of the market through the New Economic Policy, or the temporary rejection of world revolution in the name of 'socialism in one country' – was regarded by the 'signpost-changers' as being legitimate and inevitable. "Of course, Lenin remains himself as he makes all these concessions," Ustryalov wrote, "but at the same time he undoubtedly 'evolves,' i.e. out of tactical considerations he takes steps that would inevitably have been taken by a regime hostile to Bolshevism. In order to save the soviets, Moscow is sacrificing communism."[23]

The Bolsheviks, having assumed the burden of state power and while regarding it as a dangerous instrument from the moral point of view ("using Beelzebub against Satan," in Lukács's expression), started becoming transformed into its agents. Their revolutionary practice, undertaken from outside the state, had attempted to subordinate it to the goals of an anti-state and liberating moral order. But the dictatorship of the proletariat was gradually reduced to the condition of a dictatorship of the bureaucracy over the proletariat. Under the influence of circumstances, the means were victorious over the goal. One could say that the revolutionary Kantianism of the Bolsheviks (acting in despite of the circumstances) lost out to the conservative Hegelianism represented by the 'signpost-changers' (that is, the new revolutionary authorities subordinated themselves to the spirit of the national state, in contradiction of their own deliberate intentions).

The resurrection of Russia, according to the 'signpost-changers,' required the involvement of the finest forces of the patriotic intelligentsia, which had been in emigration since the end of the Civil War. The Bolsheviks' ability to accept this hand held out to them was integral to the moral question posed by the events of 1917: was it permissible to involve in the running of the state those who sought to strengthen it and not destroy it?

A special resolution passed at the twelfth conference of the Russian Communist Party (Bolsheviks), in August 1922, confirmed that "the so-called change of signposts movement has so far played and can still play an objectively progressive role. It … unifies those groups of the emigration who have 'come to terms' with Soviet regime and are willing to work with it for the revival of the country."[24]

It is important to note that the 'signpost-changers' did not capitulate, admitting the historical correctness of the new regime but, on the contrary, stated openly that the regime itself had been obliged to capitulate to their principles. They were not fellow travelers, but bearers of other convictions, the incarnate 'truth of the class enemy' that was required in order to assess one's own strength at a historical turning point. This was a test of the revolution's faithfulness to itself.

Anatoly Lunacharksy characterized the 'signpost-changers' as people "of the more or less rightist camp, i.e. by no means infected with absurd democratic prejudices, who even in the period of their counterrevolutionary work, have risen to a genuine breadth of social and state thought." They saw that "not only had the Bolsheviks not frittered Russia away, but, with only absolutely insignificant exceptions, they had united the territory of the former empire in the form of a free union of peoples." Of course, in making this political overture, Lunacharsky mentioned that the hopes of this section of the right intelligentsia that the Soviet regime would degenerate were vain. Nonetheless, on behalf of the Bolsheviks he declared their willingness to accept the challenge of this "genuine, authentic bourgeois patriotism" which represented "what remains of the vital energy of the individualistic groups and classes."[25]

There was something more to this openness to the challenge of 'signpost-changing' than instrumental political calculation. It was the Bolsheviks' clear awareness of the possibility of their own Thermidor, of the victory of circumstances over principles, of politics over morality. In attempting to predict destiny, the heroes of the Russian revolution often tried on the costumes of the French revolution. Even more than that, the revolution of 1917 was carried out bearing in mind the tragedy of 1794 – in awareness of the schism between 'given and essential,' between the revolution's notion of its moral goal and a genuine, tragic defeat.

The nontransparency of the heritage

The possibility of the appearance of Stalin, the proletarian Bonaparte, as the self-negation of the revolution and the rebirth of the old tyrannical state in a new form, crushing in its absolute totalitarianism, was integral to the conscious moral decision taken by the Bolsheviks at the moment when they decided to seize state power.

Ultimately this is precisely what renders the Russian revolution's heritage, which has no obvious heirs, so difficult. Its significance does not lie in raising anew the fallen banner to signify a simple kind of political continuity. Jacques Derrida once wrote of the Marxist tradition: "If the meaning of the heritage represented a certain given, something natural, transparent and unambiguous, if it did not require interpretation and also destroy it at one and the same time, then there would be nothing to inherit. In that case our connection with the heritage would be one of a cause-and-effect or genetic type. Whereas we always actually inherit a certain mystery that says to us: "read me, if you can, but can you read me at all?"[26]

The question of the heritage of the Russian revolution is the mystery of the power of an event that cannot be purged of the history of its own subsequent degeneration and betrayal. But it is the very impossibility of such purging that constitutes the purity of its moral force, the ability to act, even while assuming that one's chances of success are insignificant.

Notes

1 Putin: the revolution of 1917 should be given "a profound, objective assessment." http://ria.ru/politics/20141105/1031839813.html#ixzz3frIXEQIc

2 Rosa Luxemburg, *Selected Political Writings (Writings of the Left)*. Edited and introduced by Robert Looker. New York: Random House 1972, p. 227.

3 *The Gramsci Reader: Selected Writings 1916–1935*, New York: New York University Press, 2000, p. 32

4 Ibid., P.36

5 An emphasis on the role of the self-organization of the workers of St Petersburg, which often forced the Bolshevik party to review its tactical stances, is important for the 'revisionist' tradition of American historians who have studied the Russian Revolution. For instance: Alexander Rabinowitch, *The Bolsheviks Come to Power: The Revolution of 1917 in Petrograd*, Chicago: Haymarket Books, 2009, and D. Mandel, *The St Petersburg Workers and the Fall of the Old Regime: From the February Revolution to the July Days, 1917*, Palgrave Macmillan,1983.

6 G. Lukács, *Political Texts*, Moscow: Three Squares Publishers, 2006, pp. 5–14 (in Russian). For an English translation of the article, see: György Lukács, "Bolshevism as a Moral Problem," in *Social Research*, vol. 44, no. 3 (Autumn 1977), pp. 416–24

7 Ibid., p. 18 (in Russian text). In "Bolshevism as a Moral Problem."

8 Ibid., p. 72 (in Russian text). In "Tactics and Ethics."

9 Ibid, p.10 (in Russian text). In "Bolshevism as a Moral Problem."

10 W. Benjamin, "Towards the Critique of Violence," in: Walter Benjamin, *The Doctrine of The Similar. Works on the aesthetics of the media*, Russian State University for the Humanities, 2012, pp. 66–98 (in Russian). For an English translation of this essay, see: "Critique of Violence," in Walter Benjamin, *Reflections: Essays, Aphorisms, Autobiographical Writings*, edited with an introduction by Peter Demetz, transl. Edmund Jephcott, New York: 'Schocken Books, 1986

11 V. I. Lenin, *Complete Collected Works*, Moscow, 1967, vol. 33, p. 39 ("State and Revolution," chapter 3) (in Russian). For an English translation, see: V. I. Lenin, *State and Revolution*, annotated and introduced by Todd Chretien, Chicago, Haymarket Books, 2014.

12 A. Gramsci. *Parties, State, Society. From the Prison Notebooks*, www.hrono.ru/libris/lib_g/gramsci04.html (in Russian). For an English translation of Gramsci, see: Antonio Gramsci, *Selections from the Prison Notebooks*, ed. Quintin Hoare and Geoffrey Nowell Smith, International Publishers Co., 1989 edn.

13 G. Lukács, *Socialist Realism Today. A. I. Solzhenitsyn in the mirror of Marxist criticism*, http://scepsis.net/library/id_693.html (in Russian), For an English translation of Lukács's writing on Solzhenitsyn, see: György Lukács, *Solzhenitsyn*, translated by W. D. Graf, 'Merlin Press,1971.

14 See, for instance: M. Molostvov, Revisionism-58 (http://scepsis.net/library/id_1328.html) (in Russian) and B. Vail, *Especially Dangerous*, Kharkov 2005, p. 199 (in Russian).

15 A speech by Vladimir Medinsky at the round table "100 years of the Great Russian Revolution: an interpretation in the name of consolidation," May 2015, www.pravmir.ru/osmyislenie-vo-imya-konsolidatsii-k-100-letiyu-revolyutsii-1917-goda/ (in Russian).

16 Vladimir Medinsky: "By 1917 Syria was already ours. And then Lenin appeared." www.kp.ru/daily/26466.3/3335111/ (in Russian).

17 Joseph de Maistre, *Considerations on France*, chapter 2. www.e-reading.club/chapter.php/97551/4/de_Mestr_-_Rassuzhdeniya_o_Francii.html (in Russian). For an English translation of de Maistre's work see: Joseph De Maistre, *Considerations on France*, ed. Richard A. Lebrun, Cambridge University Press, 2009.

18 A. de Tocqueville, *The Ancien Regime and the Revolution*. St Petersburg: Aleteia Publishers, 2008, p. 20 (in Russian). For an English translation of this work, see: Alexis de Tocqueville, *The Ancien Regime and the Revolution*, transl. and introduced by Gerald Bevan, Penguin Classics, 2008.

19 François Furet, *Interpreting the French Revolution*, St Petersburg: INAPRESS, 1998 (in Russian). For an English translation of Furet's book, see: François Furet, *Interpreting the French Revolution*, transl. Elborg Forster, Cambridge University Press, 1981.

20 *To Canossa. A Political History of the Russian Emigration. 1920–1940. Documents and Materials*, Moscow, 1999, pp. 190-5 (in Russian).

21 N. Ustryalov, *Russia (At the Carriage Window)* http://lib.ru/POLITOLOG/USTRYALOV/rossia.txt_with-big-pictures.html (in Russian).

22 N. Ustryalov, *The Concept of a State*: www.lib.ru/POLITOLOG/USTRYALOV/ustrqlow7.txt_with-big-pictures.html (in Russian).

23 N. Ustryalov, *Patriotica*, "A Change of Signposts," Prague, 1921 (in Russian).

24 Resolution "On anti-Soviet parties and movements." *The All-Russian Conference of the Russian Communist Party (Bolsheviks), Decrees and Resolutions*, Moscow, 1922 (in Russian).

25 A. Lunacharsky, *The Changing Signposts of the Intelligentsia Community* www.magister.msk.ru/library/politica/lunachar/lunaa004.htm (in Russian).

26 J. Derrida, *Specters of Marx,* Moscow 2006, p. 32 (in Russian). For an English translation of Derrida's book, see: Jacques Derrida, *Specters of Marx: The State of the Debt, The Work of Mourning and the New International,* Routledge, 2006.

19

Dmitry Venkov

KRISIS: A FILM SCRIPT

ANDREY

My leftist friends are upset: bad Ukrainians tore down the monument to the good-hearted dreamer grandpa Lenin. Don't worry, darlings, soon we will see restored the monument to the kind uncle Felix (Dzerzhinsky) – the friend of all orphans and comrade of Lenin, a monument previously destroyed by similar thugs. What a joy it will be!

KSENIA

I want to see this person! The one who is upset over Lenin.

ANDREY

I have. It's an affable person.

VICTOR

This is heathen, infantile, and fetishist at once. Tearing down statues won't solve problems. This will only add to the litter to be cleaned up.

NIKOLAY

(to Victor) By the leftist friends, of course!

KSENIA

Let the litter be in the streets but not in the minds.

VASILISA

(to Andrey) First, read about those who tore it down, then about the beating and robbery of union activists by Nazis. Before raising this brouhaha over the toppling of the evil Lenin, you need to look into it a bit more. I understand the picture is pretty but I think Nazis in power are much worse than the statue of Lenin, although you once said they are the same.

ANDREY

True. It is the same. But now I mean those who grieve, not those who tore it down.

VASILISA

And I mean those who rejoice. Put up a Kapur.

MAXIM

A yellow square on a blue background has already been proposed.

The statue of Lenin apparently is some kind of a sacred object. So sacred that the liberals who condone its demolition turn a blind eye to those who did it. Fascists, anti-Semites, homophobes, disgusting bastards. Only a bullet can do them justice. You don't give a fuck! It's all about the statue of Lenin!

KSENIA

I don't condone them but people should be glad when two predators devour each other.

VASILISA

Then you should be OK with their incinerators, why not?

KSENIA

I don't see a reason to be horrified unless they beat people up.

VASILISA

They did! Lenin is like a red rag to a bull. You are completely blind.

KSENIA

I don't advocate for their beatings but don't mind them toppling monuments.

MAXIM

Nonsense! No one grieves over the monument. But many do over Nazis' victory in a protest movement. What fools they are!

ANDREY

You are all so sweet!

VICTOR

The tensions are running high! They will soon be fighting each other with monuments. A sculpture battle!

VICTOR

Now is a very interesting time when we would never agree on a personality for a monument.

ANDREY

Fascists without incinerators and beatings. And how about communists? Let them be as long as they are docile and don't have Kolyma? We have a lot of those among our friends. They are upset over the Lenin statue but still are shy to deplore the Dzerzhinsky one.

VASILISA

I think our docile communists are on great terms with both you and me, and Kolyma never comes up.

ANDREY

Well, you believe there is no clear connection between Kolyma and our leftist friends but you see it in the case of nationalists. It is a matter of taste. By the way, Bolsheviks were on great terms with Social Revolutionaries and Mensheviks before executing them for reasons of the revolutionary imperative.

VASILISA

What taste are you talking about? Do you seriously believe that the principle of national purity is commensurate in its cruelty with Marx's ideas? But let's drop this subject and go back to your support of the Svoboda party in the Ukraine.

ANDREY

Firstly, what does Marx have to do with that? By 1917 he was long gone.

Secondly, it is a question of taste to try not to see a connection between the economic and political principles upheld by our friends and the GULAG. This connection is as obvious as the one between neo-Nazis and incinerators.

IVAN

He doesn't see the difference between the dismantlement
and the demolition of a monument. As an artist, you really
don't care when a work of art is destroyed? This is your
understanding of European values? Europe has monuments
to absolute monarchs, war chiefs, and other tyrants. Should
we destroy everything starting from antiquity? Let's leave
monuments only to highly moral heroes with impeccable
biographies who comply with all the legal norms of
contemporary Europe? Then Europe will have no monuments
left. Only memorials to victims of such and such a regime.

ANDREY

No, I don't care. I'm no kind of an aesthete.

IVAN

Then forgive me but your mentality is not European but rather
Asian. You are no different from the Bolsheviks whom you
fiercely criticize. They didn't care either and destroyed many
monuments to their ideological foes.

ANDREY

No. In Europe, Nazi monuments and symbols were destroyed.
And monuments to Franco and Ceausescu. But the ones to all
those Louis and Davids for some reason were left standing. You
know that perfectly well. So cut the bullshit.

IVAN

Who's bullshitting? I precisely wrote that Europe has
monuments to all those Louis and Neros. They were Hitlers and
Mussolinis of their time. But according to your logic they must
be destroyed. How was Lenin worse than Caligula or Nero?

By the way, that comparison with Hitler is fucking annoying. There was the Nuremberg trial in his case. But in the case of Lenin and Caligula …

MAXIM

Wonderful. I love him for his treason. There is no better act than "betraying" an imperialist battle. Doesn't it give a good name to Lenin all of a sudden?

ANDREY

The thing is, luckily for the Finns, Bolsheviks didn't win in Finland. And the monument was probably put up privately, not by the state.

MAXIM

Private capitalist Finns. This is even more telling! And by the way, it was the Bolsheviks who gave up Russian imperialist ambitions for Finland, so you know.

ANDREY

Aha. Also for the Baltics, the Ukraine, and Transcaucasia. What they couldn't devour right away, they said, "We didn't want it anyway." They gave up their ambitions for a full twenty years.

MAXIM

So you seriously believe that Soviet Russia in 1918 is the same state as Stalin's empire twenty years later? Well well.

ANDREY

I don't believe so. I know so. Stalin developed the system created by Lenin. There were no other ways of development. Lenin just didn't have the resources and capabilities at the start. This has little to do with personality. Such a system can function only on mass terror and coercion.

MAXIM

This is simply not true. Lenin simply didn't have the time to create a system. I am critical of the Bolsheviks but I'm sorry your analysis is an anti-historical delusion.

ANTON

You are currently fighting the wrong enemy. I think celebrating the fact that Nazis took down the monument, and they did it not just as a symbol of the colonial policies of the USSR, is a loss of the sense of history and of the threats it contains. What do you think these people will install in place of the Lenin monument? I doubt it will be a monument to all kinds of repression or something equally politically correct. You seem to believe that the demolished symbol of an ideology will reveal underneath it a mythical tabula rasa of rationality and clean urban space. While there is history, it will never happen.

ANDREY

(to Anton) I am not really celebrating. And I certainly don't believe in a tabula rasa. I am simply unable to deplore the demolition of the monument to the dictator and executioner, theorist and organizer of mass killings of my compatriots, even if bad people took it down.

ANTON

It's just that what you perceive as a symbolic gesture of pure negation of the Soviets is not a pure negation in this situation. This gesture, besides anti-imperial and anti-Russian connotations, implies many things that would horrify you.

SERKHIY

Even if bad people took it down. In this case, it doesn't matter what was taken down by bad people, what does is their right to tear down anything. And to smash any heads.

It's impossible to talk about the empty pedestal while ignoring that, which is climbing there now. And, so that you know, the anti-communism seen yesterday is closely related to anti-liberalism.

20

Gleb Napreenko

QUESTIONS WITHOUT ANSWERS, ANSWERS WITHOUT QUESTIONS

1995. The action *The First Glove*. The war in Chechnya is going on. To express his protest, the artist Alexander Brener, dressed as a boxer, goes up onto the stone platform of the *Lobnoye mesto* in Red Square (in old times a site for the proclamation of the tsar's *ukazes*), and shouts out challenges to that "pitiful coward" Boris Yeltsin to fight. His shouts are addressed to the mute Kremlin walls, which are incapable of answering him. For quite a long time no one reacts to his appeals and his provocative behavior. It takes several minutes for a militia car to show up (the police were still called 'militia' then): the guardians of law and order who have arrived in it try to understand what is happening and take Brener off to the station – but soon release him.

2013. The action *Fixation*. During the third presidential term of the politician Vladimir Putin, everything is coming to resemble authoritarian government more and more. The artist Pyotr Pavlensky, symbolically diagnosing the apathy that has gripped society since the mass civil protests of 2011–12, nails his scrotum to a cobblestone in Red Square. Members of the police are quick to approach the artist. Administrative proceedings are taken against Pavlensky for "petty hooliganism," and five days later a criminal case is opened and he is made to give a written undertaking not to leave the city.

The moods of these two individual actions that occurred at the same place (Red Square), separated by a gap of eighteen years, are very different. At one pole we have Brener's tragicomic shouts addressed to emptiness: a summons to action and struggle that is drowned in the absence of a reply from the person to whom it is addressed. At the other pole – Pavlensky's masochistic and at the same time morally instructive act, unambiguously stating the impossibility of movement – is instantly met with a predictable response from the authorities.

How can we describe in structural terms the difference between these two actions, each of which was, in its own way, emblematic of its time? It is easier to make sense of the wide variety of ethical and political positions taken by Russian action artists in the period from the 1990s to the present if we regard them as acts and statements in the field of the Other, that is, as different versions of an appeal to a symbolic order, as different ways of relating to the law that regulates our existence, to its weaknesses and its strength. The symbolic law, naturally, has a material substrate, in which society and the state are the key instances for actionism.

The Other in Brener's action is a weak Other, the fragmented post-Soviet state of the 1990s (its fragmentation has been described, among others, by the sociologist Vadim Volkov in his book *Violent Entrepreneurs*). This state was far less concerned with the affairs of its citizens and the affairs of society than with its own survival and dividing up Russian capital.

With the end of the USSR this Other – that is, the state – to a significant degree abandoned its citizens to sink or swim. And Brener's actions of the 1990s existed in a state of indeterminacy of the field of the Other. This indeterminacy can be read either as the long-awaited liberal freedom or as the loss of legitimate reference points and social guarantees. And therefore Brener's actions, like many other actions of the 1990s (for instance, the collective action *Barricade* on Nikitskaya Street in Moscow, 1998), can be seen as a check on the reality of this Other, as an attempt to clarify by experimental means the new, still unarticulated laws of existence in the city and the state.

At the level of the content of his statement, Brener has a precise political agenda: a protest against the war in Chechnya. This content, and also the entire image of the boxer-warrior, are deliberately masculine and heroic. However, at the level of the act of the statement, *The First Glove* includes indeterminacy and intentional weakness: the question of exactly what reply Brener is expecting from the Other, and whether this reply is possible in principle, is left up in the air. This suspended state can be called the 'aesthetics' of Brener's action in the sense in which this term is used by the philosopher Jacques Rancière: in speaking of aesthetics what happens here is the suspension of the knowledge of how to feel correctly, how to read and understand a work correctly. To put it another way, in *The First Glove* the gap between the act and the statement is of the essence – this gap is the aesthetics.

Brener projected a similar 'state of suspension' onto the whole of the new post-Soviet social order in his action *What David Didn't Finish* (1995), by lining up a whole series of uncompleted utterances, beginning with the very title of the action. Standing near the former KGB building on Lyubanka Street, on the empty site of Dzerzhinsky's statue, which was pulled down by protesters in 1991, Brener shouted out, as if he were addressing the cars swirling round him as they turned on the square: "Everything is all right! Carry on working! I am your new commercial director. Everything is all right." In essence, Brener was giving voice to the unspoken imperatives of the new post-Soviet capitalist order. By insistently attempting to persuade the absent audience to his speech that "everything is all right," he inevitably made people suspicious – was everything really all right? Was the site where Dzerzhinsky, that symbol of power, used to stand, really empty? The interminable swirling of the cars was expressive of the flow of time in which these questions had been suspended without an answer.

Pavlensky's actions are also an emphatically male performance, like the actions of Brener – but they don't contain any paradoxical and potentially bewildering dialectic of the phallic and castration, the heroic and the comic, strength and weakness, the content and the act of the statement – a dialectic that was intrinsic to Brener. Rather than that, Pavlensky bears tautological witness to his place in the space of the Other's law, thereby challenging it – as in *Fixation*, where Pavlensky use his gesture like a signature, attesting to the fact of public apathy that he spoke about in his commentary on this action.

I will take the liberty of quoting a rather large fragment of my own article "What has Pavlensky overlooked?"[1]

In Pyotr Pavlensky's action, which, according to the artist's own statements, should make people think and provoke unpredictable consequences, an ethics can be detected, in which what is written down dominates what is not written down.

On 27 April 2016, at the request of Pavlensky, who was under criminal investigation concerning accusations of vandalism for the actions *Freedom* and *Threat*, his lawyer

Dmitry Dinze brought the women whom the artist had presented as "prostitutes" to the court as witnesses for the defense. In Dinze's retelling, Pavlensky regards prostitutes and the homeless as the only free people in Russia and therefore as being exactly the individuals who are entitled to state their opinion publicly in court.

The predictability of the authorities' response and the media effect has been a component in all of Pavlensky's works. But whereas in Pavlensky's actions the artist participated face to face with the state, in the trial he imposed a predetermined role not only on himself and the representatives of authority, but also on the women who had been invited as witnesses. These women (and their predictably negative opinion of modern actionism) found themselves overshadowed by the signifier "prostitute," which was taken up enthusiastically by the media. Pavlensky's actions do not function as paradoxes, but as a triumphant 'quod erat demonstrandum.' One more time: according to Pavlensky, in modern Russian society it is only possible to have access to freedom if you are situated on the fringes of this society by virtue of being a sex worker or homeless person. In this model of Pavlensky's the defining contours of society are neatly mapped out and everyone is assigned his/her own role (conformist/protester, sex worker/ policeman, free/not free …). But this very notion of the social order as a system of written-down, predictable roles excludes freedom, and it was this very notion that Pavlensky himself reproduced in criticizing Russian justice.

The scene with the "prostitutes" in court revealed the presence in all of Pavlensky's art of an ethics founded on the total recording of social roles. In his actions Pavlensky has always attested to the impasse of the political situation in Russia, effectively doubling it up by nailing down all of its participants in their places, as he nailed his own body to Red Square in the action *Fixation*. But in so doing he has only reproduced the impossibility of ambiguity and the impossibility of a halt to the universal accounting that underlies the power of the state. However in that case the unpredictable breakthrough, which he proclaims as an inspiration in his texts, cannot come about. Pavlensky's actions do not function as paradoxes, but as a triumphant 'quod erat demonstrandum'; in shying away from indeterminacy, they lead desire into a blind alley.

In Pavlensky's action, the collapsing and reduction of what I referred to above as "aesthetics" is symptomatic not only of a change in art, but also of a change in the state's position with regard to its citizens – a change in the Other with whom they have to deal. Essentially without granting its citizens any new social guarantees, the state is attempting ever more vigorously to interfere in their personal affairs – the legislative proposals on "prohibiting the propaganda of homosexuality to minors," "insulting the feelings of believers," and the abolition of free abortions, etc. can serve as examples of this.

Changes in the ruling regime have a direct effect on the poetics and prospects of political actionism. As my co-author Sasha Novozhenova and I wrote in an article on Russian actionism in the daily realities of the city in the 1990s,[2] the beginning of the first period of post-Soviet actionism, when the state Other was weak and not yet fully delineated, can be taken as the cancellation, resulting from the collapse of the USSR, of the criminal proceedings that had already begun against the participants in the *ETI-text* action by the ETI movement (the acronym ETI stands for Expropriation of the Territory of Art, and also spells out the Russian word for 'these'). The participants spelled out the word *Hui* ('Prick') with their bodies on Red Square. Three events can be noted as marking the end of this first period. Firstly, the criminal prosecution in 1998 of Avdei Ter-Oganyan for his action *Young Atheist*, in the course of which he chopped up reproductions of icons from the Art-Manège exhibition; in order to avoid prosecution the artist fled the country. Secondly, the FSB's pursuit of the organizers of the occupation of Lenin's mausoleum in the course of an action by the Against All movement (which advocates the reinclusion in election ballots of the option "against all"), as a result of which one of the pioneers of the movement stopped engaging in actionism. Thirdly, the criminal prosecution of Oleg Mavromatti for the action *Don't Believe Your Eyes* in 2000, in the course of which the artist was nailed to a cross; like Avdei Ter-Oganyan, Mavromatti fled the country in order to avoid trial. And so, in the late 1990s the state asserted its authority and its control over the public space – and the word 'actionism' began to be associated with persecution by the authorities. In the new era political action artists required new working methods for dealing with the strengthened Other.

Of course, Pavlensky's strategy is by no means the only way for Russian actionism to deal with this new persecuting state, which is not inclined to let artists' escapades go without a substantial response. Pavlensky espouses direct confrontation with the state, certifying with his acts the seriousness of the Other's law: it is one or the other – either face-to-face resistance or submission. In contrast, many of the actions of the group Voina ('War') and of Pussy Riot have instead been clownish or tricksterish in nature, mocking the authorities and their laws and showing how they can be evaded playfully. An indicative instance is the action by a member of Voina, Leonid Nikolaev (unfortunately recently deceased) in which he ran up onto and across a Federal Guards Service car beside the Kremlin with two buckets over his head – and then evaded capture and escaped (*Fuckhead Lyonya Runs on the Feds' Roof*). Or the action in which another member of Voina, Elena Kostyleva, carried a frozen chicken out of a supermarket in her own body – inside her vagina (*Why the Chicken Was Pinched*, or *The Tale of How the Cunt Fed the War*, 2010). Or Pussy Riot's actions from the series *Free the Flagstone* (2012), in which the members of the punk group clambered up and hid from police under the roofs of metro stations or on top of a trolleybus and sang songs from there, scattering around the down taken from pillows.

War and Pussy Riot seem to be competing with agents of the state to see who is wilier. They show how it is possible to evade taboos and prohibitions wittily and to demystify power by demonstrating that it is built on ruses which are in principle no different from their own anarchical gimmicks. Tricks or special contrivances that allow them to outwit the authorities are a major component of their actions. This is a fundamental difference between the actionism of the 2000s and 2010s and the action art of the 1990s.

The actionism of the 1990s was like a clump of naked life, tossed into the uncertainty of the post-Soviet city – like a stray dog, the alter ego of the artist Oleg Kulik, or Brener's naked body. The reaction of the authorities (for instance, the militia), when it occurred, was not an integral part of the action itself – it was, rather, the end of the action, the point at which it broke off. In the same way as the crane driver and the crane which carried out Anatoly Osmolovsky's request to hoist him up onto the shoulder of the statue of Mayakovsky were not part of the action in *The Journey of Netseziudik to the Land of the Brobdingnagians*: the content of the action was simply the image of Osmolovsky sitting on the shoulder of the proletarian poet. In the 2000s, when the gap between citizens' bodies and the state was filled by media for implementing state power, action artists started expropriating these media, fighting against the Other for those symbols, facilities and inventions through which their relationship with it was mediated. For instance, the Liteiny leaf bridge in St Petersburg, which is raised in accordance with a strict timetable, was expropriated from the state as the medium for an action by the group Voina entitled *Prick Captured by FSB* (2010), and a metro-train carriage trundled round the metro, literally carrying the same group's joint action with the Bombily ('Blitzers') under the title *Feast (A Wake for Prigov)* (2007).

But what is the role of agents of society in these actions? We have spoken above primarily about the Other of actionism as being the state, its institutions and agents – but not about society. And this is significant – the most clearly perceptible aspect of Russian political actionism is an appeal (as in the 1990s) or a challenge (beginning from the 2000s) to the authorities and the state. In the 1990s seemingly no place was envisaged for any kind of focused image or representative of society – the action artists went out into society as if it were a raw, indistinct reality, addressing every chance passer-by in the manner of Oleg Kulik, who flung himself at people like a dog. Society appeared to action artists as a clearly defined and structured target, not raw and arbitrary, from the moment when the behavior of the state was first clarified, when the state of social suspension of the 1990s came to an end. And the question of intermediaries, of media, became crucial for the action artists' relationship with society, just as it had been for their relationship with the state. And whereas in the relationship with the state these intermediaries were special stunts, lures, captured ordnance and instruments of escape, in the relationship with society they were the news media.

Even in our day action artists (Pussy Riot, Pavlensky) are inclined to ignore members of society who happen by chance to be nearby during an action, whether they are candle-sellers in the Cathedral of Christ the Savior or simply passers-by. The only exceptions are the crucial ones of agents of the authorities (the police) and journalists: the immediate reality of the action is sacrificed to its media image. For the artists the news media are more or less the only fully legitimate representatives of society.

And precisely thanks to the efforts of the news media, an action is neatly divided into two components: an act of stating, which has been reduced to the level of scandal, and the content of the statement (frequently distorted, especially in the official media) – a kind of political message that can be written down in words. As filtered through the news media, the act and the content of the statement are devoid of the paradoxical relations that were inherent to the actionism of the 1990s: today the act merely serves as the instrument for propagating the content. And therefore, the more an action relies on making an impact via the news media, the less 'aesthetics' (in Rancière's sense) it possesses. For instance, this is precisely the structure of Pavlensky's actions, which lay claim to the status of a monumental example and a reproach that is disseminated via thousands of repostings on the internet. To a much lesser degree, this also applies to the group Voina.

The 1990s in Russia were a time of protracted capitalist (counter)revolution. Against the background of the collapse and reassembly of society, the artistic actions of the 1990s did not stand out very noticeably among the large number of disorienting events and shocking crimes. It is no accident that stories about artistic actions were quite often published in the newspapers' city events pages. In this situation, artistic actions were attempts to determine the still unclear, unfamiliar borders of a new social order – attempts that were impossible in a time of changes on such a scale. This impossibility of achieving certainty was at the origin of the energy and poetics of the actionism of the 1990s. When Russian authoritarian state capitalism was firmly established, actionism acquired a new function. Its acts became acts of setting limits to the law – a rehearsal for revolutionary acts, made alone or in a narrow circle of close associates and fellow thinkers. And this is already a form of transgressive acts that is far more familiar to bourgeois society – these impatient attempts to play out a revolution – and also a far more familiar form of impossibility – the impossibility of carrying out this revolution in earnest.

Notes

1   Gleb Napreenko, "What has Pavlensky overlooked?" *Raznoglasiya* no. 4. 'A puffy eye. The ethics committee.' www.colta.ru/articles/raznoglasiya/11139], in which I wrote in detail about these properties of the artist's ethical position.
2   Gleb Napreenko and Alexandra Novozhenova. "Moscow actionism under a fragmentary state." Unpublished.

21

Gluklya / Natalia Pershina-Yakimanskaya

THE UTOPIAN UNION OF THE UNEMPLOYED

The Utopian Union of the Unemployed is a project that brings together migrants, artists and institutions in the united aim of developing a pilot model for a new type of work that exists at the junction of art, economics, progressive pedagogy, and the social sciences. The goals and objectives of the project are these: to research new methods for using art and a poetic outlook to integrate newly arrived refugees into the European Community.

At long, long last the "Theater for Migrants" has started moving my way. Although some experts don't like this name, this is what I have decided to call my project after all. After the initial projects – "Wings of Migrants" in St Petersburg and "Dumped Dreams" in Zurich – it was already clear that working briefly, that is, coming to a place for two weeks, spending a huge amount of energy on overcoming fear of the other, building up a relationship with the participants so that they open up and become my friends, even like family, and then never seeing them again and not knowing if this experiment has added something positive to their lives or not, makes no sense. You see, it turns out that the main monster now dwells in the fact that short courses with people on the fringes of society are a product. That very product which the bloodthirsty system craves, and nothing like a process that makes us alive and able to resist. This is that weak link in neoliberalism comparable with the situation in Hemingway's novel, where an old man does battle with a huge fish, but afterwards the sharks eat it anyway. In order to make sure that the sharks don't eat our big, beautiful fish we – artists who have realized that art is in very deep crisis and who therefore work with people from beyond the art community, with people who are really suffering – in order to make sure that the neoliberalism that gives us money for our work with refugees and migrants and other weak people, doesn't gobble up our efforts, we have to fight for long-term projects, no matter what it takes.

In my particular case an approximation to this ideal only became possible thanks to my meeting Agent Magical Bird. That's what I call the fragile young woman who agreed to welcome into the space of her small gallery my fantasies on the transformation of society entitled "The Utopian Union of the Unemployed."

05.09.16

If I wrote a novel, I'd begin it with Marzia's intense gaze. Marzia is the name of the director of Xenia – an organization that saves refugees. She is the most involved director of any organization that I have ever seen in my life. Her husband is one of the refugees that she has saved, and together they adopted a boy from Afghanistan, who was sent to Italy by his parents – simply put on the bus with his things – so that he would grow up and send them money. The boy is difficult and he resists Marzia with all his might, a frail little soldier whom she fell for with an acute, agonizing love. I met her at the moment when he had just started demanding autonomy, something that was hard for his mother's heart to accept. It was as if seven knives had been thrust into her heart at once. In Italian churches there are images of the Madonna with a heart impaled on knives – the canons of Catholicism permit suffering to be depicted in this way. Each knife signifies a specific degree of the suffering of Christ, her son, but it seems to me that, as often happens with inspired images that have appeared in our world, we can perceive them all at once, there is a pain that is like seven knives at once, and nothing can be done about it. I told her about my project and said we wanted to ask her to help us with finding participants.

She advised us to try several people. The migrants mentioned included a shaman who had arrived from Senegal and could foretell the future and a writer who was writing the story of his life and working 80 hours a week in seven jobs in order to feed a large family in Afghanistan, where he sent most of his pay. Several women were also on the list, but Marzia wasn't sure if we'd be able to cope with them, because they lived with conflict inside them and one way or another it always crept out. "They unconsciously provoke conflict, because they were subjected to violence in their childhood or youth," Marzia said. For instance, one of the women had witnessed the murder of her father and brothers in Bosnia, and also seen her mother being dragged away, and then she heard screams and she never saw her mother again. She was a very good worker but, for instance, she never came to meetings at the office, any relations beyond the bounds of the man–machine function threw her off balance. "You won't be able to cope with her, she'll destroy everything for you. You won't be able to cope with her in such a short space of time," Marzia said.

06.09.16

As always, projects of this kind begin with thrashing out the ethical norms accepted on the territory of the neoliberal community. Since we carry a deep sense of guilt for the exploitation of slaves in former colonies, we can't be their teachers.

I don't know what to do, because now everyone keeps telling me in a single voice that no one must be coerced, and it's not very likely that they will draw. And what if they don't want to draw? Mama mia! But this is always a challenge. We'll see. There is no art without risk.

The most important problem that bothers me is whether imagination and a sense of humor can help the newcomers achieve a condition not only of safety, but what I would call suprematist freedom. Social workers talk repeatedly about the security they must offer to the migrants, whatever it takes. But that's not enough to oppose the structure of society, is it?

A rose has to have thorns, and migrants have to have imagination and the will to transform themselves and society.

Or is this a sheer waste of time? Can the methods that artists usually employ, such as fantasy, imagination, escaping to different worlds, or orbiting round other realities – be useful to migrants when it comes to integration? Can poetry help them when it comes to integration?

07.09.16

For the third day in a row now my thinking keeps coming back to the moment when a friend – the director of a small European art institution – casually dropped into a conversation that he understood why I work with migrants: because I'm searching for new energy. Somehow the way he said that made me feel terribly afraid – what if he really saw my goal as being only that? I'm actually searching for a new faith as well. And a new platform, the meaning of art.

08.09.16

I don't have time to write it all down – everything's spinning so fast, there's so much of everything going on all around – every individual demands attention, and the information they're giving out penetrates into every layer of my cells.

Joyful news – our Manifesto has been translated into Italian!

09.09.16

My favorite amusement is to walk along under the porticos and drop into a café every fifteen minutes to drink a little cup of coffee. That's how I celebrate my arrival in Italy.

I dream of doing it some time with our guys from Nigeria who are taking part in the workshop. And I also think about how we'll give those T-shirts we're going to print to illegal immigrants, and how that will be a genuine performance.

10.09.16

Today there are more illegals, and they all stand there holding out their caps.

I should say that every day the way their standing is choreographed changes a bit. Probably behind the scenes a social worker gives them advice, or perhaps they come to an agreement among themselves? Yesterday, for instance, they were all standing in a suprematistically passive pose, but today they are holding their caps out rather determinedly. If it wasn't a tragedy, it would be very much like an organized flashmob. Every time my perverse imagination suggests different variations on the theme of recasting this sign of the times into the status of a performance.

For instance, if we give them all T-shirts with statements like *Unemployment is a state of mind*, will it turn out that the beggars are automatically transformed into citizens, if only for a short time? But then again, doubts about the effectiveness of this brief spell prevent me dashing into realizing this particular option

11.09.16

I think it started when, after stepping onto the marble floor of the apartment I've been housed in and walking on and on under the porticos of Bologna into the yellowish-gentle orange-pink haze of that same Bologna, which has the oldest university in the world, and St Luke's Hill, to which pilgrims used to come to ask to be cured of difficult illnesses, but now instead athletes run up the hill, and I saw the unfortunate *newcomers* begging, holding out napkins, and some simply standing there, dejectedly selling flowers. For some reason I never give them money, and at the same time I feel terribly ashamed, I try not to look at them and hold out. On especially sensitive days I cry at the sight of them. I tell myself then: you have to walk without looking round, I walk and I cry, but I still don't give them money. A creep, in short. On those days of self-hatred, all I do is make myself feel even worse.

12.09.16

I really don't know at all why I do this. It's very painful and frightening for me. I'm not better in any way, I'm a lot worse than these people, whom I am planning (O, God!) to teach something. I'm just a filthy swine, that's all. What can I do?

15.09.16

I had a dream that reconciled me with reality in a paradoxical
kind of way. I know what to start the workshop with today.

The point is, it was a dream about a migrant from the
previous project in a different Italian city, where the author's
residency turned out to be intensively punk. Any result was
declared unnecessary, and that reduced me to total frustration.
I couldn't do anything about it, but then again I started getting
dreams that featured characters from the residency, mixed up
together with *newcomers*. By the way, that was where the term
newcomers appeared: during the animated debates the Italian
activists promoted this term, and the Palestinian activists
replied furiously that it wasn't a recognized term, and after all
we should call a spade a spade, so let's keep the good old word
refugee. Maybe it isn't politically correct, but it's honest, the
Palestinians claimed. But I took a liking to the term *newcomers*.
I think that's exactly what the migrants can be called. Although,
to be honest, all this song and dance about what to call them is
exaggerated. For me they are messiahs who have come to tell us
the truth. In Marx's terms I would actually call them the very
class which, together with the artists, will make the revolution.

But I'll go back to the dream: I dreamed of Toslim, a
fugitive from Bangladesh, a sad, introverted individual, who
turned out to be a brilliant actor, although he couldn't read and
write, even in his own language.

What happened was this. In my dream Toslim tells me
about a dream that he has had several times, and every time
it began in the same way. Toslim found himself in an unusual
garden filled with plants that looked like reeds, but with
strange flowers. These flowers were like little fingers with little
manicured red nails. The further he went into the garden, the
deeper these flowers pierced into him, as if they wanted to grow

through him. It wasn't painful, quite the opposite actually – in the dream he had a feeling of delight and anticipation – if not of a miracle, then of some adventure that was definitely unusual.

I'm thinking of starting to get to know the participants in the workshop with this dream.

By the way, Toslim drew my portrait.

It's interesting that here I appear as a person with four eyes.

16.09.16

I don't remember very well where I got the idea of printing, that is, not dancing or eating together (a method for involving people in the process, which is used by artists in participatory projects), or even my usual ploy with clothing, but precisely this technique, but I am very pleased and I think that it's an excellent way to counter the difficult situation of idleness to which the migrants are condemned. They have to bear the test of the status of being 'no one.' You are no one in this society, and until we accept that you can be someone, you can't work, you can only observe our life unobtrusively. This state of being *totally becalmed in uncertainty*, into which they are plunged, requires genuine courage.

It's interesting that artists artificially create this kind of condition of *susceptibility* for themselves. You could say it requires a certain effort for them to approach the status of *no one*. The muses of inspiration find excellent nourishment in conditions like this, and they call it autonomy. Consequently, the artist in society is the only figure that a newly arrived migrant can relate to. A good artist looks in the mirror and sees a migrant. Not himself. He is not equal to a migrant, of course, because potentially he has the opportunity to find himself a job, for instance, as a yard keeper or someone else, that is, to stop being an artist. But a newcomer has no alternatives.

AMB also confessed to me that she's taking a great risk by paying them for working. That apparently just recently there was a raid on a big shop in the city. The police discovered that the owner of the shop was hiring illegals and paying them, and they closed it. AMB is taking a great risk by getting involved with me. If they close her gallery, all the blame will fall on my shoulders, of course.

17.09.16

Today was the first day when all our participants came. Tony, Prince and Precious. It was very difficult. Prince is still kind of all right, a cheerful kind of guy, like nothing gets to him. But Tony is really terrible. It's like talking to a rock. And the rock actually paralyzes you. But I resist, of course, we don't have any other way. That's the poignant aftertaste of misery and misfortune. Mama mia!

But actually, even Tony isn't really as difficult as Precious, who has taken on the entire grief of the Nigerian nation. They all came from small towns in Nigeria. So far all I know about them is that they won't tell me immediately what happened to them. And I don't ask. And we're not going to get in touch with the organizers, because they'll immediately forbid them to come and won't let them go anywhere at all, after all, *they're not allowed to work*. Plus, I really was feeling very bad. The level of iron in my organism had fallen catastrophically. The girls from the Academy of Art bent over double and drew little sketches of the models for about two hours, very clumsily and completely off the subject. They spent the other hour and a half smoking and chattering in Italian.

In the end I went so far as to express minimal criticism of their drawing and the fact that they weren't making the slightest effort to get any closer to the newcomers.

But then I was cheered up by the young male students. Giovanni suggested the slogan "Fear of Integration," and Fabrizio suggested printing the parts of the constitution where it says everyone is guaranteed equal rights.

18.09.16

The girls from the Academy of Art didn't show up. So okay. In utopian alliances there's always someone who falls away. And that's what happened this time. But the ones who stay are the ones who really need it. Yesterday I asked Prince for the clothes in which they sailed from Libya to Italy on those boats: T-shirts or anything at all. They said they'd think about it and frowned.

I said perhaps it could be valuable to show the clothes of people who didn't drown in the sea, but reached the shore safely. Usually talking about their clothes helps people to open up and start talking about their problems. But this time it's probably better to focus on producing drawings to print.

19.09.16

This is what I've managed to find out about Tony. He grew up in a village in Delta State, Nigeria. His mother died when he was five. He was raised by his father. "He looked good after me," Tony said. His father was a hard-working farmer, and then he fell ill and died. Tony used to go to church on Sundays, someone had taken him there once. Even now he likes reading the Bible. Basically, there are two books in his life: *Italiano di Base* (Basic Italian) and the Bible. One fine day (this was what he said: *on the happiest day of my life*) a man came up to him and asked: 'Do you want to go to Europe? I can take you with me." And he took Tony to Libya. Tony asked him: "Why have you brought me here, and not to Italy, as you promised?" The man said that after

Tony worked for a while, washing the mud off trucks, he would take him to Italy. Obviously, those were the same trucks that drive across the desert crammed to the limit, and sometimes someone tumbles out along the way and dies. Tony started working, but he was detained by the police for three months.

When he got out of jail, he came to Italy by sailing over in a boat. But it's only Tony who has come clean about himself. The others have completely clammed up and we don't know anything about them. That's why we need long projects, in order to understand more about these people, and not just work brazenly: do this, do that.

Short projects are what capitalism needs.

20.09.16

Tony has created a masterpiece. He put down his mobile phone and simply drew round it. All I had to do was write in "phone" to make it read "Iphone" and transfer it to a sheet of film.

A telephone is the most precious thing that a migrant has. You could say that he drew his own God.

21.09.16

The workshop went amazingly well today. Why? Because Tony opened my sketchpad (all on his own, no one made him do it) and started painstakingly copying my pencil portrait of Olya Zhitlina. Obviously it wasn't a waste of time. Then I showed them the video *The Utopian Union of the Unemployed*! The very first part, with the voice of the poet Osminkin and Tsaplya doing the montage. We made that video in the old premises of the Center for Independent Social Research in St Petersburg, before they were declared a foreign agent. The point is that in this video ballerinas teach unemployed men, and then the other way round. The point was equality. And the fact that, firstly, this is the only reality for us and, secondly, it is like a dance, the pirouettes and pliés are there in order to achieve this elegantly, taking each other's subtle nuances into account. Grace? How great it is that the guys took it the right way. They saw me copying their drawings, transferring them to the film for silk screening, and they took that to mean they could copy my drawings too. I was so delighted because Tony did it himself. Usually the most difficult thing about them is that they're clenched up tight and don't do anything without being asked or supervised. I have to keep asking and urging them on a countless number of times.

22.09.16

From the exchange of texts about "What's up?" between Agent Magical Bird and Tony:

AMB: What are you doing?

Tony: Having supper.

AMB: What exactly are you eating?

Tony: Bread.

AMB: What, just bread?

Tony: Yes, yes, just bread.

AMB: Just bread and nothing else?

Tony: Yes, just bread and nothing else.

23.09.16

I read that in 2010 Nigeria was the hungriest country in the world. I don't think that anything has changed radically in 2016. But I have to read more about it, of course. I also noticed that the guys lie down a lot. After all, they don't have anything to do.

They showed me a photo of their apartment. Not too bad, in principle.

They really like that they have a television there. And in our gallery they draw for all they're worth. All my concerns were groundless. I can see that they like it and it gives them pleasure.

24.09.16

The reason for the guys' exceptionally intense despondency has become clear. It turns out that the man who took Tony to Libya did it in exchange for Tony sending him a large sum of money once he got settled in Europe. Tony won't say how much.

He only said that he gets 75 euros a month from the Italian authorities while they're waiting for confirmation of their status. It's the same for Prince. I don't know about Precious. It has also become clear that they are so extremely unforthcoming and reluctant to tell us anything about themselves out of fear that we might be connected with human trafficking and sex slavery. There are women in Italy who hire guys like these and turn them into slaves. Now I understand the reasons why Tony never reacts to my jokes. For him any frivolity or sense of humor is associated with the sphere of bodily pleasure. If someone talks to you and jokes, it means they want something. And what could a white, charismatic woman want? It stands to reason!

25.09.16

The workshop happened yesterday!

We even printed with our feet! Our boys finally went away cheerful!

It's all due to the exceptional vitality of a girl from Belarus (who has preferred to remain anonymous). While I was sitting at the table, copying Tony and Prince's drawings, and had lost control of what was going on, a joyful orgy was taking place in the next room. The girl from Belarus took the guys' feet and dunked them into black paint. The great tradition of hospitality suddenly came to life.

They told us about being hungry too. They accepted everything and are willing to go to the restaurant with us!

26.09.16

Today after our activities Tony sent me a text: "My father teached me that I can not do bad things. Do not still and do not still the wife of other man."

27.09.16

I'd just come out of the gallery to buy some pills in the chemist's to ward off a cold coming on, when I saw Prince beside a supermarket, standing there cap in hand in the celebrated pose of a beggar. I was so embarrassed that I went on into the supermarket, vowing determinedly that when I came out I'd present him with a heap of money and invite him to the gallery again.

The thoughts were swirling round in my head like a tornado. In the supermarket the abundance of food fogged up my brain so badly that, after getting totally confused with the new automated tills, when I finally came back out, I didn't find Prince there, he had disappeared. Imagine my surprise when I was struck completely out of the blue by the doubt that perhaps he had never really been there and the whole thing was nothing but hallucinations. I immediately ran to the girls in the gallery and told them everything. There had just been a workshop in which a state of unity was achieved, and now all of a sudden, just like that, everything had gone to pieces! Reality had spat in our faces! Were our feeble efforts worth anything at all?

28.09.16

I have to stop telling Agent Magical Bird about anything and everything. There, I've gone and told her the way things are and now she looks at me strangely, and she has a sad air. In fact her face very often looks exhausted, but when I tell her that, she never admits anything, never, never, she always denies it and says she has loads of strength. I'm afraid all the time that the moment will come when she'll collapse like a scythed reed. She told me her grandfather was killed by Poles who had just been released from a camp, when they tried to steal jewelry from his shop. Her grandfather used to sell jewelry. He ran out after the thieves and they killed him.

29.09.16

I've overdone the work a bit, probably, and I need to go to the swimming pool urgently.

But when I got to the pool, they wouldn't let me in. You can only buy a pass for a year. You can go just once of course, but that would be for 70 euros. That's really a bit too much when Tony and Prince are eating just bread and standing with their hands held out on the other days. I'd better just have a hug with Veronica and it will all pass off.

And now Marzia is proposing to set up a factory to make clothes based on the patterns of clothing from the migrants' countries.

30.09.16

Last night I had a strange dream. We were swimming in the pool – AMB, and all the friends of the gallery, and the newcomers. But for some reason Tony wasn't swimming. I felt awkward that he was sitting there and examining us, but then I got used to it. In the middle of the swimming session Tony suddenly stood up at full height on the edge of the pool and said: *I have to tell you that I'm very much afraid that you'll use me as a sex slave and I'll never be able to pay the man who brought me here 30,000 euros.*

31.09.16

I enjoy working with the guys and I don't worry any longer now about what it's for and how to do it. Basically I think this is the only way to protect yourself against the emptiness of art. I think we enrich each other. But of course you have to unite the totally vulnerable ones and the stronger ones. What I mean is that the Utopian Union of the Unemployed is always an association of the strong and the weak, and in this particular case it's no accident, of course, that the activist Raffaello appeared. I'm not a genuine therapist, after all, I create a situation and sort of supervise it, but I don't promise anyone any answers. Today I signed a contract with the gallery for two years. During that time all the gallery's artists must work with *newcomers* in one way or another. That means, if artists don't want to do work on the subject of migration or involve participants, then they're obliged at least to tell newcomers about their art. And in addition we concluded a separate contract that lists the conditions for the future owner of the silkscreen printing board.

The future owner can print as much as he likes, make as many prints as he likes, but at the same time he or she is obliged, according to one condition stipulated in the contract, to transfer the money from the sale of these prints to the organization Xenia, which undertakes in turn to send newly arrived migrants to the art gallery or directly to the artists.

The contract was one of the items in the exhibition, we gave it the status of a work of art. We enlarged the text of the contract, printed it in one meter by one meter size and hung it on the wall. "Next time we'll print it on marble," said AMB.

1.10.16

The great day has finally arrived!

The performance "Hunger Strike" has taken place! It happened like this. Raffaello, a documentary film maker and activist who has visited refugee camps several times, came three hours before the beginning and shot the preparations. This got in the way a bit, but intellectually I realized that it was kind of the right thing to do and I even managed to say something to camera in the process of ironing the banner "Fear of integration," made by the student Giovanni. "Bologna is not a restaurant" was our basic slogan. We also wore white clothes with "Kabulonia" written on them, made by Ian from Kabul, the same one who works 80 hours a week to send his money to his family. There were other slogans: "Unemployment is a state of mind," and little white frocks.

We walked out of the gallery like the full-start cast of the Utopian Union: 4 newcomers, 4 students from the academy, 2 cameramen, AMB, the student sociologist Marzia, who was talking on the phone all the time, and me.

We paraded solemnly through the streets of the city of Bologna, across the main square, past the citizens dining demurely at the most sacred hour – between eight and nine in the evening. The citizens chewing and hardly even reacting to us (only occasionally was it possible to catch a sympathetic glance) only energized our drive. We reached the main square, went past the cathedral that was left unfinished because the Pope didn't want there to be a cathedral anywhere bigger than in Rome, and walked into a restaurant. We sat down at a table and asked for water. We hardly spoke to each other at all. And if there is happiness in this world, it was then, at the moment of solidarity, when we were united by the idea of resistance. The waiters sensed the intensity and seriousness of the people sitting at the table, and after approaching us with the menu a few times they moved away and stood in the corner of the room, talking to each other and eyeing us. I looked at Agent Magical Bird sitting opposite me and saw a Christian woman prepared to go into a cage with a lion. Tears came to my eyes. I looked at the barely breathing girl sociologist who had attached herself to us at the last moment, and then at Tony, Prince, and Precious, who were genuinely beautiful in the gravity of their drama, which sweeps away all the dross in the world, leaving only the most important thing: the exalted moment of solidarity of people around an idea that doesn't bring anyone any pragmatic benefit. So it turns out this is what I live for. My thanks to all of you, dear friends. After an hour and a bit the waiters broke down and brought us pasta. We looked at each other, got up and walked out of the restaurant.

24.09.16

I have good news!

The newcomers from the previous project have got in touch: Allilu answered me that he is alive and well, and intends to send his diary soon! Allah be praised!!!

And Tony wrote about "What's up" that he's been summoned to the committee again, and he's very worried they won't believe that the man who brought him to Italy is expecting 30,000 euros from him and he's very afraid.

Dmitry Vilensky

CHTO DELAT? AND METHOD: PRACTICING DIALECTIC

Mixing different things

The editorial and exhibition policy of Chto Delat? is often accused of inconsistency, of lacking a clear "party line." What is important for us today is to arrive at a method that would enable us to mix quite different things – reactionary form and radical content, anarchic spontaneity and organizational discipline, hedonism and asceticism, etc.

It is a matter of finding the right proportions. That is, we are once again forced to solve the old problems of composition while also not forgetting that the most faithful composition is always built on the simultaneous sublation and supercharging of contradictions.

As Master Bertolt taught us, these contra-dictions should be resolved not in the work of art, but in real life.

Apropos the polemics with Master Jean-Luc, it is worth noting that one can pace quite neatly from one shot to another and still not end up with a whole film. The question is what the third shot in the sequence will be. And how this third shot will relate to what came before the one plus one.

This, apparently, is just what Master Jean-Luc had in mind: it is always useful to emphasize the source of the whole.

On the usefulness of declarations

Everyone has long ago given up wracking their brains over the question of whether it is possible to elaborate precise rules for organizing the work of a collective. It is now quite rare to come across a new manifesto or declaration. The cult of spontaneity, reactivity, and tactics – the rejection of readymade rules – is the order of the day. Tactics, however, is something less than method. Only by uniting tactics and strategy can we arrive at method.

Hence it is a good thing to try one's hand at writing manifestos from time to time.

On the totality of capital, or playing the idiot

Today it is all the rage to say that there is nothing outside the contemporary world order. Capital and market relations are total, and even if someone or something escapes this logic, then this does not in any way negate it. This is a trait of moderately progressive consciousness: such is the opinion of leftist theorists, and the capitalists have no real objections to their equitable thesis.

We should play the idiot and simply declare this thesis a lie. We know quite well whose interests are served by it.

Being productive?

Master Bertolt said that a person should be productive. Following his method of thinking, we might boldly claim that a person should be unproductive or that a person should not be productive. We end up with a big mess. We can get ourselves out of this muddle by asking a single question: *to what end should we be productive?*

By constantly asking ourselves this question, we can resolve various working situations and understand when it is worth producing something and when it is not.

On compromises

Politically engaged artists inevitably face the question of compromise in their practices. It primarily arises when they have to decide whether to take money from one or another source, or participate in one project or another.

There are several readymade decisions to which artists resort. Some artists keen endlessly that it is impossible to stay pure in an unclean world and so they constantly wind up covered in shit. Other artists regard themselves as rays of light in the kingdom of darkness. They are quite afraid of relinquishing their radiant purity, which no one could care less about except they themselves.

The conversation about the balance between purity and impurity is banal, although finding this balance is in fact the principal element of art making.

Master Bertolt suggested us to "drink wine and water from different glasses."

On working with institutions

It is too little to postulate that collaborating with cultural institutions is a good thing or, on the contrary, that it is a bad thing. We should always remember that it is worth getting mixed up in such relations only when we try to change these institutions themselves, so that those who come after us will not need to waste their time on such silly matters and will immediately be able to get down to more essential work.

On subjugation to the dominant class

We cannot deny the fact that the great artworks of the past were produced *despite* the subjugated position of their creators.

As we recognize this fact today we should emphasize the vital proviso "despite." We thus constantly remind ourselves what art could and should be if the subjugation to the dominant classes and tastes could disappear.

On the historicity of art

Like everything else in the world, art is historical. What does this mean?

First of all, it does not mean that what was created in the past has no meaning today.

Master Bertolt and Master Jean-Luc demonstrated that art is something that arises from difficulties and rouses us to action.

Those who deny art's dependence on the powers that be are stupid.

Those who do not see that people's creative powers never dry up, even in the face of slavery and hopelessness, are blind.

The essence of the great method is to assist the *power of creativity* in overcoming its dependence on the system of art.

The formula of dialectical cinema

As Master Jean-Luc quite aptly noted, "Art is not the reflection of reality, but the reality of this reflection."

To this we should add that this reality is transformative. It has less to do with life as it is, and more to do with how the conditions of people's lives can and must change.

On financing

Master Jean-Luc unexpectedly spoke out in favor of "ten-dollar financing" for authentic films over Hollywood-style budgets.

At first glance this idea sounds like mockery. Upon more careful reflection, however, we realize that the master was not promoting the total absence of financing. And he made no mention of the sources of this financing.

On the boundaries of the disciplines

It is believed that we should have long ago put an end to the division of knowledge into separate disciplines. The mantra "knowledge is one" is hugely popular with many progressive people. They say that there is only one kind of knowledge, which serves the cause of emancipation.

And they are right insofar as there is hardly any sense in using the proud word knowledge to describe methods for enslaving consciousness.

It is a good cause to use all our powers to bring closer that day when the disciplinary divisions will disappear, but it is premature to speak of this today.

We should say rather that knowledge is one, but *for the time being* it consists of many disciplines. We must try and achieve perfection in each of them.

For now this is the most important contribution we can make to the cause of emancipation.

On the question of self-education

More and more often we hear that all imposed forms of education are unavoidably evil, that we should close all schools and organize ourselves into nonhierarchical circles in which there would be no difference between the learned and the ignorant, old and young, man and woman, the person born in misery and the person born with a silver spoon. All this sounds nice and of course we know the historical origins of such ideas.

Born at a certain historical moment, they played a supremely important role in transforming all of society and shifting capitalism to a new stage – the knowledge economy, the flexible labor market, exploitation of the general intellect, etc. Does it make sense for those who see all the dead ends of this path of development to repeat these new truisms of capital?

Let us leave the rhetoric of self-education to the corporations, which have such a need for the newly flexible worker willing to engage in lifelong learning.

Why shouldn't we again think hard about creating a methodology of learning and teaching that takes account of the contemporary moment?

I see nothing bad about having all children study Marxist dialectics, value theory, the history of the workers movement, and art history. The problem is how to make such obligatory courses thrilling and entertaining, how to combine discipline and freedom.

If we are unwilling to think in this direction, however, that means we have already lost.

On the theory of the weakest link

The question of where a breakthrough is possible, in what countries – that is, where it will be possible to create new relations outside the dominion of private property and the egotistical interests of individuals – is the most vital question.

The theory of the weakest link proved its utility in the past. Can it prove workable again? On the one hand, we are witnesses to capital's unbelievable experiments in the development of technology and new forms of life. On the other, we see clearly that the period of prosperity in the First World, paid for with the slave labor of the rest of the world, led to a situation in which *even oppressed people in the First World* were embourgeoised. Their class consciousness, even in the most progressive circles, is bourgeois consciousness. In the west, even the most out-and-out punk is bourgeois to a certain extent.

The situation outside the First World, however, looks just as hopeless. Since the emergence of cognitive capitalism, the colonial hegemony of western countries has only grown. Detecting new emancipatory potential in the Third World is no less difficult than in the First World, despite the fact that it is precisely here that forms of collective consciousness have been preserved.

We should pay close attention to newly emergent enclaves of the Third World within the First World and of the First World on the periphery. If they cooperate in the future they might become a revolutionary force capable of changing the world.

And of course we should carefully analyze everything that is happening in Latin America.

On the withering away of art

To create an art that withers away – that is, a powerful art that disappears as its functions disappear, an art that reduces its own success to naught – we should build its institutions dialectically. That is, to begin with we need to generate a healthy conflict and then devise a mechanism that would enable us to abolish the gap between the act of creativity and the system that represents it.

This is only possible, however, given a total transformation of the entire system of power and political relations. Here the forces of art (even an art that is withering away) are insufficient. Although we also should affirm that unless art's function is changed *right now*, any transformation of power relations will prove impossible.

One artist – Master Di-Gu – believed that his works were
so autonomous that they could be exhibited in any context
without losing any of their power. In all likelihood, he greatly
exaggerated their autonomy. The ease with which his works
turned up in any number of the most dubious contexts finally
called into question all his utterances. Unfortunately, his fate
was typical for most practitioners of critical art, who for some
reason considered themselves independent.

Another master – An-Os – suddenly decided that only by
resurrecting the object's commodity aura could the struggle
in art be continued. He failed to take one factor into account,
however: the commodity aura had not gone away during the
time it took for him to learn this expression. Following this
path, he thus became one of the multitude of artists who are as
difficult to count as the grains of sand on a beach.

On the utility of reading, viewing and the supreme privilege

Many people greatly enjoy reading, viewing films, and visiting
museums. There is nothing wrong with this.

What is wrong is that in our society only a tiny minority is
capable of creating something from their experience of reading
books, watching films, and visiting museums.

There is an old argument. Should art dissolve into life, or
should it, on the contrary, absorb the entire experience of life
and express it in new forms? Which position is the most correct
one today?

Art should absorb the entire experience of life and express it
in new forms. The principal task of these new forms – to come
back transformed and dissolve into life, thus provoking life's

transformation – is to change the world, the thing that everyone so loves talking about.

Ideas and the masses

Ideas mean nothing unless they seize the consciousness of people. Does this principle allow us to judge the quality of ideas? No, it does not. History teaches us that ideas need time in order to possess the consciousness of many people; it is a lengthy process. We can say with certainty, however, that ideas that *do nothing* to possess people's consciousness mean very little.

Therefore we have only ourselves to blame for the fact that we have remained unpersuasive.

On universality

A universal method might well be applied to a multitude of particular cases.

But the great method is unlikely to arise from a multitude of particular cases.

On world art

Everyone remembers how the Great Teacher wrote in a manifesto about the origin of world literature. Who would be so bold as to talk about world art today? Of course this would sound totalizing and bombastic. Statements of this sort will always appear suspicious.

It is just for this reason that we should try to speak of world art.

On leaders

Even in the most horizontally democratic organization the police can fairly quickly determine who they should arrest in order to paralyze its work.

We should consider organizational models in which this situation would be inconceivable. We don't need an absence of leaders, but a surplus. Only when each of us becomes a leader can we reject this notion itself. For the time being, however, we should not forget that our leaders need special protection from the police.

The brightest minds are willing to write and meditate on the dialectic, but only a few of them are capable of doing this dialectically.

The best artists make works on politics, inequality, and ordinary people, but only a few of them do this politically.

The best politicians try to mitigate people's hardships – to guarantee that their rights and freedoms are observed, to help the weak and the sick – but only a few of them are capable of questioning the very system of relations that destroys, robs, and cripples people.

On defamiliarization and subversive affirmation

Nothing has so spoiled the consciousness of the handful of politically minded contemporary artists than using the method of subversive affirmation. Many of them have decided that this is the most appropriate method for critiquing society and raising consciousness. But is this the case?

It is as if everyone has forgotten that capital has no sense of shame, that it is essentially pornographic. Of course it's tempting to turn soft porn into hardcore, but what does this change? This does not mean that we should discard these methods altogether. We should simply always employ them in the right proportions. It is not enough to make shit look shittier and smell smellier. It is vital to convince the viewer that there is also something that is different from shit.

And we shouldn't count on the fact that viewers will figure this out for themselves.

Is it possible to make love politically?

Master Bertolt said that love between two people becomes meaningful when a common cause arises between them – serving the revolutionary cause or something of the sort. Only then are they able to overcome their finitude in bed as well.

The most vivid example of dialectical affirmation in history is Benjamin's thesis that communists answer the fascist "aestheticization of politics" with a "politicization of art." It turns out that aesthetics is on the side of fascism, while art is on the side of the communists. I think that we shouldn't so easily farm out aesthetics to history's brown-shirted forces. Today we should reexamine this thesis and, most likely, conclude that we really lack an *aesthetics of the politicization of art.*

Only in this case we will have the chance to see, perhaps, the emergence of something comparable in power to the Marseillaise.

23

Yevgeny Granilshchikov

WEAKNESS: A SCENARIO FOR TWO ACTORS AND ONE CAMERA

'that she's married to a doctor, who acts with her in the serial, but in the serial she plays his daughter. Something like that, merely an illustration.'

'what does that have to do with our conversation?'

'well, that you'll be played by an actor.'

'you know, it really is quite difficult. Basically, I'm not sure that I can explain to someone why they ought to take part in this. And I think that's actually a good thing, and the video will be about this weakness of the director, do you understand? I can't explain anything, and so something else is needed here.'

'then, on the one hand, what you get is a film that's making itself. That is, right now, as we're talking … That is, the production is included in the actual work. And in that way you've already dodged criticism. But I don't quite understand what the viewers are supposed to see. What story are they following?'

'the viewers should see this as a documentary story, as if this conversation is taking place and being recorded right now, it shouldn't look like I recorded the conversation first, then edited it and then asked two actors to play it. In short, it should look like a documentary story played out by actors.'

'okay, so why don't we try to play it out now?'

'excellent. Let's do that. Right now. We need to get into the mood.'

'no, it won't work that way, we have to switch moods immediately. Just like that.'

'okay, let's go.'

'tell me about the film.'

'well, you see, I'm not planning to shoot anything that might look like a film. It's not a traditional form. I think it should be an improvisation. Basically, I thought up a little video work in which a conversation takes place between the director and an actress. But there's one problem. She has decided in advance that she's going to decline the offer to take part in this, although she has come to the meeting. And she asks him what the film is about and why it ought to be made. Basically, she asks really difficult questions, which he – that is, I – find hard to answer. And there's another thing, it's to do with politics … At one point it becomes clear that this isn't an entirely innocuous film, if you take my meaning.'

'no, hang on, that's a bit too complicated somehow, why don't we imagine instead that we're already in this situation, OK? Already in the film …'

'you're right, let's do that.'

'it's just that there are too many layers, and none of them have been thought right through. That is, we start speaking the text for the actors who are supposed to play us afterwards … And we start imagining how they would perform this …'

'and we'll have to go back to the beginning, where you remember again about this serial.'

'that she's married to a doctor, who acts with her in the serial, but in the serial she plays his daughter. All right, let's do it as if we're already acting … Basically that idea's not entirely clear to me. What's the most important thing about this story for you?'

'I'm going to call this film *Weakness*. Also bearing in mind the condition you experience just before the onset of an illness.'

'and what do you think the weakness of this film is?'

'it's the fact that I don't know how to defend it, to explain the idea so that you agree to do it.'

'you know, there's this idiotic game called squash. In tennis, for instance, the opponents face each other, but in squash the game is mediated, so to speak. The opponents hit the ball against a wall, and they stand beside each other, almost shoulder to shoulder. So tell me, why am I the one who has to take part in this?'

'i realize it's not really very convincing, but just consider it an intuition.'

'what exactly is supposed to happen in this film? I'm thinking of some kind of pivotal moment. Is the point here that you're not sure about anything and you're trying to turn that into your advantage? Or is the point that …'

'the point is that I'm not sure about the actual method. I think everything needs to be changed. Perhaps this is my last attempt to shoot anything in this vein and I'll never come back to it again.'

'and that is your pivotal point?'

'no, but it could become some kind of starting point.'

'this text that we're recording right now, will you really give it to actors afterwards?'

'possibly.'

'then the viewers won't understand what they're up against … the documentation of a real scene or something staged. You

could even say that right now we *are* actors who are speaking
a text as if it has already been written by someone. And even
if that isn't true, and it isn't – even so, we're still playing parts,
that is, the situation we're in is already like one on-screen.'

'basically yes, you're absolutely right. I want to make a video
that could be a disaster and my last film.'

'and then afterwards you'll decipher all the lines that we've
recorded and maybe add something that you write. Maybe
you'll put in a phrase that I never said. And your actors, who
are going to play me, and even the two of us, who are already
acting, we won't be able to tell what was said and what wasn't.
And when I say 'I,' I'm not even sure about my own identity, do
you understand?'

'all right, but you're confusing the situation yourself now.
Despite the fact that you decided in advance to decline the
offer of this part, if seems like now you've finally got interested
in it …'

'I didn't say that I'd decided in advance to decline.'

'true, that was my assumption.'

'well, all right. Can you explain to me what the viewers will
see? Two actors speaking this text?'

'initially I thought there had to be a long shot with a chase.
Imagine you're on your way back home and I'm following
you and filming you. But you don't notice me, I just walk
along after you … And while you're walking, we hear this
conversation in the background.'

'you mean, we hear a dialogue that is constantly testing its
own plausibility! Or, more accurately, we're testing the very
possibility of writing a scenario in that precise fashion.'

'yes, while the actual visual sequence couldn't be more
simple.'

'and it only has one of the characters in it.'

'no, it has both characters in it. You and the camera. Your relationship.'

'all right, and are we in the film right now, or are we sorting out the technical side of things?'

'a little bit earlier we agreed that we're in the film.'

'you really are closer than ever before to disaster. All right, let's assume that I didn't want to accept the offer, but now I've got interested.'

'that's what I was counting on.'

'you were counting on your doubts having an influence on me?'

'yes, I was hoping.'

'weren't you saying something about politics and this film not being entirely innocuous?'

'yes, and that's a particularly difficult point.'

'well, let's assume that I anticipated something of the kind. What kind of politics are you talking about? Will I have to deliver a political monologue that you've written?'

'not exactly that, you will deliver a monologue that hasn't been written yet …'

'I think that first of all we need to understand if our political views are in agreement.'

'that's what I was afraid of: that you'd start trying to find out if our political views are in agreement and everything would fall to pieces, and on top of that you'd stop being an actress. That can happen when the subject of political cinema comes up …'

'because the actor becomes an accomplice. This is one of those cases when it matters to me to what extent my personal political position and the position of my character will coincide.'

'but an actor can't play Macbeth without experiencing that kind of doubt!'

'let's assume that he can …'

'you mean, you can repeat Macbeth's line of development, but you can't deliver a monologue in my film?'

'when it comes to political cinema, a film isn't just someone's story.'

'you mean, you wouldn't argue with Shakespeare's lines, but you could edit lines from my scenario?'

'no, I don't intend to edit them, I just think that doubt is appropriate here.'

'and our political views have to be in agreement?'

'no, not necessarily. But I want to understand in whose name I'm speaking …

And apart from that, there is no political cinema without opposition between director and actor.'

'you mean you think that in a political film the figure of the director should be placed in doubt?'

'yes, in that case our social or, to be more precise, professional roles are accentuated.'

'you haven't confirmed that you'll take part in the film yet, but you've already played through the first act.'

'right now I don't understand in what way I am going to participate in your project.'

'you already started participating when you said that any political film should start from doubt.'

'don't you agree with that?'

'i do. I would be doubtful too. But sometimes it can be a hindrance. It leads me to the thought that political cinema is anti-auteur cinema. But I'd like to make a film the way I conceived it.'

'but you haven't conceived anything. You suggested that we should meet up and have a talk. And you said that our conversation could possibly become the starting point for a scenario … Right now are things turning out the way you conceived them?'

'i thought you wouldn't agree and that would become part of the storyline.'

'but I really haven't agreed yet.'

'okay, you can agree and try to play yourself, or decline, and then a different actor will play you.'

'you're still intending to write a scenario based on our conversation?'

'i'm thinking about it, but I haven't decided yet.'

'then I don't understand my part.'

'the most important thing is that you're doubtful, for instance about whether you should act in this or not. But in a certain sense you're already acting in it. We're already doing the job, and the only way you can really not take part is to leave right now.'

'you mean that if I tell you I'm leaving and start explaining why, that will become part of the film?'

'yes, all your doubt is what gets the film moving.'

'that's just like constantly calling attention to the passing of time.'

'i think what this film illustrates is precisely the idea that it's impossible to remain on the sidelines and avoid politics. With the single difference that you can still get up and leave and not take part in this film, but the people living in Russia today can't leave, they can't go anywhere. And the bottom line is that everything we're talking about right now – whether you want to act or you don't – is trivial.'

'okay, you say it's impossible to stay on the sidelines and try to fool yourself that politics doesn't concern you and you can remain unnoticed. But what will happen to your film or scenario if I leave right this very moment?'

'it will be a disaster, there won't be any film.'

'all right, I get it, let's get back to the actors. Do you still want us to be played by actors after all?'

'right now I'm trying to understand what exactly will change in the material if these lines of ours are spoken by actors. After all, they won't know if our meeting ever really happened and you spoke these words, or if I wrote them in myself later.'

'does the question of sincerity interest you at all? Right now we're talking and everything's happening for real. But if you write a scenario and give it to actors, they'll have to play our parts. What will change in that case?'

'it seems to me that in a political film there has to be some kind of manipulation.'

'getting back to the title … Maybe you interpreted or construed the meaning of the title *Weakness* wrongly at the beginning of our conversation?'

'i didn't take into account the point that you might get infected by this weakness.'

'the boundary between acting and being here is totally blurred here. I think we're following rules of some kind, but I'm not sure you know what they are.'

'maybe we're taking our motivation from clichés?'

'now I understand why this film is about politics. Only it's not squash, now it's more like a game of chess.'

'you asked where the pivotal point is here …'

'we skipped through that a page ago. But now that everything's in place, there are two ways we can go. Carry on until the end of time or wrap this dialogue up right here and now.'

'what would you prefer?'

'to know who's going to play our parts!'

'all right, I'll tell you, only remind me what that business with the doctor was all about …'

'i said that she was married to a doctor who acted with her in a serial. But in the serial she played his daughter. Something like that. Merely an illustration.'

Part Five

Future futures

In this post-utopian era we question the notion of progress and restrain ourselves from visions of a better future. Many current theoretical and artistic concerns are tasked with reimagining the human subject and its position in the world. Our visions of the future are heavily loaded with conceptions of the anthropocene, of irreversible ecological changes, the growing abyss between rich and poor and the accelerating automatisation of labour. What is the artistic response to our sense of attachment and connection to a world shared with others: humans, animals, minerals, objects, machines?

24

Oxana Timofeeva

ULTRA BLACK: BRIEF NOTES TOWARDS A MATERIALIST THEORY OF OIL

People think that they sell oil, but in fact they are becoming oil.
VIKTOR PELEVIN

How is it possible, if possible at all, to be a materialist today?
The question could be addressed to those who proclaim
themselves the only true materialists and build their argument
on the critique of the wrongness of the materialism of the
others. Is there a better name for this epic battle for the flag
of materialism than "philosophy of nature"? Such naming,
however, seems to be compromised in today's theory, as any
synthesis of knowledge about the living and the nonliving world
under the head of philosophy of nature threatens to awaken the
specter of classical Western metaphysics that is already labeled
as idealism in all philosophy schoolbooks. And yet the question
of nature, or material reality, is a stumbling block of ontology,
philosophy of science, political economy, and psychoanalysis.
The main difference is that today's philosophers of nature do

not present their subject matter as a mirror of spirit, a universe of God's creatures or something of this kind, but seek to discover nature as such, to think about the very nature of nature that is naturally independent of thought, if not opposite to it.

About a hundred years ago Alfred North Whitehead, a famous English philosopher and mathematician, formulated the problem as follows: "Thus in a sense nature is independent of thought. By this statement no metaphysical pronouncement is intended. What I mean is that we can think about nature without thinking about thought. I shall say that then we are thinking 'homogeneously' about nature. Of course it is possible to think nature in conjunction with thought about the fact that nature is thought about. In such a case I shall say that we are thinking 'heterogeneously' about nature."[1] Nature is not thought, says Whitehead, and it is difficult not to agree with this statement. Thinking homogeneously about nature is, according to Whitehead, inherent to natural sciences. It seems that now philosophy joins this thread and paves various ways of thinking nature that is not thought as it naturally is. These ways are called materialisms, new materialisms, and realisms. However, with over- or underprecision, we can still qualify them as new philosophies of nature.

The concept of nature revolves around the concept of the human, in various directions, including the transhuman, the nonhuman, the antihuman, the posthuman, or the inhuman. The nature of nature as such can be thought as agential (Karen Barad's agential realism); as ancestral or real that was already there before us (Quentin Meillassoux); as objectal – when everything, subjects included, turns into objects (Graham Harman), or even hyperobjects – global warming, etc. – that now, at the end of the world, rise beyond all our measurements (Timothy Morton). It can be described in older oppositions of subject and substance, or subject and object, or subject and thing (materialist dialectics and transcendental materialism, critical Marxism, or psychoanalysis). It can be approached as forms of life (vitalism), as bodies (corporeal, transcorporeal and incorporeal materialisms, or what Alain Badiou ironically calls "democratic materialism"), or as media and technology. It can be dialectically or nondialectically opposed to technology, or identified with it. It can be represented and symbolized as a constant lack – a lack of resources (extractive economy), a lack of desire (libidinal economy), etc. – but at the same time as an irreducible excess; as a realm of need and necessity, or of hyperchaos and contingency; as something to be defended and preserved (ecophilosophy, deep ecology), or as a threat, as a complex of unknown, blind and potentially destructive forces (dark materialism).

In his book *In the Dust of This Planet*, Eugene Thacker presents a dark materialist philosophy of nature through the lenses of horror. The word "world" has, according to Thacker, three different meanings. The first is the *world-for-us*, or simply the *World*; the second is the *world-in-itself*, or the *Earth*, and the third is the *world-without-us*, or the *Planet*. The World is anthropocentric, the Earth is natural, and the horrifying Planet is supranatural, or fantastic. About the Earth, or nature, that in a significant part is "grounded by scientific enquiry." Thacker says that it is "a paradoxical concept; the moment we think it and attempt to act on it, it ceases to be the world-it-itself and becomes the world-for-us."[2] The author is more interested in the last, supranatural world, from the (non)understanding of which he is trying to remove all the anthropomorphic projections. He claims that thought is not human, that nature is not natural, that life does not belong to living beings but is rather alien to them, and that perhaps the future of philosophy lies in the mysticism of an inhuman, uncanny dark matter. Such mysticism of nowadays is not theological, but climatological, and devolves "upon the radical disjunction and indifference of the self and the world."[3]

Without sharing the mystical spirit of Thaker's philosophy of nature (any horror makes serious sense to me only when it turns into a comedy, which is a stronger weapon that demystifies not only everything that exists but also everything that does not, without reducing it all to a mere data of positivist inventory), I generally find this division useful and productive. However, I would like to suggest that the world-for-us, the world-in-itself, and the world-without-us are not three separate entities. I rather imagine them as three concentric circles: the smallest inside is the World, the bigger the Earth, and the biggest the Planet – although, after all, these three circles might be of the same size and even occupy the same place: their difference is not geometrical, but topological. The first circle is like the home where we live. In this home, everything is familiar; we are surrounded by things that belong to us. We open the doors of this circle and go out: there is a second circle there, where animals and plants dwell without thinking and being thought. This is nature as such, or the world-in-itself, or – to borrow the name that Quentin Meillassoux gives to things-in-themselves outside any subjective relation – the Great Outdoors.[4] We grab something there (some food, some wood to make fire, some water, etc.) and go back inside. But we know that there are yet other doors, the doors of nature, that lead towards a Greater Outdoors where even the wildest of beasts do not dare to go, let alone humans. It is populated by gods, demons, dark forces, hyperobjects, and other entities that, for some unknown reason, we cannot or do not want to explain rationally even if we created them ourselves.

The cosmic utopia wants to conquer not only nature, but that Greater Outdoors, too. It wants to make it ours – contrary to mysticism that keeps it secret: in this sense, Russian cosmism presents an interesting alternative to the dark materialism. Revolution is not possible in one separate country, but the worldwide revolution is not enough, too, as it only involves humanity. Bolsheviks dreamed of revolutionizing not just society, but nature itself, for nature was considered a realm of unfreedom, inequality, injustice, need, exploitation, and death.[5] Turning rivers, blasting mountains, making animals speak: the idea was to transform the Earth by means of technology in order to make it, as Andrey Platonov says, more "kind to us."[6] But even this does not seem satisfactory, as revolution tends to expand further, and to become planetary, or cosmic.

Doesn't this desire to conquer the Greater Outdoors tell us that the triple circle of the World, the Earth, and the Planet is still structured like the human habitat with its composite inner and outer spaces, connected by doors that lead in and out? In ancient Greece, the outer part of this structure was called *cosmos*, and the inner one – *oikos*. The latter has several meanings – a house, a household, a family, but also a family's property including slaves. Today these meanings are kept in paronymous words – *economy* and *ecology*. Both economy and ecology are dealing with nature – either as a living world, environment, *Umwelt*, or as a source and resource. They are conjugate: beyond ecology there is always economy, and vice versa: this is our earthly home; here we keep slaves and exchange oil for money. But this is not the whole story, as beyond the doors nature the Greater Outdoors stands and creates anxiety. How is it possible, the world-without-us?

My argument would be that this uncanny space or cosmos does not stand out or around the canny space of the oikos that we share with other natural creatures, but paradoxically emerges at the very heart of it. Without is within. What appears to us as absolutely alien and monstrous is to be found there where we would never think of searching for it. As Alenka Zupancic puts it very precisely: "the great Outside is the fantasy that covers up the Real that is already right here."[7] The fact that it is a phantasy does not mean that it can be neglected. As psychoanalysis teaches us, phantasy is no less, but may be even more important than what we call reality. The phantasmatic world-without-us is not only attached to the world-for-us, but presents its internal truth. It is *un*canny as it is *un*human and *un*natural, where the prefix *un-* does not merely negate, but produces a kind of displacement that dialectically turns canny, natural, human, etc. into their opposites, but still keeps the former, so to say, in that negative form.

The etymologies of the words *heimlich* (canny) and *unheimlich* (uncanny), both deriving from *das Heim* – the home, the domestic hearth, – was analyzed by Freud, who underlined the ambivalence of *Heimlich*, which, on the one hand, "means what is familiar and agreeable, and on the other, what is concealed and kept out of sight."[8] Freud referred to Schelling's definition of *unheimlich* as "everything that ought to have remained secret and hidden but has come to light."[9] According to Freud, the feeling of uncannyness – this special kind of fear – relates to "something repressed which recurs" and thus it is "nothing new or alien, but something which is familiar and old-established in the mind and which has become alienated from it only through the process of repression."[10] The *un*conscious is not a mysterious substantial reality beyond our psychic life, but a structural formation of the process of repression which, as Lacan explains,[11] coincides with the return of the repressed. Similarly to that, the inhuman and unnatural planetary outside of the world can be regarded as at the same time its very innermost, that returns from the depths of the oblivion in a scary shape that we do not recognize. The world constantly turns inside out, and we are the hole through which it does so (by "we" I do not mean exclusively humans, but a much bigger collective of beings that precedes concrete species).[12]

As Georges Bataille writes in his very short essay "Materialism" (1929): "Materialism will be seen as a senile idealism to the extent that it is not immediately based on psychological or social facts, instead of on artificially isolated physical phenomena. Thus it is from Freud, among others – rather than from long-dead physicists, whose ideas today have no meaning – that a representation of matter must be taken."[13] In this sense, Alberto Toscano is right when he says that Meillassoux's concept of the Great Outdoors, or ancestral real, indifferent to humans and animals, is "ultimately idealist in form."[14] It is not random that Simon Critchley evokes Bataille's spirit in his critique of Meillassoux. He recalls a conversation between Bataille and A. J. Ayer, a British proponent of logical positivism, which took place in a Paris bar in 1951:

[It] lasted until three in the morning. The thesis under discussion was very simple: did the sun exist before the appearance of humans? Ayer saw no reason to doubt that it did, whereas Bataille thought the whole proposition meaningless. For a philosopher committed to scientific realism, like Ayer, it makes evident sense to utter ancestral statements such as "The sun existed prior to the appearance of humans," whereas, for a correlationist like Bataille, more versed in Hegel and phenomenology, physical objects must be perceived by an observer in order to be said to exist.[15]

To be precise, Bataille's sun does not really need an observer. "Observer" is may be not the right word here: one cannot, as Bataille constantly repeats, "observe" the sun, at least directly – because it burns the eyes. The sun is that cosmic object that makes me blind, insane, dizzy. The psychological aspect of matter, which Bataille tries to take into account in his own conception of base materialism, should not be underestimated. Matter is principally ambivalent and heterogeneous, as is the unconscious, and cannot be reduced to anything within an epistemic framework. Later, in his book *The Accursed Share*, Bataille expands his critique of political economy on the planetary scale and articulates the need "to recognize in the economy – in the production and use of wealth – a particular aspect of terrestrial activity regarded as a cosmic phenomenon."[16] This planetary activity is called "general economy" and is opposed to a "restricted" economy that only registers the activity of human beings on Earth. Restricted economy is the movement of labor and accumulation (of goods, of capital), whereas the general, planetary economy consists in expenditure and the nonproductive consumption. The more we try to accumulate inside, the more destruction comes from the outside: a volcano explodes and we cannot do anything about that. An ultimately destructive cosmic activity is, of course, totally indifferent to humans, but we are involved in it (as one is involved in a crime – if you know Bataille's set of metaphors …). If we regard this theory as an economic refraction of Bataille's earlier base materialist insights (which is, I think, theoretically legitimate), then we have to admit that the general cosmic activity is material, and thus corresponds to the unconscious that itself, in Bataille, is rather posthuman. To put it in more psychoanalytic terms, there is a libidinal dimension of planetary ecology and economy, where a universal death drive underlies all other drives.

In the world-for-us, where things operate according to the domestic laws of restricted economy, the unconscious becomes the capitalist unconscious.[17] Existence under the capitalist regime is bound to a general equivalent, or a value-form that can be attached to any piece of living and nonliving matter. The world as we know it consists of commodities, and among commodities there is one for which all other commodities can be exchanged: money. Money is both abstract and real; it is real abstraction that, even if it does not really exist, produces effects in reality. However, this does not give us an entire picture of the structure of the world-for-us. The fact is that money is not an ultimate commodity. It is not an autonomous being. Behind money, there are three main commodities upon which it grows: the first is matter, the second is labor, and the third is time. Here, I am only talking about the first.

In contrast to money, matter is not an abstraction, otherwise this would not be matter, but an idea – this is the sense of what Bataille calls "senile idealism." Matter as an ultimate commodity is a concrete piece of substance, to which money clings in order to prove that it is real. Such a piece of substance historically stands for the whole material world exchanged for money. It is a material side of the general equivalent, or the Thing of economy. In the old times, the general equivalent was represented by gold. Now such a commodity is – not 'officially,' but conventionally – oil.

"Oil is the life-blood throbbing through the arteries of war," says Hitler in Julian Semenov's famous novel *Seventeen Moments of Spring*.[18] Today, especially with the war crisis in the Middle East, this sounds even more evident. Thus, in Reza Negarestani's *Cyclonopedia* it is oil that allows grasping war as a machine, or rather two machines: on the one side there is an Abrahamic monotheism, or jihad war, on the other – Technocapitalist war, or the War on Terror:

> To grasp war as a machine, or in other words, to inquire into the Abrahamic war machine in its relation to the Technocapitalist war machine, we must first realize which components allow Technocapitalism and Abrahamic monotheism to reciprocate at all, even on a synergistically hostile level. The answer is oil: War on Terror cannot be radically and technically grasped as a machine without consideration of the oil that greases its parts and recomposes its flows; such consideration must begin with the twilight of hydrocarbon and the very dawn of the Earth.[19]

Negarestani presents a set of ideas of the nature and origination of oil, or its "hyperstitional entities." Among other representations, he touches upon a popular comparison between oil and blood and relates it to the "myth of fossil fuels, according to which hydrocarbons constitute the origin of petroleum."[20] Both oil and blood contain porphyrin, an organic compound that serves as an "evidence of a common lineage, the hydrocarbon," and, in the eyes of the "advocates of the myth of fossil fuels," proves that oil as a blood of Earth is not just a metaphor. Politico-economic explications of the theory of fossil fuels are that the sources of oil are finite, and in the petroleum wars blood is the price of oil. To put it very simply, the fossil fuels theory, categorized by Negarestani as myth, suggests that oil was produced from organic matter – from decomposition of various living organisms, from bacteria to dinosaurs.

As Negarestani notes very briefly apropos this theory, the idea that "petroleum was formed as a Tellurian entity under unimaginable pressure and heat in the absence of oxygen and between the strata, in absolute isolation" comprises "a typical Freudian Oedipal case."[21] Negarestani is clearly not very interested in this case, because, as emphasized by Melanie Doherty,[22] he aims, in a rather post-Deleuzian vein, to outline a theory of the non-Oedipal, inorganic unconscious that underlies planetary economy and world military politics. Negarestani's oil is a part of a sort of diabolic cosmic conspiracy, which brings together all existing narrations. But the very link between the oil and the unconscious is what I find important.

My first associations with oil are definitely "organic." When I was little, my family lived in Surgut, one of the centers of the oil industry in the northwest of Siberia. As a schoolgirl, I was very familiar with the "dinosaurs" myth. It was my mother who told me that the oil was made of their bodies which were decomposing beneath the ground and the layers of permafrost. On my way to school there was a shallow swamp. Each time I crossed it I had a feeling that the ground is in fact never really solid, not only here but everywhere, also there where we think it is solid – it just covers this tenacious black liquid of the subterranean cemetery of enormous animals that inhabited the Earth long before us. I guess I even believed that the scary dinosaurs could reemerge from a swamp created by an oil spill, similarly to a Loch Ness monster protruding from the waters of the lake. Somehow, oil kept something from that organic life the death of which was its origin. The oil of my childhood was organic, that is, neither living nor dead, but a living dead, an Undead, or an uncanny and utterly inhuman afterlife of ancestral animals. Was it there, similarly to the sun, before us, as a proponent of a philosophical realism – or a schoolgirl like me in 1986, right before the collapse of the Soviet Union – would suggest? Or should we admit, in a Bataillean manner, that this proposition is meaningless, not because this substance must be observed, but because, like the sun, it burns?

"The Black Corpse of the Sun" is one of the names given to oil in Negarestani's book. It makes me think about the color of oil. I saw it spilled around. Nothing can be compared to the blackness of it. Oil is ultra-black. More black than death. More black than the black laborer. More black than the slaves from Mother Africa brought to Americas in the era of colonialism. More black than the black market today, where slaves are an illegal commodity hidden somewhere underground, in the basements of houses. Remember Marx, who, in his *Economic and Philosophic Manuscripts* of 1844 does not really make a big difference between a worker and a slave: the point is that exploitation transforms a living labor into a dead capital. What do a slave, a worker, and oil have in common? That very fact that they are not only the repressed, the unconscious layer of the society in which we exchange matter, labor, and time for money, but that they are exploited, or the oppressed. The worker is exploited as a labor force, the slave is exploited as a black labor force, and the oil is exploited as a natural resource. If we want to grasp oil, as Hegel would say, "not only as substance, but also as subject," not only as the thing from the Greater outdoors, but as "the Real that is already right here," we must admit that oil, which now stands behind money for the whole material universe, is not a master, but a kind of ultimately inhuman black slave, that literally occupies the lowest – and the biggest – stratum of the pyramid of exploitation, and creates the very core of our capitalist unconscious. If you search for a subject of a cosmic revolution, go preach to the oil.

Notes

1   A. N. Whitehead, *Concept of Nature*, Cambridge: Cambridge University Press, 1964, p. 3.

2   E. Thacker, *In the Dust of This Planet [Horror of Philosophy, Vol. 1]*. Winchester: Zero Books, 2011, pp. 4–7.

3   Ibid., p. 158.

4   Q. Meillassoux, *After Finitude: An Essay on the Necessity of Contingency*, trans. R. Brassier, London: Continuum, 2009.

5   See on this, for example: O. Timofeeva and L. Chiesa, "(Post)Socialist Animals and Plants," in *UMBR(a): A Journal of the Unconscious*, 2012. Technology, 115–28.

6   A. Platonov, "On the First Socialist Tragedy," trans. Tony Wood, *New Left Review*, 2011, vol. 69, p. 312.

7   A. Zupancic, "Realism in Psychoanalysis," *European Journal of Psychoanalysis*, 32 (2011), p. 33.

8   S. Freud, "The Uncanny," *New Literary History*, Spring 1976, vol. 7, no. 3, pp. 623–4.

9   Ibid.

10 Ibid., p. 634.

11 *The Seminar of Jacques Lacan, Book 1: Freud's Papers on Technique 1953–4*, trans. John Forrester, London: W. W. Norton & Company, 1991, p. 191.

12 See O. Timofeeva, "Unconscious Desire for Communism," in: *Identities: Journal for Politics, Gender, and Culture*, no. 11, pp. 32–48.

13 G. Bataille, *Visions of Excess: Selected Writings 1927–1939*, trans. Allan Stoekl, Carl R. Lovitt, and Donald M. Leslie Jr, Minneapolis: University of Minnesota Press, 1985, p. 15.

14 A. Toscano, "Against Speculation, or, A Critique of the Critique of Critique: A Remark on Quentin Meillassoux's After Finitude (After Colletti)," in L. Bryant, N. Srnicek and G. Harman, eds., *The Speculative Turn: Continental Materialism and Realism*. Melbourne: re.press, 2011, p. 87.

15 S. Critchley, "Back to the Great Outdoors," *Times Literary Supplement*, 28 February 2009: 28.

16 G. Bataille, *The Accursed Share*, Vol. 1, trans. Robert Hurley, New York: Zone, 1991, p. 21.

17 Capitalist unconscious is analyzed by Samo Tomsic in his book *The Capitalist Unconscious: Marx and Lacan*, London: Verso, 2015.

18 J. Semyenov, *Seventeen Moments of Spring*, trans. Katherine Judelson, London and New York: John Calder Riverrun Press. www.semenov-foundation.org/lib/17moments1.pdf

19 R. Negarestani, *Cyclonopedia: Complicity With Anonymous Materials*, Melbourne: re.press, 2008, pp. 16–17.

20 Ibid., p. 28.

21 Ibid.

22 M. Doherty, "Non-Oedipal Networks and the Inorganic Unconscious," in: Ed Keller, Nicola Masciandaro, and Eugene Thacker, eds., *Leper Creativity: Cyclonopedia Symposium*, New York: Punctum Books, 2012, p. 122.

25

Arseny Zhilyaev

DEMAND FULL AUTOMATION OF CONTEMPORARY ART

Only very recently even the most optimistic forecasts concerning the prospects of automation spoke of the impossibility of imagining, for instance, a self-driving automobile. For a long time, navigation in the conditions of real traffic seemed too complicated to be formalized as a computer program. Even the possibility of the visual identification of moving automobiles, with their geometry constantly shifting according to the viewer's location, was seen as an insoluble problem for machines, although for the human brain it is one of the fully automated functions of perception, requiring no additional effort. But today debates on the consequences of the transition to automated transportation for the economics of roadside cafés and the families of long-distance lorry drivers are already taken completely for granted. And the epoch-making defeat of Gary Kasparov by the supercomputer Deep Blue in 2006 already seems like distant history, seen from the viewpoint of the development of computing technology. Ten years later, even a common gaming app for a mobile phone can provide serious competition for flesh-and-blood grandmasters.

For a long time the final bastion of resistance to artificial intelligence in the field of board games was the Japanese game Go, owing to the wide range of various possible moves and the substantial dimensions of the playing board. But even in this area, in the mid 2010s the computer program AlphaGo, constructed using neural networks, proved too good for the finest representatives of the human race. The automated processing of requests for financial loans, writing of texts such as press releases (or even imitative poetry), and development of new collections of mass-market clothing have already become reality. Next in line is medical diagnosis, and after that comes the development of robots capable of duplicating the fine motor skills of human beings, such as moving up and down a ladder or cooking food, which, according to Moravec's paradox ("contrary to traditional assumptions, high-level reasoning requires very little computation, but low-level sensorimotor skills require enormous computational resources") remain a more difficult problem than intellectual activity.

However, there is one form of human activity that is regarded by definition as immune to automation. This is creative activity in general and, in particular, contemporary art, which, as distinct from various kinds of art that emphasize craftsmanship and technical skills, long ago formulated its fundamental rule as the absence of all rules and its fundamental skill as the ability to develop new skills. Beginning from the twentieth century it became the norm to consider that as soon as the pattern according to which any given work by an artist is produced has been identified, any further use of that pattern becomes pointless. At least, that is the way that things happen for the history of art, which plays the role of an authority

qualified to identify and preserve cultural messages, correlating
them with the inventory of what is already known, with what
has become the rule and demands specific skills. The artist's
gamble is to produce a work of art that is as difficult as possible
to identify, by playing on the boundary between what is already
known and what is not yet known, with the constant risk of
being left unidentified, outside the inventory of art. But one
way or another, the factor that determines the value of a work
is precisely the intensity of its novelty. Consequently, in the
case of art we are dealing with an activity undertaken to create
patterns that are ever more difficult to identify and to develop
an ever more complicated system for identifying them.

One can imagine how difficult it is to create a self-driving
car for moving along a road on which there is no visual and,
at times, no conceptual correspondence between the moving
objects, and the traffic regulations are determined by a
consistent rejection of everything that has ever been identified
as a rule. It should be noted that, compared with other types
of activity involving pattern recognition, contemporary art is
significantly less homogenous. It incorporates a high level of
elements that are extraneous, even though they are drawn from
the funds of a classical set – painting, sculpture and performative
practices. Beginning from the 1970s and the advent of what
Rosalind Krauss called the 'post-medium' condition of art,
the only thing that holds works together is precisely the
methodology of their creation and the identification of the
previously unidentified. The limit in this game of ever-higher
stakes is the transcendence of art as a distinct form of activity,
whether through its annihilation, as the Dadaists demanded, or
through the rethinking of life as a whole in accordance with the
rational laws of artistic production, as demanded by the Soviet
constructivists. At this point the history of art, with its inventory

of items that defy indexing, must coincide with human history, and thereafter with history understood as activity undertaken for the development of the universe as a whole.

The role of the artist in this model of art is the role of a generator of patterns that resist instant identification, which cannot be identified as art on the basis of what is already known about art. In and of itself, this conception of artistic activity bears the imprint of Romanticism, with its faith in the ultimate freedom of the creative genius, and it has its own precise historical boundaries and sociopolitical determinacy. In contemporary interpretations the human being already proves inadequate to the role of a generator of the unidentifiable. He/she is too determined by his own history and physiology, too constrained by the specifics of a system of economic production that require him to search for ways and means to survive and, to top things off, he is corrupted by his connection with a history of art that holds out a promise of immortality, even if it is only virtual. But one way or another, to this day precisely the ability to produce nonautomated solutions, which result in the production of art with new patterns, previously unidentified by the history of art, is still recognized as one of the determining and distinctive features of the human being. And if the moment comes when the human being proves incapable of demonstrating the required level of creative freedom, but a machine is capable of doing it, then the machine will become more human than a human being, who will, in turn, begin to be perceived as more machinelike than a machine. Analogous examples of machines that are too human and human beings who are too mechanical and automated abound in contemporary science fiction literature and cinema.

But is contemporary art genuinely unexplored territory, where the ultimate human qualities of creative freedom are realized, as is generally believed? Even from what has been said above, it is possible to draw the conclusion that this is not entirely the case. Market relations and capitalism in general have produced exactly the same changes with regard to art that they have produced with regard to other particular aspects of production in the feudal system. That is, they have revolutionized relations of production by formalizing and desacralizing them. It has to be acknowledged, however, that art, as distinct from other forms of the production of added value, still retains the archaic features of artisanal activity. Even now it remains difficult for us to imagine the assembly-line production of art, and, with a certain degree of license, the relations between collector and institutional patron can be likened to the relations between a feudal lord and his dependent vassals.

The actual consequences of the capitalist transformation of art are negatively marked, not because they are connected with a vicious system of exploitation – the illegitimate appropriation of added value also occurs in artistic production – but because of their destructive influence on the fetishized, pre-capitalist aspects of the organization of artistic labor. The belief exists that artisanal production and craft-based self-organization are invariably positively marked, and they are defended, together with more humanitarian labor conditions and more archaic forms of exploitation.

The basic reproach that one often hears with regard to the consequences of capitalist organization for contemporary art concerns art's bureaucratization. The number of artists in the world whose recipes for the creation of contemporary art are becoming accessible on a mass scale is increasing, and the difference between a capitalized education system and cost-free interaction on the internet is gradually disappearing. Instead

of receiving unique works by individual geniuses, more and
more often we find ourselves dealing with the mass production
of an artistic product, possessing a value that equals the
institutionally protected history of art. As a potential response
to the situation that has come about, one hears appeals for the
creation of artisanal, self-organized educational institutions
or even unique local dialects of art that have not yet been
appropriated or automated by the industry that produces
contemporary art. But is not this argument similar to the
conservative position of the Luddites, who smashed machines
because they were forcing flesh-and-blood human beings out of
their jobs? The response from the left to this kind of criticism
could be to support the capitalist industrialization of artistic
production, which, despite all its negative aspects, is better than
feudal vassalage and will, sooner or later, offer the chance of a
revolutionary transformation of the situation. Yes, we have fewer
unique patterns of contemporary art, but it becomes available
for mass production. Yes, we no longer have the comfort of
human interaction with the collector or the individual who
commissions art works, but we are not dependent on them to
such a great extent, etc.

Whether we like it or not, today contemporary art is a social
institution with its own economy and machinery of production.
As compared with a work's relations with the history of art,
the relations of purchase and sale are subject to a significantly
greater degree of inertia, which implies a demonstrably lesser
amount of the unknown. As a rule, in order to be bought a
work must correspond to a precise set of criteria, from the
state of the market to the banal ability to be displayed on a
collector's wall. The actual process of an artist's own formation
is linked to a set of procedures that presuppose capitalist
formalization. Education in the sphere of contemporary art is

linked, to an even greater degree than the once simple relations
between master and apprentice, to a specific set of expectations
and aesthetic, economic, and social obligations. And although
in a certain sense training in contemporary art as the
development of skill in creating what cannot be reduced to skill
is contradictory in and of itself, a total repudiation of training
leads to the endless replication of a set of personal traumas and
the most common clichés of artistic self-expression, which are
merely the socially accepted tokens of creative freedom.

But the history of contemporary art itself fails the test for
containing unformalized, absolutely innovative works. In the
last 100 to 150 years the world has seen only a small number
of substantial transformations, which, at best, have developed
through the creative rejigging of well-known discoveries of
the past. It would be no great exaggeration to assert that to
this day contemporary art is still nourished by the heritage of
modernism and, in exceptional cases, of the avant-garde, which
have defined the overall scope for the perception of artistic
activity in the twentieth and early twenty-first centuries. And if
that is so, then, despite a high level of 'internal' mutations, the
scope of its potential manifestations may actually be susceptible
to formalization and computation, although it would require
the indexing of a gigantic number of possible variations. Yes of
course, this is a goal that has never been set. On the contrary,
as stated above, the very fact of this possibility's existence is
regarded as contradicting the logic of contemporary art. But
it is obvious that a certain level of automation is, in itself, an
excluded compromise that guarantees art's existence and its
very recognition as a human activity that cannot be automated
in principle.

For the human being, the fact that concessions are made
concerning the absolute newness of what is produced allows

wide scope for speculating and recombining in various ways
what is already known, which, depending on the specifics of
any particular moment, may possess a rather high level of
legitimation on the territory of the history of art. Thus, the
twentieth century has already seen the Russian avant-garde,
the American avant-garde, the second avant-garde, the postwar
avant-garde, the neo-avant-garde, the trans-avant-garde and so
forth. For a computer – let us call it a robot artist – this signifies
the possibility of creating, by means of formalization, a gigantic
number of series of works that remain as yet unrealized, but are
permissible from the viewpoint of the history of art.

In the case of the human being, the open use of already
known patterns for the creation of works of art is perceived as
kitsch or an expression of the corrupt nature of the market,
which is described as the main obstacle in the path of the
imagination. "Zombie formalism" is a pejorative label, not only
for the variations on abstract painting that constantly come
back round again, thanks to commodity fetishism, but overall
for an art that is accused of bureaucratizing its own production,
denigrating the Romantic, accenting the mechanical and
automating the basic principle of the way art works (after all,
the artist's labor really does retain within itself dead capital
– education, the capitalization of the name and so forth).
However, for a robot artist even this level of creative activity
could be a giant step forward and the beginning of a great
journey. Roboformalism could exploit this dead capital that is
contained in a work of art, not exclusively for earning money or
winning recognition by the history of art, which is characteristic
of our species, but in order to go beyond the human being and
the specific features of his artistic activity.

The automation and formalization of contemporary art
allow us to speak of the creation of a complete archive of

the history of art (future and past), that is, a list not only of actual, but also of potential works of art, created on the basis of the already known (a computer learns in a similar fashion to play the classic table games, in particular Go). These works could be actualized through individual 'robographies', the histories of specific machines in specific social contexts – an anthropomorphic kind of solution. But they could also be revealed via more industrialized forms, such as the brands of the machines, with a corresponding set of features, etc. Or they could assume the form of a unified complex standing behind the authorship of artificial intelligence at a greater or lesser degree of development. And the history of art could also be transformed by using technologies similar to the mechanisms with which cryptocurrencies work, i.e. the block chain. This would make it possible to free this history of the negative consequences of human-specific features, which corrupt the recording of patterns of the as-yet-unidentified as a result of the specific traits of capitalist production. Access to the history of art opens up the possibility of the accelerated capitalization of any given work, any given artist, etc. Furthermore, we can imagine the existence of different versions of the history of art, in each of which different combinations of works are realized and their sequence varies accordingly.

At first glance such a turn of events appears rather pointless for the human being and therefore improbable. Who will want to buy and hang on his wall a monochrome work painted by a robot or admire such a work in a museum? However, concealed within this very pointlessness there may lie even more unexpected and unpleasant consequences for the human being as artist. The possibility of creating an archive of this kind and of robot artists raises a serious question about the value of human creative activity as such, at least in the form in which it manifests itself in contemporary art today. The transformation that we are interested in can be compared with the invention of photography, initially perceived as a medium capable of supplanting 'nonmechanical' human art, which at that time was based on the mimetic copying of reality. In the case of roboformalism, the most pessimistic scenario for art produced by human beings could amount to its transformation into craftwork and exclusion from the zone of artistic production as such. This could be facilitated to a considerable extent by justified criticism of human limitations in production and pattern recognition, resulting from the way in which a human being is conditioned by his specific cultural and physiological characteristics. Just as animals were once dislodged from their position as an important force of production, becoming transformed over time into a mere resource, so will human participation in the process of creating and identifying new patterns be reduced to a stylistic set of solutions, which can be used to produce the specific effect of the 'human.' However, as in the case of the automation of other spheres of capitalist production, at the initial stage automation of this kind could raise the question of a basic income and essential compensation. Thus, in a similar fashion to the way in which we now have specific food products labeled as "non-GMO" or "BIO," i.e. produced in conditions approximating those that were natural to previous centuries, it is possible to anticipate the appearance of separate sectors of art labeled as 'human-made'. This support could also, in addition, be expressed in a guaranteed dose of recognition by the machines or attention from viewers of the same sort, or financing with the purpose of preserving the specific features of human self-expression. But, most importantly, in the possibility of being freed from the requirement to produce exclusively what is new and nondetermined, which in the conditions of late capitalism will become almost obligatory. In a world that has adopted the slogan "Everyone is an artist," in which everyone is obliged to be creative, the possibility of a creative repudiation of participation in the artistic production of life is a privilege in itself. As Marx once dreamed, sooner or later, the harsh specialization typical of the early stages of capitalist production will disappear and the human being will be a production-line worker in the morning, an artist in the afternoon, and a sportsman in the evening.

However, if the current trend towards the automation of creative activity continues, it is probable that the human being will disappear, at least in the form in which we know him/her. Then, on condition that artificial intelligence is friendly to humans, we can predict the actualization of the scenario outlined in Russian cosmism and by Nikolay Fedorov. As we know, according to this philosophical doctrine, the quintessence of human creative activity is the resurrection of the dead in their complete physical form, and their subsequent settlement throughout the universe. At the same time Fedorov and a number of his followers, for instance Tsiolkovsky, pointed out that the continuation of evolution is inevitable, with the consequent transformation of the human species, in particular of its corporeal embodiment. After all, having been created as a result of specific conditions in the past, this embodiment is not necessarily adequate to the present moment. In the cosmists' opinion, first and foremost the mechanism of generations succeeding each as a result of death has ceased to fulfill its function. But that is not all. Many organs of the human body could be improved. And in this respect Russian cosmists are without question the forerunners of the modern transhumanism movement, which also notes that in the immediate future, perhaps even starting now, specific features of our body that were created at one time by nature will be replaced by new, artificially produced, more perfect forms. Not only artificial hearts and artificial limbs, but also the lungs and the digestive system, and, in the near future, intelligent colonies of nanorobots, which will provide real-time control and optimization of human existence in its organic form. The logic of this development can easily be taken to the limit by imagining the human being as a super-complex formation that has become commensurate, in and of itself, with the nonmaterial processes in the universe.

But the development of events in this vein calls into question the possibility of resurrecting the generations that have previously lived in their physical bodies and in their psychological totality. Even if a highly developed human race or its heirs, in the form of the robotized population of the planet or artificial intelligence, should wish to do this out of gratitude for the contribution that human beings have made to progress and the victory over death, the problem is that bringing back people of the past into a future in which the characteristics of the human species have practically disappeared would traumatize them irrecoverably. Eternal human life in all its imperfection – both physical and psychological – alongside their highly developed successors would mean the unbearable torment of awareness of one's own weakness. And if that is so, then a return to the past, to a form of life on earth that may be underdeveloped, but is characteristic of the species in question, would be a great reward. The result might turn out to be the reconstruction of life on earth from its inception to the advent of a machine capable of creative activity and the subsequent gradual transformation of the human being.

But another scenario is also possible. As we know, photography, as automated visual art, only indicated the need to rethink human artistic activity, it did not completely destroy it. On the contrary, it was the catalyst for processes that led to the increased complexity of this activity and the crystallization of a number of its characteristic features in contemporary art, including the reinforcement of innate, specifically human features such as a unique 'signature' and distinctive human expression, or even the opposite tendency of the mimicry of machine art or collaborative activity – geometric abstraction, the rationalization of visual forms or even production art. In a certain sense a situation in which the artist is formed together with an archive of future art is like the situation of a chess player who plays with the help of a computer that calculates the consequences of the human being's strategic decisions, but does not take decisions independently. Rodchenko already dreamed of a time when the development of technology would mean that an artist only had to imagine a specific work of art in his mind, after which it could be realized automatically. Today the mass production of images that is typical of the social networks exploits various kinds of filters as a similar kind of technology (including filters with the distinctive stylistic features of the art of the past): the user makes his/her selection each time, depending on his concept. The existence of an archive of all potential artistic forms carries this tendency to the limit. Co-creation and the coexistence of human being and robot in the field of art represent a scenario for the further development of the tendency towards automation that is optimistic for the human being, although there are no grounds for assuming that it will exist for long without the disappearance of the clear boundary between the 'natural' and the artificial.

Another important consequence of the advent of roboformalism and the creation of a complete archive of the art of the future could be the appearance of the possibility of the radicalization of some of the modernist maxims regarding the generation of new artistic forms. As we know, one of the key definitions of the postwar avant-garde, which has remained influential to this day, is its medium-specific nature, which requires that visual art, in its turn, abandon narrative, as being specific to the methodology of another type of art – literature. However, the formal innovations of artists claiming to express this requirement as fully as possible have ended up, irrespective of the artists' volition, in a position of dependence on the narrative of the history of art. This is a feature characteristic of all forms of life within our universe, because there is a direction to time and, accordingly, inertia in the unfolding of processes. For instance, the transfer of heat from a cold body to a warm one is impossible. At the same time, the human being has a tendency to create new models of relations that deny the directionality of time and historical determination. On the territory of art a model of this kind is the museum. After all, this is an institution capable of accumulating in a single space structures that were formed in different time periods, while ignoring their historical sequence, which means that it banishes the linear nature of the historical narrative, at least within arbitrarily defined limits.

The existence of an archive with a complete list of both past and future formal innovations creates the possibility of liberation from the influence of the narrative of history in the given aspect of artistic production. From being a factor that subordinates every new form, the history of art is inherently transformed into a medium, a matrix, similar to an alphabet, which is capable of creating without any reference to linear development in time (after all, words and sentences do not depend on the sequence of letters in the alphabet). A function similar to the one described has already been performed by history in the time of the historical avant-garde. Posing the question of transcending or annihilating art required the existence of an authority capable of differentiating what it was that needed to be transcended or annihilated. But the possibility of protracted existence in a mode of nonlinear narrative 'after the death of art' was not consciously considered, although to this day it remains the basis of the history of modernist and contemporary art. Every new form was declared to be the last in the chain of development and denied the potential existence of a future after itself. The consciously considered dependence of nonnarrative forms of art on the narrative of the history of art, together with the computation of all possible formal innovations, opens up the possibility of creating even more complex, freer patterns of artistic production that are not preset. And simultaneously it actualizes a scenario that is new to western modernism, the scenario of the resurrection and preservation for subsequent life of the transformational hopes expressed through 'the deaths of art'.

But it is not only the formal component of artistic production that can undergo mutation as a result of the automation of contemporary art. The field relating to content can also be significantly expanded. Thus, in the most ambitious version of modernist art, the boundaries of its content were expressed through the rejection of representation and conditioned by the specific features of the existence of the artwork and the human being as material bodies. This interpretation of art opposed it to religious art and the various forms of mimetic and representational realism. As distinct from modernism, they were declared to be too illusory, since they led away from the physical presence, here and now, of the human being and the work, that is, from the limits of the attainable. At the same time this human limit was declared to be the limit of the world and was constructed on a rather naive faith in a necessary parallelism between the microcosm (the human being and the work) and the macrocosm (the material universe). In other words, it was assumed that readdressing the limitations of the human being is actually equivalent to aspiring to the limits of the universe. Thus, in this aspect modernist art opposed itself to the art of representation, which leads away from the limits of the human being and attempts to indicate the human being's limited nature and inadequacy in terms of reception of the world, which means that it leads to the illusory and the false.

But today all that we know about the specific material characteristics of our universe is expressed through scientific representations and cannot on any account be limited by the specific nature of human existence on planet Earth without substantial distortions. Representation no longer leads away from material reality; on the contrary, it becomes the only channel of communication with it that is accessible to the human being. And, vice versa, the presumption that the world is totally accessible to the human being, via a parallelism between microcosm and macrocosm is, in and of itself, an illusion that leads away from reality. The textbook example of modernist art claiming to be a radical materialistic expression of the world is Jackson Pollock's dripping. According to the accepted point of view, in this technique the artist renounces his own specifically human nature to the maximum possible extent, in favor of forms conditioned by the material forces that form our universe. Positioning the canvas on a horizontal surface made it possible to employ the force of gravity and the attraction of the Earth as a factor determining the artistic form. The paint falls onto the canvas and spreads out across it in exactly the same way that apples fall from trees and do not go hurtling out into cosmic space. But are this type of art and this type of physics the only possible ones for attempting a materialistic description of the world? It is obvious that if Pollock had painted his pictures while in orbit round planet Earth inside a space station, the specific features of the development of form within his works would have been fundamentally different. And what once seemed to be a natural and limiting expression of the materialistic nature of artistic practice would have been shown to be merely a particular instance, representative of human nature and of the human being's natural habitat.

In the light of such a turn of events, representational art becomes an example of a more productive model of the way that art works directly with inaccessible content. Its specific formal aspects are organized on the basis of powerful contrasts that exploit the distinctive features of human perception, for instance, the creation of an effect of the sublime by means of organ music that transcends the customary acoustic range, or the use of stained-glass windows that intensify the saturation of color, thereby pointing out the limited nature of this aspect of our everyday existence, etc. In the case of mimetic realism we are dealing with inaccessibility in the here and now of a definite situation or, on the contrary, with access, by means of representation, to an understanding of one or another process in the reality of human life. The existence of an archive of artistic forms of future innovations can, in its turn, be used to create contemporary representations of the material universe that are not necessarily tied to the specific perceptual features of any species, similarly to the way in which a scientific representation of the universe is not obliged to seek any correspondence to the range of human sensitivity. The combination of an archive of formal innovations that is as complete as possible with an openness to what is not directly accessible substantially defines the horizon for the development

of art in both its human and collaborative variants, or even in
the creative work of artificially created machines independently
of the human being.

In conclusion we can note that the automation of
contemporary art does not presuppose any necessary political
transformation of the world in which it takes place. Just as
the automation of work at the beginning of the twenty-first
century does not assume the transition from capitalism to a
postcapitalist condition. Rather, we are dealing here with a
specific tendency which, depending on the various political
contexts, can lead to the actualization of various scenarios.
A large part of the above is feasible rumination on the theme
of how this tendency could develop in conjunction with
the existing state of affairs, i.e. within capitalist relations.
Furthermore, it is seen as an inevitable consequence of these
relations only insofar as it clarifies the connection between
contemporary art, in the form in which it is known to us, and
a specific type of political and economic formation. However,
in the twentieth century an attempt was made to create an
alternative trajectory for the development of transformations
of art and the specific features of its production. First and
foremost we have in mind the postrevolutionary Soviet
museums of the 1920s and 1930s, and also reflections on the
subject of the museum that were typical of Russian cosmism.
In the case of the museums, we can trace a similar movement
from individual creative activity – conditioned by the specific
features of the human species, by the relations of production in
which it finds itself, and by the development of image-making
technologies – to institutional creative activity that is collective
and industrial, based on more complex foundations. But the
most important distinguishing feature of this line is the absence
of capitalist relations. Precisely because of this, progress in the

interpretation of Nikolay Fedorov or Walter Benjamin has been marked by an important but primarily negative consequence of the existing state of affairs, until such time as the human race realizes its danger and its potential possibilities. Until such time as a revolution occurs, i.e. – in the case of Benjamin – until someone pulls the emergency brake of the locomotive of history, which is hurtling into the abyss of technological catastrophe; or – in the case of Fedorov – until fraternal equality is achieved between all warring parties, between those who have knowledge and those who don't, between town and country and, most importantly, between those who were once alive and those who gave their lives for those who are alive today. And the automation of contemporary art will become one more wonderful possibility on the way to boundless creative freedom.

26

Alex Anikina

THE ANTICHTHON

This text, or its ancestor, first appeared in a book object that physically – literally – had no beginning or end. The kind of reading temporality that it invited was very different from any other book on my shelf: much closer to a meditation than to an immersion into a narrative. Such format, I thought, was good for describing the cyclical thinking that the artistic research often employs (mostly independently from the artist). But it also invited forth a particular relation to the time and the materiality of reading, a side of this cultural technique that is often taken for granted. Departing from the idea of a very basic storage device meant to overcome the insufficiency of memory, the book became a way to develop a complex kinship with the material body of the text itself, and its particular rhythm, not unlike that of abacus or prayer beads – a kinship with another way of thinking, a tempo, a counting device for the mind.

So while this text is a finite excerpt by necessity – an abrupt cut in the previously uninterrupted kinetics – it still links back to the cyclical ways in which thought operates, not as a linear progression but as recurring spirals and feedback loops. These circuits are universal to material bodies, be it a camera, a human being, or a book. And in a book concerning revolution, a word movement that already etymologically hints at the space charged with monumental paradigmatic shifts, planetary orbits and the fragility of lives involved, this text cuts through and straight towards the materiality of the act of reading. With so many 'others' involved, on many occasions I found it necessary to put the qualifier 'human' in front of the words that seemed to already contain it: however, only then the intertwined human and nonhuman temporalities became evident, and the intimate fragility of life in the face of larger-scale events and processes could be felt again.

A thinner line
couldn't be expected to fill
the instance between my expectations
and your hopes.

But what could happen,
and is still happening,
is a workaround process of fulfilling desires
which have nothing to do
with our goals.

The thin simplicity
is conducive to things.

There are some things
that are easier imagined:
archives kept in the human graveyards,
artificial mountains,
endless films,
and others.

Being functional is defined
as the multiplicity of possibilities
combined in certain ways
with the multiplicity of skills,
and then divided by the number of
the most likely outcomes.

In other words,
dumb luck.

In other,
lamb duck.

I could go on.

Somewhere later,
or earlier,
I mention a play on words.

Sometimes
a play on play
is just an ornament,
and sometimes
it becomes a lever
which is just
long enough.

Most of the sometimes
I know which is which.

Do you?

The point is,
it is entirely impossible
to write this book in any other way,
as it is impossible
to read it
in any definitive manner.

My job is to extend
some
understanding
by means of a net.

Through filling the gaps,
I achieve nothing;
but something else happens:
the meaning turns halfway
and clicks.

The words in this text
are unsure of their meaning
for a good reason.

The whole of it
is just a 'click'
happening
in a very slow motion.

(Isn't quoting yourself
a way of reinforcing
your own existence?)

I believe that it is still possible
to describe some of the operations
which are at work
inside a human artist.

Of course, there is no way of knowing
if the order of operations is significant.

Thoroughness and curiosity
usually collide into an operation, which,
mapped onto some more
unexpected temporalities
becomes a miraculous guide.

Give a coin to the guide,
so he can safely transport you
to the far bank.

Take care not to fall
into a whirlpool.

Where human artists are concerned,
other nonhuman presences
are to be expected.

My camera is easily one.

I use my camera now
as anything but:
as a divination device,
as an imperfect clock,
and as a reminder of my own mortality.

All of those are instruments
for a limited lifespan.

Limits, however,
drive growth.

In the floating consciousness,
islands appear and drift.

For them to become continents
(which then under the weight of time or reason or chance
crack and let the boiling blood show through),
something must happen.

A point of rupture, or
a point of convergence.

A point where everything at once collides
to form an imperfect whole,
which then proceeds to act
as if of its own volition.

A set of circumstances,
which, left to develop,
evolve into a moving,
acting thing.

Important here
is how not to be afraid.

For a long time I thought
that not to be afraid
meant to love.

Here,
include some darkness
in the equation.

Darkness has to be constricted somehow,
otherwise it's just darkness all around -
and then we are in deep space.

Or the underworld.

Who knows.

Well,
delayed knowledge has its perks.

A human artist
is mostly conflicted,
and only then
productive.

The conflict in the text
is always partially resolved
through the process of writing it.

So in a way,
once it is finished,
the text is also
a monument,
an act of marking.

I would like to think that
it's an act of bravery.

And as such,
an act of love.

For the mind,
any everyday word
is an effective contemplation device.

For me,
taking a walk in language
is definitely something
that's been persisting
for a long time.

When I am finished,
I will have lost my way,
as if in a deep forest
where apparently lost people always take slightly to the left,
and so will have made a full circle.

In this endless landscape
it will be almost impossible for me
to find intensity.

As I will mention,
or as I have mentioned already,
it is a very slow click.

Intensity is just another name.

I will now list some of what might be present,
however it is necessary to remember
that the list is infinite,
and that due to the lack of intensity,
it might bore you
to death.

(As I have mentioned earlier or later:
death as an effective contemplation device)

The list goes, some simple things:
internal pressure,
irresolvable conflict,
unbearable irony,
description that is just too much,
play on words,
play on meaning,
play on play,
conceptualized attraction,
indecisive surface,
strongly challenged perception,
shift in the definition of decency,
affirmation of futility,
postapocalyptic intentions.

I would always go with the last one,
but then
I am trying not to overuse it.

One really has only one shot
at Apocalypse.

And so
no things from the list,
except maybe for the play on play,
are directly present in this book.

And the pace
has to be slow.

It is necessary,
because the pages
are material and thus finite.

You will touch the pages,
and they will disintegrate
and turn into
sunflowers,
eventually.

Again,
in a text like this
there is no need for
intensity
as most understand it.

But there might be
a buildup,
a suspense,
a pause before jumping –
some circling of vultures, if you want.

Not fire itself,
but some potential
to catch on fire,
and to catch on fire
again.

Burning treasures
in a hidden chamber;
an operatic movement of the heart
that is constricted
by emotional overflow.

A sign of incoming storm
in trembling of water.

No, of poison in a cup,
to be noticed while standing
outside the gates of Athens,
in one extended second
before the hands
have brought the cup
to the expecting lips.

And then.

Ferryman!
I don't have any small change.

Ferryman,
talk to your king
and tell him how I
have been mistreated.

I'm stranded here.

Carry me in your boat,
ferryman,
merry man in a hood.

For the river is stubborn.

And the line is thickening.

And the waves are calming.
Again.

It is necessary for us
to continue in circles.

Dramatic mise-en-scènes
and transparent tragedies.

To be lulled by the narrative
into the whole
suspension of disbelief,
I am wondering now
how this affects me,
and you.

My childhood was
gone and gone again
with my mind suspended
over a book.

The sweetness
of that suspension
is something that I find difficult
to overcome.

Yet something
that I, myself,
am incredibly reluctant
to use.

As the ancient Greece
breathes down my neck,
like many necks before,
I surrender to the desire
of falling into familiar narratives.

To fall from the sun,
to descend to the underworld,
to overcome challenges,
to be punished indefinitely,
to show wisdom and cunning.

Familiar to whom?

Is it me or my other self
from beyond the slavic border?

When resuscitating a text from scratch,
feel right under its jaw
and check if it has a pulse.

If you can then follow the pulse,
and by tracing it,
to discover the shape of its living body,
I congratulate you.

Most of the time
in my book
this is what artists do.

Or at least in this book,
while it lasts.

(ha)

The correlation between
the shape of writing
and the physical shape.

The good thing about material objects
is that they have
a more or less definite
center of gravity.

Consider any book a universe of its own,
and it would be easy to see how
in gentle mockery
the pages of this book
revolve around its empty heated center.

To fall into it
is to surrender to the gravity
of the book,
and in doing so,
to reimagine the text
as a universe.

A cosmic configuration.

I would quite like to do that.

After all,
the center is also
where the tigers live.

The conditions are precarious,
and the situation is imperfect,
which is often a case
with utterances
fashioned after the Big Bang.

I would like to rethink the fall
as a concept of deep trust
interlaced with complete
understanding of its own future.

At the same time,
the orbit is not a perfect circle,
but it involves a circular motion,
a side glance
which continuously alters the course.

A straightforward plunge,
a dive,
a fall
could be one way of breaking the orbit.

But it is not the only one.

And I'm continuing to circle
around, as the state
of sustained fragility
is important for this text.

The idea is that of something happening very slowly,
for a very long time,
but just a second before
everything collapses
beautifully.

The question of being under-controlled.

The question of taking a fall for something
you trust.

The punctuation becomes important.

Since there is no definitive end or beginning,
a word to serve
as a punctuation mark.

It could mean 'And so',
or 'wait',
or 'so and so'.

And so,
if there exists
some understanding of physical time,
I am following it in circles.

The habitual human time,
the time of sunrise into the day and sunset into the night,
is a matter of motion in space.

A matter of spatial configurations,
of orbits and movements of celestial bodies.

The day and the night being a lucky
follow-up.

From here,
the orbit becomes significant.

The movement which is
projected and thrown ahead
of itself; like the projector's light,
except not in straight lines.

The light falls on the screen.

But to explain its fall
before the notion of gravity is invented,
is to circle around, endlessly,
within the text.

And this tells something
of the geometry
of operating as a human artist.

I'm circling here
partially
in order to name
my operations.

To name a thing
in this landscape
is to cause it
into being.

Although
over any
preconceived notions
of being,
I would still choose
an over-arching trust.

A trust not unlike the one
that I feel towards falling.

Or towards the the fact that
any window in the two-mile radius
would most probably contain
some form of fragile proportion of
human architecture
and moving image
of the trees in the wind.

In terms of production of finitude,
I'm driving around in circles
because we don't want to go home
just yet.

I'm only getting to know you.

Essentially what I might be doing
is painting sunflowers
over and over.

In order
to repeat the operations
of another artist
physically.

In order to know
through actions.

Even if they are simple.

I am remembering another operation,
which is un-naming;
un-naming is
happening in this book
en masse; and it is not
the opposite of naming.

In fact, these two
operations can be quite close
in functionality.

I could un-name the sunflower,
but it wouldn't change a single fact
of its constitution,
as well as the fact
that sunflowers include themselves
into the movement of celestial bodies,
and in doing so,
participate in construction of time.

A human being could
also participate in it
through making films.

If the idea of operation invokes the labour of the surgeon,
or the cut,
it only does so in this text

to reveal the ghostly presence of film
in any other activities
this human artist
might undertake
in the darkness.

The work of putting hours into
the material unfolding of
your own body is
a task on par with how not to be afraid.

On some days,
a human artist might feel
the following:
endless fury,
deep melancholy,
momentary blindness,
innocence,
excitement,
the weight of the world,
subjective experience of time.

Madness concealed
so well that it passes for
the tragicomical.

The constant alienation.

How to fall?

I watch films on fast-forward;
it makes me feel like

the omniscience
is still somehow possible,
even if shorthand
version.

An artificial mind would make
a better work of it.

But as we are still in the darkness,
it is hard to distinguish between
madness and enlightenment.

And absolutely no reason
there can't be both.

And so we continue
on our orbit.

When abstraction in the text becomes confusing,
the drive behind it returns
in the form of more narrative.

All the hard work burnt to ashes
makes space for more hard work.

The work then becomes a concept of faith,
only the congregation is deeply flawed.

In our line of work
the exalted presence
is often just a shadow
of more things to come.

The hero we left in the underworld
only needs to continue walking.

Walking
becomes an operation.

As a kind of proficiency
that only appears in
the liminal space.

Of the same kin
is the art of staying still in motion
(mastered so well by flies and trains,
often together).

The architecture of vision
becomes cinematic.

The lines extending
from the eyes to the objects
included.

Thin lines
but not
invisible.

The vision,
as one said,
is a propeller;
propeller eyes move,
rotate, film.

Machinic movement
on its own axis.

Wondrously
generated kinetics.

All calling the central region!

Calling the planet.

What better witness
to record a revolution.

Oh merciful king,
I have brought to you
more signs of disaster,
more songs of longing
and more lines of light.

My pale horse
is actually made of desire.

Dissociation of meaning
is not always humorous.

It is the dissociation of expectations
that produces the desired effect.

The naive approach.

Let's say
there is a degree of

recklessness
in our every proceeding.

Do I dare disturb the universe,
he asked.
I would say,
by all means.

So that when we approach
the hungry guard
at the gates
we can announce ourselves
properly.

So in the realm of what exactly
does our hero end up
upon coming back from the underworld?

Or, the question should be,
does the hero ever
intend to come back?

Look at the actual mirror, and not
at the image that
the mirror is forced to bear.

But then,
when is the image
one with the surface,
and when do they stay
like two brothers?

Now, there is something
that we have not considered.

 The act of witnessing
a greater scale.
 The act of inscribing
some mortal eyes
in the bigger scheme.

The human artist
might be aware
of that.

***

Perhaps, the answer
is closer to the pond's surface
like the faces of koi
who are proficient at divination,
and therefore tell no lies.

How to return, supposing we can?

The more we circle,
the tighter the orbit;
so that the hero can,
finally,
turn back home.

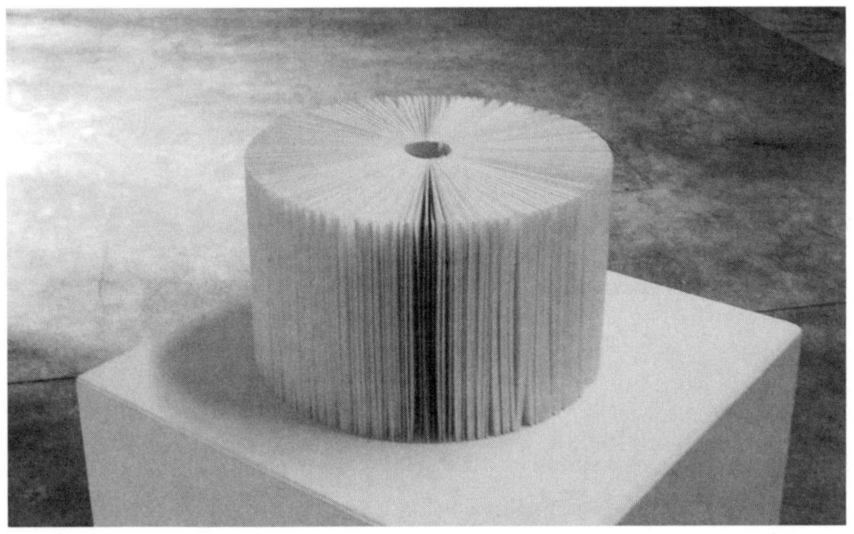

Alex Anikina. "How to Operate as a Human Artist, or the Antichthon."
2015, artist book

27

Ivan Novikov

I WANT TO BE AFRAID OF THE FOREST

Once in autumn after the rain I saw peonies with dead flower heads. The rain had hammered them down to the ground so that they spread out like octopuses cast up onto the shore and the once-lovely flowers had been transformed into a damp substance that looked repulsive and attractive at the same time. These decomposing inflorescences, which needed to be trimmed off so that the peonies would blossom again next year, gave me a glimpse into a different image of nature. A thing that used to be beautiful was turning into humus before our very eyes. Although initially this thing didn't trigger any emotional response, nonetheless somewhere inside me a clammy fear was born.

It wasn't an encounter with the horrific – after all, they were only wilted flowers, nothing more than that. But I was literally transfixed by the feeling of an encounter with the Other. I experienced nature as something that was not equal in significance and value to the human being, the way it was depicted in pictures and texts from the age of Romanticism. For a split second I was granted a glimpse of a "convulsive beauty" that had not been processed and cultivated. A creation of nature's multidirectional forces – a wet peony plant with dead blossoms – showed me plants as a "cannibalistic" otherness. I was astounded by the formlessness, the uncultivated rawness, by nature as such, which I saw so clearly for the first time. What had previously been concealed from me behind a thick layer of human, cultural activity, suddenly erupted. Even though peonies are garden flowers, I distinctly heard the echo of a certain unformalized space in them.

And whereas previously a work of art had seemed to me to be merely a product of human labor, now I saw something else in it. Like a Duchamp ready-made, the wet, skeletal plant laid bare the defects of modern artistic production. A reverential awe in the face of primordial materiality establishes a distance, which, in turn, makes possible the appearance of works of a new kind. Even if the perpetually flowing current of art, which is, in any case, focused on the realm of well-tended culture, does set itself the goal of creating some new form, it fails miserably anyway. Art only works in the field of the ready-made, in terms of both form and image. As a rule, attempts to create a new formalism only result in multiple repetitions of ready-made structures, whereas invoking the forest, nature as such, uncultivated materiality, creates the possibility of a genuinely new form. But such a development is only possible when there is distance.

Thinking along these lines, I realized that I actually need this 'fear of the forest.' But how is this fear possible nowadays? How can it be induced, even artificially? To do that you have to discover the boundary of nature as such, to see the formlessness of nature that you are seeking right here beside you. And so

I began collecting plants that had been battered by the rain and the wind in a shed. At a certain point they started rotting, and I had to dry them out in order to preserve them somehow. For the most part they were garden plants, not forest plants, but their otherness aroused fear in me anyway. This was an attempt to make myself feel afraid of the forest, using any possible means. As a result I collected several large heaps of dry branches, leaves, stalks and flower heads, the materiality of which was presented to me in its raw form. Having lost their original structure, they were nonetheless transformed into a "nonform" that now only required to be processed.

However, it is important to understand that present-day society is not afraid of nature as such. That which used to arouse fear no longer exists. The wild, primordial materiality, which frightened and enchanted human beings for thousands of years, can no longer be found. All that is left of it are skimpy little patches of parkland or, if the worst comes to the worst, occasional nature reserves. But this only confirms the contrary reality – the fear has not really passed off, it has only been masked. After all, even in the forest parks of Moscow a huge number of people get lost every year. Despite the ramified system of communication routes, despite the structures of urban security, a human being can simply disappear in the undergrowth. We think that we are protected, we live in a big city and the lights are leading us to the filling station or somewhere else. In actual fact, people can go out and lose their way almost right beside their home. The forest is a magical phenomenon, it can lure you in irretrievably.

We have stopped perceiving nature as something opposed to the human being. It seems to have been tamed and dissolved in the totality of human culture. The final spaces, both mental and real, which remain untended, are disappearing under the

pressure of cultivation. But nature does not submit totally
to human control. Today we need to rethink the slogan of
the Chinese Cultural Revolution: "The village surrounds the
town." The modern megalopolis has swallowed up the villages
and made them part of its agglomerations. But any city is
surrounded by a forest that is impossible to control, since it
actually struggles against humans. In the Anthropocene period
we have to understand this struggle and our work with nature
as political processes. The attempt to shape a new imagery
and language based on interaction with flora and fauna is now
a genuine sociohistorical act. The geochronological period
that has already begun, in which the human being plays the
determining role in the life of the entire planet, changing
the climate, the atmosphere and the directions of the ocean
currents, stipulates an understanding of politics as conscious,
meaningful activity, mediated by ecology.

In order to create new forms of art and life, we must once
again find the boundary between the human being and nature.
Following on from the age of antiquity, the line of demarcation
was not hard to define: what has not been cultivated by
human beings and precedes them, what is not culture – that is
nature. Today, however, this logic requires further refinement.
We surround ourselves with culture, constructing "neutral
territory," domesticating animals, endowing the weather
with emotional characteristics. But the "border conflict" is
exposed when we come up against the forest. Attempting to
anthropomorphize plants, we replant them in pots and carry
them into our homes. Torn out of their natural space, they give
us "an inoculation of the natural," muffling our instinctive fear
of the forest. But while we give animals, birds, and even insects
a chance to slip into the category of "the human" temporarily
(for instance, when we discover the social structures of ants

or humanize cats and dogs), plants remain pariahs. We don't want to step across that line and discover anthropomorphism in trees, flowers, and mosses.

Plants remain as the "final bastion" of authentic nature. And while, for example, killing animals and using them for food can seem problematic, with plants the same situation doesn't raise any ethical questions. It seems that the boundary between the human being and nature has been found, and it runs through the flora. Which means that in order to avoid working with images and forms that are ready-mades, we need once again to find within ourselves the fear of the forest, of the jungle, of nature as primordial materiality. Trying to find the Other in the world of plants is the only way to create a new form of art.

28

Pavel Pepperstein

THE SKYSCRAPER-CLEANER PINE MARTEN

I am a clone of the skyscraper-cleaner pine marten Haj-UB-117. The efforts of genetic engineers have adapted my body, as well as my mind, to the one and only occupation that is possible for me – maintaining absolute cleanliness and perfect order on the reserve fire-escape stairs of a gigantic skyscraper. This stairway and I are two bodies that live in a working symbiosis. Already at the developmental stage, design work on the skyscraper (which bears the proud name The Kandinsky Tower) took into account a genetic formula that could be used to produce modified pine martens, destined to become fire-escape stairway cleaners. These steps, by the way, are rarely ever used – our skyscraper has 222 lifts: there are the internal, high-speed capsules, flashing along the length of their polished pipes in a fraction of an instant; there are the external, slow, meditative platforms, seeping across the outside walls of the building like viscous balconies. And finally, there are the autonomous, maneuverable, target-seeking lifts, threading their twisting, soaring paths through the skyscraper, like a rocket-wasp stitching up a long enfilade of rooms as it pursues its impetuous flight now inside, now outside a palace.

We cloned pine marten cleaners are excluded from such exalted work as cleaning the lifts. This is performed by the so-called "invisibles," which is understandable since, after all, the interiors of some lifts are so highly complex, and the qualities of their materials are so sophisticated, that my sisters and I would not be able to cope. Well, of course not – we stupid little pine martens are nowhere near advanced enough for lifts – that's where those aristocrats the "invisibles" work! But "invisibles" are expensive, and no one's going to lavish *their* costly labor on a simple fire-escape stairway.

Since the year 3044 (when our skyscraper was erected), self-cleaning materials have appeared – the so-called "cat stuff." These materials have micro-tongues that lick their own surface clean. In my time I have suffered more than my share of aggravation from dogs and slimy dragons and golden wolf cubs (basically, from all the domestic pets that live in a skyscraper), but no one else has ever been as vicious and mean to me as cats.

Our skyscraper has 49 fire-escape stairways, and each of them is in the care of one of my sisters. It's not possible to transfer a pine marten from one stairway to another – if they decide to replace a pine marten, they destroy her. The design of the skyscraper incorporates small niches alongside the very top steps of the stairways – these are our rooms, where we can switch off during our nonworking time. I don't know if this is sleep or simply standby mode. The moment any creature, even a bird, enters the vertical, stepped-storey space (that is, the space of my stairway), I immediately wake up and mentally observe the creature's actions. My brain is organized in such a way that in my mind's eye I constantly see all the three hundred flights, I see all the landings, I see every single step – as clearly as if I am running my tongue over it. If the creature or the person introduces any flaws into the absolute cleanness of the stairway, I leave my niche (as a general rule, after waiting for the creature to remove itself from the space in my care) and slither downwards to dispose of the dirt.

The designer of the skyscraper had a reputation as a fastidious pedant with a compulsive obsession for cleanness. They say that in human beings this kind of exaggerated passion for cleanness is a symptom of schizophrenia. That is why the tittle-tattle about this great architect also claims that, although he dedicated his skyscraper to the artist Kandinsky, it has much closer karmic connections with the artist's uncle – a famous psychiatrist, who shared with his French colleague Clérambault the distinction of being the first to describe the syndrome of psychic automatism. This is an illness – which is no longer considered an illness – a person hearing voices in his mind, or receiving certain signals that seem to originate from some external source. These voices or signals incited the sick individual to carry out certain actions, and the sick individual carried them out, while complaining that alien impulses were subjecting his will to their control. This illness was masterfully described by Dr Kandinsky and Dr Clérambault, but they were unable to cure it. On the contrary, the illness became ever more prevalent and sufferers from this syndrome came to occupy ever more pivotal positions in the structures of human society. So that no one would dare to call them mentally ill, they employed technical devices actually to feed various signals into their own and other people's heads. This illness was therefore not regarded as an illness for very long: until the nineteenth century, people used to hear the voices of gods and spirits, after that they started hearing the voices of gadgets. People suffering from the Kandinsky-Clérambault syndrome (one of whom was the creator of my skyscraper) have infected the entire world with their sickness. And furthermore, they have created artificial creatures (like me), for whom the Kandinsky-Clérambault world is the only possible one. I have never observed any other form of consciousness in myself, apart from a mind that functions according to the Kandinsky-Clérambault system. I have never crept beyond the bounds of the Kandinsky skyscraper. The moment a blackbird, bullfinch or swift deposits a single tiny drop of green guano on a snow-white step, my brain receives the signal and moves me out to work.

But, in addition to the clear, functional order-signals, which I am not able to resist, I also receive others – voices slithering and gliding somewhere in the background of perception, behind the scenes, quietly whistling and babbling in the torrents of etheric noise – and I gradually learned to distinguish their obscure speech. The discerning reader will have realized that it was only thanks to these "background voices" – thanks to them alone – that I learned to think and write. It is thanks to them that I am keeping these notes. Say your "grazie molto" to these voices, dear reader, if you are democratic enough to condescend to read the memoirs of a pine marten.

I write with my tongue. My sisters and I have no legs, and the basic tools of our trade are our tongues, stomachs and tails. And, of course, the nose and ears also play their part. We have no sexual organs (nor, indeed, any sexual identity), so if I refer to myself as "she," it is purely because in my native Russian the word for pine marten happens to be feminine.

"What would these scrubbers want sex organs for?" a genetic engineer who went by the nickname of Gene Genie quipped during the process of designing our bodies.

"Their grinding will always be sterile!" guffawed his colleague who, as it happens, was entirely sterile himself, because he consisted of nothing but a thinking head which, in addition to practicing science, also enjoyed cracking a scummy joke.

In short, we are not much like those pine martens who dart about in the forests. I have never seen a single live example of my progenitors, who work for the Biosphere corporation. Of course, I envy their swift feet, their keen nose, their feeling for the forest, but I would envy them even more intensely if I knew what a forest was. Not they but the birds are the ones I really I envy. After all, I live in a skyscraper, and I often see birds – flocks, groups and solitary flyers. How I love to watch them! They are my greatest pleasure, and I am glad I was not born a genuine pine marten, one of nature's predatory patricians, who devour birds.

We have a longer body than the forest pine martens. Special glands, located on the approaches to the nose and the larynx, produce 27 varieties of detergent and scouring agents in the form of liquids, powders, lasers and acoustic vibrations. In effect, this figure – 27 – is only required for the advertising prospectuses, since 1 of the 27 is a universal cleaning agent (so the others could quite well be dispensed with).

A novel could be written about the cleansing, absorbent, polishing, scouring, surface-restoring properties of our pelts. We are capable of reaching a quite considerable speed as we move up and down the stairway – at maximum speed I climb from the ground floor to the 300th in four and a half minutes, but I only do this when my brain tells me that all the flights are empty – otherwise it could endanger the life of a human being or domestic pet loitering on the stairway. I can move not only up and down the steps, but also over the walls and even across the ceiling.

I have to clear up frequently, since my stairway is external and it is separated from the sky by nothing but an array of bright metal pipes, rather like organ pipes, but exorbitantly extended in height. The Kandinsky skyscraper is basically constructed like a gigantic, half-open book, in which each page is devoted to a particular color, but the fire-escape stairways, located on the cut ends of the skyscraper's separate "pages," are all snowy-hospital-white on the inside, so that a layer of dust, which blows in between the organ pipes, has to be continuously removed from the lower storeys. On the other hand, from every level I can see the sky, and breathe its air, and on windy days the pipes sing a song of quiet, melodic droning.

In general, however, people rarely come out onto the stairs. The most frequent visitors are children. How can they possibly be forbidden from playing on the steps? But their parents do forbid them, claiming that once a certain exceptionally slender child slipped between the pipes and fell. This is a grown-ups' lie.

It is also impossible to eradicate the couples having sex on the stairway – this tradition cannot be killed off, and I devour the bright-colored leftover scraps of their safe dating in the same way as I consume all the dirt and garbage that I encounter on the stairway – my organism ideally assimilates, or rather, incinerates, everything, transforming the trash into smoke that billows up out of my enflamed nostrils after the work is done. It is not food. I have no need of nourishment.

As for those who love to write and draw on walls, I do nothing to hinder their archaic hankering after rock paintings, instead I annihilate the fruits of their labors, restoring the perfect whiteness. The structuring of my brain forces me to remember all the drawings and inscriptions that I erase from the walls. I can reproduce them at any moment by dipping the tip of my tongue into paint or blueberry jelly. My creators programed me in this way on the crackpot assumption that this memory of mine might be of assistance to the police in certain cases, but not once in my entire life have the police asked for my help. So it was pointless and stupid to teach me to do this, but this very ability was the second reason, after the spectral voices, for the secret development of my intellect, an entirely illegitimate development that was not foreseen by the jocose genetic engineers. If someone can reproduce a text, then they can write – and I write on the walls of my little cell or on scraps of paper found on the stairway.

Once I even erased and memorized an entire poem written on the wall by an office clerk (below the hundredth floor there are only offices). Here it is:

CHILL OUT
Yet another lost weekend,
That has fallen, like a loose page,
Out of a young clerk's life.

On Saturday he did not go dancing,
He met no lovely girl as he danced,
In the chillout space his lips did not wander
Over her parted lips …

And tomorrow back to work in the bank …
In fact he thinks about that without suffering:
There are many bright rooms there. Our times
Have no place for Kafkaesque atmosphere.

And the ultramundane light plashes softly
In the little computer screen. And once again,

Slipping through the ripplings of the Paranet,
He can visit those erotic sites,
And see through heat haze on the little screen
The happy eyes of a chance-met girl,
The delicate lines of her parted lips …

Yes, instead of all the dancing and kissing,
He lay all weekend like a log in the basement
Of an empty, abandoned station-church,
Lost in reveries of golden thrones.
The orb of power weighed heavy in his hand again,
And with a single flutter of his lashes,
He kindled volcanoes, span whirlwinds into motion,
Harrowed the ocean's breast with vortexes,
Raising up off bottom shelves the ancient galleons
Of long-ago dissolved and dispersed Spaniards.

He moved the hands of all the clocks on earth,
He ruled the rising and the falling of the tide,
And bore the Moon and Sun upon his shoulders,
Like hunting birds, and never flinched.

Now it feels shameful to remember this –
A needless, foolish waste of time!
Yes, better carefree kissing with some girl
Than holding dreadful sway at the world's center,
Swirling maelstroms of bone-crushing power …

A clerk with fair hair by the name of Claire
Is over there, eating a white éclair …

This clerk's personal life was a mess, because below the waist his body had the form of a wheel of fire.

I continued stealthily developing the intellectual abilities that had been implanted in me by a blunder. I gradually became so audacious and cunning that I started cautiously roaming, not only up and down my own stairway, but across the storeys. Like any genuine cleaner, I came to know everything about the building in which I worked – the alarm systems, the offices' working hours. I also learned about doors that were not always locked – and that opened up virtually unlimited opportunities to me. On the thirteenth floor I discovered a depository of ancient books. At first I simply admired them (those rare items, books, are like birds somehow), but later I read them all, after I came across a laboratory on the 109th floor where they synthesized various substances for stimulating cerebral activity.

Although most of these stimulators were intended exclusively for the human brain, some of the substances were very helpful to me after I learned to rub them into the back of my neck using my tail (consumption via the throat and the nostrils produced no effect). These substances altered my mind, lending it flexibility, ingenuity, tenacity, the ability to classify phenomena, and a certain, almost impudent astuteness. And also, though you may not believe it, I even began having flashes of something that had previously seemed a fickle and inscrutable mystery to me – the so-called "sense of humor." For the first time the dry, narrow little corners of my black, leathery mouth began lifting upwards in the semblance of a smile at those moments when I spotted something comic in the flow of my own thoughts. And those corners of my mouth rose and my lips exposed my tubular fangs more and more often when I thought about my own mutilated, servile fate.

And the bitterness of this wry smile seemed sweeter to me than the submissive, obtuse condition I had been in previously, and which I now felt ashamed to recall. What riches! A smile had appeared on my face! And no sooner was my smile born than it became dangerous, full of secret superiority over the freaks who had created me, too, as a freak.

I shall have my revenge on you, jolly Gene Genie and Zhora the Head! And although you died long ago, I can resurrect you in order to subject you to torment. I shall transform you, Gene, into a miniature crocodile, endowed with an excruciatingly subtle sense of smell, splashing about in an ocean of shit. And they will play football with you, Zhora, as the ball, and afterwards slice you up like a watermelon.

But it was not vengeance that occupied the most important place in my aspirations. I dreamed about the sky.

I started keeping a few of the bits and pieces that I found on the stairway and hiding them in my little cell. Nobody ever looked in there, in fact nobody checked on me at all. I performed my duties impeccably and, as for the rest, no one even suspected that I was a thinking being. My cell became home to small pieces of various different materials, scraps of packaging, several plastic cable ties, and even a few technical devices that had been dropped on the steps. I was hoping to assemble this choice selection of trash into a flying machine.

This dream would have remained a foolish dream if not for one person. Yes, yes, a genuine person – an individual of the old, classical type, with two arms, two legs and one head. Of course, I never thought that I would actually associate with anyone, let alone a person. The people who lived in the Kandinsky Tower or visited it did not usually see me, but if they happened to catch sight of me occasionally, they didn't suffer a heart attack: on every flight of the fire-escape stairway a neat little sign announced that cleanness was maintained by a clone of the pine marten Jill Haj-UB-117. Children sometimes tried to play with me, but I disappeared in a flash. The adults barely even gave me a glance.

And then one day I woke up in my little cell because a picture had lit up in my brain: some person had gone out onto the fire-escape stairway on the 117th floor – at the time the coincidence with my own clone index seemed somehow mystical to me. I said the person had gone out, but more likely he had crawled out onto the stairway and immediately slumped to the floor. I could see every detail of him: a long, swarthy, haggard face, scratched all over, with tangled hair dangling down over the forehead and prominent eyes hooded by bluish-black eyelids. Not so long ago this man had clearly wished to appear fashionable. He was wearing gloves spangled with sequin-eyes, a dark-blue coat of crisp, corrugated fabric and wide brocade trousers reaching down to his ankles, with little square window-holes on the knees – and gazing out through these little windows were two skulls tattooed on his kneecaps. This romantic style of dress had only recently come into fashion, and the young man looked very trendy. But the coat was torn on his right shoulder – a whole chunk of material had been ripped out – and through the rent I could see a gaunt but muscular upper arm with the letters ZZ tattooed on it. Other details that didn't tally with the image of a dandy were the faded shirt of red mutant leather, the lace with a strange tooth dangling on it round his wrist, and the crude, but extremely expensive work boots with torsional soles (these excellent soles allow their owner to walk slightly above the earth, instead of directly on it – an indispensable item in swamps!) And in addition, a specific deformation of the index finger of his right hand hinted that he had squeezed the trigger of a biological rifle too often. Dandy or assassin, he was dying.

Something made me dash like lightning down to the 117th floor and stop in front of him. He opened his eyes with a struggle.

"You're my terrible death-bed vision, right?" he asked, barely moving his bloodless lips.

I nodded mutely at the sign.

"A cloned pine marten. God … that's just what I deserve – to see a cloned pine marten before I die. The punishment for my sins … I've killed so many little pine martens in my life – with two heads or seven tails …"

My larynx is constructed so that I cannot bark or speak. But one of the cleaning agents produced by my organism has the appearance of a completely black fluid, which evaporates into the air after several minutes, taking with it particles of dust and soot. I instructed the necessary gland to work, and immediately my tongue was impregnated with moisture that tasted like iron. I wrote quickly on the wall with my tongue:

"Are you a hunter?"

He read the words. Waited until they disappeared. Then he said:

"Dumb. But rational. So they teach you to read and write here? Yes, I was a hunter. A hunter of mutant animals. You're not a mutant, but a modified clone, so you shouldn't be offended by that. Basically, I'm a qualified ecologist … and the … bott … ats …" – his words were cut short by pain. He chewed on his lips and pressed himself up against the white wall, which seemed ruddy in comparison with his face.

"That bastard … Otto Otsovsky didn't give me anything. I've hardly got any light left," he whispered.

I knew that Otto Otsovsky, who lived on the 117th floor, was a narcolight dealer. The dying man fumbled agonizingly over his body with one hand and pulled out of his inside pocket an object that looked like a miniature gold torch with a bellmouth. On its side the torch had a button shaped like a pearl and a tiny visual display. The dandified hunter convulsively squeezed one eye shut, opened the other eye wide (it was dark and glittering), raised the little torch abruptly to the wide-open eye and pressed the button. A brief squirt of soft, smoky-golden light darted into his eye and faded away. The hunter's complexion turned fresher, a warm bloom started glowing on his emaciated cheeks, and his lips folded into a satiated smile.

"Let there be light! It really is so delicious, that light … Well then, little pine marten, everything is exactly as I was telling you – I'm a qualified ecologist, I worked for the Ministry of Wildlife Sanctuaries for many years. They used to send me into the sanctuaries to shoot individual animals with especially severe mutations. I was considered an ace at my job, the best of the best. Mutations are basically a natural process, God's work, so to speak, but ecological specialists sometimes conclude that certain individuals with especially blatant mutations should be culled in order to preserve other animals and the natural niche itself. The name Zakhar-Naum resounded through every wildlife sanctuary, great and small, in our country. That's my name, and when I shoot, I never miss. You probably couldn't find a keener-eyed marksman anywhere between Kronstadt and Omsk. I used to hunt the old-fashioned way, the noble way, without special equipment, with just an old rifle. Like the Mohicans. I went after mutants in the freezing cold and the sweltering heat, I possessed (in addition to my keen eye) a brilliant flair for hunting, good luck, and the intuition of a tracker, plus experience and knowledge. No one understands mutant animals better than I do, no one knows their ways better. I could follow a track on foot for weeks, I could construct breathtaking traps, the strength I had was staggering, and I possessed the stamina of a mule. I always hunted alone, I feared nothing, I could handle any mutant, even the most gigantic and incredibly fierce ones. Have you seen *The Mutant from Mutang*? A terrifying movie. When I was a child, it killed the very soul within me. It was to forget certain scenes from that film that I became a mutant hunter. A little boy from an Old Moscow clan, I used to wake up in the night weeping chill, inconsolable tears, shuddering in desolate despair – there it was, the abominable, calm, bright-pink face of the Mutant from Mutang, right in front of my eyes, as alive as could be. I knew that it was shameful for me, the descendant of proud men of the mountains, to be terrified by colored shadows sliding across a screen. A warrior does not dare to fear mere movie demons. But I sobbed, not so much out of fear as out of grief – I was lamenting the fate of the human race. The pink face that rose again out of the ashes of Mutang after the Americans had incinerated it told me that human beings were done for. A pink face, nothing but a pink face. Against a background of steaming jungle, against a background of cosy colonial cafés, against a background of snowy Moscow side streets. So I became a hotshot hunter. But I had a weak spot, an Achilles' heel that no one knew about. I couldn't shoot into the eyes. I never shot a single creature in the eye. And I never thought the tiny microdot of this, my only weakness, would destroy me. Six months ago I was sent to one of our most brilliant wildlife sanctuaries, which had been swamped by yet another wave of mutations among the protected animals. The specialists were particularly alarmed by four large, profoundly transformed individuals – these 'four pirates' littered the forest land with the appalling traces of their feasts, which looked more like massacres. Among other remains, two of the sanctuary's employees were discovered, torn to pieces – the torso of one was found on top of a pine tree. I set out for the place in an excellent mood, confident of my powers. I used to make notches on the stock of my rifle to mark every mutant I killed. By the time of this latest expedition there was no space left on the stock for new notches, and I bought a new old rifle. I arrived at the spot, a gigantic slab of forest, and right in the middle of it – a crummy Paranet-café called Pandeia, where the intelligentsia of the game reserve had woven a cozy nest for itself. I roamed along the paths for a while, taking the measure of the terrain. To get my eye in, I shot your sisters – pine martens are plentiful there. I used to walk into the Pandeia café, an appalling and handsome figure, stained scarlet with the blood of pine martens. Double-headed or multi-tailed, they dangled from my belt, gazing with their inverted, dead eyes at the slightly distant, but agreeable company, which was enthralled by *The Great Defeat* – the endless episodes of this interminable serial were fed directly into the brains of the café's customers. The main character – the Emperor – was always dreaming of a Great Defeat, but he simply couldn't find any worthy enemies, so he gathered together an immense army and advanced, with black-and-blue banners fluttering, into the depths of a desolate, icy waste. The Emperor looked like the gnawed core of a quince with a piercing, screeching voice, and the army consisted of semi-naked maidens who fed on each other's flesh. These delightful warrioresses chose not to put on any clothes among the eternal ice, and the only things that kept them warm there were lesbianism and cannibalism. I was unaware that a Great Defeat was in store for me, and did not vouchsafe my favor to the legends of the Quince Emperor. Neither, unfortunately, did I vouchsafe my favor to the charms of the girls in the nature reserve, who had fallen in love with

my black hair and blue eyes. On the sixth day a herd of mauled
and butchered cows was found. On the ninth day I spotted
the tracks. On the eleventh day old man Studniev's stud farm
was wiped off the face of the earth, all the horses were gobbled
up, and Studniev's head was torn off. On the nineteenth day I
saw them, standing on top of a long hill. Four of them. I came
on them unexpectedly as I roamed along the paths. Do I need
to say that they consisted entirely of eyes? Mass-eyed. Omni-
oculared. Four Monsters of the Apocalypse. Our ancient writer
Nabokov loved the word "multiple-eyed," which he applied to
butterflies, peacocks, moles, cobras, school buses, crowds of
people, and wet gardens after the rain. A magnificent writer,
but for the abomination of that word he deserves oblivion. I
loathe him for that word, a sprinkling of sugar on the surface
of a profound current of terror. They stood quite still, within
shooting distance, and looked at me with all their multiple
eyes. I didn't shoot. I ran. The taste of shame rose in my throat.
In the Pandeia café I contacted the Ministry and told them
I declined the assignment. In reply they told me I was fired.
Something happened to me then. I think I proved unequal to a
Great Defeat. A nervous breakdown or something of the sort.
I don't really want to talk about it, but I shot all the customers
in the Pandeia and smashed my new old rifle. They never saw
that bright-colored Quince Core freezing as he lay on a scrap of
black-and-blue flag among the eternal ice. They never heard his
reverberating techno-howl fading away. I came back to Russia
City and lay low, spending what money I had left like water. I
got hooked on light. No one on light lives for long. The black
ammonite will get me soon."

He glanced at the little torch.

"Only two doses left. It's the end. That Otto's a lousy son of
a bitch."

"ISN'T THAT LIGHT ENOUGH FOR YOU?" I wrote on the wall, pointing with my nose at the sun, which was declining magnificently towards the west over Russia City. A generous deluge of golden light, not pre-dosed by anyone (or rather, precisely pre-dosed in virtuoso fashion by Earth's own atmospheric cocoon) flooded the landing, which was ruled off into strips by the shadows of slim metal pipes. In this barrage of light Zakhar-Naum looked like a bundle of dark, expensive fabrics, in which his sharp features vanished.

The view of the city from there was breathtaking: birds soared and flying machines hovered in flocks in the wide-open expanse. They ranged themselves into processions, formed up into levitating garlands, spheres, pyramids …

"There's too much of that light. It's reflected in all the eyes," Zakhar-Naum declared, speaking with difficulty. "It is the beam in countless numbers of eyes."

He launched another pre-dosed raylet into his eye. His vivacity returned.

"I'm dying," he said cheerfully. "And what plans do you have?"

"TO FLY," I wrote on the wall.

He looked into the sky filled with flyers.

"Well, dying and flying are almost the same thing. You dream of flying? How do you intend to do it? You need to find Little Wing. Yes, that's it, that's the simplest way, and the best. First you have to lure Little Wing to yourself and then merge with him."

"WHAT IS LITTLE WING?" I wrote on the wall.

"You've never heard of Little Wing? You ignorant little pine marten! Everyone knows about Little Wing! Although, how to lure him to you – not many know that. But I know. That's part of my professional competence, because Little Wing is a mutant."

The hunter told me about Little Wing. To my shame, until then I had known nothing about this creature that people seldom see, but which occupies such a substantial place in their consciousness that many human children constantly draw it on paper and in sand. Other mutants, long before they appeared in reality, roamed through the expanses of human dreams and fantasies, in the vastnesses of premonition. The image of Little Wing can probably be discovered in certain ancient films and images. They give him various different names.

Little Wing, alias Winglet, Wingling, Winger, Wingo, Wing-Ding, Wing-Thing, Wingaroo, Sailwing or simply Wings. He is also known as the Faceless Angel, Swisher, Eternal Flyer, Tree Seed, Glider, Wings Without Organs, Windy, Wind, Forage Cap, Phyny Natiasy, Sinless, Silent Wings, Modest Sky, Fearquiver, Angle, Flying Zero, Uccello del Niente, Gottesvogel, Drummvogel, Restless Bird, Hollywood Eagle, Vero, Shame of Heaven, Shade of Heaven, V-Bird, Healthy Wings, Pure Levitator, Uccello Povera. I can't recall any other names at the moment, but if I knew them, even if they numbered a thousand, I would enter them respectfully in my chronicle.

Sailwing (Little Wing) is a creature that has two gliding wings, connected by a feathered gap that has no head, no legs, no tail and no other external organs. To look at, it appears to be simply a detached pair of wings soaring, seemingly forgotten in the sky by an absentminded angel. The span of the wings, as well as the color and type of feathers, are different in different individuals – Sailwings can be snow-white, chestnut-colored, magical gray, scarlet with gold trimming, they can be flamingo-pink or tar-black. They exist in endless flight and incessant soaring, and descend to the earth only after they have died (they have no legs, after all). They have no need of nourishment, do not reproduce, and have a reclusive temperament: they prefer to stay as far away as possible from people, birds and flying robots.

And so, supposedly, they avoid the society of other creatures, but … Since the time when they appeared, a legend has also been born – if a wingless creature that has reached the ultimate bounds of despair summons a Little Wing, if it invokes this earless flyer with all its heart, all its nerves, claws, fine hairs and fibers, and the trembling of its tongue, then one of the Little Wings will hear, pick up the SOS signal and fly down to the despairing creature. The Little Wing lands on the back of the creature and fuses with that back, sinking into it myriads of its own finest fibers, which are stronger than life itself. This fusion takes a minute, filled with a fierce pain that tears apart both creatures who have resolved upon a symbiotic fusion with each other. But the one who is rescued literally "sprouts wings," and for him the sky becomes a boundless highway.

This is how Jesualdo Petrov, nicknamed Christ – a famous gangster, the terror of the slums of Vyshnii Volochek – escaped when the police had him boxed into a dead end in the back alleys behind the Saga club. Jesualdo's heart screamed out to the sky, and the sky sent him Little Wing. The gangster flew away to continue his flamboyant activities in flight, and he is credited with the famous phrase "Farewell, Altai and Palermo! I have ascended on the Wings of my Native Home."

After telling me all of this, the Hunter gave me a dirty scrap of silk. Embroidered on the silk in gold thread was a text in convoluted script. The Hunter assured me that this was an incantation capable of luring Little Wing.

The Hunter casually tossed me this small silk bundle, after rummaging in his pockets for a long time to find it, then reached out for the little torch, in order to flood his eye with the final dose of light that he had left, but he never got the torch to his eye – it slipped from his grasp and went rolling across the enamel covering of the floor. The Chechen boy from Old Moscow, who used to see nightmares of the smoke-filled streets of Mutang, lay there dead in front of me.

I sat by him for a while, admiring the sky, while my program classified his corpse. Then my body gave out a brief, piercing sound. Two plumes of light, almost aromatic smoke rose out of my nostrils: quick as a flash, I drew them back into myself and incinerated the corpse. The program had identified it as: "a garbage item of complex composition, toxic and radioactive, subject to immediate liquidation." At that moment on the 111th floor a large yellow ball that had lived alone for three years on a concrete semi-balcony, surrounded by three hoops, suddenly burst.

Three days later I was flying above Russia City. As a certain mountain climber and aeronaut of ours once said: "Ascension is not the important thing. The most important thing is to launch off from the peak." That was what I had done. The incantation had worked, and as I rose into the sky, I pronounced in my mind the words: "Farewell, steps! I have ascended on the Wings of my Native Home."

Our magnificent city lay below me, with its incredible buildings soaring upwards into the air. Several of the majestic buildings, carved from the stone of flying cliffs, actually hung there, others lay on the clouds, slowly drifting. Towering up out of a honeycomb of squares and boulevards was the gigantic building of the Government of Russia – the colossal Black Cube, also known as the Malevich Tower. Squirming on the horizon, piercing through the clouds, was the bioskyscraper The Stalk (or The Monument to the Color Green), populated by floristic young people. Hanging menacingly over the city was the Falling Skyscraper (or Pisa Skyscraper) casting a long, aromatic shadow over a district of villas. Wheeling round freely above the city was the Roundelay ring of skyscrapers, in which all the buildings looked like colossal village girls, who had formed a spinning circle and were singing a Russian river song.

The gigantic, living heads that crowned many of the tower-houses sang and whispered. Monasteries hung from cloud-islands. At one moment, with my newly keen vision, I caught a fleeting glimpse of my own image – the broad, smooth sweep of my flight was reflected in the mirror-eyes of a bronze infant, amorously contemplating the heavens.

About the contributors

Alex Anikina is an artist, researcher and film-maker. Anikina is a PhD candidate at Goldsmiths, University of London, where she is writing a dissertation on algorithmic generative film. She works with experimental film, software, lecture-performances and language, addressing questions of critical posthumanism and technology. Anikina's works have been screened and exhibited internationally at VI Moscow Biennale, at Gaîté Lyrique in Paris, at Haus der Kulturen der Welt in Berlin, at Anthology Film Archives in New York, and elsewhere.

Joseph Backstein is a curator. He worked as the Commissioner of the Moscow Biennial of contemporary art from 2005 to 2016. Backstein curated the first public exhibitions of Moscow conceptualists in the Soviet Union (Moscow, 1987–9), and he was the curator of the Russian pavilion at the 48th Venice Biennale (1999). He is the founder and director of the Institute of Contemporary Art, Moscow, and an Honorary Doctor of the Gothenburg University, Sweden. Backstein is an author of books and articles on history and theory of contemporary Russian art.

Bart De Baere is the Director of M HKA in Antwerp. While working at the Museum of Contemporary Art in Ghent, 1986–2001, he curated many cutting-edge exhibitions, notably "This is the show and the show is many things" (1994). He was one of the curators of Documenta IX in Kassel; a consultant for establishing the first biennial in the city of Johannesburg; a member of the advisory council for the network of Soros Institutes in Eastern Europe; a curator of the 2015 Moscow biennial. Bart De Baere has written and published extensively on art and aesthetics.

Alexander Brener is an artist, poet, and writer. He was one of the most radical figures of Moscow art scene of the 1990s. His works often are set up as direct confrontations with the art establishment and articulate fierce protest against the system of capitalism that penetrates art. Published books include *The Art of Destruction* (2005, with Barbara Schurz), *Bukaka Spat Here* (2002, with Barbara Schurz), and more recently *The Lives of Martyred Artists* (Moscow: Hylaea, 2016), in Russian.

Ilya Budraitskis is a historian, political writer and curator, an influential Marxist thinker of a younger generation in Russia, a member of the editorial board of *Moscow Art Magazine*, and the platforms Openleft and LeftEast. He is a co-editor, together with Ekaterina Degot and Marta Dziewanska, and contributor to the book *Post-post-Soviet? Art, politics and society in Russia in the turn of the decade* (Chicago University Press, 2013). Together with Arseniy Zhilyaev he co-edited the book *Pedagogical Poem* (Marsilio Publishers, 2014). Budraitskis has contributed to *e-flux*, *WdW Review*, *Manifesta Journal*, *Colta.ru*, *Seance*, and many other publications.

Maria Chehonadskih is a theorist, writer, and curator. She holds a PhD from Kingston University, London. Her major fields of interest are Soviet Marxism and the interconnections of art, literature and philosophy. Chehonadskih is a member of the *Moscow Art Magazine* editorial board, and has published texts in that magazine as well as in *Radical Philosophy*, *Mute* and many others. The exhibition "Shadow of a Doubt" that she curated together with Ilya Budraitskis in Moscow in 2014 was dedicated to the problem of conspiracy.

Olga Chernysheva is an artist working with film, photography, drawing and text. Her work explores the increasing fragmentation of utopian narratives in contemporary Russia. She has exhibited internationally, including at BAK in Utrecht, 2011, Kunsthalle Erfurt, 2013 and M HKA, 2014. She represented Russia at the 49 Venice Biennale in 2001 and participated in the main project of 56 Venice Biennale in 2015. Her works are held at the Tate Modern, MoMA, and the Luis Vuitton Foundation, among many other public and private collections. Her book *Compossibilities* was published by Hatje Cantz, Berlin, in 2013.

Keti Chukhrov is a philosopher and artist. She is a member of the editorial board of the *Moscow Art Magazine*, and she writes widely on contemporary art in Russian and English for journals such as *Artforum*, *New Literary Review*, *Chto delat?*, *Documenta Magazine*, *e-flux*, and *Afterall*. Her books include *Pound & £* (1999), and *To Be and To Do: A Project for Theatre in a Philosophical Critique of Art* (2011). Chukhrov is an Associate Professor in the Higher School of Economy, Department of Cultural Studies, and she runs a Research Department at NCCA in Moscow.

Evgeny Granilshchikov is an artist and film-maker. While film is central to his practice, he creates elaborate continuous works using drawings, photography and collages. Granilshchikov investigates the power of the social over the individual and the possibilities for political consciousness. In 2013 he was awarded the Kandinsky Prize for his film *Positions*. His shows include "Political Populism" at Kunsthalle Wien, Vienna (2015) and the 6th Moscow Biennale of Contemporary Art (2015).

Boris Groys is a philosopher, essayist, curator and media theorist. He spent the early years of his career in Russia, in the circles of the Moscow conceptualists, and was the first critic and theorist of their work. He is a Global Distinguished Professor of Russian and Slavic Studies at New York University, a Senior Research Fellow at the Staatliche Hochschule für Gestaltung Karlsruhe, and a professor of philosophy at the European Graduate School. He is the author of more than thirty books and numerous articles on philosophy, politics, history and art theory, and criticism in English and Russian. His recent book *On the Flow* (2016) explores the fundamental changes art undergoes in the era of the internet.

Dmitry Gutov is an artist and writer. His sculptures, films, drawings, and texts explore entwining histories of art, philosophy, literature, and Marxist thought. Gutov contributes to the *Moscow Art Magazine* and to other art publications. He has exhibited extensively, including at the Venice Biennale (1995, 2007, and 2011); Documenta (2007); Manifesta (1996); the Istanbul Biennale (1992); the Valencia Biennale (2001); the Sao Paolo Biennale (2002); the Sidney Biennale (2006); and the Shanghai Biennale (2012).

lya and Emilia Kabakov. Ilya Kabakov is arguably the most prominent artist to emerge from post-Soviet Russia and is one of the leaders of Moscow conceptualism. Kabakov's first conceptualist paintings and texts span back to 1964. In the period 1968–74 he created his "Albums" which, combining image, text and temporality in a conceptual way, became classics of Russian art of the twentieth century. Since 1988 he has worked together with Emilia Kabakov. Ilya and Emilia Kabakov's work has been exhibited by major museums including MoMA, the Hirschhorn Museum, and the Stedelijk Museum. In 2017 Tate Modern runs a major show of their work. They represented Russia at the 45th Venice Biennale (1993). Their awards include the Chevalier des Arts et des Lettres, Paris, 1995, the Oscar Kokoschka Preis, Vienna, 2002, and the Premium Imperiale, Japan, 2009.

Maria Kapajeva is a feminist artist and photographer. She explores the problems of representation and expands the borders of photography by working with found images, video, and textile crafts. Her work has been exhibited internationally including at the FORMAT, Guernsey, and Chobi Mela VIII photo festivals. She was commissioned by the Photographers' Gallery in London in 2012 and took part in the Fast Forward: Women in Photography project (@womeninphoto) in collaboration with Tate Modern (since 2015). Kapajeva teaches at the University for Creative Arts at Farnham.

Andrey Kuzkin is an artist. Inspired by Moscow conceptualism, Kuzkin's brave, straightforward yet subtle performances explore existential experiences in a world full of political ruptures. He has been a participant in many collective and solo exhibitions, including the 6th Berlin

Biennale (2010), the 4th Moscow Biennale (2011), 54 and the Venice Biennale (2011).

Artemy Magun is a theorist and philosopher, and a member of the Chto Delat? group. Magun is a professor of political philosophy and theories of democracy in the European University, St Petersburg. He has published numerous articles, as well as books such as: *Unity and Solitude: The Course of Modern Political Philosophy* (NLO, 2011) and *Negative Revolution: Modern Political Subject and Its Fate after the Cold War* (Bloomsbury, 2013).

Bogdan Mamonov is an artist, curator, and writer. He works with installations, painting, videos, films and book illustrations. In 1999 he co-founded the ESCAPE group with Valery Aizenberg, Liza Morozova, and Anton Litvin. The group positioned itself as an antithesis to the loud actionism of the previous decade, quietly exploring the freedoms and ruptures of social and political landscape in the post-Soviet domain. The group represented Russia at the 51th Venice Biennale (2005). Mamonov writes extensively, and he is a member of the editorial board of and a regular contributor to *Moscow Art Magazine*.

Andrey Monastyrsky is an artist, poet, writer, and theorist, one of the central figures of Moscow conceptualism. He was the driving force behind the Collective Actions group (from 1975) which worked with collective performance, writing and debating, building a discursive platform for enabling the existence of contemporary art in the Soviet Union. Their works represented Russia at the Venice Biennale in 2011 and were included in the display collection of Tate Modern (2016). Monastyrsky had a leading role in creating the Moscow Archive

of the New Art (MANI) in 1986–1991; he was a contributor to
and editor of "Trips Out of the City" and "Dictionary of Terms
of the Moscow Conceptual School" (1998). His novel *Kashira
Highway* (1983–6, in Russian) was deemed an inauguration
of psychedelic realism and greatly influenced contemporary
Russian literature.

Gleb Napreenko is an art critic, theorist and historian of art.
Napreenko contributed as a writer and editor to numerous
publications, including *Moscow Art Magazine, Dialog of Arts,
Artchronika, Openspace* and *Colta.ru.* He was an editor-in-chief
of the online magazine *Controversies* (Raznoglasiya), dedicated
to social and cultural critique. Napreenko also teaches at the
independent art school Institute BAZA and the Rodchenko Art
School in Moscow.

Ivan Novikov is an artist. He works with installations and
abstract painting, which often include materials of nature.
Novikov has had solo and group exhibitions in Russia and
abroad, and participated in the Moscow Biennale for Young
Contemporary Art, Krasnoyarsk Biennale, Ural Industrial
Biennial, Manifesta 10, and the Garage Triennial of Russian
Contemporary Art.

Anatoly Osmolovsky is an artist, writer, curator, publicist
and theorist, one of the leaders of radical actionism in Moscow
in the 1990s, and an influential Marxist thinker. He began his
career as a writer and has been engaged in radical publishing
and collective art-making throughout his career. Osmolovsky
founded Movement ETI (Expropriation of the Territory of Art)
(1989–91); and Nezesudik Revolutionary Competitive Program
(1992–5) with Alexander Brener and Oleg Mavromaty; he was

editor-in-chief of *Radek* magazine and a guru of the eponymous
group of young artists. He is a founder and leader of the
independent art school Institute BAZA.

Pavel Peppershtein is an artist, writer, and novelist. He co-
founded the group of artists Inspection Medical Hermeneutics
(1987–2001) with Sergey Anufriev, Yury Leiderman, and Anton
Nosik. The group belonged to the generation deemed "young
conceptualists." His works have been exhibited in museums in
Russia and around the world, in the State Tretyakov Gallery in
Moscow, the Russian Museum in St Petersburg, the Louvre,
the Pompidou Centre, and others. In 2009 Pepperstein
represented Russia at the 53rd Venice Biennale (2009). He is
the author of novels and collections of short stories published
in Russian. His book *The Cold Centre of the Sun* was published
in Russian, English, and French by Hatje Cantz Verlag, in 2015.

Gluklya (Natalia Pershina-Yakimanskaya) is an artist, co-
founder and collaborative member of the Chto Delat? group.
She worked as part of the duo The Factory of Found Clothes
with Olga Egorova (Tsaplya). Gluklya is currently developing
her concept Theatre of Migrants with the idea of sharing
her method of making art with members of disadvantaged
communities. Gluklya has exhibited internationally, and her
work was included in the main project of the 56th Venice
Biennale (2015).

Dmitry Prigov (1940–2007) was an artist, poet, writer
and theorist, one of the most prominent leaders of Moscow
conceptualism. He was a prolific writer and a major voice for
the use of poetry in deconstructing official Soviet language,
having written more than 36,000 poems. During the Soviet era

his poetry was circulated underground as samizdat, and later
his installations and drawings were exhibited internationally in
major museums across the world, such as the State Hermitage
and the Pompidou Centre. He is the author of more then ten
books published in Russian. His novel *Live in Moscow* is an
influential book in contemporary Russian literature.

Masha Sumnina is an artist working with installation, collages
and language. Since 1999 she has worked together with Misha
Leykin as part of the duo MishMash. They have participated
in group and solo exhibitions in Moscow and New York, and
their works were shortlisted for the Innovation Prize (2008)
and exhibited at the 2 Moscow Biennale of Contemporary Art.
Sumnina is the author of the novels *Monument K* (1999) and
Three Megabit from New York (2008).

Oxana Timofeeva is a philosopher and theorist. She is a
member of the group Chto Delat?. Timofeeva is a senior
lecturer at the European University in St Petersburg. She
regularly contributes to *e-flux*, *Stasis*, *New Literary Observer*,
and *Moscow Art Magazine*. Timofeeva's books include *History of
Animals: An Issue on Negativity, Immanence and Freedom* (Jan van
Eyck Academie, 2012) and *Introduction to the Erotic Philosophy
of George Bataille* (Moscow, 2009).

Dmitry Venkov is an artist and independent filmmaker. His
films respond to social and political events in Russia and
abroad; one of the first works to bring him recognition was
Mad Imitators (2012), an anthropological study of a fictional
community, for which he received the Young Artist Kandinsky
Prize. Venkov teaches video art at Moscow Rodchenko School
of Photography and Multimedia.

Anton Vidokle is an artist, curator and art writer. Vidokle is a co-founder and editor of *e-flux*, a leading publishing platform in contemporary art and theory. His work has been exhibited at Tate Modern, in Documenta 13, the Venice Biennale, biennials in Lyon and Dakar. He has curated solo shows by Martha Rosler, Gustav Metzger, Adam Curtis, Andrey Monastyrsky & Collective Actions and the Agency of Unrealized Projects (jointly with Hans Ulrich Obrist). He contributes to various publications such as *October*, *Frieze* and *Artforum*.

Dmitry Vilensky is an artist, writer, publisher, and founding member of the Chto Delat? group, as well as the editor of *Chto Delat?* newspaper. As a member of the group, Vilensky contributes to collective practices in film, photography, text, installation and interventions in the public sphere. Exhibitions include Dear Art, Moderna Galerija Ljubljana, Ljubljana, 2012; 9th Gwangju Biennial, 2012; and The Lesson on DisConsent, Staatliche Kunsthalle Baden-Baden, 2011, among many others.

Vadim Zakharov is an artist, publicist and – notably – archivist of Moscow conceptualism. He joined the circles of nonofficial artists in 1979 and since then has been one of the prominent and passionate contributors to Moscow conceptualism. Zakharov established *Pastor* magazine in 1992 which was the first publishing platform for Moscow Conceptualism abroad; he is an editor of the book *Moscow Conceptual School* (2005) and a creator of the online archive www.conceptualismmoscow.org which offers comprehensive insight into the history of this movement. Zakharov exhibits internationally; he represented Russia at the 55th Venice Biennale (2013), and took part in the main project of 49 and 53 Venice Biennale (2001 and 2009) – among numerous solo and group shows around the world.

Elena Zaytseva is a curator. Before moving to London in 2008, she was a curator at the State Tretyakov Gallery, Moscow, the national museum of Russian art. She curated special projects for the Moscow Biennale in 2005 and 2007, and later worked with Pushkin House, the Russian cultural centre in London, curating exhibitions exploring the ways the institution operates in cross-cultural situations. She is the author of articles on contemporary and modern Russian art in Russian and English.

Arseny Zhilyaev is an artist and writer. His projects navigate across political, cultural, and scientific histories and explore the heritage of Russian cosmism. Zhilyaev is an editor of the acclaimed book *Avant-Garde Museology* (2015). He is a contributor to *e-flux* journal and a member of the editorial board of the *Moscow Art Magazine*. Zhilyaev exhibits internationally, including at 11 Gwangju Biennial, 8 Triennial of Contemporary Art – U3, Ljubljana (2016) and 9 Liverpool Biennial (2016).

Text credits

Translation

Andrew Bromfield translated all texts except those that were written originally in English. These are by: Bart de Baere, Elena Zaytseva, Keti Chukhov, Ilya and Emilia Kabakov, Boris Groys, Anton Vidokle, Olga Chernysheva, Artemy Magun, Dmitry Venkov, Oxana Timofeeva and Alex Anikina.

"Chto Delat? and Method" by Dmitry Vilensky was translated by Thomas Campbell.

Part One
Past futures

1. Keti Chukhrov

Chukhrov, Keti. (2009). Nomadic Theatre of a Communist (manifesto). Dead Revolutionaries E-Zine, The Manifesto Issue, Volume 1. Available at: https://web.archive.org/web/20160415053937/http://deadrevolutionariesclub.co.za/node/72 [accessed 12 June 2017]

2. Ilya and Emilia Kabakov

Kabakov, Ilya and Emilia. (2011). *Center of Cosmic Energy*. Münster: Mike Karstens, pp. 4–11.

3. Boris Groys

Groys, Boris. (2016). "The Truth of Art,", *e-flux* journal no. 71, March 2016. Available at www.eflux.com/journal/thetruthofart/ [accessed 12 June 2017]

4. Andrey Monastyrsky

Monastyrsky, Andrey. (2009). Aesteticheskie issledovaniya. [Aesthetic Investigations]. Vologda: German Titov Library, pp. 7–19. In Russian.

5. Anton Vidokle

Vidokle, Anton. (2015). "The Communist Revolution was Caused by the Sun: A Partial Script for a Short Film.", in *e-flux* journal, Supercomunity: 56th Venice Biennale. Day 60: July 2015. Available at http://supercommunity.e-flux.com/texts/notes-for-a-film-the-communist-revolution-was-caused-by-the-sun/ [accessed 12 June 2017]

Part Two

Inherited aesthetics

6. Joseph Backstein

Backstein, Joseph. (2005) "Angels of History," in *Angels of History: Moscow conceptualism and its influence*. Catalogue of exhibition. Pp. 16–25. Antwerp, MuHKA, 17 September–27 November 2005.

7. Dmitry Gutov, Anatoly Osmolovsky

Gutov, Dmitry, Osmolovsky, Anatoly (2012). "Debate II: Concerning Abstractionism," in *Three Debates*. Moscow: Grundrisse, pp. 143–251. In Russian.

9. Dmitry Prigov

Prigov, Dmitri. (2015). "Where are Our Hands, in Which Our Future Lies?" and "The Second Sacro-Cularisation," in *Wiener Slawistische Almanach*: vol. 34, 1994. Munich, pp. 293–305. In Russian.

11. Artemy Magun

Magun, Artemy (2014). "Negativity in Communism: Ontology and Politics," in *Sosciologicheskoe Obozenie (Sociological Review)*, no.1, v. 13, 2014, pp. 9–25. First publication. Republished from: Magun, Artemy (2017). Soviet Communism and the Paradox of Alienation. In:

Hlavajova, Maria, Sheikh, Simon, ed., *Former West,* Cambridge, MA and London: MIT Press, pp. 179–90.

Part Three
From the archive
14. Bogdan Mamonov

Mamonov, Bogdan. (2008). *Intimnaya Zhizn' Grigoria Speiera* [Intimate Life of Grigory Speier]. Moscow: pARTner project Gallery. Pp. 28–33. In Russian.

16. Andrey Kuzkin

Kuzkin, Andrey. (2016) Pravo na Zhizn. [The Right to Live]. Moscow Museum of Modern Art. Pp. 301–12. In Russian.

Part Four
Russia, today
22. Dmitry Vilensky

Vilensky, Dmitry. (2009). "Chto Delat? and Method", in: Chto Delat? newspaper: no. 3–27 (2009): The Great Method. Translated by Thomas Campbell. Available at: https://chtodelat.org/category/b8-newspapers/12-47/ [a14.06.2017]

Image credits

Part One

Past futures

2. Ilya and Emilia Kabakov

Exterior view of the central building (building no. 1). Courtesy of Ilya and Emilia Kabakov and Mike Karstens, Münster.

The mechanism of the viewing hall in the shape of a "throne." In the center is the top of the reservoir. Courtesy of Ilya and Emilia Kabakov and Mike Karstens, Münster.

Exterior view of the Building of Antennae (building no. 2). Courtesy of Ilya and Emilia Kabakov and Mike Karstens, Münster.

Cross-section of the Building of Research of the Noosphere. Courtesy of Ilya and Emilia Kabakov and Mike Karstens, Münster

Overall view of the Center of Cosmic Energy. Courtesy of Ilya and Emilia Kabakov and Mike Karstens, Münster.

Illustrations taken from "Center of Cosmic Energy" (2003), portfolio with 25 etchings.

Courtesy of Ilya and Emilia Kabakov and Mike Karstens, *Münster*. First exhibited at Ilya & Emilia Kabakov. The Center of Cosmic Energy, Tufts University Art Gallery, Medford, MA, USA. 6 September 2007 – 11 November 2007.

4. Andrey Monastyrsky

Andrey Monastyrsky. "The Bull on the Roof". 1986. Courtesy of Andrey Monastyrsky.

5. Anton Vidokle

Anton Vidokle, film stills from *The Communist Revolution Was Caused By The Sun*, 2015. Courtesy of the artist.

Part Two

Inherited aesthetics

8. Olga Chernysheva

Olga Chernysheva. Still from the video "A Holiday," project "Screens 2013". Courtesy of Pace London

Olga Chernysheva. Still from the video "Assembly Line," project "Screens 2013". Courtesy of Pace London

Olga Chernysheva. Still from the video "Black Dot," project "Screens 2013". Courtesy of Pace London

Olga Chernysheva. Still from the video "Exercises," project "Screens 2013". Courtesy of Pace London

Olga Chernysheva. Still from the video "It Is Said," project "Screens 2013". Courtesy of Pace London

Olga Chernysheva. Still from the video "Lion," project "Screens 2013". Courtesy of Pace London

Olga Chernysheva. Still from the video "Plastic Bags," project "Screens 2013". Courtesy of Pace London

Olga Chernysheva. Still from the video "Platform," project "Screens 2013". Courtesy of Pace London

Olga Chernysheva. Still from the video "Private Spaces," project "Screens 2013". Courtesy of Pace London

Olga Chernysheva. Still from the video "The Sound", project "Screens 2013". Courtesy of Pace London

Olga Chernysheva. Still from the video "Windowpanes," project "Screens 2013". Courtesy of Pace London

Olga Chernysheva. Still from the video "Words," project "Screens 2013". Courtesy of Pace London

Part Three

From the archive

15. Maria Kapajeva

Maria Kapajeva. *You can call him another man* (2015–2017)
The project was developed during the FATHOM residency at Four Corners Film, London in 2015 and will be published as a book in 2018.

17. Masha Sumnina

'Photographs taken in March, when everything worked.
Photo 1 "I am not here"; photo 2 "I am here"
Courtesy of MishMash (MishMash is the duo of artists Misha Leikin and
    Masha Sumnina)

Part Five
Future futures
27. Alex Anikina

Alex Anikina, 'How to Operate as a Human Artist, or the Antichthon' (2015),
    artist book. Courtesy of Alex Anikina

Index

Cosmic Shift: Russian Contemporary Art Writing was first published in 2017
by Zed Books Ltd, The Foundry, 17 Oval Way, London SE11 5RR, UK

www.zedbooks.net

The publication of this work was made possible through support from
the Kosmos Foundation.

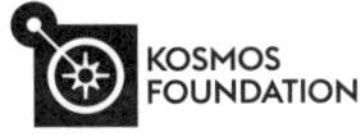

Typeset in Plantin by seagulls.net
Index by Ed Emery
Cover design by Michael Oswell

A catalogue record for this book is available from the British Library

ISBN 978-1-78699-324-3 pb
ISBN 978-1-78699-326-7 pdf
ISBN 978-1-78699-327-4 epub
ISBN 978-1-78699-328-1 mobi

ZED

Zed is a platform for marginalised voices across the globe.

It is the world's largest publishing collective and a world leading example of alternative, non-hierarchical business practice.

It has no CEO, no MD and no bosses and is owned and managed by its workers who are all on equal pay.

It makes its content available in as many languages as possible.

It publishes content critical of oppressive power structures and regimes.

It publishes content that changes its readers' thinking.

It publishes content that other publishers won't and that the establishment finds threatening.

It has been subject to repeated acts of censorship by states and corporations.

It fights all forms of censorship.

It is financially and ideologically independent of any party, corporation, state or individual.

Its books are shared all over the world.

www.zedbooks.net
@ZedBooks